"A thoughtful, compelling, and much-n disenfranchised grief, this volume is a handbook for a wide audience that should include clinicians, students, and academics familiar with or new to the topic. Take the time to truly engage with the important implications that arise from each chapter; you won't regret it."

—**Erica Goldblatt Hyatt**, *associate professor, Department of Obstetrics, Gynecology, and Reproductive Sciences in the Robert Wood Johnson Medical School at Rutgers University and author of* Grieving for the Sibling You Lost

"This edited book is a powerful must-read for helping professionals to understand the multi-faceted experiences of disenfranchised grief – especially as the sociopolitical aspects of grief are often neglected. Readers will find their hearts and minds opened to not only new information, but also to the necessity of working for a more just world."

—**Anneliese Singh**, *professor of social work and associate provost for diversity and faculty development/chief diversity officer at Tulane University and author of* The Racial Healing Handbook: Practical Activities to Help You Challenge Privilege, Confront Systemic Racism, and Engage in Collective Healing

"Disenfranchised grief often includes the types of losses that you cannot give a greeting card for; losses that often lack a name or are experienced in silence or stigma. This volume, edited by Turner and Stauffer, should be on the shelf of every clinician working with grieving individuals. As a Counselor Educator who has taught a grief counseling course for over twenty years, this book addresses a myriad of topics left out by other books, such as intersectionality and grief; COVID and disenfranchised loss; the impact of disenfranchised loss on the body; racial trauma; spiritual trauma; and how disenfranchised grief impacts communities, such as the LGBTQIA+ community, folks with disabilities, African Americans, and military families. This book is a welcome addition to the existing grief literature and will help counselors and mental health professionals learn more about death and non-death losses as they bring care and compassion to those who have experienced grief on the fringes."

—**Michael M. Kocet**, *assistant vice chancellor for graduate education at the University of Colorado, Denver, member of the AADA Grief Competencies Taskforce, and editor of* Counseling Gay Men, Adolescents, and Boys

"Disenfranchised grief is so often unattended and disregarded in clinical work. Drs Turner and Stauffer have created an exceptional and timely resource for clinicians and clinicians-in-training to change that."

—**Martha Jo Atkins**, *author of* Sign Posts of Dying: What You Need to Know

Disenfranchised Grief

Disenfranchised Grief expands the professional helper's understanding of the grief experiences that result from social, cultural, and relational oppression, microaggressions, disempowerment, and overt violence.

The authors blend trauma-informed practice and recent research on critical race theory, cultural humility, and intersectionality to both broaden mental health professionals' conceptualization of disenfranchised grief and its impacts and promote equity and inclusion among populations that have been marginalized.

Renee Blocker Turner, PhD, LPC-S, RPT-S™, is the director of the Expressive Therapies Institute, PLLC, and an author, researcher, and speaker with 20 years of experience supporting individuals and families in grief.

Sarah D. Stauffer, PhD, LPC, NCC, NCSC, RPT-S™, Psychologue-Psychothérapeute FSP, is children's services director at Association ESPAS in Switzerland and Associate Editor of the *International Journal of Play Therapy*.

Disenfranchised Grief

Examining Social, Cultural, and Relational Impacts

Edited by Renee Blocker Turner and Sarah D. Stauffer

Routledge
Taylor & Francis Group

NEW YORK AND LONDON

Designed cover image: RyanJLane © Getty Images

First published 2024
by Routledge
605 Third Avenue, New York, NY 10158

and by Routledge
4 Park Square, Milton Park, Abingdon, Oxon, OX14 4RN

Routledge is an imprint of the Taylor & Francis Group, an informa business

Library of Congress Cataloging-in-Publication Data
Names: Turner, Renee Blocker, editor. | Stauffer, Sarah, editor.
Title: Disenfranchised grief: examining social, cultural, and relational impacts / edited by Renee Blocker Turner and Sarah D. Stauffer.
Description: New York, NY : Routledge, 2024. | Includes bibliographical references and index.
Identifiers: LCCN 2023003506 (print) | LCCN 2023003507 (ebook) | ISBN 9781032268910 (hardback) | ISBN 9781032268903 (paperback) | ISBN 9781003292890 (ebook)
Subjects: LCSH: Grief—Social aspects. | Grief—Psychological aspects. | Grief.
Classification: LCC BF575.G7 D555 2024 (print) | LCC BF575.G7 (ebook) | DDC 155.9/37—dc23/eng/20230504
LC record available at https://lccn.loc.gov/2023003506
LC ebook record available at https://lccn.loc.gov/2023003507

ISBN: 9781032268910 (hbk)
ISBN: 9781032268903 (pbk)
ISBN: 9781003292890 (ebk)

DOI: 10.4324/9781003292890

Typeset in Goudy
by Apex CoVantage, LLP

To all my angels, living and passed, that have shaped my understanding of the pain and gifts associated with grief. – R.B.T.

To the generations before me that have helped me more fully understand, bear witness to, and live through the grief and disenfranchised grief experiences that have shaped me, and to my family, my children, and my friends who have helped me buffer those losses, I thank you. – S.D.S.

Contents

Foreword   xi

Preface   xv

About the contributors   xix

Part I

Foundations for understanding disenfranchised grief   1

1   Disenfranchised grief: The complicated interweave of death
and non-death losses   3
RENEE BLOCKER TURNER AND SARAH D. STAUFFER

2   Identity and loss: Where intersectionality and disenfranchised
grief converge   24
QUINN K. SMELSER

3   Our bodies: Holders of unspoken grief   42
EMILY R. KELLER

4   Wounds of spirit: The disenfranchised nature of spiritual trauma   59
RENEE BLOCKER TURNER, TINA K. BOYLES BAILEY, AND BROOKLYN GORDON

5   Untangling racial trauma and disenfranchised grief   78
CHINWÉ U. WILLIAMS AND LAYLA J. BONNER

Part II

Systemic barriers to grief   97

6   Social and systemic barriers for biracial individuals and
their families   99
CHRISTINA VILLARREAL-DAVIS

7 Complicated grief and challenges in LGBTQIA+ communities   120
DONELEY MERIS

8 The interplay of disenfranchised grief and systemic barriers
from COVID-19 for African Americans   138
THERESA LIBIOS AND EDWARD F. HUDSPETH

9 Disenfranchised grief for individuals with disabilities   155
ROCHELLE RITZI AND MARSHALL LYLES

10 The aftermath of sexual violence: Consequent grief and loss   170
MARIA HAIYASOSO

11 Addressing violence and loss in schools   187
AMANDA WINBURN AND MARY BESS W. PANNEL

Part III
Disenfranchised grief impacting families   205

12 Loss within the margins of childrearing: Disenfranchised grief
in parenting   207
MANDI MELÉNDEZ

13 African American sibling loss: A sister's perspective   222
TANGELA C. SAWYERR

14 The grief of parenting "borrowed children":
A foster parent perspective   238
THERESA FRASER

15 The sacrifice of service: Grief and loss within the
military community   256
CHRISTINA WATTS-FIGUEROA AND ALTON R. MCCALLUM, JR.

16 Ovdje nisam, a tamo me nema: The silenced complicated,
complex grief of Bosnian refugees   274
SELMA ZAKOMAC-BAĆEVAC AND MEYLEEN M. VELASQUEZ

Conclusion   293
Index   295

Foreword

The evolution of the concept
of *disenfranchised grief*

I believe that every concept has a history or personal "biography" – something that causes a new concept to develop. The concept of disenfranchised grief grew slowly and unassumingly from a comment made in a Family Therapy graduate class.

Prior to retiring, I taught for nearly 40 years at the Graduate School of The College of New Rochelle. My graduate students were generally older than recent graduates and came with considerable personal and professional experiences. It led to a rich environment of mutual learning.

In my Family Therapy course, we addressed the issue of widows and widowers. One of my students commented: "If you think widows have it rough, you ought to see what happens when an ex-spouse dies." The comment was intriguing – I had never thought about that issue. I asked the student if she was willing to share her experience. She was.

She had been married for nearly 25 years with two adolescent sons. In fact, she and her husband were planning a celebratory cruise. One day, she came home early from work to find her husband in their bed with a neighbor. Within two years of the shocking revelation, they had completed an acrimonious divorce, she had moved, the ex-husband had remarried, and then he died of pancreatic cancer.

She attended the funeral, noting that her presence seemed to cause both some discomfort and some awkwardness. Knowing of her anger throughout the divorce, some friends actually congratulated her on his death. She confronted her own ambivalence. Part of her was relieved that he had died, yet she also noted their long history – 25 years of marriage, two children, and he was her first love.

I was prompted by her account to research further, and I wondered if other ex-spouses had similar stories. I conducted a small exploratory study employing extensive interviews with a sample of a dozen widows. The results were accepted as a paper presentation at the Association for Death Education and Counseling (ADEC) national conference. As soon as I checked the program, I noted that I was sharing my paper session with Shirley Scott, who was speaking on the same topic. As soon as Shirley saw me, we decided to huddle. Though my study was an exploratory one and Shirley had sent questionnaires to a large sample, our findings were highly compatible.

In our respective studies, we found that ex-spouses experiencing grief after the death of an ex was a common experience. We also found that the ex-spouse participants tended to compare the grief experienced by the death with the grief that followed divorce. This was interesting, as generally, in discussing the psychological sequelae of divorce, grief was rarely considered.

I was further propelled by the reaction to the research to examine other circumstances where grief may be experienced but not supported or validated by others. I thought of the other side of the triangle. Suppose one is having an extramarital affair and their lover dies; how can they deal with the grief? Those of you who are research oriented can appreciate how difficult it is to find that sample. Therefore, I broadened the sample to include unmarried people in sexual relationships wherein a partner died. This included gay and straight couples cohabiting, in longtime dating relationships, and those engaged but not yet married. At the time of this research, same-sex marriage was not a legal option.

As we interviewed this second sample, a comment was oft repeated. Participants noted that they had "no right to grieve." They were, as I noted, disenfranchised.

After initially presenting the results of this research, a crowd gathered, anxious to share their stories. Though the circumstances differed, they, too, had experienced losses where they had no right to grieve. I decided that what I now call *disenfranchised grief* needed further exploration. The first edited book, *Disenfranchised Grief: Recognizing Hidden Sorrow*, published in 1989, identified three contexts of disenfranchised grief: relationships that were not sanctioned, losses that were not acknowledged, and vulnerable groups, such as persons with dementia, intellectual disabilities, and forms of mental illness, the very old and the very young, people whose characteristics often led others to discount their grief as those we may try to protect.

A second book on disenfranchised grief, *Disenfranchised Grief: New Directions, Challenges, and Strategies for Practice*, published in 2002, added two additional categories: stigmatized deaths, such as those caused by AIDS, suicide, and certain homicides. I also noted that sometimes the way individuals grieve, perhaps due to grieving styles or cultural differences, their grief is disenfranchised by others.

In some ways, developing a concept is like raising a child. It grows away from you as others see new situations or possibilities in the concept. For me, that has been exciting to see. And I am especially delighted to welcome Drs. Renee Blocker Turner and Sarah D. Stauffer's new book, *Disenfranchised Grief: Social, Cultural, and Relational Impacts*. This new work really expands the concept of disenfranchised grief, offering both a significant contribution and an advancement to our understanding of such grief in several critical ways.

First, they strongly root the concept of disenfranchised grief in a social, cultural, and neurobiological context. Their emphasis on cultural context is especially important as our society deals with increasing diversity.

Second, their work explores a variety of non-death losses. By such exploration, the authors expand the importance, especially vivid in the COVID-19 pandemic, of the critical need to acknowledge that grief is about loss – not just death.

Moreover, their work widens the theoretical base of disenfranchised grief as the editors and authors draw and develop the concept from a variety of perspectives, including critical race theory and Black feminism; biracial, LGBTQIA+, spiritual, and intersecting identities; disability status; and refugee status. In addition, they explore new areas and interventions, from expanding the physical impacts of disenfranchised grief to addressing the ways that varied forms of violence, such as sexual and school-based violence, can be disenfranchised. Finally, their authors move the concept from solely considering the individual manifestation of disenfranchised grief to incorporating a family perspective.

Anyone interested in the concept of disenfranchised grief – and grief in general – should read and treasure this work. I welcome this all-so-important addition to our understanding of the holistic nature and multiple dimensions of disenfranchised grief.

Kenneth J. Doka, PhD
Senior Vice-President for Grief Programs, The Hospice
Foundation of America
Author, *Disenfranchised Grief: Recognizing Hidden Sorrow* and *Disenfranchised Grief: New Directions, Challenges, and Strategies for Practice*

Preface

In his foundational text on disenfranchised grief, Doka (1989) described how grief becomes disenfranchised when it is "not or cannot be openly acknowledged, publicly mourned, or socially supported" (p. 4), giving way to minimization and misunderstanding of different types of grief. Over 30 years later, disenfranchisement continues to deprive many people in specific segments of the population of widely socially accepted recognition of their mourning, further isolating and restricting communities to their own narrow social circles and limiting resources that would allow healing to progress for and beyond their bereaved community.

In recent years, researchers in mental health professions have proffered more liberal understandings of individuals in their intersecting identities (Crenshaw, 1989) to recognize that individual facets of a person's identity cannot be added to make up the sum of their being. Rather, each facet, as it connects to and amplifies the shine of the others, requires a vision of the whole gem, especially at these intersections. Combinations of characteristics specific to an individual may further amplify the disenfranchisement they experience and, therefore, the depth of their marginalization and grief, even if other aspects of their identities are and will continue to be privileged.

This book was born out of a discussion between the editors at a professional conference prior to the onset of the COVID-19 pandemic. Renee pitched the idea to Sarah (originally conceptualized as a children's grief book), who could not hear or acknowledge it at the time, as she was in the aftermath of three death losses during the three months prior and the (anticipated) termination of a meaningful research mandate, which severed her ties to the academe. These losses, each disenfranchised in their own unique ways, made the subject too painful for Sarah to approach at that moment. Feeling the collective weight of grief and pain triggered by the pandemic, Renee broached the subject again.

In the years since that first conversation, both editors and many contributors to this volume have experienced additional personal and community losses. Such is the nature of life. When those losses are characterized by the kinds of disenfranchisement related to discrimination, oppression, and marginalization, the impacts on individuals, communities, and society more generally create reverberations that can be felt across generations. Understanding of and advocacy for groups that have been marginalized in their disenfranchised grief is not exclusively reserved for graduate training programs or accessible only to mental health professionals.

With shared academic and clinical experience, Renee and Sarah understand the issues surrounding accessibility and representation and are committed to a conscious author selection process. Earnest efforts were made to invite authors representative of a diverse range of backgrounds and voices who also had lived personal or professional experiences related to their chapter content and insight on the intricacies presented in grief and loss. Renee and Sarah were also sharply aware of their own privilege. They made intentional efforts to mitigate the blind spots their privilege creates by involving contributors in a collective creative process. For example, each chapter underwent a blind peer-review process to reduce potential bias. Also, as two White women, the editors consciously chose the powerful image on this book's front cover, to represent the fragmentation associated with disenfranchised grief. We were delighted to find an image that not only evokes this sense but also includes diversity, a contrast in a field of book covers that are disproportionately represented by people with light skin. In another effort to check their bias, the editors sought feedback about the image from many chapter contributors who felt validated by the image choice, stating it was affirming to see "people who look like me" on a cover.

Part of the hardest work in co-editing this book has been helping many of the authors write what they can about the subjects they chose to expose in their chapters, to lay bare in black and white on the page what is private and vulnerable. Because most of them wrote from personal perspectives with the material they offered, this was neither an easy task nor one they or we took lightly. Some of the chapters that could not be included in this volume required further "digestion" from the authors based on the intersection of their direct experiences, discrimination, and systemic oppression. Indeed, keeping an objective perspective that would be helpful in the professional context that we are aiming to impact with this work required further development of personal resources that have been particularly taxed during the unprecedented times of this pandemic. Yet, we fully accept and embrace where people are with their own stories and capacities to convey them at this time. We did our best in this regard to help each of them "polish" their "precious gems" to bring them to light in this format.

How the book is organized

It is impossible to capture every type of disenfranchised grief in a volume of this length, and even more impossible to capture the felt experience of each individual at every intersection of identity. With this knowledge, the editors focused on identifying groups that have been disenfranchised and have received the least amount of focus and attention from researchers and scholars.

Part I explores the holistic foundations of disenfranchised grief. Chapter 1 expands the notion of disenfranchised grief to include concepts related to discrimination, oppression, and marginalization. The remaining chapters in Part I present a holistic viewpoint of disenfranchised grief that is rarely discussed in the literature related to grief or disenfranchised grief. Chapter 2 relates intersectionality to the complicated nature of disenfranchised grief with pointed examples of the interplay between identity, marginalization, and grief. Chapter 3 invites readers to consider the embodied nature of grief and the importance of clinically attending to a client's somatic experience of loss. Chapter 4 discusses the role of spiritual and religious grief and trauma, moral injury, and pathways for clinicians to therapeutically integrate faith and spirituality into their practice. Chapter 5 boldly addresses the historical influence of racial trauma and the resultant patterns of disenfranchised grief among African Americans.

Part II addresses some of the systemic and social barriers that perpetuate discrimination, oppression, and marginalization that directly influence the grief trajectories of vulnerable populations. In this volume, the authors thoughtfully address biracial individuals and interracial couples and families (Chapter 6), the LGBTQIA+ community (Chapter 7), historical oppression and the effects of the COVID-19 pandemic on African Americans (Chapter 8), individuals with disabilities (Chapter 9), survivors of sexual violence (Chapter 10), and youth confronting violence in school settings (Chapter 11).

Part III takes a vital and novel glimpse at the influence of disenfranchised grief within the family system. This unique section addresses a significant paucity in the literature directly relating to parenting (Chapter 12), sibling loss (Chapter 13), foster families (Chapter 14), military families (Chapter 15), and the impact of war and refugee resettlement on family systems (Chapter 16).

Advancing the discussion about the systemic barriers levied against these vulnerable groups requires a social justice consciousness that implements cultural humility in acknowledging clients' intersecting identities and circumstances, which translates to action and accountability in employing direct allyship with them and advocacy for them. For example, we prioritized the use of person-first language to describe groups/communities/identities/people *who have been minoritized/marginalized*. This language emphasizes that people who have been minoritized are *not less than* those in dominant groups; rather, they have been subject to power-over social structures that discriminate against, oppress, and marginalize them.

The authors of each chapter examined *social, cultural,* and *relational* aspects of disenfranchised grief germane to the population or subject they described. The authors discussed *advocacy and allyship* approaches to empower clinicians to be more effective in recognizing and addressing the cumulative consequences of their clients' disenfranchised grief across the lifespan. They presented *ethical considerations* and offered clinical *strategies and interventions* to support the integration of disenfranchised grief. Finally, they asked *questions for reflective practice* and listed *supplemental electronic resources* to guide clinicians' examination of their relationship with their own grief and disenfranchised grief experiences. Part of this introspection necessitates simultaneously acknowledging the privilege clinicians carry into the therapeutic relationship. This privilege could pertain to their individual characteristics (e.g., race, ethnicity, gender identity and expression, sexual orientation, speaker of one of their nation's native languages, identification with a religious or political majority, socioeconomic status, etc.) and to the opportunities that they have been afforded to be able to pursue and complete higher education and/or mental health licensure, when these are the cases.

In this volume, the authors courageously tackled subjects that are complex, nuanced, and important for working through grief and disenfranchisement with clients. We proudly stand with them and behind them in their treatment of these sensitive subjects and encourage readers to use the information contained within this volume to raise their awareness of the issues and to follow the ethical dictates of their mental health professions in providing the highest standard of grief care for their clients.

Renee Blocker Turner, PhD
Sarah D. Stauffer, PhD

About the contributors

Rev. Dr. Tina K. Boyles Bailey, Dmin, EXAT, Chaplain, is a trauma-informed visual and performing artist, ordained minister, and endorsed chaplain working cross-culturally. Dr. Bailey enjoys guiding people to discover their creative potential through integrating and healing the whole self. Tina has used visual and performing arts in response to traumatic situations following the Bali bombings and the Asian tsunami, with West African refugees, and with displaced people in northern Iraq and eastern Indonesia. She helps prisoners develop skills and process trauma through painting, drawing, and dance. Tina has also worked with church trauma both inside and outside the church.

Layla J. Bonner, PhD, LMFT (Tennessee), NCC, is an assistant professor in the Mental Health Counseling program at Belmont University. Dr. Bonner is an American Association for Marriage and Family Therapy Clinical Fellow and Approved Supervisor. She is trained in EMDR (Levels I and II), Brainspotting (Phase 1), and has completed the EFT externship. She teaches counseling techniques, counseling theories, group, family systems, and practicum/internship. She specializes in attachment wounds, childhood trauma, relational conflict, depression, anxiety, infidelity, grief/loss, and supervision of pre-licensed counselors. Dr. Bonner publishes on race-based trauma, mental health, and coping strategies in the African American community, general trauma, and crisis interventions.

Theresa Fraser, PhD (Candidate), CYC-P, CPT-S, MA, RP, RCT, RT, is a trauma specialist who has also completed birth and death doula training. She teaches in child and youth care programs, play therapy programs, and grief and loss programs. She is an international presenter and supervises therapists in Canada and the United States. She has won provincial, national, and international awards for her mental health service provision.

Brooklyn Gordon is a proud Black woman counselor, who is passionate about holistic healing. Brooke earned her bachelor's in psychology from HBCU Huston-Tillotson University, her master's degree in clinical mental health counseling from the University of Mary Hardin-Baylor. Brooklyn is the co-founder of RE[ME]DY Retreats, LLC, creating brave spaces for Persons of Color to heal in community. Brooklyn is a Licensed Professional Counselor and a Licensed Chemical Dependency Counselor-Intern. Brooklyn is trained in EMDR and specializes in working with Persons of Color, poverty, trauma/grief/loss, and mental illness/substance use. Brooklyn received the 2020 DFPS Champion of Children, Family, and Community Services Award and the 2021 Ancestors' Wildest Dreams Award from TAHDOE.

Maria Haiyasoso, PhD, LPC-S, RPT™, NCC is an associate professor in the Professional Counseling Program at Texas State University. Dr. Haiyasoso serves as secretary for the Texas Association for Play Therapy and a committee member for the International Association for Resilience and Trauma Counseling. She publishes regularly and provides trainings on topics related to applying relational-cultural theory (RCT) and working with survivors of trauma. Further, she owns and operates a private practice where she provides counseling and play therapy for survivors of trauma, primarily survivors of child sexual abuse, sexual assault, and/or intimate partner violence.

Edward (Franc) Hudspeth, PhD, NCC, LPC-S, ACS, RPT-S™, RPh, is Chair and Associate Professor of Counselor Education at Sacred Heart University in Fairfield, Connecticut. He is the editor of the *International Journal of Play Therapy*, the co-editor of the *Journal of Military and Government Counseling*, and an editorial board member for the *Journal of Creativity in Mental Health* and *The Professional Counselor*. He serves as the past president of the Association for Creativity in Counseling and president-elect of the Military and Government Counseling Association. His writing and research interests include creative applications in mental health, telemental health, ethical and legal issues, neuroscience influences on play therapy, trauma's impact on brain development, and psychopharmacology.

Emily R. Keller, PhD, LPCC, NCC, RPT-S™, works with individuals, couples, children, families, and groups in her private practice. She specializes in offering play therapy, sand tray therapy, expressive arts therapy, and redecision therapy to clients who are dealing with grief, trauma, and major life changes. She offers play therapy training and supervision focused on family play therapy and emotional regulation. She lives in California with her husband and four sons and is a regular practitioner of yoga.

Theresa Libios, PhD (ABD), LPC, is a mental health specialist at Leander Independent School District, the director and clinician at Blaine Counseling and Consulting (BCC), a non-profit mental health agency in Texas. She specializes in EMDR, play therapy, crisis intervention, and psycho-education. She is an adjunct professor at Henderson University, formed BCC to decrease mental barriers, and writes self-guided journals.

Marshall Lyles, MA, LMFT-S, LPC-S, RPT-S™, EMDRIA Approved Consultant, has over 20 years of practice in family and play therapy. Drawing on lessons learned from working with attachment trauma in a variety of mental health settings, Marshall regularly teaches on sand tray therapy, other expressive modalities such as poetry, and attachment-informed family work around the globe. In addition to co-authoring the book *Advanced Sandtray Therapy: Digging Deeper into Clinical Practice*, he has contributed multiple chapters and articles to publications.

Alton R. McCallum Jr., Ed.D., LPC, NCC, is the founder of Insight Counseling and Training Center with offices in Belton and Georgetown, Texas. Alton specializes in counseling leaders and emerging leaders, men coming of age, trauma, emotionally healthy leadership, and emotional literacy. He works extensively with military, veterans, and emergency response. Alton is a retired army officer, a veteran of Operation Iraqi Freedom and Operation Enduring Freedom, and a recipient of the Purple Heart. He completed his undergraduate degree at the United States Military Academy; his master's at the University of Mary Hardin-Baylor (UMHB); and his doctorate at Johns Hopkins University.

Mandi Meléndez, MA, LMFT-S, LPC-S, RPT-S™, is the owner of Nurture Family Counseling with locations in and around Austin, Texas. She is a child and family therapist specializing in creative and expressive therapies, an author, an international speaker, and the clinical editor of *Play Therapy*™ Magazine.

Doneley Meris, MA, MSW, is a grief psychotherapist and training-educational consultant. He is the founder and executive director of HIV Arts Network – a supportive organization that provides free mental health services to men and women living with HIV/AIDS and their support networks. He specializes in human – LGBTQIA+ sexuality and complicated grief (HIV/AIDS, COVID, and others) and consults with mental health and hospice care organizations to facilitate dignified patient end-of-life care and life transitions for death-loss survivors. He has been an adjunct instructor in applied psychology and clinical social work at New York University, CUNY Hunter College, and Columbia University.

Mary Bess W. Pannel is Associate Professor of Counselor Education and Psychology at Delta State University. Dr. Pannel earned her Ph.D. in counselor education and supervision with an emphasis in school counseling (Mississippi State University, 2016). Dr. Pannel holds two master's degrees and an education specialist degree (Mississippi College – 2007, 2006, and 2003) and a bachelor's degree (Louisiana State University-2002). She has taught, supervised, and served in various roles in higher education for the past 15 years. Dr. Pannel is a licensed professional counselor and a national certified counselor. Her research interests include child and adolescent groups, data-driven practices, and creative techniques in counseling.

Rochelle Ritzi, PhD, is a Licensed Professional Counselor Supervisor, National Certified Counselor, Registered Play Therapist – Supervisor™, Certified First Responder Counselor, and an adjunct professor at the University of North Texas and Palo Alto University. Dr. Ritzi is a co-owner/founder of Bright Spot Counseling Center in the Dallas area. Her areas of expertise include play therapy, activity therapy, group counseling, and working with individuals with disabilities. Dr. Ritzi enjoys being involved in the Deaf/hard of hearing culture and offers counseling in American Sign Language. Dr. Ritzi has conducted research, published, and presented regionally and internationally in the field of counseling.

Tangela C. Sawyerr, DSW, MA, MSW, is a Licensed Social Worker with decades of experience engaging the most vulnerable segments of our society, including pregnant and post-partum mothers on methadone maintenance, individuals experiencing homelessness, and abused/ neglected children. She is Assistant Professor at the Rutgers University School of Social Work, and her qualitative research has been published in the *Journal of Ethnicity in Criminal Justice*. Tangela's research interests focus on adult sibling bereavement, intersectionality, and the impact of structural inequities on minoritized communities.

Quinn K. Smelser, PhD, NCC, LPC-S, RPT-S™, is a lecturer at the George Washington University and a private practitioner in Maryland. In addition to her published research, she has a clinical background in grief and loss and trauma treatment for children and adolescents. She has worked in residential treatment, hospice, with military families, and with youth and families experiencing traumatic grief and loss. Quinn completed her doctorate in counseling and human development at the George Washington University, her master's degree in counseling from Texas State University, and her bachelor's degree in psychology from the University of Texas at Austin.

Sarah D. Stauffer, PhD, LPC, NCC, NCSC, RPT-S™, Psychologue-Psychothérapeute FSP, Art-thérapeute APSAT, is Clinical Director of Children's Psychotherapy Services, Director of Research and Teaching, and lead crisis intervention specialist at the non-profit Association ESPAS (Espace de Soutien et Prévention – Abus Sexuels) for the cantons of Vaud and Valais, Switzerland. She specializes in play therapy, crisis intervention, and psychological trauma treatment for people of all ages. She is an instructor and supervisor of play therapy, family therapy, and trauma treatment; an author; an international speaker; and an associate editor of the *International Journal of Play Therapy*.

Renee Blocker Turner, PhD, LPC-S, RPT-S™, is Director of the Expressive Therapies Institute, PLLC, an author, a researcher, a speaker, and a private practitioner in San Antonio, Texas, with 20 years of experience supporting individuals and families in grief. She publishes on grief and loss, trauma, play therapy, and counselor development. Renee is the past president of the Texas Association for Play Therapy and has held numerous leadership positions within the Association for Play Therapy. She has been recognized by state and national associations for excellence in scholarship, service, and teaching. She practices from a relational Gestalt framework, using sand tray and expressive therapies to help clients integrate experiences.

Meyleen M. Velasquez, DSW, LICSW, RPT-S™, PMH-C, is an immigrant Latinx psychotherapist specializing in perinatal and infant mental health. Her practice supports birthing people and clinicians working from an anti-oppressive framework. Meyleen identified as a Brown person for most of her life until several years ago, when vitiligo changed how she navigates the world. She is on the board of the Washington Association for Infant Mental Health. She served as the chair for the Florida Chapter of Postpartum Support International and as president of the Florida Association for Play Therapy.

Christina Villarreal-Davis, PhD, LPC-S, NCC, RPT-S™, is an Assistant Professor at Liberty University and the Clinical Director of Wellspring of Life Counseling and Play Therapy Center, PLLC, in San Antonio, Texas. She specializes in working with all ages, utilizing play therapy, expressive arts, and sand tray therapy. Her teaching and research interests include play and sand tray therapy, child–parent relationship therapy, family therapy, children in foster care, military families, PTSD/trauma, multiculturalism/diversity, and merging creativity in counseling supervision. She is an author and international speaker and has served as the President of Texas APT and Chair of APT's Leadership Academy.

Christina Watts-Figueroa, MA, LMFT-S, LPC, RPT-S™, EMDRIA Approved Consultant, is the co-owner of Yellow Ribbon Counseling PLLC in Kileen, Texas. She specializes in play therapy, EMDR therapy, sand tray therapy, and family therapy with all ages, and her primary clinical population is the military and veteran community and their families. She is a trainer, speaker, author, and doctoral student at Walden University in the Counselor Education and Supervision program. She also serves in various roles on national, state, and local mental health associations and co-founded the Central Texas Chapter of the Texas Association for Play Therapy.

Chinwé U. Williams, PhD, LPC, NCC, CPCS, is a board-certified EMDR therapist and owner of Meaningful Solutions Counseling and Consulting in Roswell, GA. She has taught at Georgia State University, Argosy University, the University of Central Florida, and Rollins College; has served as a high school counselor, group facilitator, and executive coach; and currently works as a therapist and consultant for schools, non-profit, and corporate work settings. Dr. Williams specializes in grief and trauma resolution, stress/anxiety management, and women's wellness. She is a published author and a featured blog and podcast contributor on trauma, grief, race, and parenting. She received the 2009 Courtland C. Lee Multicultural Excellence in Scholarship Award.

Dr. Amanda Winburn is currently serving as an Associate Professor at the University of Mississippi within the Department of Leadership and Counselor Education. She is a licensed educator, counselor, and administrator with over a decade of experience working with children in various settings. She currently serves as the Program Coordinator for the Ed.S. in Counselor Education (Play Therapy Specialization Track). Dr. Winburn has been actively involved in play therapy at the University of Mississippi, both in the clinical setting and in actively conducting research within the field. Other research interests include school counseling, bullying, and advocacy.

Selma Zakomac-Baćevac, MA, LMHC, is a licensed psychotherapist, consultant, and clinical supervisor in Florida, United States. She consults with providers and patients from around the world, working to heal intergenerational wounds caused by interpersonal and war trauma. She specializes in the generational effects of war on interpersonal relationships between parents and children. She is also a children's book author, providing a therapeutic way to speak about war and refugees to young children.

Part I

Foundations for understanding disenfranchised grief

Disenfranchised grief

The complicated interweave of death and non-death losses

Renee Blocker Turner and Sarah D. Stauffer

Grief is perhaps life's most complex phenomenon because, despite its universal nature, the grief experience is unique to each individual and sensitive to internal and external influences. As such, no two grief experiences are the same. Although grief models highlight different aspects of the grief process (e.g., cognitive, attachment, narrative), the importance of connection and emotional support is undisputed. Research consistently indicates that social isolation, disconnection, and poor support systems negatively influence outcomes. From this, validation and acknowledgment are necessary to process grief. However, *disenfranchised grief* is socially invalidated and unacknowledged (Doka, 2008), thus lacking the necessary components to navigate the grief journey. Given the importance of connection to process, integrate, and heal the many wounds of grief, it is not surprising that disenfranchised grief is present in grief scenarios with poorer outcomes.

Disenfranchised grief

Doka (1989) suggested that disenfranchised grief occurred across three typologies: (1) the relationship is not recognized, (2) the loss is not acknowledged, and (3) the griever is excluded. He later added (4) the cause of death is stigmatized by society and (5) the way griever processes their grief (Doka, 2008).

The relationship is not recognized

In the first category, others do not *recognize the relationship*, reducing the likelihood that the griever will be supported and thus denying the opportunity to express and process the loss. This vast category often overlaps with the other

DOI: 10.4324/9781003292890-2

types of disenfranchised losses. Grief related to non-kin losses (e.g., stepparents, foster parents, neighbors, co-workers, caregivers, friends, and lovers) is often assumed to not have high levels of attachment by others; thus, it does not receive the same empathic response provided to kinship losses (Doka, 2008). When met with this reaction, individuals may question their right to grieve or may feel judged by a grief response that is outside social, cultural, or relational expectations.

For example, the loss of a partner identifying within the LGBTQIA+ community (see Chapter 7) in a cultural or social system that does not recognize the relationship inhibits the griever's outward expression of mourning. In this scenario, the social and cultural dynamics of marginalization and oppression directly influence the level of disenfranchised grief the surviving partner experiences. However, the griever may also experience disenfranchisement from their family and the legal system when the relationship is not publicly or legally acknowledged, creating additional secondary losses.

Another aspect of this loss typology is a "grief reaction [that] brings finality to [an] earlier loss, ending any remaining contact or fantasy of reconciliation or reinvolvement" (Doka, 2008, p. 231). Here, an individual may grieve the death of a childhood abuser (see Chapter 10). The client can experience competing and confusing emotions when, for example, their father, who sexually abused them for many years, dies in prison. Despite the trauma injury, clients can still feel intense sorrow and mourning for the attachment that once existed or the loss of an attachment that never was.

The grief is not acknowledged

The second type of disenfranchised grief, *lack of acknowledgment*, is the most pervasive and includes a large portion of non-death losses, many of which are discussed in subsequent chapters. Social standards and cultural attitudes heavily influence losses in this category. The division of these grief scenarios is complex and ranges from discounted attachment (e.g., pet loss, miscarriages) and marginalization (e.g., racism, political losses) to physical losses (e.g., disability, infertility). In another example, a child may experience feelings of grief after the divorce of their biological or adoptive parent from a stepparent. Society may incorrectly assume the child does not grieve this loss because the stepparent (who is still alive) was not their biological parent and thus no attachment exists.

The griever is excluded

The third category of loss relates to grievers who are *excluded from the grief process*. This category traditionally contains children and individuals with disabilities, who are assumed to lack the cognitive or emotional ability to understand and process grief. However, from a social perspective, losses may also include being non-native speakers, immigrants, and refugees (see Chapter 16), many of whom may not have the financial or legal means or support to advocate for or travel to their home countries to participate in funeral rites performed at the time prescribed by cultural or religious customs. Corporate policies related to bereavement leave also prohibit extended bereavement leave when the loss is not a parent, spouse, or child, which discounts the cultural importance of extended family.

The death is stigmatized

Doka's (2008) fourth category of disenfranchised grief is related to the *stigmatization* of the method and manner of death. The authors have well documented the disenfranchised experience of deaths linked to suicide and homicide. Guilt and shame are key aspects of the stigma associated with these types of deaths. Similarly, grief related to substance abuse (Valentine et al., 2016), abortion (e.g., due to a fetal anomaly; Goldblatt Hyatt, 2021), incarceration of family members and families of death row inmates (Jones & Beck, 2006), deaths after police contact (Baker et al., 2021), and family members of sex offenders (Bailey, 2018) also carry social stigmatization.

How the griever grieves

The fifth type of loss relates to *how the griever grieves*. Initially proposed through a gendered lens (Martin & Doka, 1999), there was some discussion around the influence of culture as a mediator of how a person grieves. Recent understanding of the current viewpoint of gender through a non-binary lens and culture through a lens of cultural humility emphasizes the need to recognize a client's intersecting identities (see Chapters 2, 6, and 13) when counseling them through grief reactions and processes. Cultural and religious rites and practices that have been marginalized, misunderstood, or considered threatening are often stigmatized, disenfranchised, and even legally prohibited. For example, African Diaspora devotees outside of the African continent have experienced rights infringements in the form of physical assaults on their person, their homes, and their places of worship, and have been disenfranchised through the prohibition of different religious practices (Boaz, 2021a).

Expanding the viewpoint on disenfranchised grief

We propose a sixth typology of disenfranchised grief to contribute to and advance practitioners' current understanding of disenfranchised grief, as Doka stated in the Foreword to this volume. We suggest that non-death *losses specifically related to discrimination, marginalization, and oppression* comprise another unique typology for consideration in the context of disenfranchised grief and are the emphasis of this book. Although the combined six typologies serve as a practical conceptual framework, clinicians should not assume they are mutually exclusive or comprehensive. Instead, readers should consider the complex interweaving of losses to gain a more holistic understanding of loss that destigmatizes the internal experiences of grief and disenfranchised grief on the body and the mind.

The neurobiology of grief

In this holistic view, it is essential to consider how the brain and nervous system shape around death and non-death losses rather than consider grief and loss as an external experience. In communities that have been disenfranchised and marginalized, like the ones presented in this book, individuals also may bear the burden of unresolved intergenerational trauma and loss or chronic oppression, thereby amplifying the neurological impact of grief.

In 1969, Bowlby identified the role of attachment as a mediator in the grief process. Since then, researchers have consistently confirmed the myriad ways attachment styles influence the grief process and outcomes. Advances in neuroscience establish a deeper understanding of *how* the brain experiences and processes grief, pointing to specific components of attachment useful for grief practitioners. Briefly, attachment is rooted in the organism's experience of attunement and reciprocity, leading to synchronicity and co-regulation, which encourage the development of a neural network with the ability to self-regulate and self-soothe within a system that is predictable and safe (Porges, 2011; Siegel, 2020). However, attachment styles and patterns are not fixed and are subject to ongoing relational ruptures, unresolved losses, and traumas across the lifespan.

According to Siegel (2020), unresolved trauma and losses, including non-death losses (e.g., divorce, abandonment, or abuse), can create long-term impairments in self-regulation and functioning. Furthermore,

> unresolved trauma or loss leaves the individual with a deep sense of incoherence in autonoetic consciousness, which tries to make sense of the past, organize the future, and chart the future . . . and can produce lasting effects through the lifespan.
>
> (Siegel, 2020, p. 406)

Because "experience directly shapes regulation" (Siegel, 2020, p. 38), individuals and communities that have been marginalized may lack the necessary foundation and relational support to withstand the high levels of stress associated with disenfranchised grief.

The concepts of neuroception and social engagement influence regulation patterns and help-seeking behaviors during times of perceived threat (Porges, 2011), such as during grief. At the most basic level, *neuroception* is the process by which the nervous system detects safety and threats to safety based on sensory cues from the environment (external) and viscera (internal; viz. Porges, 2011). In healthy, adaptive nervous systems, defenses reduce, allowing for social engagement, the precursor for co-regulation. Unfortunately, individuals surrounding the griever do not always attune and respond to the griever's needs, resulting in an empathic failure. *Empathic failure* is a response to the griever that "subtly or obviously invalidates the bereaved person, family, or community's distinctive narrative of the loss" (Neimeyer & Jordan, 2002, p. 95) and is inherent to disenfranchised grief.

Relatedly, mental mapping (see Chapter 3) is how people understand their surroundings and relationships and is the thread weaving together the past, present, and future (O'Connor, 2022). The merging of past and present into one experience complicates grief. The lack of acknowledgment associated with disenfranchised grief can be jarring and intensely painful when support is expected or part of the mental map. Without the desired or anticipated relational or emotional support, it is easy for individuals to get lost in their journey.

Non-death losses

Individuals experiencing non-death losses may not believe they have the right to grieve, such as foster children, foster parents, and biological and adopted children in foster families (see Chapter 14) or people born with or who develop disabilities (see Chapter 9). Other non-death losses resulting from situational changes, such as becoming a parent (see Chapter 12) or being discharged from the military (see Chapter 15), also incite disenfranchised grief on many levels. Instead of being viewed through the lens of grief, non-death losses are frequently identified as symptoms of depression or anxiety (Papa et al., 2014; Sabin & Daniels, 2017). As such, few opportunities exist to process and integrate these losses.

However, accumulated psychological and social grief likely account for significantly more grief history when viewed across the lifespan. Moreover, an overarching feature of non-death losses is the psychosocial aspect of loss. Rando (1984) described psychosocial losses as *symbolic losses*. Symbolic losses are not tangible and often abstract in nature, such as the loss of a "dream," "future," or "freedom," and are bound by cultural and social norms and mores unique to the griever. Psychosocial losses may also impact one's self-perception (Mitchell, 2017). Papa et al. (2014) found an overlap in symptoms in bereaved individuals who also experienced non-death grief stemming from job loss or divorce; participants had elevated prolonged grief symptoms in four areas of analysis: longing/yearning, feeling stunned/shocked/dazed by the event, trouble accepting what happened, and avoidance of reminders of the event. Without the apparent signaling of a death-loss event, clinicians may misdiagnose grief from non-death losses as clinical depression, for example, and thus inaccurately treat the client.

Discrimination, oppression, and marginalization

As a general concept, disenfranchisement is related to the deprivation of a right (e.g., to vote) or a privilege (e.g., to legal counsel), or is a felt disconnection (e.g., not sharing a sense of belonging) within a specified context (e.g., a democracy, a criminal or civil trial, or a school setting). Disenfranchisement results from discrimination, oppression, and marginalization. Researchers have documented the intergenerational epigenetic and environmental impacts of historical trauma and historical unresolved grief in populations that have been resettled and marginalized, such as Indigenous Americans (e.g., Brave Heart & DeBruyn, 1998), African Americans (e.g., Wilkins et al., 2013; Williams, 2016), Jewish Holocaust survivors (e.g., Kellerman, 2013; Yehuda & Lehrner, 2018), and war trauma survivors (e.g., Bezo & Maggi, 2015; Ramo-Fernández et al., 2015), the current effects of which include symptoms of posttraumatic stress disorder (PTSD; Williams et al., 2018).

When this discrimination, oppression, and marginalization happen at the juncture of several facets of a person's identity, it may hinder their integration and acceptance into larger society. For example, forms of *religious racism*, the prejudice that sits at the intersection of religious intolerance and racism (Boaz, 2021a, 2021b), continue today in prohibiting the right to wear or use symbols of religious attire in public places such as schools, courtrooms, and places of employment (also the military), including locks or dreadlocks hairstyles for devotees to African Diaspora religions (e.g., Boaz, 2021b), a niqab (face veil) in Islam (e.g., Zempi, 2019), or yarmulkes in Judaism and turbans in Sikhism (Green, 2018). Naturally, chronic feelings of marginalization and oppression have pervasive impacts, including on how one identifies and navigates through their grief.

Populations that have been minoritized underutilize mental health services and are reticent to consult mental health practitioners due to the stigma attached to mental illness (Ward et al., 2013) and a sense of discrimination (Burgess et al., 2008), and they may prematurely terminate at higher rates than clients who have not been minoritized (Leong & Lau, 2001). Mistrust that people who have been minoritized feel is not unfounded and may be part of a historical systemic echo propagated through the field of mental health itself:

> The field of psychiatry developed at the time of colonialism and slavery when myths of racism were being integrated into European culture. . . . In America, the Abolitionist and Civil Rights movements were met with mistrust and prejudice by mental health practitioners.
> (Medlock et al., 2016, p. 13)

Prior to the American Civil War, European colonialism imposed social change that contributed to cultural disruption for Indigenous Americans (Brave Heart & DeBruyn, 1998) and arguably for other stolen and resettled peoples. Practitioner bias led to societal dismissal of Indigenous peoples' right to grieve (Brave Heart & DeBruyn, 1998) and continues to affect clinical decision making (Klassen et al., 2002) and the overdiagnosis of mental health disorders for people who have been racially minoritized (Medlock et al., 2016).

Health disparities

Health disparities for populations that have been minoritized are well documented, including "unequal access to salubrious resources and exposures to health risks" due to racial inequalities that contribute to greater prevalence and severity of illnesses and higher death rates (Homan & Brown,

2022, p. 219). Societal discrimination (as opposed to specific healthcare discrimination) contributes to underutilization of healthcare services in general for groups that have been minoritized (Burgess et al., 2008). In the US, the COVID-19 pandemic united these factors in a perfect storm of health disparity and social disenfranchisement that resulted in Indigenous American, Pacific Islander American, Latinx American, and African Americans' mortality rates surpassing their European American and Asian American counterparts' rates in the first two years of the pandemic, when accounting for age by race/ethnicity (Gawthrop, 2022), which had "no modern precedent" for Indigenous Americans (Lopez & Wu, 2022). Hill and Artiga (2022) argued that although the numbers of COVID-19 cases and deaths have varied by race/ethnicity over time, "the underlying structural inequities in health and health care and social and economic factors that placed people of color [sic] at increased risk at the outset of the pandemic remain" (para. 4; see Chapter 8). These social and economic factors include being able to afford insurance and healthcare, initiating help-seeking behaviors, and activating personal and interpersonal resources (e.g., Bindley et al., 2019), which adds further layers of disenfranchisement to the pursuit of wellbeing for People of Color.

Systemic inequities influence and increase grief inequity across racial, social, and gender lines. Because disenfranchisement goes unrecognized by definition, differentiating grief from trauma and other mental health diagnoses and presenting concerns should be among clinicians' top priorities. However, Kim and Ali (2022) argued that medicalizing grief is also controversial because non-death losses are not included in criteria for a persistent complex bereavement disorder diagnosis, for instance, creating a further access barrier by limiting the possibility of medical insurance reimbursement for these types of losses.

Social, cultural, and relational influences

Disenfranchisement and marginalization are influenced by social, cultural, and relational expectations and cannot be overlooked when conceptualizing the subjective experience of grief. With this understanding, authors throughout this text examine the social, cultural, and relational implications of disenfranchised grief. For the purposes of this text, we define *social* as the macro-level systemic influences that condition societies to believe and act in a prescribed way, *cultural* as mezzo-level influences that define expectations for individuals living within in-groups, and *relational* as the interpersonal manifestations of social and cultural influences on an individual's worldview, emotional expression, and behavioral pattern.

Social influences

Power-over social structures cause trauma (Haines, 2019) and subsequent grief. Haines (2019) elaborated that power-over systems assume that some people are more worthy than others of dignity, respect, and safety; those who are less worthy are subject to inequalities in wealth distribution, violence, and exploitation. Becker et al. (2022) found that "deeper grief after bereavement leads not only to more physical problems but also to decreased productivity, more down time, and more medical/social service dependency" (p. 685) in addition to poverty exacerbating lost work time for health reasons and increased pharmacy reliance in Japanese mourners. Social disenfranchisement deepens grief, and grief perpetuates further disparity like a snake biting its tail.

In the context of grief, systemic oppression (e.g., racism, classism, ableism, poverty, etc.) exerts external forces on whole swaths of society and creates barriers to their full participation therein, oftentimes eliminating personal agency at these intersections. For example, meatpackers, as essential workers in the US during the COVID-19 pandemic, may have been forced to choose between working in unsafe conditions (i.e., crowded environments, lack of personal protective equipment) or losing their jobs, many being People of Color and already working for low wages (Kim & Ali, 2022).

Additionally, living under the weight of systemic oppression may lead to individuals adopting behaviors consistent with *internalized oppression* (Freire, 1970/2005), or a "devaluation or an inferiorization of one's self and one's group" (David & Derthick, 2013, p. 2). Internalized oppression may give rise to individuals self-disenfranchising their grief by suppressing the grief process and not allowing themselves to grieve (Kauffman, 2002). Shame is at the root of self-disenfranchisement as a result of comparing oneself to dominant social and cultural norms (e.g., Brave Heart & DeBruyn, 1998).

The process of mourning is "intricately social" (Neimeyer et al., 2014, p. 485) and beseeches the bereaved to find or appropriate meaning within the concentric circles touched by the loss, "from personal and familial, but also broader community and even cultural spheres" (p. 485). However, with disenfranchised grief, meaning making is often not possible because the underlying causes of the grief are also the reasons it is disenfranchised. In these cases, acknowledging the causes and the disenfranchisement are necessary for processing the grief in culturally appropriate ways.

Cultural influences

Culture and identity are inextricably linked. Culture often prescribes how and if grief may be expressed, for example, outwardly projected or unobtrusively manifested. Culture also dictates a timeline on which different rites and rituals may be performed in the case of death losses (i.e., funeral and burial rites) and sometimes for non-death losses, as well (e.g., introducing children to a new partner after divorce). The aspects of one's intersecting identities with which they most identify will inform the person of required or recommended cultural expectations. Following those prescriptions may bring comfort and a sense of belonging during a difficult time, offering an anchoring point for resilience. However, conflicting views may create personal dissonance and a sense of disenfranchised grief in *not* wishing to participate in or perform certain acts, rituals, or activities associated with the loss or in being or feeling excluded from doing so (see Chapter 4).

Relational influences

In the wake of loss, an individual is embedded in their entourage, community, culture, and society. Grievers often seek community with whom to mourn in the case of death losses or with whom to commiserate and feel heard and understood in the aftermath of oppressive, discriminatory, and marginalizing experiences. Peskin (2019) observed:

> Permission to grieve belongs to a relational process of recognizing loss through the real or virtual company of others and is more essential to the process of mourning than we often let ourselves know. Even without public display, grief is dialogic, representing a simultaneous need to listen and be listened to – to give comfort and be comforted – about the meaning of the loss.
>
> (p. 479)

Interestingly, in Peskin's (2019) analysis, grief can become further disenfranchised when one or more people usurp one's right to grieve, "deem[ing] themselves more appropriate to suffer object loss" (p. 477), or self-disenfranchised when one defers their mourning to another in conceding to a social hierarchy within the relationships between those experiencing it. This deference circumscribes efforts to integrate the losses, which "can be one of the many faces of intrapsychic delay that covertly prolongs grief" (Peskin, 2019, p. 477).

Once it manifests, this grief deferred, much like the "dream deferred" that Langston Hughes (1951) described in *Harlem*, could wither inside the person, weigh on them individually, or provoke conflict if it explodes in anger or aggression. Haines (2019) explained:

> Because of oppressive social conditions, there are fundamental skills that many [people] don't learn to embody . . . having boundaries that take care of [self] and others, mutual contact and intimacy, moving toward what is important to you, or building trust amidst conflict. Other survival skills become embodied, including: hypervigilance and distrust, appeasing, and aggression. Trauma and oppression can leave people with a deep sense of powerlessness, isolation, and shame.
>
> (p. 30)

To overcome the loss of connection and attachment, grievers must begin by acknowledging the multiple levels of losses associated with their disenfranchisement to bear witness to their own suffering. Working with a grief practitioner to disentangle and dismantle internalized messages of oppression can be helpful in this process and provide an external witness to this suffering and advocate for mitigating its effects in the person's lifespan and life-space.

General clinical approaches

Despite the ubiquitous nature of grief, clinicians struggle to engage clients in meaningful methods for processing their grief. Without a comprehensive understanding of the whole person, including social, cultural, and relational influences, clinicians can easily miss subtle themes of grief and disenfranchisement. Treatment conceptualization should begin with clinical training and include specific training and supervision on grief, disenfranchised grief, and psychological trauma. From that solid base of support, practitioners can help clients process their experiences from the perspective of cultural humility, acknowledge clients' hitherto unrecognized identities and needs, and design trauma-informed strategies for optimal care. The authors of each chapter identify ethical considerations, allyship and advocacy, and treatment strategies specific to the population of focus. However, a few general areas warrant discussion.

Clinical training programs

Researchers suggest that many training programs do not provide foundational training in bereavement and grief practices. Wheat et al. (2022) identified a lack of consistent or available grief-focused coursework in 61 counselor educator programs, meaning many entry-level clinicians are not adequately prepared to support complex grief cases. Part of the educational negligence observed in the paucity of grief classes being offered may parallel the consistent barriers King (2021) identified as "plaguing the multicultural counseling literature: (a) It is broad, aspirational, and often vague, and (b) it can occasion counselor resistance and self-protective defense strategies" (p. 88). To effectively ally with clients in their intersecting identities and the multitude of stressors that contribute to their disenfranchised grief, counselors-in-training must be taught to "translate course experiences into actionable skills" (King, 2021, p. 88). King (2021) suggested *broaching* issues with clients by openly discussing issues such as race/ethnicity, racism, culture, and power, despite the discomfort both Black and White practitioners have demonstrated when working with people of different cultural backgrounds. The same discomfort exists for grief practitioners.

Hay et al. (2021) found a significant gap between grief knowledge and practice among 140 bereavement practitioners worldwide. The top three reported deficit areas were (1) supporting clients' growth, resilience, and recovery through the grief process, (2) distinguishing grief from mental health issues (e.g., depression, PTSD, anxiety), and (3) learning to recognize complicated grief more quickly (Hay et al., 2021, p. 337). Broaching both cultural identity and grief issues with clients will help practitioners make more accurate differential diagnoses and plan treatment strategies to address the underlying issues more acutely.

Cohen Konrad (2010) found that preparing social workers with bereavement competencies, such as relational and communication skills and cultural and self-reflective capacities, allowed them to "transition from anxiety, to curiosity, to appreciating how 'suffering with' can make their clients' difficult life circumstances more bearable and their mourning more conducive to healing" (p. 27). Self-reflection promoted students' self-awareness of the impact "suffering with" clients had on their own wellbeing, bolstering their "appreciation for the centrality of culturally attuned and compassionate communication and also for the importance of being patient with others and loving with themselves" (Cohen Konrad, 2010, p. 25).

Finally, Breen (2011) noted a disparity between academics and clinicians in accessibility to affordable scholarly material and everyday clinician concerns. If general grief and bereavement are absent from most graduate training programs, then discussions about disenfranchised grief are also likely absent from initial training and, perhaps, continuing education levels. Broaching grief, loss, and cultural content holistically as part of diversity or trauma coursework may fulfill accreditation standards without requiring additional coursework.

Trauma-informed care

Although not all grief is traumatic, all trauma contains partial elements of grief (e.g., loss of safety, loss of an assumptive worldview). As previously indicated, health disparities influence *if* and *how* an individual seeks mental health support in response to their grief and *how* their grief is perceived by providers. Klassen et al. (2002) proffered:

> We must acknowledge that the cumulative effect of negative experiences across the life course becomes the prism through which current choices are viewed. Caregivers cannot undo a patient's past experiences, but they can be aware of the influence of those experiences on current decisions and well-being.
>
> (p. 816)

Resilience is a factor in grief that appears to promote coping with minimal disturbance in functioning (Bonanno, 2009).

For grievers with individual or collective histories embedded with trauma and marginalization, the core conditions creating resilience may be lacking, preventing the griever from grieving well. Considering the interplay of intersectionality (Crenshaw, 1989) in a holistic view of grief, it is obvious that some grievers are prone to disenfranchised grief. In their research, Taku et al. (2008) found the following factors facilitated *posttraumatic growth*: personal strength, relating to others, new possibilities, appreciation of life, and spiritual and existential change. Pliske et al. (2022) also emphasized the importance of relationships for nurturing creative expression and posttraumatic growth subsequent to the trauma and grief that accompany adverse childhood experiences (ACEs; Felitti et al., 1998; see also Anda et al., 2006; Finkelhor et al., 2015). Unfortunately, these factors and means are not socially accessible to all individuals.

For example, an individual oppressed by intergenerational trauma or poverty may genuinely not *see* new possibilities, and their opportunity for positively relating to others may not be reciprocated. Witnessing violence significantly impacts the mind and nervous system (Siegel, 2020). Interpersonal violence, war, and similar events activate the sympathetic nervous system (fight or flight) and parasympathetic nervous system (freeze and faint) responses (van der Kolk, 2015). Additionally, the ease of media accessibility increases one's exposure to potentially traumatic content, bringing the plight of individuals who have been marginalized to light more than ever before.

Millions of people watched George Floyd take his last breath. Watching this or the police response to the Uvalde school shooting burns into viewers' minds and bodies. Even if viewers did not know George Floyd or the individuals killed in Uvalde personally (kin attachment), their bodies responded nonetheless to the threat and the grief these situations provoked: the racial trauma of Black bodies dying after a police encounter (see Chapter 5) and children and teachers being killed at school (see Chapter 11). These experiences stay in the nervous system and may be amplified by increased identification with the victims or situations, leaving populations that have been marginalized and oppressed in further mental health precarity. In these cases, disenfranchisement is doubled down with more disenfranchisement.

To counter the effects of "dissociation, minimization, and numbing [as] normal responses to trauma, oppression, and difficult life experiences" (Haines, 2019, p. 24) that contribute to mental health precarity, grief practitioners need to help clients recognize their disenfranchised grief, acknowledge it, and speak the unspoken. This will help survivors interrupt their fight or flight and freeze or faint responses to promote *flow*, an end-outcome term used by Seng and the Complex ACES and Complex Aid (CAsCAid) Group (2019) to describe a "positive state of embodied (or physical or somatic) recovery" (p. 200), "an active state, useful for daily life, attainable more routinely, and sustainable by trauma survivors" (p. 203).

Addressing shame and self-esteem

Feelings of shame and worthlessness are natural byproducts of chronic oppression and marginalization cited repeatedly throughout this book. In the context of grief, pre-existing shame patterns present in intergenerational trauma constrict one's expression of normal grief responses, resulting in compounded feelings of inadequacy, low self-esteem, and self-blame. Although previous research was inconclusive, emerging research suggests that shame and low self-esteem are likely linked to symptoms of prolonged grief (Dellmann, 2018). Considering the characteristics of Doka's (1989, 2008) disenfranchised grief typologies, it is reasonable to hypothesize that individuals experiencing disenfranchised grief are more susceptible to the impacts of shame.

Shame produces a profound feeling of self-deficiency, causing individuals to withdraw from others. This is poignantly represented in Chaoseum's (2021) lyrics from *Leaving Paradise*: "Like an ugly kid, drowning in his shame/I feel my goodness die/In my loneliness, I continue to scream your name/But you're already out of my sight." Deep in the cycle of shame, individuals may defer their grief to others, block their feelings of grief, or feel guilty for not grieving the right way (Rosbrow, 2019). Shame also impacts the belief that the griever has the right to grieve, amplifying self-disenfranchisement (Kauffman, 2002). However, a healthy and safe connection is the antidote to shame. Normalizing and validating the client's experience are essential elements of addressing shame as clients navigate their disenfranchised grief and non-death losses.

Summary

Grief is universal, yet individually or collectively experienced through social, cultural, and relational influences. Misattunement between grievers and their support system, community, culture, or society can impact their individual experience of neurobiological alignment and interpersonal interactions. When the griever experiences discrimination, oppression, and marginalization at the juncture of their intersecting identities, they are at increased risk of experiencing disenfranchised grief. However, it is possible that a client has internalized dominant social or cultural norms and may not realize they are experiencing grief.

Grief practitioners must be willing to invite the whole person of their client into the room, to recognize their intersecting identities, and to acknowledge their grief and the disenfranchisement in their grief processes and experiences. Broaching may be helpful in overcoming the cultural and bereavement gaps that exist for mental health professionals in addressing clients' shame and in promoting their self-esteem. Clinical training and supervision on grief, disenfranchised grief, psychological trauma, and cultural humility provide a springboard for promoting clinicians' efforts to provide a minimum ethical standard of care and to activate allyship and advocacy functions. These subjects can be integrated into existing trauma or diversity coursework to meet accreditation standards without expanding program requirements.

References

Anda, R. F., Felitti, V. J., Bremner, D., Walker, J. D., Whitfield, C., Perry, B. D., Dube, S. R., & Giles, W. H. (2006). The enduring effects of abuse and related adverse experiences in childhood: A convergence of evidence from neurobiology and epidemiology. *European Archives Psychiatry and Clinical Neuroscience*, *256*(3), 174–186. https://doi.org/10.1007/s00406-005-0624-4

Bailey, D. J. S. (2018). A life of grief: An exploration of disenfranchised grief in sex offender significant others. *American Journal of Criminal Justice: The Journal of* the *Southern Criminal Justice Association, 43*(3), 641–667. https://doi.org/10.1007/s12103-017-9416-4

Baker, D., Norris, D., & Cherneva, V. (2021). Disenfranchised grief and families' experiences of death after police contact in the United States. *OMEGA – Journal of Death and Dying, 83*(2), 239–256. https://doi.org/10.1177/0030222819846420

Becker, C. B., Taniyama, Y., Kondo-Arita, M., Yamada, S., & Yamamoto, K. (2022). How grief, funerals, and poverty affect bereaved health, productivity, and medical dependence in Japan. *OMEGA – Journal of Death and Dying, 85*(3), 669–689. https://doi.org/10.1177/0030222820947573

Bezo, B., & Maggi, S. (2015). Living in "survival mode:" Intergenerational transmission of trauma from the Holodomor genocide of 1932–1933 in Ukraine. *Social Science and Medicine, 134*, 87–94. https://doi.org/10.1016/j.socscimed.2015.04.009

Bindley, K., Lewis, J., Travaglia, J., & DiGiacomo, M. (2019). Disadvantaged and disenfranchised in bereavement: A scoping review of social and structural inequity following expected death. *Social Science and Medicine, 242*, 1–16. https://doi.org/10.1016/j.socscimed.2019.112599

Boaz, D. N. (2021a). *Banning Black gods: Law and religions of the African Diaspora*. Penn State University Press.

Boaz, D. N. (2021b, September 13). Law, religious racism, and religions of the African Diaspora [Interview]. *The Religious Studies Project*. www.religiousstudiesproject.com/wp-content/uploads/2021/09/369-Reg.mp3

Bonanno, G. A. (2009). *The other side of sadness: What the new science of bereavement tells us about life after loss*. Basic Books.

Bowlby, J. (1969). *Attachment and loss: Attachment (Vol 1)*. Hogarth Press and the Institute of Psycho-Analysis.

Brave Heart, M. Y. H., & DeBruyn, L. M. (1998). The American Indian Holocaust: Healing historical unresolved grief. *American Indian and Alaska Native Mental Health Research, 8*(2), 60–82.

Breen, L. J. (2011). Professionals' experiences of grief counseling: Implications for bridging the gap between research and practice. *OMEGA – Journal of Death and Dying, 62*(3), 285–303. https://doi.org/10.2190/OM.62.3.e

Burgess, D. J., Ding, Y., Hargreaves, M., van Ryn, M., & Phelan, S. (2008). The association between perceived discrimination and underutilization of needed medical and mental health care in a multi-ethnic community sample. *Journal of Health Care for the Poor and Underserved, 19*(3), 894–911. https://doi.org/10.1353/hpu.0.0063

Chaoseum. (2021). Leaving paradise [Song]. On *Second Skin: Alive in Studio*. Chaoseum.

Cohen Konrad, S. (2010). Relational learning in social work education: Transformative education for teaching a course on loss, grief and death. *Journal of Teaching in Social Work, 30*(1), 15–28. https://doi.org/10.1080/08841230903479458

Crenshaw, K. (1989). Demarginalizing the intersection of race and sex: A Black feminist critique of antidiscrimination doctrine. *University of Chicago Legal Forum, 1989*(1), 139–168. http://chicagounbound.uchicago.edu/uclf/vol1989/iss1/8

David, E. J. R., & Derthick, A. O. (2013). What is internalized oppression and so what? In E. J. R. David (Ed.), *Internalized oppression: The psychology of marginalized groups* (pp. 1–30). Springer.

Dellmann, T. (2018). Are shame and self-esteem risk factors in prolonged grief after death of a spouse? *Death Studies, 42*(6), 371–382. https://doi.org/10.1080/07481187.2017.1351501

Doka, K. J. (1989). *Disenfranchised grief: Recognizing hidden sorrow.* Wiley.

Doka, K. J. (2008). Disenfranchised grief in historical and cultural perspective. In M. S. Stroebe, R. O. Hansson, H. Schut, & W. Stroebe (Eds.), *Handbook of bereavement research and practice: Advances in theory and intervention* (pp. 223–240). American Psychological Association. https://doi.org/10.1037/14498-011

Felitti, V. J., Anda, R. F., Nordenberg, D., Williamson, D. F., Spitz, A. M., Edwards, V., Koss, M. P., & Marks, J. S. (1998). Relationship of childhood abuse and household dysfunction to man of the leading causes of death in adults: The adverse childhood experiences (ACE) study. *American Journal of Preventative Medicine, 14*(4), 245–258. https://doi.org/10.1016/s0749-3797(98)00017-8

Finkelhor, D., Shattuck, A., Turner, H., & Hamby, S. (2015). A revised inventory of adverse childhood experiences. *Child Abuse and Neglect, 45,* 13–21. https://doi.org/10.1016/j.chiabu.2015.07.011

Freire, P. (2005). *Pedagogy of the oppressed* (30th anniversary ed.). Seabury Press. (Original work published 1970).

Gawthrop, E. (2022, September 14). The color of coronavirus: COVID-19 deaths by race and ethnicity in the U.S. *APM Research Lab.* www.apmresearchlab.org/covid/deaths-by-race

Goldblatt Hyatt, E. D. (2021). Counseling women who have terminated a pregnancy due to fetal anomaly (TOPFA): The ACCEPT model. *Clinical Social Work Journal, 49*(1), 52–63. https://doi.org/10.1007/s10615-019-00732-0

Green, K. L. (2018). Courts rule too narrowly regarding the right to wear religious clothing in public. *Hastings Women's Law Journal, 29*(2), 261–296. https://repository.uchastings.edu/cgi/viewcontent.cgi?article=1239&context=hwlj

Haines, S. K. (2019). *The politics of trauma.* North Atlantic Books.

Hay, A., Hall, C. W., Sealey, M., Lobb, E. A., & Breen, L. J. (2021). Developing a practice-based research agenda for grief and bereavement care. *Death Studies*, 45(5), 331–341. https://doi.org/10.1080/07481187.2019.1636897

Hill, L., & Artiga, S. (2022, August 22). COVID-19 cases and deaths by race/ethnicity: Current data and changes over time. Kaiser Family Foundation. www.kff.org/coronavirus-covid-19/issue-brief/covid-19-cases-and-deaths-by-race-ethnicity-current-data-and-changes-over-time/

Homan, P. A., & Brown, T. H. (2022). Sick and tired of being excluded: Structural racism in disenfranchisement as a threat to population heath equity. *Health Affairs*, 41(2), 219–227. https://doi.org/10.1377/hlthaff.2021.01414

Hughes, L. (1951). Harlem. In L. Hughes (Ed.), *Montage of a deferred dream* (p. 268). Holt.

Jones, S. J., & Beck, E. (2006). Disenfranchised grief and nonfinite loss as experienced by the families of death row inmates. *OMEGA – Journal of Death and Dying*, 54(4), 281–299. https://doi.org/10.2190/a327-66k6-p362-6988

Kauffman, J. (2002). The psychology of disenfranchised grief: Liberation, shame and self-disenfranchisement. In K. J. Doka (Ed.), *Disenfranchised grief: New directions, challenges, and strategies for practice* (pp. 61–77). Research Press.

Kellerman, N. P. (2013). Epigenetic transmission of Holocaust trauma: Can nightmares be inherited? *Israel Journal of Psychiatry and Related Sciences*, 50(1), 33–39.

Kim, J. Y., & Ali, S. R. (2022). Expanding the constructs of grief and loss in capturing the human experiences: Essential workers in the meatpacking industry and the pandemic. *Professional Psychology: Research and Practice*, 53(1), 90–98. https://doi.org/10.1037/pro0000432

King, K. M. (2021). "I want to, but how?" Defining counseling broaching tenets and debated components. *Journal of Multicultural Counseling and Development*, 49(2), 87–100. https://doi.org/10.1002/jmcd.12208

Klassen, A. C., Hall, A. G., Saksvig, B., Curbow, B., & Klassen, D. K. (2002). Relationship between patients' perceptions of disadvantage and discrimination and listing for kidney transplantation. *American Journal of Public Health*, 92(5), 811–817. https://doi.org/10.2105/ajph.92.5.811

Leong, F. T. L., & Lau, A. S. L. (2001). Barriers to providing effective mental health services to Asian Americans. *Mental Health Services Research*, 3(4), 201–214. https://doi.org/10.1023/a:1013177014788

Lopez, G., & Wu, A. (2022, September 10). How Covid reduced Native Americans' life expectancy. *New York Times*, A16.

Martin, T., & Doka, K. (1999). *Men don't cry, women do: Transcending gender stereotypes of grief*. Brunner/Mazel.

Medlock, M., Weissman, A., Shucheng Wong, S., & Carlo, A. D. (2016). Addressing the legacy of racism in psychiatric training. *The American Journal of Psychiatry Residents' Journal, 11*(2), 13.

Mitchell, M. B. (2017). "No one acknowledged my loss and hurt": Non-death loss, grief, and trauma in foster care. *Child and Adolescent Social Work Journal, 35*(1), 1–9. https://doi.org/10.1007/s10560-017-0502-8

Neimeyer, R. A., & Jordan, J. R. (2002). Disenfranchisement as empathic failure: Grief therapy and the co-construction of meaning. In K. J. Doka (Ed.), *Disenfranchised grief: New directions, challenges, and strategies for practice* (pp. 95–117). Research Press.

Neimeyer, R. A., Klass, D., & Dennis, M. R. (2014). A social constructionist account of grief: Loss and the narration of meaning. *Death Studies, 38*(8), 485–498. https://doi.org/10.1080/07481187.2014.913454

O'Connor, M.-F. (2022). *The grieving brain: The surprising science of how we learn from love and loss.* HarperOne.

Papa, A., Lancaster, N. G., & Kahler, J. (2014). Commonalities in grief responding across bereavement and non-bereavement losses. *Journal of Affective Disorders, 161*, 136–143. https://doi.org/10.1016/j.jad.2014.03.018

Peskin, H. (2019). Who has the right to mourn? Relational deference and the ranking of grief. *Psychoanalytic Dialogues, 29*(4), 477–492. https://doi.org/10.1080/10481885.2019.16326., Werner-Lin, A., & Stauffer, S. D. (2022). Posttraumatic growth following ad55

Pliske, M. Mverse childhood experiences: "My creative arts teacher got me through it." *Psychology and Behavioral Sciences, 11*(4), 105–115. https://doi.org/10.11648/j.pbs.20221104.11

Porges, S. W. (2011). *The polyvagal theory: Neurophysiological foundations of emotions, attachment, communication, and self-regulation.* Norton.

Ramo-Fernández, L., Schneider, A., Wilker, S., & Kolassa, I.-T. (2015). Epigenetic alterations associated with war trauma and childhood maltreatment. *Behavioral Sciences and Law, 33*(5), 701–721. https://doi.org/10.1002/bsl.2200

Rando, T. (1984). *Grief, dying, and death: Clinical interventions for caregivers.* Research Press.

Rosbrow, T. (2019). On grief, guilt, shame, and nostalgia. Discussion of "Who has the right to mourn?: Relational deference and the ranking of grief." *Psychoanalytic Dialogues, 29*(4), 501–506. https://doi.org/10.1080/10481885.2019.1632656

Sabin, J. E., & Daniels, N. (2017). Seeking legitimacy for DSM-5: The bereavement exception as an example of failed process. *AMA Journal of Ethics, 19*(2), 192–198.

Siegel, D. J. (2020). *The developing mind: How relationships and the brain interact to share who we are* (3rd ed.). Guilford Press.

Taku, K., Cann, A., Calhoun, L. G., & Tedeschi, R. G. (2008). The factor structure of the Posttraumatic Growth Inventory: A comparison of five models using confirmatory factor analysis. *Journal of Traumatic Stress, 21*(2), 158–164. https://doi.org/10.1002/jts.20305

Valentine, C., Bauld, L., & Walter, T. (2016). Bereavement following substance misuse: A disenfranchised grief. *OMEGA – Journal of Death and Dying, 72*(4), 283–301. https://doi.org/10.1177/0030222815625174

van der Kolk, B. (2015). *The body keeps the score: Brain, mind, and body in the healing of trauma*. Penguin.

Ward, E. C., Wiltshire, J. C., Detry, M. A., & Brown, R. L. (2013). African American men and women's attitude toward mental illness, perceptions of stigma, and preferred coping behaviors. *Nursing Research, 62*(3), 185–194. https://doi.org/10.1097/NNR.0b013e31827bf533

Wheat, L. S., Matthews, J. J., & Whiting, P. P. (2022). Grief content inclusion in CACREP-accredited counselor education programs. *Journal of Counselor Preparation and Supervision, 15*(2), 277–305. https://digitalcommons.sacredheart.edu/jcps/vol15/iss2/14

Wilkins, E. J., Whiting, J. B., Watson, M. F., Russon, J. M., & Moncrief, A. M. (2013). Residual effects of slavery: What clinicians need to know. *Contemporary Family Therapy, 35*(1), 14–28. https://doi.org/10.1007/s10591-012-9219-1

Williams, M. T., Printz, D. M. B., & DeLapp, R. C. T. (2018). Assessing racial trauma with the Trauma Symptoms of Discrimination Scale. *Psychology of Violence, 8*(6), 735–747. https://doi.org/10.1037/vio0000212

Williams, R. K. (2016). Toward a theorization of Black maternal grief as analytic. *Transforming Anthropology, 24*(1), 17–30. https://doi.org/10.1111/traa.12057

Yehuda, R., & Lehrner, A. (2018). Intergenerational transmission of trauma effects: Putative role of epigenetic mechanisms. *World Psychiatry, 17*(3), 243–257. https://doi.org/10.1002/wps.20568

Zempi, I. (2019). Veiled Muslim women's views on law banning the wearing of the niqab (face veil) in public. *Ethnic and Racial Studies, 42*(15), 2585–2602. https://doi.org/10.1080/01419870.2019.1588985

Questions for reflective practice

(1) Create a personal grief timeline, including non-death and secondary losses. Which losses were acknowledged and by whom? Which were not acknowledged, and by whom would this acknowledgment be helpful?

(2) Considering your grief timeline and the unacknowledged losses, what did you need to support your grief at that time? What do you need in the present moment?

(3) What themes or patterns in your grief timeline do you correlate with your social, cultural, and relational domains?

(4) How do your cultural identity and social and relational standing influence your ability to grieve well?

(5) If you are a graduate or post-graduate educator, how do you plan to interweave your understanding of death and non-death losses into your current curriculum?

Supplementary electronic resources

- The Dana Foundation (philanthropic organization; advances neuroscience): www.dana.org
- International Commission to Combat Religious Racism (ICCRR; nonprofit organization): www.religiousracism.org/about
- National Alliance for Children's Grief: https://nacg.org
- National Organization for Victim Assistance (NOVA): https://trynova.org
- National Suicide Prevention hotline (US; free, confidential, 24/7): Telephone 988, Text GO to 74174
- Neurobiology of Grief International Network (NOGIN): https://research.arizona.edu/events/15461-neurobiology-grief-international-network-nogin

2

Identity and loss

Where intersectionality and disenfranchised grief converge

Quinn K. Smelser

Over 30 years ago, Kimberlé Crenshaw (1989) coined the term *intersectionality* in an analysis arguing that experiences of Black women were "erase[d]" in feminist and antiracist theories because of the "single-axis framework" upon which these theories were built (p. 140). Through commentary on a series of court cases, Crenshaw (1989) demonstrated the multiple burdens that emerge from intersecting identity discriminations. For example, Black women members of the LGBTQIA+ community, who have overlapping social identities, are often viewed through singular siphoned lenses (Crenshaw, 1989), thereby marginalizing their discrimination and inequality experiences. Historically, social identities, such as race, class, gender, sexuality, or immigrant status, have been used to create systemic oppressive power structures in society. For example, the practice of redlining loan applications and other financial services by banks, frontline communities bearing the brunt of pollution as industrial facilities are built in their neighborhoods, and the wage gap that exists across gender, sexuality, race, and ethnicity illustrate this systematic oppression.

When we focus on singular identities, we fail to see how this oppression compounds as these identities intersect with one another. Carbado et al. (2013) considered intersectionality as a framework through which people may be understood in various disciplines and contexts. The current author applies the framework of intersectionality to conceptualize disenfranchised grief as a response to the loss of identity and to highlight the influence of intersectionality in response to disenfranchised and ambiguous losses. From this perspective, it is clear that intersecting identities must be attended to when helping a client process disenfranchised grief. Similarly, marginalization of one or more aspects of a client's identity might be the underlying cause of their disenfranchised grief, which needs to be acknowledged to give weight and credence to suggested strategies.

DOI: 10.4324/9781003292890-3

Definitions and background

Crenshaw's (1989) argument highlights the opportunity to embrace intersectionality and to view ambiguous loss as inherent when intersecting identities are not celebrated, given voice to, and instead are marginalized or erased. Carbado et al. (2013) expressed hope that intersectionality will continue to be an interactive and fluid concept applicable internationally and across disciplines. Additionally, Love's (2010) *liberatory consciousness* model embraces social justice and recognizes historical perspectives of oppression as sources of disenfranchised grief that affect people today, such as "colonialism, genocide, enforced involuntary servitude, dislocation due to immigration, and forced migration. These [social justice] perspectives provide important parameters and guidelines for survival and flourishing," particularly for Black women (Love & Jiggetts, 2019, p. xi).

Intersectionality

Intersectionality recognizes that every oppression and discrimination experience is different, and the multiple identities a person carries (e.g., gender, ethnicity, class, sexual orientation, and physical ability) do not coexist in isolation from one another but influence each other. Intersectionality emphasizes that social identities operate on several different levels, creating individual and unique experiences, opportunities, and barriers for every individual. The concept of intersectionality has its roots in Black feminist and critical race theories (Carbado et al., 2013). Intersectionality highlights that historically there has been a segregation of legal issues and social issues, such as sex-based discrimination first lobbied for White women and race-based discrimination first lobbied for Black men. Siloing these issues eliminates the plight of Black women at the intersection of these discriminations based on race and sex (Crenshaw, 1989). Activists, academics, and professionals have since applied the concept of intersectionality as a framework for understanding social identities, privilege and power in systems, and legal and political structures, and this concept continues to traverse disciplines.

Disenfranchised grief and ambiguous loss

Disenfranchised grief often occurs in tandem with ambiguous loss, a loss of a sense of self, or a loss of identity. Doka (1999) defined *disenfranchised grief* as the response to "a loss that is not, or cannot be, openly acknowledged, publicly mourned or socially supported" (p. 37). Disenfranchised grief may occur due to a lack of recognition of a relationship, lack of recognition of a loss itself, and lack of recognition of the significance to the griever (Doka, 1989). It is a grief that goes unvalidated by social norms, is minimized, and is not supported by others, leaving a person with potential depression, anxiety, traumatization, and/or interpersonal conflicts (Doka, 1989). Because of this, an ambiguous loss can be traumatic.

In traditional grief therapies, the goal is to help the client make meaning out of the loss and find some closure or sense of mastery over the loss. However, disenfranchised grief may freeze or pose a barrier to meaning making because an individual's grief process may stall or remain unresolved, creating confusion in decision making and coping processes (Boss, 2010). Without closure, a person may feel helpless, hopeless, and exhausted. The loss and grief potentially continue for years as coping and meaning making are blocked by the marginalization of the grief and the lack of closure (Boss, 2010).

Relatedly, ambiguous loss is defined as a loss that occurs without the closure provided by a death certificate or end-of-life/death ritual (e.g., funeral, memorial; Boss, 2000). Ambiguous loss leaves people with uncertainty, stress, and unresolved grief because the loss is incomplete and hard to understand (Boss, 2000). Similar to non-death rituals that symbolize transition (e.g., going-away parties, graduation), after a death, families often participate in some sort of memorializing ritual or funeral to symbolically process the loss and signal a transition forward. However, in the case of ambiguous loss, the person still faces the societal expectations to carry on, restructure their lives and their family life, if needed, and to cope with the intensity of emotion without the social support present after death losses and without a clear way forward.

Boss (2000) outlined two types of ambiguous loss. The first is when a person is physically present, but psychologically absent, such as in the case of patients with dementia, traumatic brain injury (TBI), severe mental illness, developmental disorders, or addiction. A second type of ambiguous loss is when a person is physically absent, but psychologically present, as occurs in a missing persons case, kidnapping, natural disaster, war, divorce, adoption, abandonment, immigration, or status as a new refugee. In both types of ambiguous loss, counselors must see the client in the context of how the client's intersecting identities are interacting with their grief. Further, when a client has lost or experienced marginalization of an aspect of their identity, counselors must also consider this as an absence/erasure with a psychological presence for the client and honor this disenfranchised grief as a response to the loss of that intersection of their identity. Just as intersectional identity markers have been socially constructed, ambiguous loss is externally caused and not the root of a person's pathology (Boss, 2010).

Intersectionality in processing disenfranchised grief

In many high-income countries, there are structural and social inequalities that create layers of disadvantage and disenfranchisement in a person's bereavement experience (Bindley et al., 2019). Bindley et al. (2019) reviewed studies about social and structural barriers, such as: (1) *sexism*, where women more often face financial insecurity after a loss; (2) *classism*, where those already living in poverty experience even more of an income drop following a loss, as well as facing barriers to acquiring benefits in bereavement; (3) *heterosexism*, where the bereaved partner faces both legal and financial stress due to unequal social status and fears of disclosure and less access for formal/informal support; (4) *ethnocentrism*, where financial strain following a loss was worse based on one's ethnicity; and (5) *"bereavism,"* where the person faced institutional inequities, such as employment loss, based on being a griever (p. 11).

After a death or an ambiguous loss, intersecting identities will impact how a person's grief is systemically disenfranchised, as well as how they process that grief. Additionally, the bereaved person adds a new identity of "griever" that intersects with their other social, relational, or cultural identities.

African American widow

Consider the intersecting identities of an African American woman following her husband's death. As Love and Jiggetts (2019) explained, "jumping double-dutch, facing and managing the challenges and difficulties of racism and sexism has been the experience of Black women" (p. xii). Compounding those challenges is the reality that, historically, the life of African American men has been stereotyped and viewed as less meaningful than the life of European American men (Taylor et al., 2019). Society's erasure of her husband as having had a meaningful existence already sets the stage for this Black woman's grief to be disenfranchised. Further, Bindley et al. (2019) suggested that grieving Black women remain single for longer periods of time than their grieving White counterparts.

Because Black women also face systemic oppression in U.S. institutions, on average, they tend to have fewer financial resources and less access to resources like protected bereavement leave, insurance benefits, and institutional supports and are not offered or made aware of potential resources they might have access to compared to White women (Bindley et al., 2019). When Black women become widowed early in life, the financial strain compounds over the years (Bindley et al., 2019). Systems have already marginalized the Black woman along the intersection of her race, sex, and new identity as a griever. She must now navigate these structural and social inequalities that disenfranchise her grief while further diminishing the worth of her loss due to society's bias that the lives of Black men are somehow less valuable than those of White men (Taylor et al., 2019).

Partner infidelity

In another example, consider a client who has ended a 10+ year relationship after their partner's infidelity. The loss of this relationship might be socially disenfranchised because the partner was a "bad" person; they committed a hurtful act, and therefore the client *should be happy* the relationship ended. Then, imagine this was a queer relationship, illustrating a further intersection where oppression and marginalization of the relationship may have already occurred in the client's family, community, or greater societal context. Perhaps the client and the former partner lived together and shared finances but did not have the legal protections afforded to heterosexual couples, which is still the case in many parts of the world. The potential exists for this client's grief to be diminished by systemic structures, by societal opinions about affairs, and by their support system. Further, the client is likely experiencing the ambiguous loss that occurs with the psychological presence of their partner, though the partner has physically left the home.

Each person in these vignettes had multiple intersecting identities compounded by experiences of disenfranchised grief and/or ambiguous loss. If the Black woman is widowed early in life, the financial strain of living on one income may last longer. Importantly, she likely already started at a lower socioeconomic status (SES), both due to sex and race discrimination; paying for funeral and burial expenses will only worsen that strain. For the queer mourner, the societal attitude that devalues infidelity, including any victim-blaming that may arise from this, erases the loss in the eye of the beholder and potentially blames the client for the grief they are feeling, further disenfranchising their grief.

Disenfranchised grief as a response to identity loss

An individual's cultural identity is rarely "one set of values tied to one identity," and is rather a multitude of identities that inform one another (Chan et al., 2018, p. 61). Therefore, a person may experience privilege for one identity, but oppression for another. When a part of one's identity is erased or marginalized, or the intersection of identities is not considered, a person often experiences this loss internally as disenfranchised grief, such as in the case of the person experiencing partner infidelity.

The lack of acknowledgment and marginalization of one's intersecting identities over time can be traumatizing (Ali & Lee, 2019). Someone experiencing disenfranchised grief because a part of their identity has been repressed or ignored might struggle to examine intersecting identities due to a block caused by this pain and trauma. When a facet of identity is diminished or oppressed, that pain can make it difficult to carry. For this reason, it is important that clinicians remain vigilant in treating therapeutic blockages that could arise for clients or from parallel experiences and systemic grief resonances that emerge for therapists from the interaction.

In graduate and post-graduate training, both the student and the educator must attend to their own counselor identity development within the context of multiple identities they each carry. Chan et al. (2018) argued that counselor education programs could improve by focusing on multiculturalism and on the understanding and acknowledgment of the intersection of identities that each individual carries using a cultural humility posture. These authors illustrated how an individual's sexual or gender identity may impact how they navigate their ethnic group, which then might impact their developing counselor identity (Chan et al., 2018). Without examining this intersection, the student faces further potential oppression, and this compounds their potential disenfranchised grief; in turn, this may affect the work they do with clients.

Cumulative impacts of disenfranchised grief across the lifespan

The complex nature of disenfranchised grief is rarely connected to a single event. Similar to complex or chronic posttraumatic stress disorder (PTSD), disenfranchised losses are experienced repeatedly, compounding and further complicating the grief experience. Walter and McCoyd (2015) analyzed the biopsychosocial effects of grief over the lifetime. These authors studied the body's biological responses to stress, psychological responses to an individual's response to loss, and changes in relationships that arise from loss (Walter & McCoyd, 2015). Ambiguous losses and disenfranchised grief encountered repeatedly over the lifespan take a physical toll on the body in the form of chronic stress (van der Kolk, 2015; Walter & McCoyd, 2015). Further, Walter and McCoyd (2015) identified *maturational losses*, those experienced due to developmental differences in identity, as another form of disenfranchised grief. These might be due to missing developmental milestones or to the first unrecognized loss in the human experience, being thrust out of the safety of the womb (Walter & McCoyd, 2015). No matter the reason for the loss or disenfranchised grief, the cumulative effect of all these losses and grieving seasons over a lifespan can become debilitating to some.

Intersecting identity strategies for processing disenfranchised grief

Cultural identity, relational identity, and social identity affect therapists' encounters with clients (Smid et al., 2018). Clinicians must assess clients' cultural traditions related to death, bereavement, loss, and mourning in addition to their help-seeking behaviors, relational support systems, and ways of coping. The intersection of a client's many identities and cultural traditions creates a unique grief experience for each client who seeks treatment. Boss (2000) reminded mental health professionals to:

> Listen to family members as they tell us what their ambiguous losses mean to them, for their stories will vary with culture, gender, race, ethnicity, sexual orientation, and even age. In their narratives will be clues about the source of their distress and thereby the meaning of it. . . . By listening to their stories, we would gain not only an understanding of what they are experiencing, but also a real appreciation for their ability to survive and even transcend the pressure thrust upon them by outside forces.
>
> (p. 132)

"Disenfranchised grief tends to occur for people in social categories that are not as privileged, and thus, oppressed" (Curtin & Garrison, 2018, p. 265). Mental health professionals should be aware of the intersecting levels of privilege in grief work. Privilege exists first in being able to openly acknowledge and celebrate all of one's intersecting identities. It also exists in being able to withstand the loss financially, ritualize the loss within a spiritual or religious community, seek support from a group of other grievers, and receive condolences from friends and family (Curtin & Garrison, 2018). For instance, the same grief privileges are not afforded to a Latinx man who identifies as gay, is spiritual but non-religious, and earns a low income in a historically oppressed community. This man may not have a spiritual community within which he can openly ritualize his grief, and he also may lack the financial resources for therapy or grief support groups. In contrast, more resources would likely be available for a heterosexual, Catholic Latino with the same income level, living in the same community.

Theories of grief and grief therapy taught in graduate schools are largely built upon Western, individualized notions of bereavement in a death-loss context (e.g., Kübler-Ross, 1969). Consequently, various populations have experienced stigmatization and disenfranchisement of grief for not following the norm of these models (Harris & Bordere, 2016), which is why other authors proposed alternative models that could include death and non-death losses alike (e.g., Boss, 2006; Tonkin, 1996; Worden, 2018). Counselors working with clients and disenfranchised grief must remember that working solely with Western models could contribute to further oppression, especially if clinicians' and clients' privilege and intersectional identities remain unexamined. Additionally, traditional grief therapies will not lessen the disenfranchised grief associated with ambiguous loss because those therapies are built on finding closure in stages that are not present with ambiguous loss (Boss, 2010).

Curtin and Garrison (2018) recommend processing disenfranchised grief on three systemic levels: micro (individual, social identity), mezzo (relational identity), and macro (cultural and societal). Disenfranchised grief can be processed through all three of these levels by using Worden's (2018) task approach, Boss's (2006) approach to treating ambiguous loss, relational-cultural theory (e.g., Duffey & Somody, 2011), and the cultural-context model (e.g., Almeida & Durkin, 1999).

Worden's tasks

The first level of processing disenfranchised grief is at a micro-system or individual/social identity level. This means helping a client with intrapersonal work through a model like Worden's tasks of mourning, which may apply to disenfranchised grief (Curtin & Garrison, 2018). However, whether or not the client values processing at an individual level based on their social or cultural identities should be considered before applying Worden's tasks of mourning. Worden (2018) identified four non-linear tasks for mourners.

First, a person must accept that there has been a loss on both an intellectual and an emotional level, which takes time (Worden, 2018). From an intersectional perspective, this would include accepting that there was a loss that is affecting myriad identities a person carries. Acceptance at the individual level may be nearly impossible to complete because it would involve accepting society's disenfranchisement of an aspect of one's identity. It might also mean accepting that a part of a person's identity has been erased by their family (interactions between personal and familial micro-systems comprise this mezzo-system level) or their greater community (macro-system level), and that loss must be acknowledged (Curtin & Garrison, 2018). In instances of disenfranchised grief and identity, the goal should be to acknowledge the loss rather than accepting it in the way Worden (2018) proposed.

In Worden's second task, a griever must process the pain from this loss, something he stated society may impede because people are uncomfortable with the mourner's expression of pain. This can be especially true when the grief is already disenfranchised or a relational, cultural, or social identity has been marginalized. In the third task, one must adjust to a world without the person, place, or identity that was lost. These mean potentially adjusting one's relationships with others and/or adjusting one's identity within a greater societal context. Finally, a person must find a meaningful connection with what was lost while continuing to live (Worden, 2018). This can be the most difficult task in processing disenfranchised grief because it often means holding two truths: clinicians must help a griever connect with all aspects of their identities while also reconciling the erasures and grief they have experienced because of these (lost) identities.

Boss's approach

Similar to Worden's tasks, Boss (2006) offered strategies to help a client process their disenfranchised grief at a micro- or individual-level of processing. These strategies underscore the task of meaning making with disenfranchised grief. Similar to Worden's first task, Boss (2006) recommended first helping a client understand what has been lost and define what disenfranchised grief is to facilitate meaning making. Boss (2006) cautioned that perceptions of loss matter, and that these are often culturally or socially based. It is vital to understand a client's perception of the loss as well as how one's identities are working in conjunction to influence this perception.

Mental health professionals must remember that truth is relative, especially in cases of disenfranchised grief and ambiguous loss (Boss, 2006). Meaning making with disenfranchised grief presents an extra obstacle. Systemic oppressive forces exist without good reason and therefore render making logical sense of them impossible. So, a griever must attempt to make meaning of their loss within a meaningless system (Boss, 2006). This meaning making might happen on a micro- or individual-level and may influence how a client finds meaning in their relationships. Clinicians must view the client's perception of their loss through the client's intersecting lenses of identities, help the client make meaning of what might feel meaningless, and validate the loss and subsequent grief via empathy and acceptance. All of this is done while also helping a client sit with the ambiguity and lack of closure for this kind of grief, similar to Worden's (2018) task of processing the pain.

Resilience is built in treating disenfranchised grief through normalizing feelings of ambivalence and increasing a client's tolerance for ambiguity (Boss, 2006). However, there can be cultural differences in one's tolerance for ambiguity and experience of ambivalence. For instance, there are religious cultures that do not accept ambiguity in their religious texts and, thus, discriminate against LGBTQIA+ persons (Boss, 2006). A religious LGBTQIA+ client might experience disenfranchised grief for their religious values conflicting with their gender identity or expression and/or their sexual identity. Simultaneously, they might be experiencing disenfranchised grief for the loss of an unrecognized relationship. Tolerating this much ambiguity is a monumental task.

Boss (2006) also spoke of restructuring one's identities while processing the loss, similar to Worden's (2018) fourth task of continuing to live and making meaning. Loss of any type often brings cultural, social, and relational identities more sharply into view, because these identities have to be redefined with the loss in mind. Stigma and discrimination around these identities and around the type of loss and grief experienced can sometimes block this process (Boss, 2006). In the case of disenfranchised grief due to the erasure of an identity, redefining and reclaiming this identity is crucial. Clients must learn to let go while holding on (Boss, 2006). Consequently, clinicians might need to help clients revise their attachments to people, places, or things when processing their disenfranchised grief (Curtin & Garrison, 2018). Clinicians could also process a griever's or group of grievers' experiences with overt or covert discrimination when working through disenfranchised grief (Curtin & Garrison, 2018).

Relational-cultural theory

Processing disenfranchised grief has a large relational component, because it is in relationships with other people that a grief or a loss went unrecognized and became disenfranchised. Identities are culturally, socially, and relationally based. Miller's (1976) relational cultural theory (RCT) focuses on how people develop connections with others while considering sociopolitical diversity. RCT grew out of studying the connection and the context of the experiences of women and other devalued groups (Duffey & Somody, 2011).

Miller's (1976) theory deemphasizes pathology and instead focuses on how a client's context and life experiences have shaped current behaviors and attitudes. Further, it is an approach that values clients' relational development across the lifespan rather than Western notions of separation, autonomy, and individuation (Duffey & Somody, 2011). Because RCT emphasizes client relationships, cultural identities, and social identities, it is an ideal theory for grief therapists to use to support their clients by working through an intersectional lens.

RCT focuses on growth-fostering relationships built on mutual empathy and authenticity between clinician and client, between clients in groups, and within the client (Duffey & Somody, 2011). Olivier and Monroe (2021) used RCT as a therapeutic approach to treat clients experiencing perinatal loss, a type of ambiguous loss with disenfranchised grief. One of the worst experiences that comes with any type of grief is feeling isolated (Doka, 1989). In RCT terms, this is called *relational disconnection* (Duffey & Somody, 2011; Miller, 1976).

Persons in groups that have been marginalized may carry shame, feel like they are failures because of social injustices, and feel unworthy of connecting with others, and this can lead to a chronic feeling of relational disconnection (Duffey & Somody, 2011). RCT focuses on the relational images people create when something triggers feelings of injustice and shame in relationships, such as a trauma trigger (Olivier & Monroe, 2021). RCT emphasizes separating these triggers from the individuals who may have caused the client distress so clients begin to understand the layered identities of people around them as well. As a person builds connections through RCT, relational resilience and competence build, steering clients away from feelings of isolation and towards fulfilling connections in their relational, cultural, and social identities. RCT therapists hope clients gain empathy for others through experiencing empathy, and they also gain self-empathy and feelings of empowerment (Duffey & Somody, 2011; Olivier & Monroe, 2021).

Cultural context model

Almeida and Durkin (1999) proposed a model for therapy that honored intersectionality in group and communal settings for processing things like grief at a macro or societal level. The cultural context model of therapy is not concerned with presenting problems, such as disenfranchised grief or trauma, but rather it focuses on the range of challenges shared across cultural backgrounds. These authors proposed "healing circles," or therapeutic group-type treatments, where people develop relationships across intersecting identities (Almeida & Durkin, 1999). Using a cultural context, the healing circles provide opportunities for clients to engage with individuals representing a wide range of demographics and diversity (i.e., ethnicity, abilities, sexual orientation, gender identity and expression, and socioeconomic classes). This intersectional treatment approach recognizes individuals' intersecting identities and encourages participant engagement on a broad range of issues with the hope that people connect with one another beyond the societal walls by which they are often separated (Almeida & Durkin, 1999).

Moore et al. (2022) emphasized using this cultural context model in working with grieving Black Americans. Because Almeida and Durkin's (1999) model uses an intersectional lens and a non-traditional approach, it honors varying experiences within cultural groups and allows clients to see that groups such as Black Americans are not monolithic (Moore et al., 2022). The cultural context model values the fact that people do not live out one individual identity and offers space for clients to engage in the pantheon of intersectional identities and issues that exist in society. This perspective provides grief therapists an opportunity to recognize historical trauma and the treatment of oppressed groups as another intersecting layer of a client's identity, disenfranchised grief, and societal marginalization. (Moore et al., 2022). A cultural context model offers a space for clients to explore identities they might feel have been erased.

Grief therapists can integrate Worden's (2018) and Boss's (2006) approaches and a relational-cultural theoretical perspective in conjunction with a cultural context model to produce strategies for working with intersectionality and disenfranchised grief. Because of the social, cultural, and relational nature of disenfranchised grief, clinicians should ethically consider their work with clients along individual, relational, and societal lines. This means working not only with the individual client but also with the therapist-client relationship as a conduit for clients to extend their healing beyond the therapy space. It also means working as an ally or advocate when not working in one-on-one or group settings with clients.

Allyship and advocacy

The American Counseling Association (ACA, 2014) called on counselors to advocate for their clients. Boss (2006) furthered that connecting clients experiencing disenfranchised grief with family members or community members who are supportive is integral. Connection with others experiencing similar grief is essential for normalizing disenfranchised grief. Doing so supports clients at the macro/societal-level of processing (Curtin & Garrison, 2018). Additionally, Harris and Bordere (2016) discussed the need for advocacy on policy issues where mental health professionals can address structural vulnerabilities in response to loss, as well as connecting clients with community-based approaches within their cultural context.

The liberatory consciousness framework also may be important in inspiring mental health professionals and professionals-in-training to constantly confront discrimination that is experienced directly or in internalized manners (Love & Jiggetts, 2019). Liberatory consciousness is comprised of four elements: awareness, analysis, action, and accountability/allyship. Although Love and Jiggetts (2019) specifically mentioned Black women, the current author believes this paradigm to be key in helping clients with an array of intersecting identities "hold a vision of themselves as belonging, of institutions as capable of supporting their participation, and institutional members as capable of supporting their inclusion, all the while confronting and transforming the daily instances when that vision was shortchanged" (Love & Jiggetts, 2019, p. xiii).

From a liberatory consciousness perspective, mental health professionals must use their *awareness* to observe how their clients have been impacted by historical and current trends. *Analyzing* their observations critically involves them accounting for their own biases and remaining culturally humble and curious when their perspectives and life experiences differ from those of their clients. Taking *action* based on one's awareness and analysis is at the crux of allyship and advocacy efforts, and may include implementing interventions on micro-, mezzo-, or macro-systemic levels. Finally, as Love and Jiggetts (2019) implored, "Accountability . . . requires the individual to accept accountability to self and community for the consequences of the action that has been taken or not taken" (p. xiii) "to act in responsive ways to transform institutions and society to accomplish goals of fairness, justice, and equity" (p. xiv).

Ethical considerations

As a framework, intersectionality was introduced to mental health professions through the field of social psychology. Early social psychology scientists studied social issues, such as segregation or gender discrimination, to further illuminate how intersectional identities have been overlooked (Goff & Kahn, 2013). However, social psychology scholars failed to look at how "race and gender mutually construct each other" (Goff & Kahn, 2013, p. 365). In this shortcoming, Goff and Kahn (2013) argued that social psychologists might inherently examine research through a racist or sexist lens. Clinicians also must be vigilant in how they explore identities within teaching, research, and clinical application. Embracing intersectionality is a step to ensuring grief therapists are practicing ethically.

The ACA (2014) called on counselors to be culturally and ethically competent by honoring each client's individual background. All individuals have multiple identity facets (e.g., ethnicity, religion, gender, SES, etc.). Researchers using intersectional perspectives posit that these facets of identity interact with one another to influence the entirety of one's identity (Ali & Lee, 2019). For example, a person raised in relative wealth might have a series of events that lead them to experience poverty as an adult (Ali & Lee, 2019). From a loss perspective, a change in socioeconomic status might cause this person to consider how their relative privilege, or loss thereof, could trigger feelings of guilt or shame. This person may also experience grief about the places or things they no longer have financial access to and how that grief may bring on feelings of guilt or shame. Ethically, grief therapists must attend to each of these facets and intersections within the context of the life of the client they are treating. Clinicians also must be in constant examination of their own intersectional identities, blind spots to privileged identities, and awareness of privilege and oppression in society.

Summary

As individuals move through the lifespan, they acquire various cultural, relational, and social identities. These identities, along with life experiences, continually inform and influence one another. Social forces influence the degree to which these identities can or cannot be expressed, honored, and celebrated, resulting in the marginalization of the individual and their experiences. By embracing an approach to treating disenfranchised grief from an intersectional perspective, counselors shield their clients from experiencing further marginalization.

Disenfranchised grief caused by an ambiguous loss might occur from the marginalization of an identity, from oppression experienced in society, from structural and systemic inequities that impede grief processing, from societal norms and opinions about a loss, and from the internalization of guilt or shame when a person's own intersecting identities are in conflict with one another. Throughout this book, readers will encounter different forms of disenfranchised grief across varying social, relational, and cultural identities. Without viewing these groups from an intersectional and contextual lens, this grief cannot be fully understood and, therefore, properly acknowledged. Using affirming and trauma-informed cultural-contextual and relational-cultural models, grief therapists can better understand and ethically honor the multitude of facets of themselves that each of their clients bring to session.

References

Ali, S., & Lee, C. C. (2019). Using creativity to explore intersectionality in counseling. *Journal of Creativity in Mental Health*, 14(4), 510–518. https://doi.org/10.1080/15401383.2019.1632767

Almeida, R. V., & Durkin, T. (1999). The cultural context model: Therapy for couples with domestic violence. *Journal of Marital and Family Therapy*, 25(3), 313–324. https://doi.org/10.1111/j.1752-0606.1999.tb00250.x

American Counseling Association. (2014). *ACA code of ethics*. www.counseling.org/resources/aca-code-of-ethics.pdf

Bindley, K., Lewis, J., Travaglia, J., & DiGiacomo, M. (2019). Disadvantaged and disenfranchised in bereavement: A scoping review of social and structural inequity following expected death. *Social Science and Medicine*, 242, 1–16. https://doi.org/10.1016/j.socscimed.2019.112599

Boss, P. (2000). *Ambiguous loss: Learning to live with unresolved grief*. Harvard University Press.

Boss, P. (2006). *Loss, trauma, and resilience: Therapeutic work with ambiguous loss*. Norton.

Boss, P. (2010). The trauma and complicated grief of ambiguous loss. *Pastoral Psychology*, 59(2), 137–145. https://doi.org/10.1007/s11089-009-0264-0

Carbado, D. W., Crenshaw, K. W., Mays, V. M., & Tomlinson, B. (2013). Intersectionality: Mapping the movements of a theory. *Du Bois Review: Social Science Research on Race*, 10(2), 303–312. https://doi.org/10.1017/S1742058X13000349

Chan, C. D., Cor, D. N., & Band, M. P. (2018). Privilege and oppression in counselor education: An intersectionality framework. *Journal of Multicultural Counseling and Development*, 46(1), 58–73. https://doi.org/10.1002/jmcd.12092

Crenshaw, K. (1989). Demarginalizing the intersection of race and sex: A Black feminist critique of antidiscrimination doctrine. *University of Chicago Legal Forum*, 1989(1),139–168. http://chicagounbound.uchicago.edu/uclf/vol1989/iss1/8

Curtin, N., & Garrison, M. (2018). "She was more than a friend": Clinical intervention strategies for effectively addressing disenfranchised grief issues for same-sex couples. *Journal of Gay and Lesbian Social Services, 30*(3), 261–281. https://doi.org/10.1080/10538720.2018.1463885

Doka, K. J. (1989). *Disenfranchised grief: Recognizing hidden sorrow*. Lexington Books.

Doka, K. J. (1999). Disenfranchised grief. *Bereavement Care, 18*(3), 37–39. https://doi.org/10.1080/02682629908657467

Duffey, T., & Somody, C. (2011). The role of relational-cultural theory in mental health counseling. *Journal of Mental Health Counseling, 33*(3), 223–242. https://doi.org/jbpw

Goff, P. A., & Kahn, K. B. (2013). How psychological science impedes intersectional thinking. *Du Bois Review: Social Science Research on Race, 10*(2), 365–384. https://doi.org/10.1017/S1742058X13000313

Harris, D. L., & Bordere, T. C. (Eds.). (2016). *Handbook of social justice in loss and grief: Exploring diversity, equity, and inclusion*. Routledge.

Kübler-Ross, E. (1969). *On death and dying*. Macmillan.

Love, B. J. (2010). Developing a liberatory consciousness. In M. Adams, W. J. Blumenfeld, C. Castañeda, H. W. Hackman, M. L. Peters, & X. Zúñiga (Eds.), *Readings for diversity and social justice: An anthology on racism, sexism, anti-Semitism, heterosexism, classism, and ableism* (pp. 470–474). Routledge.

Love, B. J., & Jiggetts, V. D. (2019). Black women rising: Jumping double-Dutch with a liberatory consciousness [Foreword]. In S. Y. Evans, A. D. Dominique, & T. D. Mitchell (Eds.), *Black women and social justice education: Legacies and lessons* (pp. xi–xx). SUNY Press.

Miller, J. B. (1976). *Toward a new psychology of women*. Beacon Press.

Moore, S. E., Jones-Eversley, S. D., Tolliver, W. F., Wilson, B., & Harmon, D. K. (2022). Cultural responses to loss and grief among Black Americans: Theory and practice implications for clinicians. *Death Studies, 46*(1), 189–199. https://doi.org/10.1080/07481187.2020.1725930

Olivier, H., & Monroe, B. (2021). Relational-cultural theory as a therapeutic approach to perinatal loss. *Journal of Prenatal and Perinatal Psychology and Health, 35*(1), 77–88.

Smid, G. E., Groen, S., de la Rie, S. M., Kooper, S., & Boelen, P. A. (2018). Toward cultural assessment of grief and grief-related psychopathology. *Psychiatric Services, 69*(10), 1050–1052. https://doi.org/10.1176/appi.ps.201700422

Taylor, E., Guy-Walls, P., Wilkerson, P., & Addae, R. (2019). The historical perspectives of stereotypes on African-American males. *Journal of Human Rights and Social Work, 4*, 213–225. https://doi.org/10.1007/s41134-019-00096-y

Tonkin, L. (1996). Growing around grief – another way of looking at grief and recovery. *Bereavement Care, 15*(1), 10. https://doi.org/10.1080/02682629608657376

van der Kolk, B. A. (2015). *The body keeps the score: Brain, mind, and body in the healing of trauma*. Penguin Books.

Walter, C. A., & McCoyd, J. L. M. (2015). *Grief and loss across the lifespan: A biopsychosocial perspective* (2nd ed.). Springer.

Worden, J. W. (2018). *Grief counseling and grief therapy: A handbook for the mental health practitioner* (5th ed.). Springer.

Questions for reflective practice

1. Analyze your identities and your awareness of how they intersect. Have you experienced vulnerabilities and systemic oppression that impact your identity? What disenfranchised grief may you have experienced resulting from the amplification of the discrimination at these intersections?
2. Have you experienced one identity not being considered in context with another? Reflect upon the historical aspects of these identities and whether you may have experienced privilege for one and oppression for another.
3. Have vulnerabilities or oppression you or your clients have experienced across the lifespan changed the connection you or your clients feel between two or more of these identities? How has it changed in your family context? In your larger community context? As a mental health professional, what actions could you take through advocacy and allyship to improve the lives of your clients and others in the community?
4. How do your social identities impact how you grieve? Are there norms about how you are "supposed" to grieve that are attached to possible systemic forms of oppression?
5. Reflect on a time you may have experienced ambiguous loss. What type of ambiguous loss was it (i.e., physically present but psychologically absent, physically absent but psychologically present)? Were you able to mourn your loss and have it recognized by others? If so, how? If not, what were the barriers that prevented or altered mourning? Were the intersections of your identities honored, and if so, how?

Supplemental electronic resources

- Crenshaw, K. (7 December 2016). *The urgency of* intersectionality [Video]. TED Conferences. www.ted.com/talks/kimberle_crenshaw_the_urgency_of_intersectionality
- Feminist Freedom Warriors Digital Toolkit: http://feministfreedomwarriors.org
- Learning for Justice "Toolkit for Teaching at the Intersections"|: www.learningforjustice.org/magazine/summer-2016/toolkit-for-teaching-at-the-intersections
- NPR Code Switch® "Race. In your face." Podcast: www.npr.org/sections/codeswitch/
- What's Your Grief?: https://whatsyourgrief.com/disenfranchised-grief/

3
Our bodies

Holders of unspoken grief

Emily R. Keller

> I get up to walk to my writing desk where I will sit and write this chapter. Expecting my dog, I step over an absent hill. The next morning, I laced up my tennis shoes and braced for the tongue-dangled excitement that didn't arrive. At the desk, I reach down to pet her nest of fur and find emptiness. I return to make sense of notes on grief and the body even as my body holds the memory of Sierra.

The mental map I have of Sierra in my world hasn't adjusted to the reality of her absence. This mental map, stored in my hippocampus (O'Connor, 2022), is the same one I would use to navigate a dark room in the middle of the night. I could find my way because I knew what to expect and when. Because of this map, I continue to expect a dog, her habits, and our habitual daily interactions even though I know she is gone. The physical bond we had is broken, yet the attachment we had prompts me to look for her. This attachment need asks, "Where is she?" O'Connor (2022) described this as our need for the "comfort and safety of our loved ones" (p. 13). The dog is gone; the map is still adjusting; and this is the case for all of us who grieve.

For those who experience disenfranchised grief, however, the natural process of adjustment is complicated. Doka (1989) used the term "disenfranchised grief" to refer to grief that occurs when a person experiences a loss that is not acknowledged, validated by society, or mourned publicly. In this chapter, the author explores various ways that disenfranchised grief manifests itself in the body. She will also explore the impacts of disenfranchised grief on the body and how those impacts may be exacerbated and mitigated based on social relationships as well as marginalization.

Our muscle memory is well worn, like traffic patterns on a living room rug. Our arms may reach out automatically and discover, again, that they are not there. Eventually, our internally stored mental maps adjust. Until then, our expectations for connection are unmet. Instead of contact, we find emptiness. This

DOI: 10.4324/9781003292890-4

invites grief as a normal and natural response to their absence. We experience grief in many ways. We may feel a silent welling of psychic (emotional) tears that have their own neural pathways. Unlike basal tears that lubricate and reflexive tears that form in response to an irritant, psychic tears can escape the preventive measures of anesthetization (Huron, 2018). We may feel as if we've been "plunged into an ocean of grief" (Helbert, 2015, p. 40) and may respond by wailing, a social cue that invites those around us to respond in pre-determined ways cultivated over years of evolution.

Disenfranchised grief

Some clients seek therapy to address grief specifically. Other clients are in therapy when something else happens in their lives, altering the course of their current therapy to accommodate their grief. Still, other clients discover hidden layers of unexpressed grief from years ago as they pursue their healing journey. Despite the reasons for beginning therapy, when clinical progress stalls, it may be a sign of unexpressed grief. Grief can be thought of as fallen leaves blocking a river's flow, and other mental health professionals concur. Holinger (2020) wrote that, in her experience, anxiety and depression sometimes hide disenfranchised grief. In the preface to her book, she specified that "grief, whether delayed or forbidden, was being expressed through the body as physical symptoms, or through emotions and behaviors that indicated psychological problems" (p. x). Iyengar (1966) pondered, "Where does the body end and the mind begin? Where does the mind end and the spirit begin? They cannot be divided as they are inter-related and different aspects of the same all-pervading divine consciousness" (p. 41).

The effects of grief on the body can be of two types: physical symptoms of grief and physical communications of grief. Physical communications of grief include the various ways in which the subconscious expresses grief through the body and may manifest as a lack of congruence between verbal and non-verbal expression. One example of this incongruence is when a client shakes her head from side to side, indicating "no," as she says, "I feel ready to move on after my grandmother's recent death." Similarly, I tell my friends and family that I am well, but every time I prepare to go for what used to be my daily walk, I become paralyzed. I feel both empty and heavy at the same time. Rather than stepping through the door, I close it. My body tells me I'm not ready to walk without Sierra. I seek comfort in stillness.

Incongruence is often outside of a client's awareness and doesn't always communicate grief. However, grief and disenfranchised grief may be worth exploring because, sometimes, some parts are ready to communicate something of which other parts are unaware. Grieving is a social process. Therefore, a sense of being understood – the process of expressing our feelings and having them heard – is essential to grieving and to recognizing disenfranchisement. However, the degree to which a mental health care provider confronts a client with an awareness gained from observing the client's body depends on both the quality of the therapeutic relationship and the therapist's intuitive sense of timing in the moment. A clinician may ask themselves, "Would my bringing this into the client's awareness *at this moment* facilitate or impede the current process?"

Stroebe (2018) adapted Stroebe et al.'s (2017) work to create a list of grief symptoms, placing them into four categories: affective, behavioral, cognitive, and physiological-somatic. The physical symptoms include loss of appetite, sleep disturbances, energy loss, exhaustion, somatic complaints, physical complaints similar to the deceased's former complaints, immunological and endocrine changes, and susceptibility to illness, disease, and mortality (p. 72). Despite the use of the word "symptoms," which may imply pathology (Stroebe, 2018), grief is a normal response to loss. It is especially associated with the loss of important people in our lives (O'Connor, 2022).

Casellato (2022) discussed the relevance of Bowlby's (1969) attachment research, explaining that mourning is not only a response to the loss of a person but also the experience of broken attachment bonds. Furthermore, grief that stems from love that went unacknowledged or unrecognized is disenfranchised. Research indicates that pet loss is associated with disenfranchised grief (Park et al., 2021). Many pet owners, including myself, experience dissonance due to the unconditional love from their pets on the one hand and, on the other hand, a sense of embarrassment and loneliness related to their feelings surrounding pet loss (Park et al., 2021). Before diving into the content of this chapter, I probably would not have noticed the way I decided not to speak up about the loss of my dog until after a friend mentioned the loss of her grandmother. My pain seemed embarrassing in comparison to hers, so I swallowed the words I had planned to share, thus isolating myself.

Holinger (2020) specified that disenfranchised grief goes unrecognized by the person's family, friends, culture, religion, or society (p. 33). According to Doka (1989), non-recognition of the relationship, the loss, or the person grieving are three paths that lead to disenfranchised grief. Grief that remains unnamed and unrecognized deprives the grievers of a sense of being seen, heard, and understood in their pain. This loss of empathetic observation and response from those most dear to the griever stalls their process of healing and growing through their grief.

Social impacts of disenfranchised grief

Levine (2015) suggested that social emotions have two primary functions: to signal to ourselves and to others what we are feeling and needing. He explained that this inter-related functioning creates an opportunity for inter-subjectivity, a felt sense of one's own internal experience as well as that of another's. As such, grieving is a social process. One's facial expressions and body postures invite others to know their internal pain and to help. Sometimes, the assistance offered is the act of resonating with the griever's pain and acknowledging both the griever and their grief.

The denial of social recognition and response to grief is not only unnatural, but it also leads to complications of disenfranchised grief. These complications may be exacerbated for individuals and populations that do not feel a sense of belonging and connection to the larger community, thus potentially worsening the physical effects of grief on the body. Common physical manifestations of grief include a sense of longing, heaviness, emptiness, pain, aches, tightness, and a general lack of energy (Dominquez, 2018). Grievers may describe feeling as if they have a hole in their heart, and that, oftentimes, these feelings wash over them like waves (Dominguez, 2018).

Researchers have suggested that threats to belonging may threaten long-term physical health outcomes (Jaremka & Sunami, 2018). In one study, researchers demonstrated that Blackfeet Reservation Indigenous people reporting a lower sense of belonging had a statistically significant association between adverse childhood experiences (ACEs) and immune system inflammation markers (John-Henderson et al., 2020). In fact, a lack of social bonds has been linked to increased bodily inflammation (Peña-Vargas et al., 2021). Attachment and relationships are central to both the experience of grief and its relief, adding further support to the premise that grieving is largely a social process. Consequently, social rules shape who has permission to express their grief and how, many of which are unspoken. Furthermore, these rules determine who is likely and unlikely to experience being held in their grief.

Similarly, social ideas of what and who is valued also shape experiences of grief. Although society tends to agree that the loss of a child is one of the most difficult pains to experience, unborn children or children born with severe disabilities may not be held in the same regard. Society tends to attach quality of life and quantity of time alive to worth and value in relationships. However, people tend to discount the value of that which goes unacknowledged. This discounting removes us from the social support we could be offering to those who are grieving. In exploring some of these social rules throughout this chapter, it is important to remember that the more implicit the rule, the more resistant it is to change. This is likely because implicit rules exist to reinforce the stories one tells oneself about who they are and who others are.

Men provide one example of a group of people with different levels of social approval and acceptance of grief. Generally, men have permission to express anger and are encouraged not to express more vulnerable emotions, which include grief. Helbert (2015) warned that the consequences of such overlooked and unexpressed grief could be "disastrous," including "isolation, denial or repression of feelings, . . . [decreased] intimacy, increased potential to medicate the experience of grief through substance overuse or abuse, an imbalance of anger resulting in abusive or destructive behavior toward self and others" (p. 239).

Siblings are another example of a group of people who do not have the same social acknowledgment of their grief. In a "roundup" of bereavement literature on sibling loss and disenfranchised grief, Davidson (2018) cited a study that suggested male and female siblings demonstrated similar rates of trauma. However, the female siblings reported more grief.

A third group of people whose grief may not be socially sanctioned and therefore supported are those who suffer perinatal loss. Lack of acknowledgment of a perinatal loss can exacerbate the symptoms of grief. For example, Lang et al. (2011) emphasized that care providers may exacerbate parental grief among vulnerable patients when they do not consider the impact of their words and actions: "Just as comforting words of kindness and touches have the potential to have long-lasting healing effects, callousness and indifference (often unintentional) can severely compound an already difficult experience for the bereaved" (p. 185). Not acknowledging their physical sensations of emptiness and aching may further disenfranchise their grief.

Cultural impacts of disenfranchised grief

Social justice is considered the "fifth force" in counseling (Ratts, 2009). Social justice invites counselors to understand the impact of privilege and oppression on clients (Ratts & Pedersen, 2014). Oppression refers to how groups of people use their power and privilege to maintain domination over others (Wong et al., 2014). Dominant cultural group norms incontrovertibly impact non-dominant cultural groups. A social justice lens will consider the impact of culture on disenfranchised grief. It will also invite exploration into how one's cultural experience opens doors to grief and trauma.

Grief and trauma associated with oppression, inequality, and discrimination can be experienced at multiple levels. Jones (2000) defined them as interpersonal, institutional, and internalized. Interpersonal oppression occurs between people. Institutional oppression is baked into systems through their policies. Internalized oppression comes in the form of messages internalized from societal norms and dictates.

Rather than acknowledging pain and trauma resulting from unhealthy and unjust institutions, people in power tend to place blame on the victim, leading to further disenfranchisement. Furthermore, grief and trauma both involve loss and often overlap. Doka (2017) noted that trauma, no matter the cause, can lead to grief disenfranchisement (p. 377). Allen (2017) characterized grief and bereavement as "deeply social experiences" that must be recognized and acknowledged to "counter the impact of structural oppression on those who are grieving. We are reminded of the importance of addressing oppression and discrimination, which can result in Social and equality exclusion and disenfranchised or suffocated grief" (p. 98).

Though invisible, such grief is not inconsequential. Rather, it is a silent stalker of peace, preventing opportunities for rest, restoration, and healing. Parker (2020) identified some of the effects of the scars of dehumanization as posttraumatic responses, such as hypervigilance to threats, nightmares, aversion to certain people or experiences, flashbacks, headaches, stomach disorders, rapid heartbeat, insomnia, anxiety, and depression (p. 56). Parker (2020) suggested that during the practice of restorative yoga for treating race-based trauma, nervous systems learn to "release the contraction and to feel safe coming into deep states of rest that support repair, rejuvenation, and resilience" (p. 37).

Additionally, race-based trauma affects victims' children. DeGruy Leary (2005) coined the term *posttraumatic slave syndrome* in her book by the same name. The author described the generational effects of slavery as:

> A condition that exists when a population has experienced multigenerational trauma resulting from centuries of slavery and continues to experience oppression and institutionalized racism today. Added to this condition is a belief (real or imagined) that the benefits of the society in which they live are not accessible to them.
>
> (p. 109)

Therefore, the cultural impact of disenfranchised grief (and trauma) affects minority groups disproportionately, and it also has the potential to affect future generations. The theory of epigenetics is broadening our understanding of how organisms' experiences, shaped by environments and relationships, affect the expression of genes without changing their DNA structure. Researchers are working to understand how epigenetics might explain how human parents' experiences can be passed on to their children, though current biochemical understanding does not permit a full explanation or proof of this hypothesis (Szyf, 2022).

Relational aspects of disenfranchised grief

To enter a relationship is to open oneself up to vulnerability. Relationships are the starting point of felt loss. When welcoming lovers, children, friends, or pets into our lives, we open ourselves up to the safety and security of relational bonds. However, at the same time, we open ourselves to the loss of those bonds. While relationships come with the vulnerability of their eventual end, they also fortify us during these difficult experiences. Relationships offer psychological and physiological comfort.

Jakubiak and Feeney (2019) described how perceived threats push adults to "instinctively seek proximity – especially romantic partners – and often disclose the problem and their distress in an effort to regulate their emotions" (p. 2919). The psychological comfort inherent in healthy relationships has its roots in physiological comfort. Relational bonds are not physical tethers, but it may feel as though they are woven throughout the physical body.

Spitz's research (1945) suggested that infants who are not touched fail to thrive, and, in some instances, they die. Modern neuroscience supports the concept that touch is critical to healthy physical and psychological wellbeing. Moreover, it supports the developmental significance of touch during infancy. Touch is central to forming healthy attachment bonds and styles. Neuroscience researchers point to the importance of physical touch for the stimulation of healthy infant development (Cascio, 2010), including social-emotional wellbeing (Field, 2010). The lack of touch has also been connected to neurodevelopmental delays. The attachment styles formed with early caregivers will shape relationships, especially the important ones, throughout one's life.

The closer one is to a person genetically and the more responsibility the person has for them, the more severely the former will experience grief concerning the latter (O'Connor, 2019). However, there is also a subjective component concerning who one deems important and who is not. That subjective component is one of the reasons that disenfranchised grief develops. Relationships that are not apparent to others and are taboo may be easier to hide, for example, referring to a same-sex lover as a "friend." Similarly, subjectivity invites space for others to not acknowledge a griever's pain, either covertly or overtly.

Additionally, moments of caring interactions come in many forms. They can be deep and enduring. They can also be short and in passing. An example of the latter came from strangers outside the veterinarian's office, who observed me grieving the loss of a pet who had died in my arms. After we used a gurney to wheel my dog's body into the vet's office, people I had never met wrote notes and attached them to my car. They offered care and concern through their anonymous messages, which brought a small measure of relief to me.

Care and concern come in the form of nonverbal communication, like touch or eye contact, and through written or spoken words. Much of our right-brain processing relies on nonverbal communication to send and receive messages related to whether a person matters to us or not. This process of witnessing or beholding one's pain offers both physical and psychological relief. Physical closeness has been demonstrated to reduce overall levels of stress (Conradi et al., 2020; Robinson et al., 2015), lower the heart rate, and reduce blood pressure (Light et al., 2005).

A sense of mattering is an important relational experience and helps meet our fundamental human need for belonging. When we are not interacting with others, we wonder whether we matter at all. Further isolation and a lack of social support intensify the disenfranchised griever's pain surrounding their unacknowledged grief.

Cumulative impacts of disenfranchised grief on the body across the lifespan

Yin yoga practitioner Paul Grilley (2012) observed that "we imagine that by masking our emotions they are not affecting us" (p. 29). He added that masking only succeeds in suppressing the outward expression of one's emotions. Meanwhile, "our bodies are still taking a beating" (Grilley, 2012, p. 29). When disenfranchised grief and trauma go unaddressed, the body continues to take "beatings," which have a cumulative impact across the lifespan.

Over time, unaddressed disenfranchised grief can drive long-lasting reactive patterns that are maladaptive (Levine, 2015). Levine (2015) explained that persistent procedural memories underlie "all trauma, as well as many problematic social and relationship issues" (p. 37). Additionally, van der Kolk (2015) identified the following somatic symptoms of suppressed or unaddressed emotions: "chronic back pain and neck pain, fibromyalgia, migraines, digestive problems, spastic colon irritable bowel syndrome, chronic fatigue, and some forms of asthma" (p. 97). van der Kolk (2015) also posited that a long-term impact of unaddressed trauma is that it erases one's ability to determine what is good and bad for them. In addition to bodily harm, it further opens the doors to reliance on external sources of emotional regulation, such as "medication, drugs like alcohol, constant reassurance, or compulsive compliance with the wishes of others" (van der Kolk, 2015, p. 97).

Eisenberger (2012) reported research about the overlapping circuitry of social pain and physical pain: "Following the death of a loved one – arguably one of the most devastating forms of social pain – bereaved people report feeling intense psychological pain and often complain of somatic symptoms" (p. 422). Though we may think of body processes and experiences on the gross-motor level, such as facial expressions and body postures, body-based memory and emotions are stored in both neurons and cells. Levine (2015) explained that "emotional memories interface, well below the level of conscious awareness, with procedural ('body') memories" (p. 21).

Trauma imprints are not stored as episodic memories with cohesive narratives that make sense to us about something that happened in the past (Levine, 2015). Rather, they are stored in our procedural – or body – memories and are experienced as physical sensations that are happening in the present. The psychosomatic medicine field has identified several physical mechanisms that explain how bereavement and medical outcomes are related (O'Connor, 2019), including those in the autonomic, endocrine, and immune systems.

Allyship and advocacy

The processing and movement of raw trauma-related emotions depends on connection and communication with others (Levine, 2015). Without connected communication, trauma memories may not move into "a future built upon new information, experiences, and possibilities" (Levine, 2015, p. 16). It is important to honor that when working with disenfranchised clients who are members of communities that have been oppressed. We may be working with people experiencing being in connected communication about their grief for the first time.

The healing spaces we create have been referred to as sacred. Sacredness implies separateness. For some people, the separateness of this healing space and the space of their lived experiences is so wide that our work barely bridges the gap. As mental health professionals, we understand that advocacy is a pillar of social justice. To advocate for a client involves arguing or acting on their behalf for social justice (Chang et al., 2010, p. 84).

Liberation psychology criticizes traditional psychology for explaining human behavior separate from the contexts of the sociopolitical, historical, and cultural (Martín-Baró, 1994). Martín-Baró (1994) criticized the attribution of pathological characteristics and labels found in society to the individual. This includes describing clients, many of whom are doing their best to adapt to unhealthy societies, in pathological terms and not considering them as a person first. According to Martín-Baró (1994), societies that have been oppressed carry the pathology. He suggested that it is not enough for mental healthcare workers to seek change at the individual level without addressing change at the social level. He furthered that because society is a system that is more than the sum of its parts, social change demands structural change beyond the summation of changes at the individual level. Real change occurs at the social level (Martín-Baró, 1994, p. 37).

Being an advocate for clients requires one to see the person, not the labels. It also requires one to see the person embedded within their unique experience of society and its hierarchies and oppressions. It requires that we name them and acknowledge them. For example, a Black client in her fifties described the "craziness" she felt during a racially motivated incident with a White woman. She had not identified the event as such. Instead, I named it. I wondered aloud if the White woman would have said the same thing to another White woman or if, perhaps, she felt permission to be dismissive of my client's feelings and needs because of her Black skin. My client's shoulders softened, and she sighed. "I wasn't sure if I was reading too much into this or not," she said, "but hearing you say it, of course race did." Our work shifted from her exploring the craziness she felt in response to her strong body reaction to exploring the grief she feels about the loss of safety and connection to others due to racial oppression based on her skin color.

As mental health workers, it is imperative that we take action to attribute labels where they belong. In this case, the *incident* was crazy making, not my client's natural response to the situation. Furthermore, it is imperative that mental health providers take action to bring about change in society that offers healing to all populations, especially those that carry an unequal amount of the burden of living in the shadows of oppression. Mental health professionals can practice allyship by supporting friends, colleagues, and fellow healers who are creating healing spaces through monetary donations, by joining in the practice of cultural humility as a learner, and by promoting their creative spaces, especially when those spaces include efforts directed at community building, community arts, dance, and, of course, yoga.

Ethical considerations

When working through disenfranchised grief with clients, it is important to consider the whole person. There are underlying conditions that may be attributed to emotional processes that traditional medical professionals would better serve. For example, treatment of thyroid dysfunction has been demonstrated to alleviate mood disorders (Bauer & Whybrow, 2021). Additionally, when considering alternative approaches to addressing the body, it is imperative that mental health clinicians practice due diligence and research the evidence that supports nontraditional approaches. Specifically, when considering a referral to massage therapy or another service involving touch, it is important to understand that touch can trigger strong memories and emotional responses. Touch may invite psychological defense and regressive behavior and may be counterproductive.

Furthermore, we must not overlook a client's healing traditions, especially those that are embedded within their communities, as a source of emotional support. Community expressions of grief and trauma offer powerful avenues for connected communication and expression of emotions that offer healing to grief, especially disenfranchised grief. The very nature of oppression in societies that have been minoritized by dominant societies may restrict one's access to these approaches.

Strategies and interventions

In a study on the effectiveness of dance therapy to treat disenfranchised grief, Dominguez (2018) described how "the body in relationship served as the primary tool of re-establishing connection and provided the opportunity for expression and validation of disenfranchised grief" (p. 265). Furthermore, researchers have validated that changing breathing patterns can positively affect emotions such as anger and depression (van der Kolk, 2015).

A client sits in her chair. Either her breath is shallow or she's holding it. "Breathe," a clinician says. The client inhales. Exhales. Shoulders drop. Her tears flow. The clinician prompts her to "make all the noise you need." The client begins to wail.

Holding one's breath is one way to block emotional experiences, such as grief. Inviting breath encourages contact with and flow of the held emotion. In his translation of the *Yoga Status of Pantanjali*, Satchidananda (1984) quoted Saint Thirumular: "Wherever the mind goes, the prana follows" (pp. 54–55). Prana is often defined as vital energy. Pranayama is the control of this vital force through breath control. When prana is regulated, so is the mind. Controlled breathing can be used to bring tranquility to the mind.

van der Kolk (2015) highlighted that yoga has a positive impact on the body, affirming that it positively affects high blood pressure, stress, asthma, and even lower back pain. Pyles (2020) concurred, citing research that links certain behaviors with stress reduction, such as "spending time in nature; connecting with community; or engaging in the creative arts, exercise, mindfulness, conscious breathing, drumming, spiritual practices, and journaling" (p. 180).

Yoga is described as

> the yoking together of mind, body and spirit. A great part of this union, and one of the benefits of yoga, is the increased ability of the practitioner to become more aware of the workings of both mind and body and of the intimate connection between the two.
>
> (Helbert, 2015, p. 12)

Similarly, Powers (2008) asserted that "yoga can be understood as a set of behaviors that develops a holistic experience of the body, heart, and mind. It is a process of fully inhabiting ourselves and our life in a radically engaging and inquisitive way" (p. 3).

Yoga is a way of life that simultaneously connects us to aspects of ourselves and to "something greater than ourselves" (Helbert, 2015, p. 12). People refer to this greater power as "God, the Universe, Spirit, the Divine, our Higher Selves, the True Self" (Helbert, 2015, p. 12). It helps people become aware of one person's connectedness to another in body, mind, soul, and to a higher power. It also helps people discover that disconnections are myths. Helbert (2015) wrote that the experience of grief distorts one's perception of connection. Rather than feeling connected, we feel disconnected. Yoga reveals that "reunification is not a distant dream or imagined hope. It teaches and shows us that we are already unified; that in fact we were never parted" (Helbert, 2015, p. 15).

Though we may conceive of our life experiences as separate circuits – physical, mental, emotional, spiritual – they are indeed one. When one is impacted by grief, the whole self, and all the ways in which we dissect our experiences, are impacted. Similarly, yoga impacts all of one's experiences of self. Indeed, a regular practice of yoga yokes our experiences into one. Neimeyer (2015) cited several "brand-name" styles of yoga as "well suited for grief-work" (i.e., Kripalu, Phoenix Rising, LifeForce Yoga for Depression, and Yin Yoga) and other "generic" styles as "appropriate" (i.e., gentle yoga, the no-impact "restorative yoga," p. 145).

Summary

As suggested by the research in this chapter, it's a disservice to think of our bodies and minds as separate. Feelings do not affect our minds alone. Rather, they are experienced, expressed, and even suppressed throughout our bodies. An understanding of body-mind interconnectedness can enhance our work with clients experiencing disenfranchised grief.

Yesterday, I picked up Sierra's keepsakes: a wooden box with her ashes and a ceramic disc with her paw print. I held the weight of her ashes in my arms, a mere shadow of the 100-pound dog I once nuzzled. I am learning to move forward while making space for integrating the loss. I find that space on the yoga mat.

References

Allen, J. (2017). Women's contribution to classical sociology. In N. Thompson & G. R. Cox (Eds.), *Handbook of the sociology of death, grief, and bereavement: A guide to theory and practice* (pp. 85–100). Taylor & Francis.

Bauer, M., & Whybrow, P. C. (2021). Role of thyroid hormone therapy in depressive disorders. *Journal of Endocrinological Investigation*, 44(11), 2341–2347. https://doi.org/10.1007/s40618-021-01600-w

Bowlby, J. (1969). *Attachment and loss, Vol. I: Attachment.* Hogarth Press and the Institute of Psycho-Analysis.

Cascio, C. J. (2010). Somatosensory processing in neurodevelopmental disorders. *Journal of Neurodevelopmental Disorders*, 2(2), 62–69. https://doi.org/10.1007/s11689-010-9046-3

Casellato, G. (2022). Grief and identity. In G. Casellato (Ed.), *Disenfranchised grief in contemporary society* (pp. 25–38). Summo Editorial.

Chang, C. Y., Crethar, H. C., & Ratts, M. J. (2010). Social justice: A national imperative for counselor education and supervision. *Counselor Education and Supervision*, 50(2), 82–87. https://doi.org/10.1002/j.1556-6978.2010.tb00110.x

Conradi, H. J., Noordhof, A., & Arntz, A. (2020). Improvement of conflict handling: Hand-holding during and after conflict discussions affects heart rate, mood, and observed communication behavior in romantic partners. *Journal of Sex and Marital Therapy*, 46(5), 419–434. https://doi.org/10.1080/0092623X.2020.1748778

Davidson, D. (2018). Sibling loss – disenfranchised grief and forgotten mourners. *Bereavement Care*, 37(3), 124–130. https://doi.org/10.1080/02682621.2018.1535882

DeGruy Leary, J. (2005). *Post-traumatic slave syndrome: America's legacy of enduring injury*. Joy DeGruy.

Doka, K. J. (1989). Disenfranchised grief. In K. J. Doka (Ed.), *Recognizing hidden sorrow* (pp. 3–11). Lexington Books.

Doka, K. J. (2017). *Grief is a journey: Finding your path through loss*. Simon & Schuster.

Dominguez, K. M. (2018). Encountering disenfranchised grief: An investigation of the clinical lived experiences in dance/movement therapy. *American Journal of Dance Therapy*, 40(2), 254–276.

Eisenberger, N. I. (2012). The pain of social disconnection: Examining the shared neural underpinnings of physical and social pain. *Nature Reviews Neuroscience*, 13(6), 421–434.

Field, T. (2010). Touch for socioemotional and physical well-being: A review. *Developmental Review*, 30(4), 367–383. https://doi.org/10.1016/j.dr.2011.01.001

Grilley, P. (2012). *Yin yoga: Principles and practice*. White Cloud Press.

Helbert, K. (2015). *Yoga for grief and loss: Poses, meditation, devotion, self-reflection, selfless acts, ritual*. Singing Dragon.

Holinger, D. P. (2020). *The anatomy of grief*. Yale University Press.

Huron, D. (2018). On the functions of sadness and grief. In H.C. Lench (Ed.), *The function of emotions: When and why emotions help us* (pp. 59–91). Springer International.

Iyengar, B. K. S. (1966). *Light on yoga: The definitive guide to yoga practice*. Shocken Books.

Jakubiak, B. K., & Feeney, B. C. (2019). Interpersonal touch as a resource to facilitate positive personal and relational outcomes during stress discussions. *Journal of Social and Personal Relationships*, 36(9), 2918–2936. https://doi.org/10.1177/0265407518804666

Jaremka, L. M., & Sunami, N. (2018). Threats to belonging threaten health: Policy implications for improving physical well-being. *Policy Insights from the Behavioral and Brain Sciences*, 5(1), 90–97. https://doi.org/10.1177/2372732217747005

John-Henderson, N. A., Henderson-Matthews, B., Ollinger, S. R., Racine, J., Gordon, M. R., Higgins, A. A., Horn, W. C., Reevis, S. A., Running Wolf, J. A., Grant, D., & Rynda-Apple, A. (2020). Adverse childhood experiences and immune system inflammation in adults residing on the Blackfeet reservation: The moderating role of sense of belonging to the community. *Annals of Behavioral Medicine*, 54(2), 87–93. https://doi.org/10.1093/abm/kaz029

Jones, C. P. (2000). Levels of racism: A theoretic framework and a gardener's tale. *American Journal of Public Health*, 90(8), 1212–1215. https://doi.org/10.2105/ajph.90.8.1212

Lang, A., Fleiszer, A. R., Duhamel, F., Sword, W., Gilbert, K. R., & Corsini-Munt, S. (2011). Perinatal loss and parental grief: The challenge of ambiguity and disenfranchised grief. *OMEGA – Journal of Death and Dying*, 63(2), 183–196. https://doi.org/10.2190/om.63.2.e

Levine, P. A. (2015). *Trauma and memory: Brain and body in a search for the living past: A practical guide for understanding and working with traumatic memory*. North Atlantic Books.

Light, K. C., Grewen, K. M., & Amico, J. A. (2005). More frequent partner hugs and higher oxytocin levels are linked to lower blood pressure. *Biological Psychology*, 69(1), 5–21. https://doi.org/10.1016/j.biopsycho.2004.11.002

Martín-Baró, I. (1994). *Writings for a liberation psychology*. Harvard University Press.

Neimeyer, R. A. (Ed.). (2015). *Techniques of grief therapy: Assessment and intervention*. Routledge.

O'Connor, M.-F. (2019). Grief: A brief history of research on how body, mind, and brain adapt. *Psychosomatic Medicine*, 81(8), 731. https://doi.org/10.1097/PSY.0000000000000717

O'Connor, M. F. (2022). *The grieving brain: The surprising science of how we learn from love and loss*. Harper Collins.

Park, R. M., Royal, K. D., & Gruen, M. E. (2021). A literature review: Pet bereavement and coping mechanisms. *Journal of Applied Animal Welfare Science*, 1–15.

Parker, G. (2020). *Restorative yoga for ethnic and race-based stress and trauma*. Singing Dragon.

Peña-Vargas, C., Armaiz-Peña, G., & Castro-Figueroa, E. (2021). A biopsychosocial approach to grief, depression, and the role of emotional regulation. *Behavioral Sciences*, 11(8), 110. https://doi.org/10.3390/bs11080110

Powers, S. (2008). *Insight yoga: An innovative synthesis of traditional yoga, meditation, and Eastern approaches to healing and well-being*. Shambhala Publications.

Pyles, L. (2020). Healing justice, transformative justice, and holistic self-care for social workers. *Social Work*, 65(2), 178–187. https://doi.org/10.1093/sw/swaa013

Ratts, M. J. (2009). Social justice counseling: Toward the development of a fifth force among counseling paradigms. *The Journal of Humanistic Counseling, Education and Development*, 48(2), 160–172. https://doi.org/10.1002/j.2161-1939.2009.tb00076.x

Ratts, M. J., & Pedersen, P. B. (2014). *Counseling for multiculturalism and social justice: Integration, theory, and application*. Wiley.

Robinson, K. J., Hoplock, L. B., & Cameron, J. J. (2015). When in doubt, reach out: Touch is a covert but effective mode of soliciting and providing social support. *Social Psychological and Personality Science*, 6, 831–839. https://doi.org/10.1177/1948550615584197

Satchidananda, S. (1984). *The yoga sutras of Patanjali* (Sri Swami Satchidananda, Trans.). Integral Yoga Publications.

Spitz, R. A. (1945). Hospitalism: An inquiry into the genesis of psychiatric conditions in early childhood. *The Psychoanalytic Study of the Child*, 1(1), 53–74. https://doi.org/10.1080/00797308.1945.11823126

Stroebe, M. (2018). The poetry of grief: Beyond scientific portrayal. OMEGA – *Journal of Death and Dying*, 78(1), 67–96. https://doi.org/10.1177/0030222818792706

Stroebe, M., Schut, H., & Boerner, K. (2017). Cautioning health care professionals: Bereaved persons are misguided through the stages of grief. OMEGA – *Journal of Death and Dying*, 74, 455–473. https://doi.org/10.1177/0030222817691870

Szyf, M. (2022). The epigenetics of early life adversity and trauma inheritance: An interview with Moshe Szyf. *Epigenomics*, 14(6), 309–314. https://doi.org/10.2217/epi-2021-0483

van der Kolk, B. A. (2015). *The body keeps the score: Brain, mind, and body in the healing of trauma*. Penguin Books.

Wong, G., Derthick, A. O., David, E. J. R., Saw, A., & Okazaki, S. (2014). The what, the why, and the how: A review of racial microaggressions research in psychology. *Race and Social Problems*, 6, 181–200. https://doi.org/10.1007/s12552-013-9107-9

Questions for reflective practice

1. Based on an understanding of the manifestations of disenfranchised grief in the body, how can we shift the framework that guides treatment plan development in a way that honors the individual and collective bodies' role in healing?
2. Reflect on the role of acknowledging and feeling grief to help resolve it. Discuss the impact of unacknowledged microaggressions on individuals and the discounting of racial and social injustice built into social systems, the experiences of which may lead to a sense of loss and grief.

3. Think about a recent loss you experienced. How did an experience of belonging or lack thereof affect your grieving process? In which area(s) of your life can you invite belonging, and how?

Supplemental electronic resources

- Allied Media Projects: https://alliedmedia.org/resources/healing-justice-principles-guidelines
- Connected Warriors Inc., offers trauma-informed yoga services to active-duty personnel and veterans: https://connectedwarriors.org/
- Yoga is Dead, a podcast that explores race, class, and commercialization in the yoga community: www.yogaisdeadpodcast.com/home

4
Wounds of spirit

The disenfranchised nature of spiritual trauma

Renee Blocker Turner, Tina K. Boyles Bailey, and Brooklyn Gordon

Religious faith and spirituality are often a source of strength for many individuals during grief and loss. Researchers have indicated that religiosity and spiritual faith are often a resource or protective factor (Ballard, 2017; Khan & Ungar, 2021), which may also improve wellbeing and quality of life (Brown et al., 2021). Further, public worship and a strong adherence to religious values can improve mental health (Garssen et al., 2020). Spirituality also serves as a foundation for existential meaning making, a process necessary for posttraumatic growth (Zeligman et al., 2020). In a meta-analysis of 103 studies, Prati and Pietrantoni (2009) found that spirituality was a moderate predictor of posttraumatic growth and that religious coping strongly predicted posttraumatic growth.

Across faith traditions, many experience spirituality as a consistent central resource. However, the function of spirituality or religiosity as a resource may be reduced, eliminated, or turned into a source of pain when an individual's faith community causes harm or when spiritual beliefs contradict an individual's actions, as in the case of moral injury. These conditions facilitate a crisis of faith, referred to in the literature as *complicated spiritual grief* (CSG), in which one questions their meaning, purpose, and relationship with God and faith communities (Burke et al., 2014). Common feelings associated with CSG include betrayal, anger at God, not feeling safe and protected by God, not being able to pray, and not feeling comforted by one's faith (Burke et al., 2014). Although research in this area is emerging, it appears grievers are at risk of experiencing CSG following grief situations that challenge spiritual or religious beliefs, such as divorce, suicide (Mason, 2021), homicide (Burke et al., 2011), or abortion (Coyle & Rue, 2015). Likewise, individuals whose gender or sexual identity is not accepted by prescribed faith norms (Jones et al., 2022) also may experience an elevated risk of CSG. In these situations, individuals can experience profound secondary losses of spiritual networks

DOI: 10.4324/9781003292890-5

and spiritual practices, potentially thwarting their ability to make meaning out of loss, a vital aspect of posttraumatic growth.

Unfortunately, the scant research examining the role of religiosity and spirituality on mental health offers inconsistent and sometimes conflicting results. Consequently, many clinicians remain hesitant about broaching the subject of spirituality. In doing so, they risk bypassing a critical component of the client's grief and trauma narrative. In many ways, this is understandable, especially for clinicians who lack integrated training in working within the spiritual domains of wellbeing and mental health and fear offending clients or otherwise damaging the therapeutic relationship. Moreover, philosophical and semantic differences exist between the definitions of faith, spirituality, and religiosity, creating the potential for relational ruptures and mishaps when not handled with sensitivity.

For this chapter, the authors conceptualize *spirituality* as the "universal human capacity to experience self-transcendence and awareness of sacred immanence" (Young & Cashwell, 2011, p. 7) and *religious faith* as the expression of one's spirituality tied to a specific religion. Of course, defining *spiritual trauma* is an even more difficult task, because individual experiences are vastly unique and deeply personal; however, Panchuk (2018) broadly captured a range of backgrounds and clinical presentations in the following definition:

> Religious [and spiritual] trauma refer to a broad category of traumatic experiences that includes (but is not limited to) putative experiences of the divine being, religious practice, religious dogma, or religious community that transform an individual in a way that diminishes their capacity for participation in religious life . . . First, the trauma is caused by something that the individual closely associates with the religion. Second, the survivor usually perceives the religion to have played a positive or negative causal role in the experience's coming about, either by motivating the perpetrator, justifying the behavior, or failing to forbid or protect against it. And third, some of the posttraumatic effects have a religious trigger or object.
>
> (p. 608)

Using Panchuk's definition, there are countless and common scenarios in which an individual can experience trauma and grief directly from their faith-based communities due to perceived rejection or betrayal and the subsequent loss of support networks. For example, religious-based LGBTQIA+ conversion practices impact the "spiritual dimensions of self-identity, ability to construct existential meaning, a person's relationship to the divine and/or their religious community, and a person's ability to develop spiritually" (Jones et al., 2022, p. 2). Others experience spiritual trauma and grief resulting from unanswered prayers or violations of the fundamental belief that good things happen to good people and bad things happen to bad people (Attig, 1996) after a traumatic life event (e.g., life-threatening illnesses, suicide, or fatal accident of a loved one). Still, others may experience a sense of being betrayed or outcasted by a God or a higher power. Individuals and religious institutions can also manipulate spirituality or faith to psychologically bypass painful emotions, so that spirituality becomes a psychological defense mechanism and ultimately a barrier against identifying and processing painful situations or emotional help-seeking (Fox et al., 2017).

Moreover, Fox et al. (2017) noted that religious institutions may also cause harm when they discourage the engagement of psychological and medical support. Such an attitude (spoken or unspoken) negatively influences help-seeking behaviors, producing a barrier to addressing psychological trauma. When an individual needs and cannot obtain support beyond the scope of religious institutions, the likelihood of disenfranchised grief increases. As a result, researchers have indicated that spiritual struggles and negative religious coping are risk factors for suicidality (Rosmarin et al., 2013). Panchuk (2018) observed:

> The survivor may be distrustful of God and religious communities, believe that clergy are especially likely to be predators, or believe that they are doomed to be rejected by religious individuals. They might experience intrusive memories triggered by religious practices, feel extreme fear, distrust, or revulsion toward the divine being, or internalize a deep sense of shame as the result of religious doctrines.
>
> (p. 608)

When individuals experience what Panchuk (2018) described they are prone to generalizing their experience, a typical trauma response, effectively eliminating the resilience found in spirituality or faith. Spiritual trauma occurs in myriad ways, further complicating a clear definition. Thus, the clinician's role involves carefully listening for disenfranchised losses in the client's lived experiences.

Dynamics of spiritual grief and trauma

The experience and impact of spiritual grief and trauma create a narrative unique to each individual. Therefore, the present authors' intent is not to generalize or invalidate the experiences of others not reflected in this chapter. Instead, the authors present dominant areas of discourse emerging in the literature related to spiritual trauma and disenfranchised grief. Additionally, the authors emphasize Judeo-Christian faith practices as is their lived experience.

Readers should note their clients' faith backgrounds and engage cultural humility in practice, wherein they educate themselves and remain open to and actively explore the client's unique intersectionality, particularly where existential shattering may be present.

Existential shattering

Existential shattering is a "devastating, unexpected, irreversible event, . . . in which one's fundamental meaning and relating systems are irreparably shattered" (Greening, as cited in Hoffman et al., 2013, p. 2). For generations, existential philosophers have discussed the fundamental tenet that individuals can bear any *how* with the support of a meaningful *why* (Frankl, 1959), as one's spiritual or religious foundation serves as an integral source of meaning making in the wake of a crisis. However, the result of spiritual trauma is most often grief. It could be argued that many individuals who have walked away from their faith or spiritual communities have experienced existential shattering.

Following Hoffman et al.'s (2013) reasoning, after such an experience, individuals may be left at existential ground zero, searching for ways to integrate a new sense of self as they refine themselves and their worldview. Without a feeling of solidarity and community, individuals experience a sense of groundlessness, with no anchor to tether them to meaning and purpose. Unsurprisingly, a position without meaning and purpose is susceptible to a cascade of mental health and relational difficulties. Unfortunately, the existential aspects of trauma remain underdeveloped (Hoffman et al., 2013).

Similar to existential shattering is the concept of *shattered assumptions*, a term Attig (1996) coined in which the individual must reconcile, reintegrate, and ultimately *relearn* their world in the context of the reality of the grief. For those shunned or rejected by their faith communities, relearning is a significant task missing from the fundamental grounding provided by one's spirituality. As individuals recover from spiritual trauma, they are not only relearning the world on a shaken spiritual terrain, but they are also often relearning it absent from their community or through the lens of distrust or fear.

Moral injury

Related to spiritual trauma is the concept of *moral injury*, which arose from Johnathon Shay's observation of war veterans recovering from the psychological impacts of war and combat (Shay & Munroe, 1999). The initial conceptualization of moral injury focused on psychological trauma, which occurs when an individual holds legitimate authority or control over the actions of self and others and commits acts that betray their sense of what is right or moral. Like spiritual trauma, moral injury results in a deep sense of existential shattering as one attempts to reconcile their actions with their values and spiritual or religious beliefs, often resulting in feelings of shame and worthlessness. The substantial impacts of moral injury can increase negative spiritual coping, which is consistently linked to higher rates of suicidality in veterans (Currier et al., 2017; Ogden et al., 2011).

Over time, however, the concept has been expanded to include those without control over the event, including victims and bystanders, extending to anyone who experiences a sense of betrayal from their core values and beliefs. This expansion contains helping professionals (e.g., healthcare workers, mental health practitioners, first responders, clergy) and situations (e.g., abortion, family violence, rape) that result in symptoms synonymous with moral injury (Koenig & Al Zaben, 2021). Specific to religious and spiritual institutions, *sacred moral injury* is defined as:

> A trauma syndrome with lasting biological, psychological, social, organizational, and spiritual effects which emerges from the experience of betrayal of a sacred trust by a perpetrator of a religious organization whom the victim perceives as representing God. Typically, the religious organization supports the perpetrator by covering up the event [or] invalidating the victim.
>
> (Sperry, 2021, p. 117)

Sacred moral injury may be present in clergy, church personnel, or chaplains who participate in practices that feel inherently wrong, leading to myriad symptoms of guilt, shame, and disillusionment. Clinicians should also recognize that clergy members may experience false accusations leading to symptoms of posttraumatic stress (Goldblatt Hyatt, 2019).

Patriarchal hierarchy

Embedded in many religions is a spoken and unspoken patriarchal hierarchy (Wood, 2019) that may overlook, minimize, or ostracize the grief experiences of women, especially non-death losses. Although researchers have indicated some women are able to negotiate their agency and autonomy in patriarchal hierarchies, other women experience frustration with tightly bound and limiting gender roles (Burke, 2012). Researchers also have suggested that queer women and women of color may experience additional mental health challenges and cognitive dissonance as they continually negotiate their identity with the predominant church culture (Lockett et al., 2022).

Marginalization and oppression stemming from a historically patriarchal hierarchy may influence education, career, marriage, divorce, reproduction, and sexuality (French, 1985). As a result, women may experience inequity to the extent that it impacts grief equity. For example, women may perceive or lose the right to grieve things, such as their divorce, missed educational or career opportunities, or their partner's infidelity. The inability to grieve these relational and social experiences facilitates disenfranchised grief at a profound level. In some cases, the patriarchal hierarchy lacks culpability for men while more harshly punishing or judging women.

In extreme cases, the patriarchal hierarchy can endorse and perpetuate abuse. According to Bent-Goodley and Fowler (2006), more than 85% of religious and spiritual abuse victims are women. Of course, this number is hard to quantify as the term "abuse" depends upon subjective perceptions. Of importance is the fact that many women of color reach out to their faith communities before they seek help from mental health providers or legal support. Unfortunately, women of color may also experience rejection by their faith leaders and encouragement to remain in harmful relationships based on biblical interpretations (Bent-Goodley & Fowler, 2006).

In their research, Bent-Goodley and Fowler (2006) found that African American/Black women felt as if "clergy missed opportunities to stop violence in the home and the clergy sometimes helped perpetuate the violence because of their own sexism and sex-role perceptions" (p. 288). Although this experience is cofounded by perceived sexism, it clearly illustrates the compounded oppression experienced through intersecting identities. Moreover, participants in the study emphasized how their power and decision-making were disenfranchised as women in the church, which amplified their feelings of trauma and helplessness. Bent-Goodley and Fowler's (2006) results suggested that women experiencing domestic violence may choose to silence themselves to avoid shame and judgment from fellow parishioners and faith leaders. Women in the study also identified the increased difficulty in overcoming spiritual abuse compared to physical abuse, stating that "spirituality speaks to the foundation of your being, the essence of who you are" (p. 289).

Case studies

The following case studies illustrate the aforementioned areas of spiritual trauma experienced by the second and third authors. These case studies are not intended to generalize to the greater population, and the experiences only illustrate spiritual trauma from a Christian perspective. Below, the first author invited the second and third authors' respective answers as case study participants.

Spiritual journey and significant milestones

The second and third authors were asked to "describe your spiritual journey and significant milestones."

Brooklyn

All I've ever known is the church. All I've ever known is God. My spiritual journey, like many others, was marked by fear of hell. So, I've lived my life trying to DO all the right things and BE all the right things so that I don't go to hell. Looking back, I acted out of fear of not being accepted or loved. I accepted my call to gospel preaching ministry at 15 years old. I preached my first sermon and was licensed. Everyone was so proud. I remember like yesterday that feeling deep in my soul that this is what God was calling me to do. Everyone celebrated.

It was incredible and my grooming and training began: how to preach; how to teach and pay attention to language, tone, and performance. It always felt a little inauthentic to me. It didn't feel like my voice, but I didn't know anything other than submitting to leadership. I hurt a lot of people due to the harmful, toxic, patriarchal, and misogynistic theology. As proud as I am of my ministry work, it has brought me much grief because I don't even know who I am authentically as a minister of the gospel.

I worked in an abusive (verbal, emotional, spiritual) environment at the church I grew up in. After being hospitalized for stress-related medical issues, I was rejected by the very church family that "loved" me. The members cut me off, and leadership and others spread rumors and lies about me, and I was alone. I am still grieving this, 11 years later. Leaving the church has been pivotal in my spiritual journey.

I prayed and asked God to show me who God really is, and it has been a beautiful journey of discovering my own divinity, power, strength and healing the parts of me wounded by religion. But in doing so, I now see God in everything.

Tina

I have been a part of a faith community as far back as I can remember. I grew up a Southern Baptist and became a youth minister at my home church when I went to college. Following that, I went to seminary. While I was in seminary, the fundamentalists took over and I left Southern Baptists for a more moderate group that welcomed women in ministry. Yet, even there, the more traditional gender roles still impact thoughts and policies. During seminary, I got married, and afterward my husband and I began a career in international cross-cultural ministry. During these years, my work has taken me to and through many traumatic situations, some from the spiritual community and some from manmade and natural disasters. These years have formed and shaped me. I earned a doctorate in ministry focusing on the intersection of art and spirituality, became a prison chaplain, and my work has grown to include trauma-informed practices in expressive arts therapy.

Grief and disenfranchised grief experiences and faith

The second and third authors responded to the question, "How have you experienced grief and disenfranchised grief in the context of your faith?"

Brooklyn

I chose to leave my faith community because it was unhealthy and abusive. When I left, I lost the only community and family I'd ever known. I also felt a loss of identity. I often wondered who I am apart from this community of faith, the people I did life with on a consistent basis. I felt lost. I felt angry. I felt afraid. I felt disappointed and that I was a disappointment. No one acknowledges the grief in letting go of what is no longer serving you, letting go of what's harmful, letting go of conditioning; and the audacity of choosing YOU. There's also another layer of grieving the disappointment you feel from God around having to disconnect from the one place/space that is supposed to be safe yet was a main source of wounding. How does one say, "I'm grieving my relationship with God, and I don't know where I stand?" It's hard. And I'm still angry. And I still hurt. And I'm still grieving. And it feels very lonely because not many people are talking about this kind of grief.

Tina

I have faced betrayal by the very institution that I put my trust in, and I found my way through it to help others heal from similar experiences. My deepest grief is from a loss of trust and belief that the faith community that shaped me will be there for me in my deepest pain.

Patriarchal influence and gender

The second and third authors answered the question, "Is any of this grief related to the patriarchal influence and your gender?"

Brooklyn

So, in the churches I grew up in, there is this patriarchy hierarchy. Within the faith community, people look to the male leader or pastor as a father figure. What we know about male church leaders is that they take the role of being a "father," oftentimes in creating structure and implementing rules and correction/discipline. In my case, this artificial father-daughter dynamic was both positive and negative. When it was good it was good. When it was bad it was bad. There was a lot of manipulation. There was a lot of conditioning, grooming, manipulation, gaslighting, public humiliation; and you dare not say anything because the Pastor/Bishop is supreme.

All the women around me were very submissive to the pastor. And everyone would do anything for him. And no one would question or challenge him. People made life-altering decisions for their families that ruptured their homes based on what the pastor advised. And the men absolutely were catered to and considered supreme. I hurt seeing the ways the women who got free were demeaned and cast away. I wanted that freedom, even if it meant losing that community.

Tina

Yes, as a woman. Being married to another minister, even though our credentials are similar, I still have been seen as less than him at times. Also, I think there is an element of male insecurity that drives this, even among men who see themselves as champions of equality. As male superiority began to dominate throughout history, the body, especially the female body, became suspect. Feminine wisdom (e.g., feelings, intuition, sensuality, imagination) became dangerous and systems began to be put into place that suppressed and devalued the body as something to be tamed and controlled, creating a perfect system for the seeds of trauma to flourish.

Moral injury and spiritual leadership

The second and third authors were asked, "Have you experienced any moral injury in either your role as a spiritual leader or member?"

Brooklyn

I've experienced moral injury countless times, notably after seeing, hearing, and experiencing what had been shared in private and confidence being spoken publicly over the sacred and holy pulpit for everyone to know. Using the sacred scripture to manipulate and coerce was hard to experience, and it was hard to watch, but it was all we knew. The betrayal was constant. And painful.

Tina

Yes, I have and still am experiencing moral injury. Policies in many religious institutions are for the good of the institution, not the good of the individual. When one finds themself in a place of hurt or crisis, there is not much room for support in contrast to a policy. This is injuring for the person impacted and for the ones enforcing it. Leaders in the church can use toxic practices to control [others] but also can be controlled by toxic practices. When either hold up a religious ideal as justification to do harm and to control another person, citing "the voice of God as authority for their actions," they are potentially moving into toxic spirituality practices.

Toxic spirituality is always a risk when [U.S.] religious institutions are allowed discrimination practices in hiring and policies that could never be allowed in other settings due to their protected status under the First Amendment. It mixes control of a person's private life with job status and security. This happens in many ways and is often communicated in a manner that speaks of what is acceptable in a traditional sense, but often is about keeping the status quo and not addressing the need at hand. Toxic spirituality is most apparent in gender roles, race relations, sexual orientation, marital status, right to adopt a child tied to sexual orientation or marital status, and other areas of discrimination. When these issues are tied to employment in a religious institution then the risk of harm is increased substantially.

Disenfranchised grief, culture, and faith

The second and third authors responded to the question, "For you, what is your experience of the connection between disenfranchised grief and culture as it pertains to faith and faith institutions?"

Brooklyn

Well, within my [Southern Black American] culture, grief is very complex and not something that we deal with directly. Historically, faith has been the anchor of Black folks' survival. What's difficult is that it's also been the source of our pain and grief. I never realized that I needed to *decolonize* my faith, which is a whole other level of grieving and letting go.

Within faith institutions, there is not a lot of room for any type of grief because we are supposed to have faith. There is so much shame around feeling raw authentic emotion and around grief because there's this implication of lack of trust or faith in God versus the reality of pain. Within my culture, there's a silent implication of weakness, like we shouldn't grieve certain things. We should have tougher skin. There's no realization of the complexities of grief and how anything can be grieved.

Tina

As a spiritual leader, there is often an expectation of strength and perfection; so, many times, there is a dilemma of how open you can be about your pain. Ministers often suffer in silence. The grief can be buried and can impact health and relationships. But because it goes on so long due to fear of exposure, the wounds felt and inflicted on others can become very toxic, often hidden behind a mask of faith.

When grief is not processed in a healthy and open way, it becomes embedded and toxic. So, a facade of strength is built. When paired with spirituality and leadership, the myth that is played out is, "I must be strong," or "I am not a good example for others," while at the same time feeling, "I am dying inside resulting in a fear of abandonment and rejection if I reveal my truth."

Embracing vulnerability and the shame that comes from facing one's humanity takes courage. This is how I survive and find resilience. I have learned that my failures are actually my strengths when I allow myself to see the big picture. It is only a toxic myth that says we must be perfect to be acceptable.

Case study summary

These case examples illustrate a commonplace narrative of spiritual grief and trauma. The influence of culture, gender, patriarchal hierarchy, moral injury, and toxic spirituality shaped Brooklyn and Tina's worldview, perspective, beliefs, and even their sense of self and agency. Unfortunately, the scenarios highlighted in the case examples are frequently minimized or rationalized by faith leaders and communities as unintentional and harmless, leaving little recourse for victims. Add the cumulative impacts of these countless small scars, and the result is fertile ground for cultivating disenfranchised grief.

Allyship and advocacy

Readers can cultivate allyship and advocacy, above all, by creating a safe and open environment supportive of diverse religious and spiritual perspectives that promote inclusivity (Smigelsky et al., 2022). Practitioners must recognize that there is often a deep sense of shame, and possible denial, affiliated with traumatized spiritual needs. Therefore, naming and acknowledging the trauma and grief as genuine and valid, guided by the client's language, may be the first step to processing and integrating spiritual grief.

Meeting clients with a stance of curiosity about their spiritual needs supports deeper conversations about the values held by the client and the client's family/culture. Establish a safe place for deeper conversations to occur and do not force meaning making. Provide permission for the client to separate from a previously held belief system if it no longer serves them. Meaning making is a slow process and happens over time as individuals re-appraise who they are with and without their faith and reconcile their previously held beliefs.

Ethical considerations

Given a historical lack of training, conflicting research, and old attitudes that discourage dialogue about religion, it is understandable why some clinicians feel uncomfortable navigating conversations related to spirituality. Only recently did the *Association for Spiritual, Ethical, and Religious Values in Counseling* (ASERVIC) establish competencies for practice (Cashwell & Watts, 2010), outlining domains about culture and worldview, counselor self-awareness, human and spiritual development, communication, assessment, and diagnosis and treatment. A lack of competence in any of these domains increases the potential for countertransference issues that could result in the clinician projecting their thoughts or beliefs or deflecting essential aspects of the client's narrative.

Countertransference related to grief and spiritual trauma can arise in many ways. The most obvious is avoiding, minimizing, or deflecting content about the client's spiritual world out of fear of offending the client, rooted in a lack of training to facilitate topics of spiritual grief. This lack of competence may lead the clinician to avoid essential themes necessary to process the client's grief or trauma. Failure to hear and affirm the client's struggles related to spiritual trauma will likely further disenfranchise the grief and prevent working with the client holistically. Equally damaging is making assumptions about the client's worldview. If the therapist and client share a faith background, the therapist may assume they understand or share their client's values, which can blur the lines of objectivity.

Clinicians should note that while one's faith may inform values, those values are contained within a greater context of the whole person. Instead, clinicians can adopt an existential approach and take an inventory of the client's values to facilitate conversations about how their faith tradition supports or contradicts their values. Furthermore, a lack of understanding of one's spiritual development is inextricably tied to the potential for countertransference. Thus, mental health practitioners must explore their own spiritual development to provide competent care.

Finally, clinicians must remain aware of their boundaries related to spiritual discussions and seek supervision when they lack adequate training to provide competent mental health support. Supervision in this context should not be viewed through a deficit model but rather embraced as a growth model. Supervision should center on increasing clinician awareness of personal spiritual development, addressing biases and stereotypes, and relating the client's worldview to treatment through a lens of cultural humility with an understanding of intersecting identities.

Strategies and interventions

Addressing shame is central to healing from spiritual trauma, spiritual abuse, or moral injury. For some clients, this shame is consistent with developmental trauma as it relates to rejection, abandonment, or betrayal from an attachment lens. In their research, Smigelsky et al. (2022) found that group counseling had a profound impact on reducing shame for individuals struggling with moral injury. The importance of validation and normalization for ameliorating spiritual trauma and abuse symptoms in individual and group contexts cannot be overstated.

When spiritual grief or trauma is identified, clinicians can utilize the *Inventory of Complicated Spiritual Grief* (ICSG; see link in Supplemental Resources, Burke et al., 2014) to determine specific areas of clinical focus. The ICSG is divided into two subscales: *Insecurity with God*, characterized by confusion, anger, and betrayal toward God, and *Disruption of Spiritual Practice*, which relates to the connection to and expression of spiritual beliefs and practices. Each of these domains contains critical points for exploration, which can enhance treatment goals and direction. Neimeyer and colleagues (2021) found that individuals with elevated scores on the ICSG inventory had increased difficulty making meaning of and integrating the loss. These findings are consistent with research suggesting that individuals with negative spiritual coping are at increased risk for suicidality (e.g., Currier et al., 2017; Rosmarin et al., 2013). Thus, it is essential that clinicians identify the possibility of and track suicidal ideation as a potential/planned consideration for those wracked with hopelessness from a lack of meaning and purpose.

Specific strategies include replacing lost rituals, which may aid spiritual recovery (Ramsay, 2019). In reference to death loss, Doka (2012) suggested that "rituals can be a bridge to the client's culture or spirituality" (p. 342), which may facilitate the client's reconnection with their identity and sense of self. While spiritual grief or trauma is not always connected to death loss, establishing rituals (e.g., meditation, contemplative prayer, convening with nature) bridges lost spiritual needs and practices with the client's shifting narrative. Generally, rituals provide comfort and consistency, helpful in grounding one in meaning and faith. However, after spiritual grief or trauma, clinicians may need to assist clients in revisioning rituals that support emerging spiritual needs in the wake of disenfranchised grief.

Finally, processing unfinished business (Zinker, 1977) through empty chair work allows clients to speak the unspoken, a necessary characteristic of disenfranchised grief. Zinker (1977) wrote that the empty chair technique is "an effective device for reclaiming . . . what one had disowned" (p. 150); hence, it is a viable intervention to process disenfranchised grief and integration. Using this technique, clients can place individuals, whole religious institutions, or even their higher power "in the chair" to elicit unexpressed thoughts and emotions.

Summary

The experience of spiritual and religious grief and trauma is as unique as the diverse demographics they represent. Recent literature offers compelling evidence of the pervasive impact of spiritual and religious trauma on most domains of functioning. However, society retains a cultural belief of avoiding the topic of spirituality in "polite" conversation, resulting in stalled grief and disenfranchising the grief over time. Clinicians willing to explore the influence of spiritual trauma and clients' subsequent grief experiences gain holistic data, which may positively influence the course of treatment. Though not exhaustive, the authors offered clinical points of exploration and demonstrated a stance of openness and curiosity. Through active and open conversations, clinicians give clients the opportunity to reconcile their faith, allowing it to resume its place as a source of strength, or to resolve their experiences, allowing for new resources to emerge.

References

Attig, T. (1996). *How we grieve: Relearning the world.* Oxford University Press.

Ballard, B. (2017). The rationality of faith and the benefits of religion. *International Journal for Philosophy of Religion, 81*(1–2), 213–227. https://doi.org/10.1007/s11153-016-9599-5

Bent-Goodley, T. B., & Fowler, D. N. (2006). Spiritual and religious abuse: Expanding what is known about domestic violence. *Affilia, 21*(3), 282–295. https://doi.org/10.1177%2F0886109906288901

Brown, J. E., van Mulukom, V., Charles, S. J., & Farias, M. (2021). Do you need religion to enjoy the benefits of Church services? Social bonding, morality and quality of life among religious and secular congregations. *Psychology of Religion and Spirituality*. Advance online publication. https://psycnet.apa.org/record/2021-98450-001

Burke, K. C. (2012). Women's agency in gender-traditional religions: A review of four approaches. *Sociology Compass*, 6(2), 122–133. https://doi.org./10.1111/j.1751-9020.2011.00439.x

Burke, L. A., Neimeyer, R. A., Holland, J., Dennard, S., Oliver, L., & Shear, M. K. (2014). Inventory of Complicated Spiritual Grief: Development and validation of a new measure. *Death Studies*, 38(4), 239–250. https://doi.org/10.1080/0748118 7.2013.810098

Burke, L. A., Neimeyer, R. A., McDevitt-Murphy, M. E., Ippolito, M. R., & Roberts, J. M. (2011). Faith in the wake of homicide: Religious coping and bereavement distress in an African American sample. *The International Journal for the Psychology of Religion*, 21(4), 289–307. https://doi.org/10.1080/10508619.2011.607416

Cashwell, C. S., & Watts, R. E. (2010). The new ASERVIC competencies for addressing spiritual and religious issues in counseling. *Counseling and Values*, 55(1), 2–5. https://doi.org/10.1002/j.2161-007X.2010.tb00018.x

Coyle, C. T., & Rue, V. M. (2015). A thematic analysis of men's experience with a partner's elective abortion. *Counseling and Values*, 60(2), 138–150. https://doi.org/10.1002/cvj.12010

Currier, J. M., Smith, P., & Kuhlman, S. (2017). Assessing the unique role of religious coping in suicidal behavior among U.S. Iraq and Afghanistan veterans. *Psychology of Religion and Spirituality*, 9(1), 118–123. https://doi.org/10.1037/rel0000055

Doka, K. (2012). Therapeutic ritual. In R. Niemeyer (Ed.), *Techniques of grief therapy: Creative practices for counseling the bereaved* (pp. 341–434). Routledge.

Fox, J., Cashwell, C. S., & Picciotto, G. (2017). The opiate of the masses: Measuring spiritual bypass and its relationship to spirituality, religion, mindfulness, psychological distress, and personality. *Spirituality in Clinical Practice*, 4, 274–287. https://doi.org/10.1037/scp0000141

Frankl, V. (1959). *Man's search for meaning*. Washington Square Press.

French, M. (1985). *Beyond power: On women, men, and morals*. Ballantine Books.

Garssen, B., Visser, A., & Pool, G. (2020). Does spirituality or religion positively affect mental health? Meta-analysis of longitudinal studies. *The International Journal for the Psychology of Religion*, 31(1), 4–20. https://doi.org/10.1080/10508619.2020.17 29570

Goldblatt Hyatt, E. D. (2019). Falsely accused clergy in therapy: A case study. *Social Work and Christianity*, 46(4), 87–103. https://doi.org/10.34043/swc.v46i4.64

Hoffman, L., Cleare-Hoffman, H. P., & Vallejos, L. (2013, July 31–August 4). Existential issues in trauma: Implications for assessment and treatment. In I. Serlin (Chair), *Developing resiliency: Compassion fatigue and regeneration* [Symposium]. American Psychological Association 121st Annual Convention, Honolulu, HI, United States.

Jones, T. W., Power, J., & Jones, M. J. (2022). Religious trauma and moral injury from LBGTQA+ conversion practices. *Social Science and Medicine, 305*, Article 115040. https://doi.org/10.1016/j.socscimed.2022.115040

Khan, A., & Ungar, M. (2021). Resilience to self-harm: A scoping review of protective factors that aid in recovery among marginalized young people. *Crisis: The Journal of Crisis Intervention and Suicide Prevention, 44*(1), 61–69. https://doi.org/10.1027/0227-5910/a000831

Koenig, H. G., & Al Zaben, F. (2021). Moral injury: An increasingly recognized and widespread syndrome. *Journal of Religion and Health, 60*, 2989–3011. https://doi.org/10.1007/s10943-021-01328-0

Lockett, G. M., Brooks, J. E., Abreu, R. L., & Sostre, J. P. (2022). "I want to go to a place that's openly talking about the experiences of people of color who also identify as LGBTQ+": Cultural, religious, and spiritual experiences of LGBTQ people of color. *Spirituality in Clinical Practice.* https://psycnet.apa.org/doiLanding?doi=10.1037%2Fscp0000288

Mason, K. (2021). Suicide stigma in Christian faith communities: A qualitative study. *Religions, 12*(7), Article 540. https://doi.org/10.3390/rel12070540

Neimeyer, R. A., Testoni, I., Ronconi, L., Biancalani, G., Antonellini, M., & Dal Corso, L. (2021). The integration of stressful life experiences scale and the Inventory of Complicated Spiritual Grief: The Italian validation of two instruments for meaning-focused assessments of bereavement. *Behavioral Sciences, 11*(11), Article 149. https://doi.org/10.3390/bs11110149

Ogden, H., Harris, J. I., Erbes, C. R., Engdahl, B. E., Olson, R. H. A., Winskowski, A. M., & McMahill, J. (2011). Religious functioning and trauma outcomes among combat veterans. *Counselling and Spirituality/Counseling et spiritualité, 30*(1), 71–89.

Panchuk, M. (2018). The shattered spiritual self: A philosophical exploration of religious trauma. *Res Philosophica, 95*(3), 505–530. https://doi.org//10.11612/resphil.1684

Prati, G., & Pietrantoni, L. (2009). Optimism, social support, and coping strategies as factors contributing to posttraumatic growth: A meta-analysis. *Journal of Loss and Trauma, 14*, 364–388. https://doi.org/10.1080/15325020902724271

Ramsay, N. J. (2019). Moral injury as loss and grief with attention to ritual resources for care. *Pastoral Psychology, 68*(1), 107–125. https://doi.org/10.1007/s11089-018-0854-9

Rosmarin, D. H., Bigda-Peyton, J. S., Öngur, D., Pargament, K. I., & Björgvinsson, T. (2013). Religious coping among psychotic patients: Relevance to suicidality and treatment outcomes. *Psychiatry Research, 210*(1), 182–187. https://doi.org/10.1016/j.psychres.2013.03.023

Shay, J., & Munroe, J. (1999). Group and milieu therapy for veterans with complex posttraumatic stress disorder. In P. A. Saigh & J. D. Bremner (Eds.), *Posttraumatic stress disorder: A comprehensive text* (pp. 391–413). Allyn & Bacon.

Smigelsky, M. A., Trimm, V., Meador, K. G., Jackson, G. L., Wortmann, J. H., & Nieuwsma, J. A. (2022). Core components of moral injury groups co-facilitated by mental health providers and chaplains. *Spirituality in Clinical Practice, 9*(3), 159–174. https://doi.org/10.1037/scp0000297

Sperry, L. (2021). Moral injury in Christian settings: Sacred moral injury. In J. Peteet, S. Moffic, A. Hankir, & H. Koenig (Eds.), *Christianity and psychiatry* (pp. 113–127). Springer. https://doi.org/10.1007/978-3-030-80854-9_8

Wood, H. J. (2019). Gender inequality: The problem of harmful, patriarchal, traditional and cultural gender practices in the church, *HTS Teologiese Studies/Theological Studies 75*(1), Article a5177. https://doi.org/10.4102/hts.v75i1.5177

Young, J. S., & Cashwell, C. S. (2011). Integrating spirituality and religion into counseling: An introduction. In C. S. Cashwell & J. S. Young (Eds.), *Integrating spirituality and religion into counseling: A guide to competent practice* (2nd ed., pp. 1–24). American Counseling Association.

Zeligman, M., Ataga, J., & Shaw, Z. (2020). Posttraumatic growth in trauma survivors: Associations with attachment to God and God representation. *Counseling and Values, 65*(2), 155–169. https://doi.org/10.1002/cvj.12135

Zinker, J. (1977). *Creative process in gestalt therapy.* Brunner/Mazel Publishers.

Questions for reflective practice

1. How do your personal experiences with faith and faith institutions influence your prejudices and biases related to faith as either a positive or a negative influence on wellbeing and healing?
2. Describe your personal spiritual development. How does your current spiritual development influence you as a person and helper?
3. What are some specific client religions or faith backgrounds that would be the hardest for you to work with, and why? Develop a plan for learning more about these faiths and how you can best support clients and their therapeutic processes.

4. How much time have you spent with people of other faiths? Have you ever attended services from other religions, not just different denominations of one religion but also different faiths?

Supplemental resources

- Association for Spiritual, Ethical, and Religious Values in Counseling: https://aservic.org/
- Inventory of Complicated Spiritual Grief (public domain scale): https://pdfs.semanticscholar.org/12a8/16148426af20966347f3289270182004ace6.pdf
- Interfaith literacy quiz: www.interfaithamerica.org/resources/interfaith-literacy-quiz/
- Intercommunity Peace & Justice Center: https://ipjc.org/interfaith-resources/

5
Untangling racial trauma and disenfranchised grief

Chinwé U. Williams and Layla J. Bonner

Racial trauma involves injury to an individual or an entire cultural group due to chronic and ongoing exposure and re-exposure to overt or subtle racial discrimination (Comas-Díaz et al., 2019). Exposures to racial discrimination include perceived or real threats of harm, shaming, or witnessing harm to another person of the same racial or ethnic group (Carter, 2007). Racism disenfranchises grief (Baker et al., 2021; Pabon & Basile, 2022). Furthermore, racist and oppressive societal beliefs and attitudes establish the grounds for disenfranchised grief. Universal experiences of racism can be traumatic (Comas-Díaz et al., 2019; Sotero, 2006). Generations of race-based trauma, oppression, and disenfranchised grief experiences since the brutal forced migration of Africans to America continue to add to the legacy of trauma in the African American community (Laurie & Neimeyer, 2010; Rogers & Bryant-Davis, 2020; Rosenblatt & Wallace, 2005a). Considering that racial discrimination and oppression are systemic, centuries long, and deeply ingrained issues, untangling racial trauma and disenfranchised grief will require much more work than anyone might imagine.

Historical context of disenfranchised grief for African Americans

American society has failed to acknowledge, recognize, or has outrightly denied the trauma and grief experiences of African Americans for centuries (Rogers & Bryant-Davis, 2020; Williams, 2016; Vil & Vil, 2019). From being brutalized and dehumanized on slave ships and plantations to the deaths, separations, and losses of loved ones, the grief and trauma for Africans who were stolen and brought to America remained unrecognized and invalidated (Roediger, 1981; Rogers & Bryant-Davis, 2020; Williams, 2016; Vil & Vil, 2019). *Disenfranchised grief* is, in fact, "grief that persons experience when they incur

DOI: 10.4324/9781003292890-6

a loss that is not or cannot be openly acknowledged, publicly mourned, or socially supported" (Doka, 1989, p. 4). Furthermore, it is societal forces that refuse the bereaved the right to grieve, deem one's grief illegitimate, and fail to recognize or invalidate the grief experience (Doka, 2002a). Hence, this lack of humanity and disenfranchisement was a consequence of White supremacist cultural norms and attitudes, privilege, and power that have been set from the foundations of this country.

For example, slaves' ability to publicly mourn and grieve was solely contingent upon the goodwill and approval of White slave owners (Laurie & Neimeyer, 2010; Roediger, 1981; Williams, 2016). White slave owners determined when and how it was appropriate to grieve and who was worthy to be grieved (Roediger, 1981). Furthermore, slave masters rarely approved funerals and burials, but on occasion they allowed them for their most beloved slaves (Laurie & Neimeyer, 2010; Roediger, 1981).

Likewise, slave masters validated Black motherhood insofar as a Black mother's nurturing extended to the master's family and children as their "mammy," a term that once referred to the female slave who attended to the slave owner's family in his home and was considered so devoted that she was expected to happily prioritize the master's family over her own (Johnson, 2005). Williams (2016) clarified that the "one discursive space where Black women's love and the potential to grieve loss was imaginable was the archetypal mammy" (p. 20). Therefore, if a Black mother lost her own biological child to death or to transactions between plantation owners, the White supremacist prevailing rules at the time "denied claims of affective trauma once mother and child were split apart" (Williams, 2016, p. 20). The horror and unimaginable grief of a Black mother were simply deemed illegitimate. Racist society labeled her relationship with her deceased child as insignificant, her loss as meaningless, and herself, the bereaved, as incapable of experiencing grief under such circumstances.

This racial trauma and disenfranchisement of grief of African Americans is not limited to the period of slavery; it has continued across generations. In fact, Emmett Till's 1955 death during the Civil Rights Movement demonstrates how American society has remained persistent in its devaluation of Black life, the perpetuation of racial trauma, and the disenfranchisement of grief (Williams, 2016). Likewise, more recent examples include national stories of Black men and women like George Floyd, Mike Brown, and Breona Taylor, who all died by homicide at the hands of police in racially tinged contexts (Anderson, 2015).

The psychological cost of the "Strong Black Woman" schema

The *Strong Black Woman* (SBW) schema is a race-gender schema that assigns specific roles, norms, and expectations for African American women to assume. African American women are expected to play multiple roles as caregivers and providers, to possess intractable strength, and to prioritize the care and consideration of others above themselves (Beauboeuf-Lafontant, 2007; Settles et al., 2008). Essentially, SBW serves as a cultural expectation placed on Black women to display signs of strength and nurturance, while suppressing their emotions – even in the face of traumatic grief.

Black women's emotional distress often goes unnoticed, in part because Black women internalize the message that it is noble to be strong caretakers who are too busy bearing the brunt of others' pain while rarely acknowledging their own. Although the SBW schema has adverse psychological effects, it is important to note that it is not without its advantages. For example, the SBW schema is rooted in African American emotional strength, perseverance, and resilience. Even though the SBW schema can be temporarily helpful in navigating individualized experiences of racism (Abrams et al., 2014), its internalization comes with a cost.

SBW schema has been linked to negative physical and mental health outcomes (Harrington et al., 2010), such as anxiety and depression. For example, self-silencing, a hallmark characteristic of the SBW schema, involves intentionally inhibiting outward expressions of pain and discomfort and minimizing personal needs. Practiced over time, self-silencing promotes psychological distress and depressive symptomatology (Jack, 2011). Due to cultural expectations of resilience in the face of hardship and loss, many Black women project the cultural ideal of self-sacrificial strength while simultaneously masking their own experiences of grief and trauma.

How historical oppression and racial trauma impacts help seeking

The denial of access to basic human rights, such as adequate medical treatment and economic freedom, has cultivated feelings of mistrust of the medical health system and behavioral health professionals. The impact of historical and racial trauma is instructive in exploring African Americans' psychological help-seeking experiences. Historical and contemporary experiences of racial discrimination continue to have a negative impact on the mental and physical health of African Americans, including short life spans.

Between 2018 and 2021, the Southern Poverty Law Center reported 1,341 incidents of White supremacist propaganda and pamphleteering on college campuses through its Hatewatch resource (www.splcenter.org/hatewatch). Black students at predominantly White institutions often report multiple incidents of racism, ranging from exclusion and microaggressions to direct racial hostility and intimidation (Prasad, 2014). Racialized incidents can take a toll mentally, emotionally, and physiologically on one's nervous system and undermine self-confidence and academic performance.

Discrimination across numerous institutions has detrimental psychological effects but also impacts the ways in which African Americans access care. African Americans tend to be apprehensive about seeking mental health support (Ward et al., 2013). Although Black women are more likely to report symptoms of anxiety and depression at the same rate or higher than White women, they are least likely to seek care (Nelson et al., 2020). Managing complex layers of historical and present-day trauma has a compounding effect that impacts the way Black people seek mental and emotional support.

For many African Americans, psychological help-seeking behavior begins with initial outreach to faith-based or pastoral support (Moore, 2003). However, despite many clergy members being trained to provide grief support, many have limited expertise to manage severe psychological symptoms that accompany complicated or prolonged grief (Rogers et al., 2012). Therefore, church officials will provide grieving Black church members with counseling referrals that may or may not be pursued. With the limited number of mental health professionals of color, many Black help seekers are concerned that White providers may not address their specific concerns with enough cultural humility (American Psychological Association [APA], 2017a; Nelson et al., 2020). Clinicians practicing *cultural humility* will understand the need to remain open to learning about each client's specific cultural background and unique experiences, as well as prioritize the client's lived experience over their more limited theoretical understandings (Hook et al., 2013). Due to these and multiple other factors, African Americans are less likely to seek mental health care, but are more likely to experience severe and persistent, rather than episodic, psychological conditions.

Current context of disenfranchised grief for African Americans

Racism permeates societal norms still today and continues to serve as an oppressive force in African Americans' trauma and grief experiences (Baker et al., 2021; Martin, 2005). Research supports the idea that Black families experience disenfranchised grief, especially when a loved one dies by homicide (Dutil, 2019; Lawson, 2014; Martin, 2005). For example, Lawson (2014) documented the trauma and disenfranchised grief of Blacks who lost a loved one to gun violence in Canada, where anti-Black racism also exists. Interviews revealed that families and friends experienced traumatic reactions to these deaths and simultaneously had to endure negative narratives tinged with underlying racial subtexts about their deceased loved ones. Police and media alike emphasized a narrative that suggested that the deceased was of ill repute and characterized by criminality. Racist discourses around these types of deaths stigmatize the victim, call into question who is worthy of being grieved, and suggest that only those above reproach should be grieved (Lawson, 2014; Martin, 2005).

According to Doka (2002b), stigmatized deaths are disenfranchised. These discrediting portrayals and "postmortem profiling" (Martin, 2005, p. 157) trivialize the death of the deceased, re-victimize surviving family and friends, and invalidate their tremendous pain and grief (Lawson, 2014). The American media also weaved together similar storylines stigmatizing the deaths of African Americans like Mike Brown, Trayvon Martin, George Floyd, Sandra Bland, and Breona Taylor, leaving widespread feelings of cultural trauma and disenfranchised grief within the African American community (Anderson, 2015).

Within the context of stigmatized deaths, Black boys become ineligible grievers (Dutil, 2019; Pabon & Basile, 2022). In some instances, the violent deaths of young Black males have been so normalized that key figures in their ecological system (Bronfenbrenner, 1979), like school administrators and counselors, dismiss their trauma, fail to recognize their grief, and do not attempt to provide opportunities for them to grieve (Pabon & Basile, 2022). Dutil (2019) described a 16-year-old African American male's experience that he "could not openly mourn his friend's death because of the nature of the death and messages he received from media and even family and peers" (p. 185).

Baker et al. (2021) also documented the connection between racism and grief disenfranchisement. The authors interviewed non-White U.S. citizens following the death of a loved one subsequent to contact with law enforcement. To be clear, their loved one died after being shot by police, restrained by police, or committing suicide after being in police custody. Participants reported a strong belief that racism contributed to their disenfranchised grief. In particular, they indicated that they "experienced significant levels of social prejudice, stigma, and grief invalidation due to the context of their loved one's death" and "due to their marginalized position in society" (Baker et al., 2021, p. 246).

Racist societal attitudes disenfranchised their grief due to the circumstances of the death and also because of the identity of the grievers themselves as persons of color. This perceived lower moral worth of the deceased and victim blaming form the basis of social rejection and empathic failures (Baker et al., 2021).

Black grievers are also characterized as illegitimate grievers because of their social status (Martin, 2005). Baker et al. (2021) further described African American grieving styles as being disenfranchised. Researchers revealed that African Americans express their grief more privately and more briefly (Hines & Boyd-Franklin, 1996; Laurie & Neimeyer, 2008). The authors suggested that this grieving style is rooted in grieving rules set by oppressive forces that historically denied African Americans the right to grieve. As a result of internalized social cues, African Americans continue to bury their own pain today.

Williams (2016) also highlighted the connection between historical oppression, gendered racism, and disenfranchised grief. In particular, the author examined how Black mothers were historically viewed as illegitimate grievers and denied the power to grieve because White society revoked and refused their status as actual human beings. In fact, during slavery, White supremacist cultural norms and beliefs nullified the attachment between a Black mother and her child. Williams (2016) discussed that Black mothers may now be allowed to grieve insofar as their grief remains consistent with stereotypes of the Black Matriarch or the Strong Black Woman. She pointed to Mamie Till-Mobley, Emmet Till's mother, as an example of "iconic Black maternal mourning" (Williams, 2016, p. 21). Further examples of this type of maternal mourning have emerged in the more recent deaths of unarmed Black men, such as Trayvon Martin's mother, Sybrina Fulton, or Mike Brown's mother, Lesley McSpadden (e.g., Alcindor, 2014; Purnell, 2022). These mothers' grief was public and positioned as a vehicle for social justice reform.

Williams (2016) suggested that any Black maternal grief expression that deviates from the more public grievance of these iconic mothers goes unacknowledged. The history of Black maternal grief evolved from being deemed completely illegitimate by the standards of White supremacy to being legitimized insofar as "the mother articulates her anguish through grievance" (Williams, 2016, p. 21). One well-known example of Black maternal mourning is Mamie Till-Mobley. She made the unimaginable decision to show her son's mutilated body to the nation at his funeral after he was bludgeoned to death and left unrecognizable. The images of her openly grieving alongside her slain son's open casket fueled an entire movement yet also crystallized a widely held schema about Black maternal grief. Black mothers who mobilize their anguish to fight for justice for their slain children have become the model, the stereotype even, of Black maternal grief. Any variation from this stereotyped grief expression is, thereby, disenfranchised. Black women who retreat, demonstrate less emotional fortitude, or grieve more privately are forgotten.

Self-disenfranchisement within African American grievers

According to Kauffman (2002), *self-disenfranchisement* occurs when an individual has internalized the social sanctions surrounding the norms and expectations for grievers and regulates their own grief. Piazza-Bonin et al. (2015) described a sort of self-disenfranchisement that some African Americans self-impose, possibly stemming from experiences of racism or intergenerational trauma. During the funeral ritual, which harkens back to West African death rituals, it is customary for African Americans to demonstrate strong emotions (Hines, 1991; Roediger, 1981; Rosenblatt & Wallace, 2005a). However, soon thereafter, surviving friends and family members are expected to be strong, and highly emotional grief reactions are discouraged (Hines & Boyd Franklin, 1996; Laurie & Neimeyer, 2008; Rosenblatt & Wallace, 2005a).

Furthermore, culturally, the stereotypes of African Americans as Strong Black Women and Mothers are more favorable (Williams, 2016). It is likely that this expectation developed as an adaptive coping strategy from slavery and generations of oppression (Piazza-Bonin et al., 2015; Wilkins et al., 2013). Wilkins et al. (2013) identified some of the residual effects of slavery on African Americans. African Americans may, in fact, feel strong emotional reactions, such as rage and resentment (Rosenblatt & Wallace 2005a). However, Wilkins et al. (2013) proposed that the effects of slavery may include the stifling of one's natural emotional reactions, passivity, and powerlessness. In fact, emotional strength was cited as being self-protective in nature and a necessary adaptation to surviving slavery and oppression (hooks, 1993; Laurie & Neimeyer, 2010; Piazza-Bonin et al., 2015; Wilkins et al., 2013; Williams, 2016). However, researchers have indicated that African Americans who spoke less about their grief were more likely to report greater levels of complicated grief compared to European Americans (Laurie & Neimeyer, 2008). Silencing pain is harmful and may be an adaptive survival mechanism as a consequence of historical trauma. And due to the stigma rooted in racial and historical trauma and oppression, many African Americans are not confident that they will find a trusted professional to rely on for emotional support.

Allyship and advocacy

Professional standards for mental health professionals mandate that practitioners serve in roles that extend beyond the therapy room (American Association for Marriage and Family Therapy [AAMFT], 2015; American Counseling Association [ACA], 2014; APA, 2017b). One of the most important of those is that of *advocate* (Toporek & Daniels, 2018). As part of their roles and responsibilities, counselors are expected to advocate for their clients at the client level, the community level, systemically, and within the profession (Toporek & Daniels, 2018). National counseling organizations, like ACA (2014), have established competencies to help guide practitioners in allyship and advocacy.

Lastly, counselors practice advocacy and allyship by taking action on a greater sociopolitical level. This may look like educating the public through public awareness campaigns and informing lawmakers who have the power to legislate policies that either perpetuate or confront systemic barriers for African Americans. Clinicians must understand how even the field of counseling itself has perpetrated oppression against African Americans. For example, *drapetomania* was once declared a diagnosable mental illness (Medlock et al., 2016). It is cited as a pathology that drove African slaves to escape their bondage. Moreover, since the 1970s, African Americans have been overdiagnosed or even misdiagnosed with schizophrenia, taking no cultural consideration for the traumatic and psychological effects of oppression and racism on their psyche, affect, or behavior (Suite et al., 2007). Rightfully, APA (2021) recently issued an "Apology to People of Color for APA's Role in Promoting, Perpetuating, and Failing to Challenge Racism, Racial Discrimination, and Human Hierarchy in [the] U.S." At the community level, advocacy competencies suggest that clinicians collaborate with schools, community agencies/organizations, and broader systems to address the systemic barriers that marginalized clients face.

Ethical considerations

The Association for Multicultural Counseling and Development (AMCD, 2015) drafted the *Multicultural and Social Justice Counseling Competencies*. Through Figure 16.1 in that text, Ratts et al. highlighted the ways in which both counselor and client identities and privileged or marginalized statuses intersect in therapy (as cited in AMCD, 2015, p. 4). These competencies encourage counselors to develop an awareness of their own beliefs and attitudes as well as knowledge and understanding of the client's worldview. The guide also offers action-oriented steps that practitioners and allies alike may take in working with populations that have been marginalized (AMCD, 2015).

Practitioners might also familiarize themselves with the *Competencies for Addressing Spiritual and Religious Issues in Counseling* (ASERVIC, 2014). This guide encourages counselors to consider the client's spirituality as an important source of well-being and to address themes of religion and spirituality, as this may serve as a function of hope and healing during mourning (Utsey et al., 2007). However, it is wise to consider individual differences between clients, as some African American clients may not find this to be a helpful approach.

Lastly, Toporek and Daniels's (2018) update of the American Counseling Association's *Advocacy Competencies* identified several domains as helpful in leading clinicians in their advocacy and allyship efforts: client/student empowerment, client/student advocacy, community collaboration, systems advocacy, public information, and social/political advocacy. It may be useful for clinicians to engage in a more thorough reflection of some of these areas.

Strategies and interventions

Previous authors have highlighted the negative impact of racism on the psychological well-being of African Americans. Identifying clinical interventions for processing disenfranchised grief is relevant to African American clients' mental health wellness. The following interventions will guide clinicians in helping to reduce traumatic symptoms and will create opportunities for mental health professionals to intervene in culturally specific ways.

Address the super woman schema

In a study of 194 Black females, Abrams et al. (2019) found that over 80% of participants identified with the SBW schema, reflecting the pervasiveness of this cultural construct. The need to embody this cultural ideal may contribute to the underutilization of mental health treatment among Black women. When Black people eventually decide to engage in mental health services, researchers show that they run into cultural barriers, resulting in low treatment retention rates. Therefore, given the prevalence of the schema, Black female clients may benefit from a clinician-initiated discussion of the SBW construct and how it may mask underlying symptoms of distress through negative coping strategies, such as avoidance, emotional suppression, self-silencing, and minimization (Abrams et al., 2019).

Clinicians should broach topics of race and racism and explore larger cultural factors that may be causing unhelpful cognitions and behaviors. Clinicians are encouraged to assist clients in examining how racial and structural inequities may play a role in and/or maintain the SBW schema and subsequently impact how the client processes grief. Particular attention should be placed on assisting clients in managing internal messages that they are not enough or are not *doing* enough. Moreover, clinical interventions should also focus on helping clients recognize and decrease tendencies toward perfectionism by increasing self-awareness and self-compassion.

Broach the topics of race and racism

One of the most important strategies to keep in mind when supporting African American clients who are in mourning involves broaching the topic of racism (Rosenblatt & Wallace, 2005b). Some have suggested expanding clinical understanding of the adverse conditions that impact Blacks to include historical, collective, and intergenerational trauma as well as their racial/social contexts across the lifespan (Stevens, 2015). It is imperative that clinicians process the perceived impact of racism in the life of the deceased and in the life and grief process of surviving friends and family members. According to Rosenblatt and Wallace (2005b), the harsh reality that racism impacted the death and, perhaps, even the trajectory of the deceased's attainment of life goals is overwhelming.

Provide psychoeducation and create breathing room

Grief is often unpredictable in its presentation, intensity, and course. Clinicians can provide clients with psychoeducation around the existing social norms and expectations for Black grievers through a discussion of the concept of self-disenfranchisement and its psychologically limiting nature (Piazza-Bonin et al., 2015). Stifling one's natural emotional reactions is an ineffective coping strategy that can increase levels of complicated grief. Clinicians can encourage the emotional expression of grief-related emotions by discouraging a natural tendency for some clients to suppress powerful emotion.

Clinically, mourning can be characterized as a deeply psychological process associated with remembering, experiencing, and regulating emotions (Shear, 2012). Memories of the deceased or circumstances related to a traumatic loss can sometimes activate painful emotions, such as guilt, bitterness, anger, and shame. Clinicians can support Black clients in the integration and assimilation of grief by teaching effective emotional coping and regulation strategies such as conscious breathing, which activates the body's parasympathetic nervous system and signals the brain to regulate (Shear, 2012).

Utilize spiritual coping resources

Researchers indicate that many African Americans utilize spirituality more than therapy to cope with traumatic life experiences and grief (Janowiak, 1995). At the center of Afro-centric culture and tradition is collective and spiritual coping (Greer, 2011). Collective coping refers to the reliance on group-focused activities to manage stress. Spiritual coping involves practices that deeply connect one to a higher power or with the Creator (Utsey et al., 2007).

Utsey et al. (2007) reported that African American clients who utilize spiritual coping resources (e.g., praying, meditating, attending church, and reading the *Bible*) experience more positive mental health outcomes, such as decreased anxiety and depression, and a higher quality of life. Clinicians are encouraged to consider the exploration of spiritual practices as a valid treatment option for grieving Black clients (Association for Spiritual, Ethical, & Religious Values in Counseling [ASERVIC], 2014).

Seek informal supports

African Americans are often hesitant to seek professional assistance for grief or other mental health concerns (Laurie & Neimeyer, 2008). Therefore, support from family, church leaders, or others who also have a keen understanding of the relationship between racism, trauma, and disenfranchised grief is healing for many African American grievers. Clinicians might consider engaging in outreach in spaces where African Americans gather (e.g., places of worship, community centers, traditional medical facilities, and school events) to discuss mental health benefits and introduce community and mental health resources.

Engage Black youth and young adults in treatment

Troubling trends are emerging in the suicide rate of Black children, adolescents, and college students. Recently, researchers have highlighted that the suicide rate among Black children between the ages of 5 and 11 has increased at a rate now surpassing that of their White peers (Bridge et al., 2018; Ivey-Stephenson et al., 2020). Black teenage girls outpace both White and non-White Hispanic teenage girls in suicide attempts, with 15.2% of Black 14- to 18-year-old girls reporting a suicide attempt in the previous 12 months compared with 9.4% of White teenage girls and 11.9% of Hispanic teenage girls. Suicide deaths among Black adolescent girls rose 182% between 2001 and 2017 (Ivey-Stephenson et al., 2020).

These disturbing patterns have confounded mental health researchers because suicide historically has been considered an issue faced primarily in the White community (Early & Akers, 1993). Although the debate continues regarding the reasons for such a sharp increase, Gordon (2020) found that Black youth are disproportionately affected by mental health concerns because of risk factors such as racism, trauma, gun violence, bullying, poverty, and LGBTQIA+ intolerance. Moreover, many Black youths and their families are distrustful of healthcare organizations due to institutional racism. The success rate of evidence-based treatments for depression has been mixed at best for Black teenagers (Lindsey et al., 2013), and treatment dropout rates remain high.

Therefore, clinicians can engage Black youth with a combination of strategies including spirituality, music (e.g., drumming), creative arts, and other culturally informed holistic and restorative interventions that can help process grief. Furthermore, prevention and early intervention services (e.g., routine screening for mental health disorders and suicide risk; suicide risk and safety assessments; and school counselor and teacher/staff training) are critical to addressing suicide risk factors. Given the low rates of treatment utilization among African American youth, there is a need for clinicians to engage Black youth and young adults in clinically meaningful ways in both ally and advocacy roles. However, clinicians must first identify and unpack their own implicit biases.

Summary

Racial trauma for African Americans has its historical roots in slavery and White supremacist ideologies and practices. The remnant of these oppressive forces continues to form the foundation for persistent discrimination and marginalization and has invalidated and continues to invalidate African Americans' grief experiences. The intersection of racial trauma and disenfranchised grief is most salient in the experiences of Black women and young Black males who are bereaved. It is important that clinicians are clear about the definitions of and relationship between racial trauma and disenfranchised grief, especially when working with African American clients. This understanding, paired with a posture of cultural humility and other suggested interventions, will better support African American clients and improve treatment outcomes.

References

Abrams, J. A., Hill, A., & Maxwell, M. (2019). Underneath the mask of the Strong Black Woman schema: Disentangling influences of strength and self-silencing on depressive symptoms among U.S. Black Women. *Sex Roles*, 80(9–10), 517–526. https://doi.org/10.1007/s11199-018-0956-y

Abrams, J. A., Maxwell, M., Pope, M., & Belgrave, F. Z. (2014). Carrying the world with the grace of a lady and the grit of a warrior: Deepening our understanding of the "Strong Black Woman" schema. *Psychology of Women Quarterly*, 38, 503–518. https://doi.org/10.1177/0361684314541418

Alcindor, Y. (2014, August 26). Amid furor over killing, Brown's family seeks solace. *USA Today*. www.usatoday.com/story/news/nation/2014/08/25/ferguson-michael-brown-missouri-police/14594185/

American Association for Marriage and Family Therapy. (2015). *Code of ethics*. www.aamft.org/Legal_Ethics/Code_of_Ethics.aspx

American Counseling Association. (2014). ACA *code of ethics*. www.counseling.org/resources/aca-code-of-ethics.pdf

American Psychological Association. (2017a). *Demographic characteristics of APA members by membership characteristics*. www.apa.org/workforce/publications/17-member-profiles/table-1.pdf

American Psychological Association. (2017b). *Ethical principles of psychologists and code of conduct*. www.apa.org/ethics/code#

American Psychological Association. (2021, October 29). Apology to people of color for APA's role in promoting, perpetuating, and failing to challenge racism, racial discrimination, and human hierarchy in U.S. *American Psychological Association*. www.apa.org/about/policy/racism-apology

Anderson, W. (2015, January 16). From lynching photos to Michael Brown's body: Commodifying Black death. *Truthout*. https://truthout.org/articles/from-lynching-photos-to-michael-brown-s-body-commodifying-black-death/

Association for Multicultural Counseling and Development. (2015). Multicultural and social justice counseling competencies. AMCD. www.counseling.org/docs/default-source/competencies/multicultural-and-social-justice-counseling-competencies.pdf?sfvrsn=8573422c_22

Association for Spiritual, Ethical, and Religious Values in Counseling. (2014). Competencies for addressing spiritual and religious issues in counseling. *ASERVIC*. https://aservic.org/spiritual-and-religious-competencies/

Baker, D., Norris, D., & Cherneva, V. (2021). Disenfranchised grief and families' experiences of death after police contact in the United States. *OMEGA – Journal of Death and Dying, 83*(2), 239–256. https://doi.org/10.1177/0030222819846420

Beauboeuf-Lafontant, T. (2007). You have to show strength: An explanation of gender, race, and depression. *Gender and Society, 21*(1), 28–51. https://doi.org/10.1177/0891243206294108

Bridge, J. A., Horowitz, L. M., Fontanella, C. A., Sheftall, A. H., Greenhouse, J., Kelleher, K. J., & Campo, J. V. (2018). Age-related racial disparity in suicide rates among US youths from 2001 through 2015. *JAMA Pediatrics, 172*(7), 697–699. https://doi.org/10.1001/jamapediatrics.2018.0399

Bronfenbrenner, U. (1979). *The ecology of human development: Experiments by nature and design*. Harvard University Press.

Carter, R. T. (2007). Racism and psychological and emotional injury: Recognizing and assessing race-based traumatic stress. *The Counseling Psychologist, 35*(1), 13–105. https://doi.org/10.1177/0011000006292033

Comas-Díaz, L., Hall, G. N., & Neville, H. A. (2019). Racial trauma: Theory, research, and healing: Introduction to the special issue. *American Psychologist, 74*(1), 1–5. https://doi.org/10.1037/amp0000442

Doka, K. J. (2002a). Introduction. In K. J. Doka (Ed.), *Disenfranchised grief: New directions, challenges, and strategies for practice* (pp. 5–22). Research Press.

Doka, K. J. (2002b). How we die: Stigmatized death and disenfranchised grief. In K. J. Doka (Ed.), *Disenfranchised grief: New directions, challenges, and strategies for practice* (pp. 323–336). Research Press.

Doka, K. J. (Ed.). (1989). *Disenfranchised grief: Recognizing hidden sorrow*. Lexington Books.

Dutil, S. (2019). Adolescent traumatic and disenfranchised grief: Adapting an evidence-based intervention for Black and Latinx youths in schools. *Children and Schools, 41*(3), 179–187. https://doi.org/10.1093/cs/cdz009

Early, K. E., & Akers, R. L. (1993). "It's a White thing:" An exploration of beliefs about suicide in the African-American community. *Deviant Behavior 14*(4), 277–296. https://doi.org/10.1080/01639625.1993.9967947

Gordon, J. A. (2020). Addressing the crisis of Black youth suicide. *National Institute of Mental Health*. www.nimh.nih.gov/about/director/messages/2020/addressing-the-crisis-of-black-youth-suicide.shtml

Greer, T. M. (2011). Coping strategies as moderators of the relationship between race-and-gender-based discrimination and psychological symptoms for African American women. *Journal of Black Psychology, 37*(1), 42–54. https://doi. org/10.1177/0095798410380202

Harrington, E. F., Crowther, J. H., & Shipherd, J. C. (2010). Trauma, binge eating, and the "Strong Black Woman". *Journal of Consulting and Clinical Psychology, 78*, 469–479. https://doi.org/10.1037/a0019174

Hines, P. (1991). Death and African American culture. In F. Walsh & M. McGoldrick (Eds.), *Living beyond loss: Death in the family*. Norton.

Hines, P., & Boyd-Franklin, N. (1996). African American families. In M. McGoldrick, J. Giordano, & J. K. Pearce (Eds.), *Ethnicity and family therapy* (2nd ed., pp. 66–84). Guilford Press.

Hook, J. N., Davis, D. E., Owen, J., Worthington Jr, E. L., & Utsey, S. O. (2013). Cultural humility: Measuring openness to culturally diverse clients. *Journal of Counseling Psychology, 60*(3), 353–366. https://doi.org/10.1037/a0032595

hooks, b. (1993). *Sisters of the yam: Black women and self-recovery*. South End.

Ivey-Stephenson, A. Z., Demissie, Z., Crosby, A. E., Stone, D. M., Gaylor, E., Wilkins, N., Lowry, R., & Brown, B. (2020). Suicidal ideation and behaviors among high school students – Youth Risk Behavior Survey, United States, 2019. *Morbidity and Mortality Weekly Report, 69*(1), 47–55. https://doi.org/10.15585/mmwr.su6901a6

Jack D. C. (2011). Reflections on the Silencing the Self Scale and its origins. *Psychology of Women Quarterly, 35*(3), 523–529. https://doi.org/10.1177/0361684311414824

Janowiak, S. M. (1995). Bereavement experiences of African Americans: The use of focus groups (Publication No. 9528867) [Doctoral dissertation, Indiana University of Pennsylvania]. Proquest Dissertations and Theses Global. www.proquest. com/openview/edad16e35ea38a23c1c238a4f52be331/1?pq-origsite=gscholar&cbl=18750&diss=y

Johnson, J. M. (2005). "Ye gave them a stone": African American women's clubs, the Frederick Douglass Home, and the Black Mammy monument. *Journal of Women's History, 17*(1), 62–86. https://doi.org/10.1353/jowh.2005.0009

Kauffman, J. (2002). The psychology of disenfranchised grief: Liberation, shame, and self-disenfranchisement. In K. J. Doka (Ed.), *Disenfranchised grief: New directions, challenges, and strategies for practice* (pp. 61–77). Research Press.

Laurie, A., & Neimeyer, R. A. (2008). African Americans in bereavement: Grief as a function of ethnicity. *OMEGA – Journal of Death and Dying, 57*(2), 173–193. https://doi.org/10.2190/OM.57.2.d

Laurie, A., & Neimeyer, R. A. (2010). Of broken bonds and bondage: An analysis of loss in the slave narrative collection. *Death Studies, 34*(3), 221–256. https://doi. org/10.1080/07481180903559246

Lawson, E. (2014). Disenfranchised grief and social inequality: Bereaved African Canadians and oppositional narratives about the violent deaths of friends and family members. *Ethnic and Racial Studies*, *37*(11), 2092–2109, https://doi.org/10.1080/01419870.2013.800569

Lindsey, M. A., Chambers, K., Pohle, C., Beall, P., & Lucksted, A. (2013). Understanding the behavioral determinants of mental health service use by urban, under-resourced Black youth: Adolescent and caregiver perspectives. *Journal of Child and Family Studies*, *22*(1), 107–121. https://doi.org/10.1007/s10826-012-9668-z

Martin, D. D. (2005). Acute loss and the social construction of blame. *Illness, Crisis and Loss*, *13*(2), 149–167. https://doi.org/10.1177/105413730501300206

Medlock, M., Weissman, A., Wong, S. S., & Carlo, A. D. (2016). Addressing the legacy of racism in psychiatric training. *American Journal of Psychiatry Residents' Journal*, *11*(2), 13. https://doi.org/10.1176/appi.ajp-rj.2016.110206

Moore, P. J. (2003). The Black church: A natural resource for bereavement support. *Journal of Pastoral Counseling*, *38*, 47–58.

Nelson, T., Shahid, N. N., & Cardemil, E. V. (2020). Do I really need to go and see somebody? Black women's perceptions of help-seeking for depression. *Journal of Black Psychology*, *46*(4), 263–286. https://doi.org/10.1177/0095798420931644

Pabon, A. J.-M., Basile, V. (2022). It don't affect them like it affects us: Disenfranchised grief of Black boys in the wake of peer homicide. *The Urban Review*, *54*(1), 67–82. https://doi.org/10.1007/s11256-021-00605-2

Piazza-Bonin, E., Neimeyer, R. A., Burke, L. A., McDevitt-Murphy, M. E., & Young, A. (2015). Disenfranchised grief following African American homicide loss: An inductive case study. *OMEGA – Journal of Death and Dying*, *70*(4), 404–427. https://doi.org/10.1177/0030222815573727

Prasad, A. S. (2014). Lift every voice: The counter-stories and narratives of first-generation African American students at a predominately White institution [Doctoral dissertation, Ohio State University]. OhioLINK Electronic Theses and Dissertations Center. http://rave.ohiolink.edu/etdc/view?acc_num=osu1397667313

Purnell, D. (2022, January 31). Grief over time: Sybrina Fulton, who lost her son Trayvon Martin ten years ago this month, found her painful place in history. *The Cut*. www.thecut.com/article/sybrina-fulton-trayvon-martin-interview.html

Roediger, D. R. (1981). And die in Dixie: Funerals, death, and heaven in the slave community 1700–1865. *The Massachusetts Review*, *22*(1), 163–183.

Rogers, E. B., Stanford, M., & Garland, D. R. (2012). The effects of mental illness on families within faith communities. *Mental Health, Religion and Culture*, *15*(3), 301–313. https://doi.org/10.1080/13674676.2011.573474

Rogers, G., & Bryant-Davis, T. (2020). Historical and contemporary racial trauma among Black Americans: Black wellness matters. In R. Geffner, J. W. White, L. K.

Hamberger, A. Rosenbaum, V. Vaughan-Eden, & V. I. Vieth (Eds.), *Handbook of interpersonal violence and abuse across the lifespan* (pp. 1–35). Springer. https://doi.org/10.1007/978-3-319-62122-7_338-1

Rosenblatt, P. C., & Wallace, B. R. (Eds.). (2005a). *African American grief*. Routledge.

Rosenblatt, P. C., & Wallace, B. R. (Eds.). (2005b). Narratives of grieving African-Americans about racism in the lives of deceased family members. *Death Studies*, 29(3), 217–235. https://doi.org/10.1080/07481180590916353

Settles, I. H., Pratt-Hyatt, J. S., & Buchanan, N. T. (2008). Through the lens of race: Black and White women's perceptions of womanhood. *Psychology of Women Quarterly*, 32(4), 454–468. https://doi.org/10.1111/j.1471-6402.2008.00458.x

Shear, M. K. (2012). Grief and mourning gone awry: Pathway and course of complicated grief. *Dialogues in Clinical Neuroscience*, 14(2), 119–128. https://doi.org/10.31887/DCNS.2012.14.2/mshear

Sotero, M. (2006). A conceptual model of historical trauma: Implications for public health practice and research. *Journal of Health Disparities Research and Practice*, 1(1), 93–108.

Stevens, J. (2015, April 7). Adding layers to the ACEs pyramid: What do you think? *PACES Connection*. www.pacesconnection.com/blog/adding-layers-to-the-aces-pyramid-what-do-you-think

Suite, D. H., La Bril, R., Primm, A., & Harrison-Ross, P. (2007). Beyond misdiagnosis, misunderstanding and mistrust: Relevance of the historical perspective in the medical and mental health treatment of people of color. *Journal of the National Medical Association*, 99(8), 879–885.

Toporek, R. L., & Daniels, J. (2018). American Counseling Association advocacy competencies. *American Counseling Association*. www.counseling.org/docs/default-source/competencies/aca-advocacy-competencies-updated-may-2020.pdf?sfvrsn=f410212c_4

Utsey, S. O., Bolden, M. A., Lanier, Y., Williams, O. (2007). Examining the role of culture-specific coping as a predictor of resilient outcomes in African Americans from high-risk urban communities. *Journal of Black Psychology*, 33, 75–93. https://doi.org/10.1177/0095798406295094

Vil, C. S., & Vil, N. M. S. (2019). Black trauma in the US and the pursuit of human rights: A brief history. In L. D. Butler, F. M. Critelli, & J. Carello (Eds.), *Trauma and human rights: Integrating approaches to address human suffering* (pp. 99–123). Palgrave Macmillan.

Ward, E. C., Wiltshire, J. C., Detry, M. A., & Brown, R. L. (2013). African American men and women's attitude toward mental illness, perceptions of stigma, and preferred coping behaviors. *Nursing Research*, 62(3), 185–194. https://doi.org/10.1097/NNR.0b013e31827bf533

Wilkins, E. J., Whiting, J. B., Watson, M. F., Russon, J. M., & Moncrief, A. M. (2013). Residual effects of slavery: What clinicians need to know. *Contemporary Family Therapy*, *35*(1), 14–28. https://doi.org/10.1007/s10591-012-9219-1

Williams, R. K. (2016). Toward a theorization of Black maternal grief as analytic. *Transforming Anthropology*, *24*(1), 17–30. https://doi.org/10.1111/traa.12057

Questions for reflective practice

1. Do I have an understanding of the history of oppression, systemic barriers, and microaggressions that African Americans face?
2. Do I have an understanding of the current "cultural, political, developmental, and environmental contexts" of African Americans (Toporek & Daniels, 2018, p. 7)?
3. What local groups can I support or build an alliance with to help bring about systemic change for African American clients?
4. How might my organization be harming African American clients in their practices, policies, and procedures?
5. What are the ways in which I can influence policy making in my local area, region, or nation that redress systemic barriers to better mental health and well-being for African American clients?
6. Who are the allies within my own organization who are also actively confronting systemic barriers for African American clients and other People of Color?

Supplemental electronic resources

- Office of Minority Health Resource Center. (2019). Profile: Black/ African Americans. *U.S. Department of Health and Human Services, Office of Minority Health.* www.minorityhealth.hhs.gov/omh/browse. aspx?lvl=3&lvlid=61
- Southern Poverty Law Center: www.splcenter.org

Part II
Systemic barriers to grief

6
Social and systemic barriers for biracial individuals and their families

Christina Villarreal-Davis

Since the historical 1967 U.S. Supreme Court decision that legalized inter-racial marriage in the US, *Loving v. Virginia*, interracial marriage has steadily increased (Livingston & Brown, 2017), which has also led to a steady rise in multiracial and multiethnic births. The term *intermarriage* is used by the Pew Research Center when calculating the number of U.S. newlyweds who married a spouse of a different race or ethnicity. For this review, the terms *interracial couple* and *interracial marriage* will be used to identify a relationship or marriage between two persons of a different race or ethnicity. Furthermore, the terms *biracial*, the combining of two races (e.g., White and Black, His-panic and Asian), and *bicultural*, the combining of two separate cultural atti-tudes and customs (e.g., a meal that includes foods from two distinct cultural groups) will be used to describe parenting the offspring of interracial couples/marriages. Authors have also used the terms *multiracial* or *multiethnic* (e.g., the combining of two or more races or ethnicities) and *multicultural* (e.g., the combining of two or more cultural attitudes and customs).

Most biracial identity development researchers have examined social influ-ences throughout the lifespan while overlooking the physiological and psy-chological effects of racism and various forms of racism on interracial couples and their biracial children. Furthermore, little is known about how racism and discrimination impact the grief process for these populations and subsequent generations. However, racism and its various forms have a profound impact on its victims physically, psychologically, and educationally (Paradies et al., 2015; Trent et al., 2019).

These experiences often lead to profound feelings of *disenfranchised grief*, which refers to a grieving experience that cannot be publicly expressed or acknowl-edged, nor is it validated by others and society (Doka, 1989). Though grief

DOI: 10.4324/9781003292890-8

may be a universal experience, sociocultural factors, such as cultural norms, ethnic identity, and religious affiliations, often predict and fashion the expression of grief (Silverman et al., 2021), including experiences of racialized grief and trauma and what the current author terms *racialized disenfranchised grief*.

Although authors who have written about disenfranchised grief and social injustices have focused mostly on death loss (Baker et al., 2021; Lawson, 2014), the current author will explore all types of losses experienced by interracial couples and biracial individuals, underscoring racism, discrimination, microaggressions, and social and systemic barriers leading to racialized disenfranchised grief. In full transparency, the author is a Hispanic female married to a Black male and has three biracial children.

Historical data and current trends

Interracial marriages

Prior to *Loving v. Virginia*, interracial couples in the US faced imprisonment for marrying someone outside their race. Interracial marriages and relationships have been banned in other countries, including Nazi Germany and Apartheid-era South Africa (Shields, 2017). Although explicit anti-miscegenation laws that enforce racial segregation have been scarce throughout the world, the US is the historical leader in the creation of anti-miscegenation legislation (Shields, 2017), such as the famous Jim Crow laws that required businesses and other organizations to segregate Whites from non-Whites. These harsh laws most likely resulted in People of Color and interracial couples living in fear and feeling misunderstood by the White majority culture that led to the experience of disenfranchised grief.

According to the Pew Research Center, since *Loving v. Virginia*, interracial marriages among newlyweds have risen from 3% in 1967 to 19% in 2019 (Parker & Barroso, 2021). As of 2015, the most common interracial marriage among newlyweds included one Hispanic and one White spouse (42%), followed by one White and one Asian (15%), one White and one multiracial (12%), one White and one Black (11%), one Hispanic and one Black (5%), one White and one Indigenous (3%), one Hispanic and one Asian (3%), and one Hispanic and one multiracial (3%; Livingston & Brown, 2017). Indigenous people have the highest rate of interracial marriage among all single-race groups with 58% marrying outside their race, followed by 28% of Asians, 19% of Blacks, and 7% of Whites (Wang, 2015). Asians and Hispanics are more likely to marry someone outside their race or ethnicity in the US (Livingston & Brown, 2017). Lastly, the most dramatic increases in interracial marriages have happened among Black newlyweds, which increased from 5% in 1980 to 18% in 2015 (Parker & Barroso, 2021).

Public attitudes toward interracial marriages have become more accepting over time in the US. According to a 2017 Pew Research Center survey, 39% of the adults felt interracial marriages were a *good thing* for society, which increased from 24% in 2010 (Livingston & Brown, 2017; Parker & Barroso, 2021). However, there is also a distinct partisan divide in attitudes about interracial marriage being good for society. About half (49%) of these adults indicated they were Democrats, and only 28% were Republican. In another survey, the Pew Research Center found that the opposition of non-Black adults to a close relative marrying a Black individual had significantly declined from 63% in 1990 to 14% in 2016 (Livingston & Brown, 2017). Based on these findings, interracial couples still face unacceptance by others in American society, which continues to discount their mixed-race-related discriminatory experiences and leave their grief unvalidated.

Biracial/multiracial and bicultural/multiracial individuals

Due to the lack of statistical data strictly on biracial individuals, the author reports statistical information on multicultural and multiethnic individuals. With the increase in interracial marriages has come a steady increase in multi-racial and multiethnic births, which have tripled since 1980, with 14% of U.S. infants identified as multiracial or multiethnic (Livingston, 2017). According to Parker et al. (2015), "multiracial Americans are at the cutting edge of social and demographic change in the U.S. – young, proud, tolerant, and growing at a rate three times as fast as the population as a whole" (p. 1). Furthermore, nearly half (46%) of the multiracial or multiethnic population is under the age of 18 (Parker et al., 2015). Although most of these adults (60%) are proud of their multiracial or multiethnic background, 55% of these individuals have been subjected to racial insults or jokes, and 24% have felt irritated by others' assumptions about their racial or ethnic makeup (Parker et al., 2015). As of 2020, there were 33.8 million people in America who identified as multiracial, which has nearly quadrupled from 9 million in 2010 (Jones et al., 2021).

The interracial couple

Interracial couples often experience the same relationship concerns that their monoracial counterparts undergo, but there are also unique challenges and concerns that only interracial couples encounter.

Challenges

There are distinctive issues for interracial couples that originated from their (1) current social context: lack of family and community support for their relationship or the power differential that may exist in the relationship due to racial privilege; and (2) racialized histories: level of racial identity development; experienced *microaggressions*, which are implicit and unconscious actions and/or statements that are insulting and discriminatory; and cultural patterns of communication (Leslie & Young, 2015). The divorce rate for interracial couples (41%) is also higher compared to monoracial couples (31%; Bratter & King, 2008). However, Brown et al. (2019) found that "despite interracial relationships not substantively differing from same-race couples in trajectories of relationship quality, specific Black-Hispanic interracial couples are at a higher risk of eventual separation" (p. 650).

Parenting biracial children

Parenting biracial children also has unique challenges when compared to raising monoracial children, such as how children racially identify themselves (e.g., only one race, usually the minority race; as biracial or multiracial; or as a transcendent race, meaning not choosing a race; Csizmadia & White, 2019). According to the American Academy of Child and Adolescent Psychiatry (AACAP, 2016), biracial and multiracial children have experienced bullying, whispers, and glares and are often subject to societal pressures from their peers or family members to identify with only one race. Having to make these racial identity choices as a child or adolescent can lead to the experience of disenfranchised grief. Furthermore, this identification can be traced back to the "one-drop rule" in early 20th century America, which racially categorized anyone with one Black ancestor as Black, which more than likely created and maintained the experience of disenfranchised grief by having to deny one's biracial or multiracial makeup.

Interracial couples' parenting practices are also unique. Rosen and Greif (2021) identified four themes common to interracial couples' parenting practices: preparing their children for racism/discrimination, facilitating ethnic-racial identity development through various forms of exposure, discussing skin color and recognizing and comparing skin colors of family members, and educating their child(ren) on the benefits of being biracial, multiracial, or bicultural. To help navigate the complexities biracial and multiracial children face, the AACAP (2016) recommended parents help establish open communication about race and culture in their home and permit inquisitive-ness about physical features (i.e., skin color/tone, hair texture, and facial fea-tures) among family members. The lack of open communication could lead to the experience of disenfranchised grief in children.

Interracial couple grief

To better understand the interracial couple's view of grief, mental health pro-fessionals must first understand that attitudes, beliefs, and customs regarding grief and how grief is processed vary greatly among individuals and across vari-ous cultural groups. Interracial couples appear to be at greater risk for increased experiences of racism and discrimination, which leads to increased experiences of grief and disenfranchised grief. Interracial couples are also processing grief experiences in their distinct cultural ways and customs while also collectively grieving as a couple. Mental health professionals are encouraged to work from a place of cultural humility, and they should continue to work from this place when addressing the unique experiences of grieving interracial couples.

Proposed by Tervalon and Murray-García (1998), *cultural humility* is a "life-long process of self-reflection and self-critique whereby the individual not only learns about another's culture, but one starts with an examination of her/his own beliefs and cultural identities" (Yeager & Bauer-Wu, 2013, pp. 251–252). For example, in the aftermath of the killing of George Floyd, this author, a Hispanic mother of two biracial boys (of Black and Hispanic ethnicity) expressed deep feelings of grief, loss, and sadness related to a sense of safety being lost for her biracial boys who could one day be faced with a similar situation. However, her husband was experiencing feelings of numb-ness, reporting that the killing of Black men in the media was nothing new. Although this author's experience does not reflect all interracial couples' experiences, mental health professionals must understand that the person (or persons) within the interracial couple that has/have been marginalized may have their own unique history of racism and oppression, which will contrib-ute to their distinct method of processing grief and experiences of racism. Also, the *privileged* person in the relationship, if applicable, may not have a complete understanding of their partner's experiences of racism and discrimi-nation, as was this author's experience, which possibly created her husband's own experience of disenfranchised grief. Lastly, when this author expressed her support for the Black Lives Matter movement to her conservative par-ents, she was left feeling misunderstood and unvalidated by the parents by whom she had always felt supported. In this moment, this author felt that her parents' political beliefs and conservative association was far more important than the lives of their biracial grandchildren, thus the experience of disenfranchised grief from the phrase, "All Lives Matter because Jesus settled that debate 2000 years ago on the cross."

Privilege and systemic racism

To further understand racism, it is important to understand the terms *privilege* and *systemic racism*. "Privilege is comprised of unearned advantages that are conferred upon individuals based on membership or assumed membership in a dominant group" (Israel, 2012, p. 166). Global examples of dominant groups that experience privilege include White individuals (or appearing White, including lighter hair and eyes), males, upper social class individuals, Christians, heterosexuals, able-bodied individuals, and younger individuals not considered elderly.

Moreover, privilege is enacted through societal structures, legislative systems, and daily interactions with others who explicitly or implicitly share their dominant worldviews (Israel, 2012). Through these structures, systems, and interactions come the products of privilege and *oppression*, which perpetuate the unjust treatment and control of people who have been marginalized and further usher in disenfranchised grief. These oppressive actions have morphed into legislative, societal, and systemic barriers, referred to as *systemic racism* or *institutional racism*, that are seen in educational systems, economic systems, healthcare systems, and criminal justice systems worldwide.

For example, Todd et al. (2016) found that stereotypes associating Black men with criminality and violence resulted in Black children as young as 5 years old being identified as dangerous when compared to their White counterparts. The view of Black men as violent law-breakers can be traced back to the time period of slavery in America, from illegally arresting Black men once slavery was abolished, to treating them as "thugs" that needed to be jailed in the late 1900s; however, the same treatment was not given to their privileged White counterparts (Smiley & Fakunle, 2016), including the past and continued police brutality seen with George Floyd and many others.

Systemic and social barriers

Forbidding interracial couples to marry was the most obvious systemic barrier that interracial couples faced. Livingston and Brown (2017) noted changes in attitudes toward interracial marriage, with 9% of Americans holding negative beliefs; such beliefs tied to political ideology hold a lot of power to promote and perpetuate systemic racism.

Interracial couples also experience social barriers from their community, family, and friends. Leslie and Young (2015) reported that interracial couples have to manage societal disapproval and cope with the power differential resulting from racial privilege. For example, this author experienced parental disapproval when dating outside her race. She was told, "You don't want to marry a thug [Black man]. You need to marry a *Mexicano*." Furthermore, Killian (2013) highlighted that disapproving reactions from strangers in public added additional stress for the interracial couple and may strain their relationship. A cumulation of these experiences can be overwhelming and lead to feelings of isolation. Ultimately, these barriers can create and support experiences of disenfranchised grief for interracial couples. According to Neimeyer and Jordan (2002), when viewing grief from a societal and psychological point of view, the central concern in disenfranchised grief is termed *empathic failure*, meaning "the failure of the system to understand the meaning and experience of another" (p. 96).

Meaning making for interracial couples

Researchers overwhelmingly support the quest for meaning making in the aftermath of grief experiences (Neimeyer et al., 2010), including experiences of racism, systemic racism, discrimination, and microaggressions. Meaning making for the interracial couple will be unique to each individual's culture and will merge some aspects of the two cultures to form the interracial couple's unique ways of processing racial grief and traumatic experiences. Furthermore, clinicians must also consider the family system when fostering family relationships and family resilience for grieving interracial couples and their children (Barboza et al., 2022).

Mental health professionals would be wise to employ cultural humility to become informed about the rich cultural aspects of processing interracial couples' and their children's racial grief and loss, disenfranchised grief experiences, and trauma experiences. Interracial couples have managed their racial and cultural differences and societal concerns by co-creating a narrative of "we" that transcends all others and gives birth to a shared meaning within the couple's relationship, framing differences in a way that celebrates and respects culture, communicating emotions and insecurities concerning difficult encounters with various social contexts, and positioning the "we" in relation to societal and familial context (Seshadri & Knudson-Martin, 2013).

This strong position of "we" can sustain the interracial couple experiencing disenfranchised grief when others and systems have failed to comprehend or acknowledge the unique experiences. Furthermore, "what is disenfranchised in one culture may be supported in another" (Doka, 2008, p. 227). This author would also add that even within one culture group, there can be varying accepted cultural norms, such as some Blacks supporting interracial marriages while others do not, and some Christian communities supporting gay/same-sex marriages while others do not.

The uniqueness of being biracial and bicultural

The biracial/multiracial population faces distinct challenges and stressors that monocultural populations do not experience, including navigating their biracial identity development as well as discrimination and/or microaggressions directly tied to being racially and ethnically mixed.

Biracial identity development

Pride in one's culture has been linked to healthy racial identity development. For biracial/multiracial individuals, the development of a multiracial and multiethnic pride is complex and processed differently when compared to other racial development models. Poston (1990) first argued for the need for a biracial identity development model specific to biracial individuals. Common beliefs found in various biracial identity development models include identification with a monoracial population, declaration of a cohesive multiracial identity, or acceptance of a context-specific or fluid identity (Rockquemore et al., 2009). Additionally, there are also multiple societal factors that influence biracial individuals to identify as monoracial.

Harris (2016) argued that social structures exist that perpetuate a monoracial-only perception of race, interwoven with racism. For example, numerous theorists speculate that the "principle of colorism, colloquially known as 'the one drop rule,' has influenced American racial socialization in such a way that numerous individuals primarily identify with one racial group despite having parents from two different racial backgrounds" (Harris, 2018, p. 2072). These societal structures can further lead to *identity-based challenges*, or internal pressures and complications experienced by biracial individuals when faced with pressures to conform to society's definition of race (Salahuddin & O'Brien, 2011). These challenges hinder healthy biracial identity development and put these individuals at risk for harmful psychological outcomes (Franco & O'Brien, 2018). The current author postulates that these societal structures and identity-based challenges can lead to the experience of disenfranchised grief.

When a biracial individual is denied membership in a cultural group with which they identify, this experience is known as *identity denial*. These experiences can impact healthy biracial identity development because the individual is focused on reaffirming the sense of self that is being denied. Cheryan and Morin (2005) reported that Asian Americans who were denied their American identity self-reported engagement in more American practices when compared to participants who were not denied. Being denied part of one's identity and not being accepted as a biracial/multiracial individual is a form of racism and can also lead to disenfranchised grief.

Additionally, identity denial has been associated with a myriad of psychological concerns including increased stress and depressive symptoms (Albuja et al., 2019), decreased life satisfaction (Huynh et al., 2011), and lowered motivation and self-esteem (Townsend et al., 2009). Overall, the inability to grieve and process experiences of identity denial, identity-based challenges, and having to reaffirm one's identity is exhausting and psychologically damaging. More empirical research is needed to fully understand the psychological impact.

Discrimination and microaggressions

Biracial individuals experience forms of discrimination and microaggressions similar to other groups that have been marginalized, though unique to their multiracial makeup. Johnston and Nadal (2010) identified multiracial microaggressions and *monoracism*, which included invalidation of one's multiracial identity, exclusion and isolation (when the invalidation is repeated), objectification, false assumptions that multiracial individuals are monoracial, denial of a multiracial identity and reality, and pathologizing multiracial identity. These identity concerns and challenges can transform into experiences of disenfranchised grief.

As both a person in an interracial marriage with biracial children and a clinician who has heard many client stories of discrimination and microaggressions,

I have experienced and witnessed the effects of such hurtful actions and comments. Being a Hispanic female who appears very fair-skinned with light brown hair and green eyes, I did not experience many instances of discrimination growing up due to the privilege of appearing White. I have only experienced discrimination and microaggressions in public with my Black husband and our biracial children, which included looks of disgust, being asked for a receipt when shopping with my husband, being overlooked, and being pushed aside to assist customers of the dominant culture. The lack of acknowledgment and respect at times has felt beyond disenfranchising and is downright inhumane.

Biracial and bicultural grief

Biracial and bicultural grief experiences are also unique as they face additional challenges and stressors that their monoracial and privileged counterparts do not encounter. Research on grief and disenfranchised grief experiences among biracial individuals is severely lacking. The existence of discrimination, microaggressions, and systemic racism exacerbates and increases the barriers for biracial individuals in processing the complexity of their grief and disenfranchised grief.

Nayak (2019) posited that "racism produces grief and loss and as long as there is racism, we all remain in racial grief and loss" (p. 352). Furthermore, Granek and Peleg-Sagy (2015) contended that Black Americans live in a perpetual state of grief stemming from slavery and the generational trauma that lives in the bodies of Black Americans, which is seldom acknowledged in therapy. Though experiences of severe racism have a great propensity to intensify grief, less severe experiences of microaggressions related to racial identity can also lead to elevated grief and feelings of not belonging for biracial individuals (Johnston & Nadal, 2010).

For example, a biracial person of Hispanic and Black ethnic heritage tells her Black friend that she is so excited about attending her cousin's *quinceañera*, and then the friend comments, "But you're not really Hispanic, and you don't really look Hispanic. You don't even speak Spanish. You're totally Black." This is an accumulation of several microaggressions and the outright denial of the person's biracial makeup. These experiences of identity-based challenges and feelings of confusion, exclusion, and isolation only complicate biracial identity development and lead to more significant psychological distress (Johnston & Nadal, 2010) and disenfranchised grief, even more so for those of Black-White biracial makeup (Christophe et al., 2022).

Systemic and social barriers

The U.S. monoracial paradigm is a major systemic and social barrier that biracial individuals have encountered and continue to encounter. Both the "one-drop rule" and government census monoracial categories perpetuated a socially embedded false belief that biracial people were not allowed to self-identify as biracial or multiracial. Historically, it was not until the 2000 census that Americans could choose more than one race to describe their biracial/multiracial heritage. Furthermore, it wasn't until 2020 that respondents who chose White or Black for their race could provide more information about their ethnic origins, such as African American, German, or Somali (Brown, 2020).

Systemic barriers have also been examined in America's educational system, especially how dominant culture and White supremacy ideologies are being preserved in educational systems. Critical race theory (CRT) was birthed out of this awareness. CRT began with civil rights lawyers' growing concerns "that dominant conceptions of race, racism, and equality were increasingly incapable of providing any meaningful quantum of racial justice" (Matsudo et al., 1993, p. 3) to People of Color, mainly Black Americans. CRT scholars do not subscribe to one set of beliefs, and instead advocate for several different principles, including "whiteness as property, interest convergence, intersectionality, narrative voice, and others that allow for a critique of oppressive systems embedded within the U.S. education" (Harris, 2016, p. 796). Furthermore, Harris (2016) advanced critical multiracial theory (MultiCrit) as a framework for "the inclusion of multiraciality into critical discourses, [which] allows for the introduction of a new language with which to talk about multiraciality in the academy, resulting in a breakdown of a socially constructed monoracial paradigm of race" (p. 811). CRT has been an American hot topic in recent local, state, and national political elections that present CRT as harmful, which only further discounts racism and discrimination that accompany disenfranchised grief. Given the unique nature and barriers biracial individuals and families face, it is essential for clinicians to become allies and carefully consider ethical concerns that may impede treatment.

Allyship and advocacy

In 2002, the American Counseling Association (ACA) formed an interest group that focuses on providing awareness and advocacy for professional counselors when working with multiracial/multiethnic populations. In *Competencies for Counseling the Multiracial Population,* ACA (2015) provided valuable information and guidelines for working with interracial couples, multiracial families, and multiracial individuals, including a call to action that counselors must "provide advocacy efforts at the micro, meso, and macro levels to develop consciousness-raising and public awareness of the multiracial population's concerns, history, sociopolitical influences, resilience, and strengths" (p. 21).

Advocacy also centers on key counseling skills, including empathy and validation of feelings, which would help clients address their racialized disenfranchised grief experiences. When a client's presenting problem centers on racism and discrimination, the clinician must acknowledge and validate their emotional experience(s) as well as have a complete understanding that multiracial discrimination does exist (Greig, 2015). For example, a client presents with feelings of sadness and reports that his parents have never approved of him dating his Asian girlfriend. Now they are engaged, and he fears his parents will not want to attend their wedding. The clinician should acknowledge the client's sadness and fears that he is grieving the loss of relationship acceptance, regardless of the outcome and whether his parents attend the wedding. Any comments such as, "Well, at least you have each other," or "Maybe they will come along once you have children," would not validate the client's current feeling. Furthermore, a harsher comment, such as "Well, since she's Asian, she is probably very smart, so maybe they will accept her," displays a clinician's ignorance and lack of cultural competence and humility. These comments are also examples of microaggressions.

Advocacy includes parent education on *racial socialization.* Rollins and Hunter (2013) posited "racial socialization buffers youth from racism and discrimination, giving meaning to their social locations, and provides information that aids in the development of racial identity" (p. 151). In their study, one-third of mothers felt ill-prepared to help their biracial youth navigate their biracial heritage and identity. Accordingly, they recommended parent education address the unique issues faced by biracial youth, including monoracism and racial microaggressions, strategies that help prepare biracial children to successfully navigate their racial status and potential discrimination, and ideas on how to positively support racial identity development.

These advocacy steps and many others are helpful ways of promoting social justice for both interracial couples and biracial individuals. These populations have unique experiences that appear at various levels (e.g., family, friends, communities, and systems), and mental health professionals must be aware of and acknowledge these unique experiences to process instances of racism and racialized disenfranchised grief.

Ethical considerations

Sue and colleagues (1992) described fundamental principles for multicultural counseling competencies (MCCs) that center on knowledge, awareness, and skills used with diverse populations that have been marginalized, which have been widely accepted in the US and internationally (Aga Mohd Jaladin, 2017). However, researchers have provided inconclusive findings linking MCCs to therapeutic outcomes and clinical efficacy (Dunn et al., 2006; Tao et al., 2015). Lantz et al. (2020) proposed a viewpoint for comprehending MCCs that applies social dominance theory. After sampling 362 counselors and mental health trainees, they argued that "the process of developing MCCs is not only about learning but also *unlearning . . .* beliefs developed through socialization by the dominant culture . . . and coming to understand the role of privilege in systemic oppression" (p. 142). They concluded that "awareness of privilege was significantly related to multicultural knowledge and awareness" (p. 142). Therefore, mental health professionals need to learn new knowledge, gain new awareness, develop new skills, acknowledge how privilege and oppression preserve discrimination and systemic racism, and unlearn previous socialization principles.

In their *Code of Ethics*, ACA (2014) charged counselors to "gain knowledge, personal awareness, sensitivity, dispositions, and skills pertinent to being a culturally competent counselor in working with a diverse client population" (Sect. C.2.a, p. 8). Although these codes provide valuable information related to MCCs, they do not provide a roadmap for how to get there. However, Chao et al. (2011) demonstrated that multicultural training is related to higher MCCs, and Tao et al. (2015) found that counselors with greater MCCs tend to have better client outcomes.

Lastly, there has been a recent trend toward *multicultural orientation* (MCO; Lantz et al., 2020). Owen and colleagues (2011) proposed the MCO framework, which is an extension of the MCC model. Davis et al. (2018) elaborated on three foundational MCO concepts: "a 'way of being' in session for therapists (e.g., cultural humility), a way of identifying and responding to therapeutic cultural markers in session (e.g., cultural opportunities), and a way of understanding the self in these moments (e.g., cultural comfort)" (p. 90). Practicing within an MCO framework will help counselors address and meet ACA's ethical standards. Overall, these ethical considerations will improve clinical treatment for interracial couples and biracial individuals.

Strategies and interventions

Meaning making for biracial individuals involves processing grief from one's biracial makeup as well as gaining an understanding of their unique experiences with discrimination and racialized disenfranchised grief. Although various psychotherapeutic approaches in traditional talk therapy are beneficial in processing grief and loss, this author proposes a creative, whole-brain, expressive arts approach to facilitate meaning making for biracial individuals (e.g., Beauregard, 2020; Thanasiu & Pizza, 2019).

The utilization of expressive arts, such as drawing, sand tray, writing/poetry, using clay and other art materials, provides a non-verbal modality to safely explore one's past experiences. Incorporating creative and expressive art interventions also activates both the right and the left hemispheres of the brain, which allows for the coming together of both emotional and cognitive expression (Binson & Lev-Wiesel, 2018). For example, a biracial person may find it more helpful to create a drawing or a sand tray of their racialized disenfranchised grief experiences rather than verbalizing them. Ultimately, creative and expressive interventions can help foster personal growth and greater self-awareness (Villarreal-Davis et al., 2021), as well as safe passage for stories to be held and heard.

Summary

Interracial couples and biracial individuals encounter unique concerns and challenges, including forms of racism, systemic racism, systemic and social barriers, discrimination, and microaggressions, all of which can lead to experiences of racialized disenfranchised grief. These experiences impact the interracial couple and their biracial offspring in many facets throughout their lifespan. Awareness and advocacy bring hope to those processing racialized and disenfranchised grief experiences that have often led to racial grief and, in some cases, racial trauma and posttraumatic stress disorder (PTSD). Most importantly, mental health practitioners must also practice cultural humility when engaging interracial couples and biracial individuals, not make assumptions about their struggles and concerns, and offer a supportive atmosphere that validates their unique multicultural experiences. The current author recommends that mental health clinicians operate from an MCO that emphasizes a way of *being* with their client rather than a way of *doing* and holds cultural humility as paramount in the therapeutic relationship.

References

Aga Mohd Jaladin, R. (2017). Perceived multicultural counseling competence of Malaysian counselors: An exploratory study. *Journal of Multicultural Counseling and Development, 45*(2), 127–148. https://doi.org/10.1002/jmcd.12069

Albuja, A. F., Sanchez, D. T., & Gaither, S. E. (2019). Identity denied: Comparing American or White identity denial and psychological health outcomes among bicultural and biracial people. *Personality and Social Psychology Bulletin, 45*(3), 416–430. https://doi.org/10.1177%2F0146167218788553

American Academy of Child and Adolescent Psychiatry. (2016). *Facts of families*©: *Multiracial children, Article 71.* www.aacap.org/AACAP/Families_and_Youth/ Facts_for_Families/FFF-Guide/Multiracial-Children-071.aspx

American Counseling Association. (2014). *2014 ACA code of ethics.* www.counseling. org/resources/aca-code-of-ethics.pdf

American Counseling Association. (2015). *Competencies for counseling the multiracial population.* www.counseling.org/docs/default-source/competencies/competencies-for-counseling-the-multiracial-population-2-2-15-final.pdf?sfvrsn= c7ba412c_16

Baker, D., Norris, D., & Cherneva, V. (2021). Disenfranchised grief and families' experiences of death after police contact in the United States. OMEGA – *Journal of Death and Dying, 83*(2), 239–256. https://doi.org/10.1177/0030222819846420

Barboza, J., Seedall, R., & Neimeyer, R. A. (2022). Meaning co-construction: Facilitating shared family meaning-making in bereavement. *Family Process, 61*(1), 7–24. https://doi.org/10.1111/famp.12671

Beauregard, C. (2020). Being in between: Exploring cultural bereavement and identity expression through drawing. *Journal of Creativity in Mental Health, 15*(3), 292–310. https://doi.org/10.1080/15401383.2019.1702131

Binson, B., & Lev-Wiesel, R. (2018). Promoting personal growth through experiential learning: The case of expressive arts therapy for lectures in Thailand. *Frontiers in Psychology, 8,* Article 2276. https://doi.org/10.3389/fpsyg.2017.02276

Bratter, J. L., & King, R. B. (2008). "But will it last?": Marital instability among interracial and same-race couples. *Family Relations: An Interdisciplinary Journal of Applied Family Studies, 57*(2), 160–171. https://psycnet.apa.org/ doi/10.1111/j.1741-3729.2008.00491.x

Brown, A. (2020, February 25). The changing categories the U.S. census has used to measure race. *Pew Research Center.* www.pewresearch.org/fact-tank/2020/02/25/ the-changing-categories-the-u-s-has-used-to-measure-race/

Brown, C. C., Williams, Z., & Durtschi, J. A. (2019). Trajectories of interracial heterosexual couples: A longitudinal analysis of relationship quality and separation.

Journal of Marital and Family Therapy, 45(4), 650–667. https://doi.org/10.1111/jmft.12363

Chao, R. C., Wei, M., Good, G. E., & Flores, L. Y. (2011). Race/ethnicity, color-blind racial attitudes, and multicultural counseling competence: The moderating effects of multicultural counseling training. *Journal of Counseling Psychology, 58*(1), 72–82. https://doi.org/10.1037/a0022091

Cheryan, S., & Morin, B. (2005). Where are you *really* from? Asian Americans and identity denial. *Journal of Personality and Social Psychology, 89*(5), 717–730. https://doi.org/10.1037/0022-3514.89.5.717

Christophe, N. K., Atkin, A. L., Stein, G. L., Chan, M., Abidog, C., Gabriel, A. K., Lee, R. M., Wu, C. S., & Yoo, H. C. (2022). Examining multiracial pride, identity-based challenges, and discrimination: An exploratory investigation among biracial emerging adults. *Race and Social Problems, 14*(1), 22–38. https://doi.org/10.1007/s12552-021-09325-4

Csizmadia, A., & White, S. (2019). Racial identity: Choices, context, and consequences. In R. N. Roy & A. Rollins (Eds.), *Biracial families: Crossing boundaries, blending cultures, and challenging racial ideologies* (pp. 225–245). Springer.

Davis, D. E., DeBlaere, C., Owen, J., Hook, J. N., Rivera, D. P., Choe, E., Van Tongeren, D. R., Worthington, E. L., & Placeres, V. (2018). The multicultural orientation framework: A narrative review. *Psychotherapy, 55*(1), 89–100. https://doi.org/10.1037/pst0000160

Doka, K. J. (1989). *Disenfranchised grief: Recognizing hidden sorrow.* Lexington Press.

Doka, K. J. (2008). Disenfranchised grief in historical and cultural perspective. In M. S. Stroebe, R. O. Hansson, H. Schut, & W. Stroebe (Eds.), *Handbook of bereavement research and practice: Advances in theory and intervention* (pp. 223–240). American Psychological Association.

Dunn, T. W., Smith, T. B., & Montoya, J. A. (2006). Multicultural competency instrumentation: A review of analysis and reliability generalization. *Journal of Counseling and Development, 84*(4), 471–482. https://doi.org/10.1002/j.1556-6678.2006.tb00431.x

Franco, M. G., & O'Brien, K. M. (2018). Racial identity invalidation with multiracial individuals: An instrument development study. *Cultural Diversity and Ethnic Minority Psychology, 24*(1), 112–125. https://doi.org/10.1037/cdp0000170

Granek, L., & Peleg-Sagy, T. (2015). Representations of African Americans in the grief and mourning literature from 1998 to 2014: A systemic review. *Death Studies, 39*(10), 605–632. https://doi.org/10.1080/07481187.2015.1047059

Greig, A. (2015). Understanding the stressors and types of discrimination that can affect multiracial individuals: Things to address and avoid in psychotherapy practice. *Psychotherapy Bulletin*, *50*(2), 56–60. https://societyforpsychotherapy. org/understanding-the-stressors-and-types-of-discrimination-that-can-affect-multiracial-individuals-things-to-address-and-avoid-in-psychotherapy-practice/

Harris, J. C. (2016). Toward a critical multiracial theory in education. *International Journal of Qualitative Studies in Education*, *29*(6), 795–813. https://doi.org/10.108 0/09518398.2016.1162870

Harris, K. L. (2018). Biracial American colorism: Passing for White. *American Behavioral Scientist*, *62*(14), 2072–2086. https://doi.org/10.1177%2F0002764218810747

Huynh, Q. L., Devos, T., Sanchez, L. (2011). Perpetual foreigner in one's own land: Potential implication for identity and psychological adjustment. *Journal of Social and Clinical Psychology*, *30*(2), 133–162. https://doi.org/10.1521%2Fj scp.2011.30.2.133

Israel, T. (2012). 2011 Society of Counseling Psychology presidential address: Exploring privilege in counseling psychology: Shifting the lends. *The Counseling Psychologist*, *40*(1), 158–180. https://doi.org/10.1177%2F0011000011426297

Johnston, M. P., & Nadal, K. L. (2010). Multiracial microaggressions: Exposing monoracism in everyday life and clinical practice. In D. W. Sue (Ed.), *Microaggressions and marginality: Manifestations, dynamics, and impact* (pp. 123–144). Wiley.

Jones, N., Marks, R., Ramirez, R., & Rios-Vargas, M. (2021). *Improved race and ethnicity measure reveal U.S. population is much more multiracial: 2020 Census illuminates racial and ethnic composition of the country*. United States Census Bureau. www.census.gov/library/stories/2021/08/improved-race-ethnicity-measures-reveal-united-states-population-much-more-multiracial.html

Killian, K. D. (2013). *Interracial couples, intimacy, and therapy: Crossing racial borders*. Columbia University Press.

Lantz, M. M., Pieterse, A. L., & Taylor, T. O. (2020). A social dominance theory perspective on multicultural competence. *Counseling Psychology Quarterly*, *33*(2), 142–162. https://doi.org/10.1080/09515070.2018.1500352

Lawson, E. (2014). Disenfranchised grief and social inequality: Bereaved African Canadians and oppositional narratives about the violent deaths of friends and family members. *Ethic and Racial Studies*, *37*(11), 2092–2109. https://doi.org/10.1 080/01419870.2013.800569

Leslie, L. A., & Young, J. L. (2015). Interracial couples in therapy: Common themes and issues. *Journal of Social Issues*, *71*(4), 788–803. https://doi.org/10.1111/ josi.12149

Livingston, G. (2017, June 6). The rise of multiracial and multiethnic babies in the U.S. *Pew Research Center*. www.pewresearch.org/fact-tank/2017/06/06/ the-rise-of-multiracial-and-multiethnic-babies-in-the-u-s/

Livingston, G., & Brown, A. (2017, May 18). Intermarriage in the U.S. 50 years after Loving v. Virginia. *Pew Research Center*. www.pewsocialtrends.org/wp-content/uploads/sites/3/2017/05/Intermarriage-May-2017-Full-Report.pdf

Loving v. Virginia, 388 U.S. 1 (1967). www.oyez.org/cases/1966/395

Matsudo, M. J., Lawrence, C. R., & Crenshaw, K. W. (1993). *Words that wound: Critical race theory, assaultive speech, and the First Amendment*. Westview Press. https://doi.org/10.4324/9780429502941

Nayak, S. (2019). Occupation of racial grief, loss as a resource: Learning from "The Combahee River Collective Black Feminist Statement." *Psychological Studies*, 64(3), 352–364. https://doi.org/10.1007/s12646-019-00527-w

Neimeyer, R. A., Burke, L. A., Mackay, M. M., & van Dyke Stringer, J. G. (2010). Grief therapy and the reconstruction of meaning: From principles to practice. *Journal of Contemporary Psychotherapy*, 40(2), 73–83. https://doi.org/10.1007/s10879-009-9135-3

Neimeyer, R. A., & Jordan, J. (2002). Disenfranchisement as empathic failure: Grief therapy and the co-construction of meaning. In K. Doka (Ed.), *Disenfranchised grief: New directions, challenges, and strategies for practice* (pp. 95–118). Research Press.

Owen, J. J., Tao, K., Leach, M. M., & Rodolfa, E. (2011). Clients' perceptions of their psychotherapists' multicultural orientation. *Psychotherapy*, 48(3), 274–282. https://doi.org/10.1037/a0022065

Paradies, Y., Ben, J., Denson, N., Elias, A., Priest, N., Pieterse, A., Gupta, A., Kelaher, M., & Gee, G. (2015). Racism as a determinant of health: A systematic review and meta-analysis. *PLoS ONE, 10*(9), Article e0138511. https://doi.org/10.1371/journal.pone.0138511

Parker, K., & Barroso, A. (2021, February 25). In vice president Kamala Harris, we can see how American has changed. *Pew Research Center*. www.pewresearch.org/fact-tank/2021/02/25/in-vice-president-kamala-harris-we-can-see-how-america-has-changed/

Parker, K., Horowitz, J. M., Morin, R., & Lopez, M. H. (2015, June 11). Multiracial in America: Proud, diverse, and growing in numbers. *Pew Research Center*. www.pewsocialtrends.org/wp-content/uploads/sites/3/2015/06/2015-06-11_multiracial-in-america_final-updated.pdf

Poston, W. S. C. (1990). The biracial identity development model: A needed addition. *Journal of Counseling and Development*, 69(2), 152–155. https://doi.org/10.1002/j.1556-6676.1990.tb01477.x

Rockquemore, K. A., Brunsma, D. L., & Delgado, D. J. (2009). Racing to theory or retheorizing race? Understanding the struggle to build a multiracial identity theory. *Journal of Social Issues, 76*(1), 13–34. https://doi.org/10.1111/j.1540-4560.2008.01585.x

Rollins, A., & Hunter, A. G. (2013). Racial socialization of biracial youth: Maternal messages and approaches to address discrimination. *Family Relations*, 62(1), 140–153. https://doi.org/10.1111/j.1741-3729.2012.00748.x

Rosen, J. E., & Greif, G. (2021). The voices of interracial and interethnic couples raising biracial, multiracial, and bi-ethnic children under 10 years old. *Child and Adolescent Social Work Journal*. Advanced online publication. https://doi.org/10.1007/s10560-021-00805-5

Salahuddin, N. M., & O'Brien, K. M. (2011). Challenges and resilience in the lives of urban, multiracial adults: An instrument development study. *Journal of Counseling Psychology*, 58(4), 494–507. https://doi.org/10.1037/a0024633

Seshadri, G., & Knudson-Martin, C. (2013). How couples manage interracial and intercultural differences: Implications for clinical practice. *Journal of Marital and Family Therapy*, 39(1), 43–58. https://doi.org/10.1111/j.1752-0606.2011.00262.x

Shields, J. (2017, June 12). *How has interracial marriage been treated around the world?* https://people.howstuffworks.com/culture-traditions/cultural-traditions/interracial-marriage-around-world.htm

Silverman, G. S., Baroiller, A., & Hemer, A. R. (2021). Culture and grief: Ethnographic perspectives on ritual, relationships and remembering. *Death Studies*, 45(1), 1–8. https://doi.org/10.1080/07481187.2020.1851885

Smiley, C., & Fakunle, D. (2016). From "brute" to "thug:" The demonization and criminalization of unarmed Black male victims in America. *Journal of Human Behavior in the Social Environment*, 26(3–4), 350–366. https://doi.org/10.1080/10911359.2015.1129256

Sue, D. W., Arrendondo, P., & McDavis, R. J. (1992). Multicultural counseling competencies and standards: A call to the profession. *Journal of Counseling and Development*, 20(2), 477–486. https://doi.org/10.1002/j.2161-1912.1992.tb00563.x

Tao, K. W., Owen, J., Pace, B. T., & Imel, Z. E. (2015). A meta-analysis of multicultural competencies and psychotherapy process and outcome. *Journal of Counseling Psychology*, 62(3), 337–350. https://doi.org/10.1037/cou0000086

Tervalon, M., & Murray-García, J. (1998). Cultural humility versus cultural competence: A critical distinction in defining physician training outcomes in multicultural education. *Journal of Health Care for the Poor and Underserved*, 9(2), 117–125. https://doi.org/10.1353/hpu.2010.0233

Thanasiu, P. L., & Pizza, N. (2019). Constructing culturally sensitive creative interventions for use with grieving children and adolescents. *Journal of Creativity in Mental Health*, 14(3), 270–279. https://doi.org/10.1080/15401383.2019.1589402

Todd, A. R., Thiem, K. C., & Neel, R. (2016). Does seeing the faces of young Black boys facilitate the identification of threatening stimuli? *Psychological Science*, 27(3), 384–393. https://doi.org/10.1177%2F0956797615624492

Townsend, S. S., Markus, H. R., & Bergsieker, H. B. (2009). My choice, your categories: The denial of multiracial identities. *Journal of Social Issues*, 65(1), 185–204. https://doi.org/10.1111/j.1540-4560.2008.01594.x

Trent, M., Dooley, D. G., & Douge, J. (2019). The impact of racism on child and adolescent health. *Pediatrics*, 144(2), Article e20191765. https://doi.org/10.1542/peds.2019-1765

Villarreal-Davis, C., Sartor, T. A., & McLean, L. (2021). Utilizing creativity to foster connection in online counseling supervision. *Journal of Creativity in Mental Health*, 16(2), 244–257. https://doi.org/10.1080/15401383.2020.1754989

Wang, W. (2015, June 12). Interracial marriage: Who is "marrying out?" *Pew Research Center*. www.pewresearch.org/fact-tank/2015/06/12/interracial-marriage-who-is-marrying-out/

Yeager, K. A., & Bauer-Wu, S. (2013). Cultural humility: Essential foundation for clinical researchers. *Applied Nursing Research*, 26(4), 251–256. https://doi.org/10.1016/j.apnr.2013.06.008

Questions for reflective practice

1. What is the first thing that comes to mind when you see an interracial couple and/or a biracial person? Explore your own personal beliefs and examine where they come from. Share them with a listening partner who will also challenge any negative, false beliefs.
2. Would you date and/or marry someone outside your race? Why or why not? What beliefs about interracial dating and marriage influence your decision, and why? From where did those beliefs come?
3. Review the definition of cultural humility. Imagine yourself interacting from a place of cultural humility with someone outside your race. What would that look like? How might cultural humility improve your race relations with others?

Supplemental electronic resources

Resources for interracial couples

- American Association for Marriage and Family Therapy – Multicultural Families: www.aamft.org/Consumer_Updates/Multiracial_Families.aspx
- Association for MultiEthnic Americans, Inc. (AMEA): http://ameasite.com/

Resources for parents raising biracial children

- American Academy of Child & Adolescent Psychiatry – Multiracial Children: www.aacap.org/AACAP/Families_and_Youth/Facts_for_Families/FFF-Guide/Multiracial-Children-071.aspx
- American Adoptions NEWS, 25 Helpful Resources for Transracial Adoptive Families: www.americanadoptions.com/blog/25-helpful-resources-for-transracial-adoptive-families/
- Project Race: Reclassify All Children Equally: https://projectrace.com/

7
Complicated grief and challenges in LGBTQIA+ communities

Doneley Meris

Throughout history, the diverse lesbian, gay, bisexual, transgender, queer, intersex, and asexual (LGBTQIA+) communities have been subjected to the lifelong effects of stigma, discrimination, isolation, criminalization, familial and intra-LGBTQIA+ sub-group disconnects, the ravages of the HIV/AIDS epidemic, and more recently, the COVID-19 pandemic and monkeypox. LGBTQIA+-identified individuals are challenged with trauma, ongoing multiple death losses, devastation from violence, bullying, socioeconomic and political deprivation of human rights protections, sexual and substance abuse, disproportionate rates of incarceration, insufficient medical-mental health-social services, and discrepancies in end-of-life compassionate care. Their complex death and non-death loss experiences, which are not openly acknowledged, often socially invalidated, and not publicly mourned, exemplify Doka's (2008) very definition of disenfranchised grief.

Giving voice to the disenfranchised grief, trauma, mental health, and wellness challenges of the LGBTQIA+ communities has always been at the forefront of this writer's work over four decades. As a grief psychotherapist, clinical adviser-supervisor to social work and psychology graduate students, founder and clinical executive director of the non-profit organization HIV Arts Network, and director of bereavement services at the LGBT Community Services Center in New York City, the author's primary focus in this chapter is to review and make meaning(s) of the complicated losses and essential community re-integration of these diverse populations.

The LGBTQIA+ community has achieved many successes as of late. These include obtention of same-sex marriage rights; election of LGBTQIA+-identified politicians and judges; incorporation of LGBTQIA+-culture sensitivity and advocacy trainings in medical, nursing, social work, psychology, pastoral-ministry, and several therapeutic modalities in higher education; de-pathologization of gay identities in their removal from the *Diagnostic*

DOI: 10.4324/9781003292890-9

and statistical manual for mental disorders; obtention of corporate-hierarchal strides; and attainment of greater visibility in social media. However, many in the LGBTQIA+ community continue to be disenfranchised in social justice reform and more significantly in end-of-life and palliative care services (Mortell, 2015). Compared to the heterosexual mainstream, the coping mechanisms/care for the HIV/AIDS epidemic, disasters, domestic and international violence-repression-bullying, the COVID-19 pandemic, and other global traumatic calamities have been addressed secondarily.

Examining the micro-lens of disenfranchised grief as it continues to impact the lives of LGBTQIA+-identified individuals, the massive spectrum of emotions throughout their true lived stories requires support, compassion, and cultural-gender humility. Recognizing their diverse tales will enable and foster an earnest commitment from mental health and social services (MHSS) professionals and advocates to inspire optimism while instilling the essentials of self-care, safety, and self-preservation in the diverse LGBTQIA+ communities to support them in their reintegration into a world of dignified survival and societal belonging.

Disconnected and disenfranchised LGBTQIA+ subgroups

Although it is impossible to name all the subgroups within the diverse LGBTQIA+ community, there are some whose experiences across their lifespan illustrate the cumulative impacts of disenfranchised grief. The subgroups below illustrate the social stigma, marginalized intersecting identities and racial/ethnic make-up, and the universal lack of acceptance outside of and even within the LGBTQIA+ community that add overwhelmingly to disenfranchisement.

Gay widowers from HIV/AIDS

For over four decades, HIV/AIDS has dominated the discourse on gay life and survival. The grief and rage that come with the disease and death of a loved one are universal. With HIV/AIDS, there is a particular sense of war calamity that is endured by the person dying and their survivors. The HIV/AIDS epidemic has been a profound test of humanity. Thousands of gay men have died and have left their surviving spouses to re-configure their lives. Subjected to societal prejudice and institutional oppression, they often must confront issues of partner loss while battling blood relatives. They must deal with the impact of the double stigma of gay identity and HIV/AIDS, realizing that their deceased partners have been dishonorably discharged from life.

Widowers also face challenges of self-identity, self-worth, and status in the gay community, financial strain due to loss of a second income, and are often left with staggering hospitalization and medication bills. Confronted with a reallocation of tasks, fear of sexual vulnerability (Bristowem et al., 2016), and questions of family-identity around the heterosexual ideal of "what a widower should be," they must also deal with their own mortality (HIV-positive or negative status) and reconfigure the roles and functions they are to assume in the context of a largely homophobic society.

Gay widowers' confrontation with multiple losses on a large scale exacerbates their normative grieving process (McNutt & Yakushko, 2013). The subjugation and reluctance to acknowledge their *sexual bereavement*, or sexual intimacy when predeceased (Piatczanyn et al., 2016; Radosh & Simkin, 2016), in losses related to aging, intense-hidden gay couple intimacy connections, and relationship break-ups, may cause severe negative emotional and physical consequences (Blackwood, 2019; Patlamazoglou et al., 2018, 2021). Their heterosexual widower counterparts often receive unsolicited support when loved ones die or long-term relationships end. Yet many same-sex survivors lack access to gay community support, facing a rollercoaster grieving process in isolation. Such solitary periods may result in increased feelings of vulnerability, where meaningful reconstruction could be difficult to reconcile (Wheat & Thacker, 2019).

Gay men experiences with disenfranchised grief

Facing discrimination, arrest, bullying, disease, and death, gay men have risked violence as they explore their sexuality; lost family ties and mainstream social networks; and endured sexually transmitted diseases, HIV/AIDS, and drug addictions to seek pleasure and intimacy, and same-sex sexual behavior is still criminalized in more than 70 countries (Garner, 2022). Coming out as a gay man is often met with scorn and relational disengagement; vulnerability to depression and suicidality is three times higher than the general adult population (Lee et al., 2017). For four decades, gay men have grappled with the devastation, stigma, and death toll from HIV/AIDS. New generations of gay men struggle with excessive alcohol consumption, crystal meth abuse, and compulsive sexual addictions (Derbyshire & Grant, 2015; Mangia, 2020). Global contagion of the monkeypox epidemic has primarily infected gay men, resulting in fear and frustration as the response is met with slow action (Otterman, 2022). The current moment echoes the 1980s response to the HIV/AIDS epidemic (Stack, 2022).

Trans women with histories of sex work and incarceration

Many trans women epitomize a type of individual whose needs are rarely addressed in the mainstream. Assigned male at birth, trans women frequently grow up under normative standards and conforming to rigid gender expectations; their often-turbulent transition(s) as trans women is/are never easy (Norwood, 2013). Faced with enormous oppression, rejection, transphobia, and disenfranchised grief, they take risks to claim their space and place in daily life. For some, sex work is the only viable way to financially survive after their families reject and blatantly dismiss their existence.

With sex work comes the persistent danger of violence, constant safe-sex negotiations with sex partners, the complicating influence of alcohol and other drugs, and physical threats and trips to jail where sex work is still a crime. While processing and making sense of their multiple losses, trans women often develop addictions and self-destructive behaviors. Such stressful realities leave their physical safety and mental wellbeing in question. Their quest to transition into more traditional professions and into a state of stability requires committed mentors and institutional support that may be difficult to identify or access.

Trans men experiences with complicated grief

In defining the complicated losses and grief journeys of transgender men, their plight must be viewed through tangible, visual, and sometimes trans-cultural validated losses. This could be associated with their core identities: their loss of family and friends (Coolhart et al., 2018), professional identity, social and class status, lack of suitable and positive trans-role models, disconnection from ethnic and racial identity, the challenges of *passing* as male, and their religious affiliation and identity. In this search of an authentic connection to self and community, most trans men delay their grief process in a search for meaning from their traumatic experiences. More challenging are their intangible losses, including the loss of safety, innocence, hope, freedom, dignity, humanity, and the capacity to love (Norwood, 2013).

Complex plight of intersex and bisexual persons

Many bisexual and intersex persons identify as heterosexual and often distance themselves from the diverse LGBTQIA+ communities (Alexander et al., 2015). As most self-identify as either male or female, non-binary, or intersex, there is a disconnect as to whom they may access to gain support. This process of change is a dilemma for some who are uncertain of where they belong (Jenkins & Short, 2017). To address common intersex misconceptions, mental health and social service professionals must first understand that gender is on a spectrum. Second, intersex individuals in a society still unfamiliar with their placement in the social milieu put the intersex community in a discriminatory context when they seek quality bereavement support and mental health care.

Similarly, bisexual individuals are confronted with the constant questions of where and how to fit into the psychosocial structures imposed by a heterosexist society. Equally challenging for this population is the reluctance within gay culture and even the mental health professions' grief work, to embrace and include their plight in sexual, mental health, and social support services. Although there has been incremental growth in supporting their plight, bisexuals are challenged each day with how much to share with others, resulting in self-isolation and reluctance to seek mental health and grief counseling services.

Complicated grief experiences of lesbian women

For lesbian women, the complex web of addiction is a problem that requires community support that is not always available to this vulnerable population. They have higher rates of psychological trauma and interpersonal-intimate partner violence (Dodd & Booker, 2017). Their experiences with hate crimes and rape are more frequent than for heterosexual women (Descamps et al., 2000). Lesbian women have higher percentages of alcohol, cigarette smoking, and drug use/abuse than straight-identified women (Meyer, 2003). It seems these addictions are strongly influenced by multiple factors: health inequities, injustice, lack of access to employment, housing, and quality mental health and social services care.

Many lesbian women were close friends and primary caregivers for gay men who died from HIV/AIDS. They made hospital and home visits, attended to household chores, and were protective advocates for their gay friends. As countless gay men died in their arms, they silently mourned thousands of death losses while carrying the burden of stigmatized supporters. Yet there is still a scarcity in the existing literature about their real, ongoing compassion fatigue as frontline advocates (McNutt & Yakushko, 2013). As these women continue to endure such pain, their dance with life's transitions may lead to isolation and self-loathing.

Case studies

The following composite cases emphasize the complex disenfranchised grief experiences of LGBTQIA+ individuals who are silenced and isolated by fear, stigma, and violence; describe how they navigate discriminating and unsupportive family, relational, and social networks; demonstrate how they meet punitive cultural and ethnic exclusion because of their sexual orientation or gender identity; and explain how they overcome multiple hurdles in accessing medical-mental health and social services. These cases explore unique consequences when LGBTQIA+ individuals are deprived of family, friends, and institutional validation, acknowledgment, and mourning-grieving time afforded to their heterosexual counterparts.

Edwina

Never officially transitioning as a trans woman, because she is economically unable to afford hormone therapy, reassignment surgery, and other maintenance regimens, 62-year-old "Ina" nevertheless lives and dresses as a woman and has made a living since age 19 as an exotic nail salon specialist and beautician. The Vietnam War claimed her father's life when she was four years old; her family's traumatic voyage to escape the battlefields still horrifies her today. An older brother died from gang violence, and her youngest sister was killed by this sister's boyfriend after a domestic dispute.

"Ina" was a sex worker in New York City for several years before beginning her current job. Often being ridiculed as a "freak," she has difficulty connecting with her extended Vietnamese community. Ina sought therapeutic help after suffering multiple bruises from her abusive bisexual male partner. Her ongoing struggles with not fully transitioning prevent her from being fully integrated into heterosexual circles today.

Davila

Identified as "different" at age 3, Davila, who presented as a boy but had both male and female sexual anatomy and chromosome patterns, had a rough upbringing. The third of multiple children, Davila dressed and regarded herself as a girl early on, which confused many in her social circle. Her challenges escalated during her adolescent years, when she was constantly bullied and physically harmed in school and by her brothers at home. Daily verbal and physical abuse prompted Davila to start drinking at age 14. Her entire family also consumed alcohol.

Her eldest brother overdosed on drugs and alcohol, and another sibling died instantly in a car crash while heavily intoxicated. In her college years, Davila had several blackouts, resulting in her removal from school and spending three months in a rehabilitation facility where she met her future husband. Though she remained sober for four and a half years, Davila divorced her husband after they could not conceive and following the discovery that her husband had had multiple affairs. The divorce altered her social life entirely when most of their friends, including her tennis partners, sided with her husband.

The physical and social benefits of playing tennis had deterred her from substance use, but the social disconnect prompted a deep depression, which necessitated a two-week hospitalization. During this time, Davila's mother died from lung cancer following decades of heavy smoking. Davila ended her sobriety and resumed heavy drinking, resulting in job loss and re-entry into individual therapeutic work.

Frank

Born into a family of military men and firefighters, Frank was expected to excel at hockey and other "masculine" sports. But Frank was drawn to classical music and ballet; with the encouragement of his singer-aunt, he began piano lessons and ballet classes. Bullied, Frank was shunned by the male figures in his family. He eventually left home and enrolled in a ballet school with financial scholarship support. Frank apprenticed with a major company and later joined as a corps member, becoming a soloist as his dance career advanced. Throughout this successful trajectory, his personal life was conflicted. The joy and freedom of dance was his escape from the abuse of an older male lover. He was also the victim of a street gang mugging that exacerbated a previous dance injury, causing an early retirement at age 29. Frank was devastated to lose the safe refuge that his ballet career had provided. He began seeing a counselor at an LGBT-medical/mental health clinic after he suffered from severe acute respiratory syndrome (SARS).

Emily

Emily's female companion suggested she seek counseling after receiving the sad news that her adult child, a medical doctor who volunteered to provide medical care relief to Haiti disaster survivors, was killed in an ambush attack. A beautiful 59-year-old mixed-race woman, she had been married for 28 years to a devoted husband, and they raised their only child in a bucolic part of Southern California. Throughout her marriage, she was conflicted with the emotional connection she had forged with her Latina female college roommate, silently yearning for more physical contact with women.

She suppressed these feelings until after her husband's sudden death from an aneurysm. When her child was in medical school, she reconnected with her now-out lesbian college friend, and they established a passionate relationship. However, their coupling was frowned upon by her close circle of upper-middle-class friends in her close-knit community. Many of her friends stopped socializing entirely when her female partner moved in with her. In therapy, Emily addressed her grief and tremendous losses of her only child, her husband, her largely diminished social networks, and her struggles in redefining her sexual orientation and bisexual identity.

Social/cultural aspects of disenfranchised grief

These cases, and the disconnected subgroups' similar but different plights, present wrenching displays of complicated human traumas, losses, and grief. Their stories tell the hard truth that LGBTQIA+ persons lack access to traditional family supports that most heterosexuals take for granted. For these survivors, the stigma from HIV/AIDS, suicide, drug overdose/abuse, incarceration, and LGBTQIA+ violence all too often leads to the loss of financial, emotional, and physical support (Cook et al., 2016).

Today, there is a growing movement to delegitimize what was gained by LGBTQIA+ activists and advocates in recognizing their human rights. The governments of at least eleven countries still criminalize LGBTQIA+ people with the death penalty if they are suspected of engaging in private, consensual, and same-sex sexual activities (Human Dignity Trust, 2022). Fifteen countries still regard gender identity and/or expression of transgender life as criminal and public-order offenses (Human Dignity Trust, 2022).

Renewed cultural wars over sex education, sexual orientation, and gender identity persist today. There are forbidden discussions on sexual orientation or gender identity in schools that endanger children who are secretly conflicted about their sexuality, because they realize they might not have support from their nuclear family as they grapple with their self-doubts, self-discovery, and isolation (Douthat, 2022). In 2020, for example, the state of Florida proposed CS/CS/HB 1557, informally known as the "Don't Say Gay" bill, a legislative effort camouflaged as "parental rights" used to silence LGBTQIA+ youth. Such actions squash early adolescent and young adult human sexuality-body interconnectedness, which is traumatizing youth under the guise of morality and religious-framed values. Future generations of LGBTQIA+ youth will be further disenfranchised and confront a human disconnect (Gonzalez et al., 2017). This harmful agenda is at odds with the very definition of human rights, sexual development, and diversity.

Gay men who are living long term with HIV/AIDS now live in a different era as they confront ever-changing biopsychosocial-political terrain. The stigma of AIDS has not subsided, and many still mourn the deaths of their partners, friends, and the loss of vibrant sex lives. Many now confront the realities of ageism and rejection based on their HIV-related physical appearance and difficulty in their search for age-appropriate peers as they face job discrimination, financial inequality, rejection, and oppression from the Gen Z and young gay generations (Michael, 2007).

Relational aspects of disenfranchised grief

There are tremendous interpersonal disjoints, institutional disconnects, and exclusion from a wider web of supports for LGBTQIA+ individuals throughout their lifetimes, which impact their grief trauma and recovery survival. Their death losses from suicide, hate crime, old age, HIV/AIDS, COVID-19, cancer, and other diseases are met differently. Attention to details before and after death often requires a review of human ties: nuclear or chosen family, surviving partner(s), friends, and extended community. Identifying who will assume responsibility for last rites, funeral-burial, or cremation arrangements can be a battlefield. If no one steps forward to administer such tasks, decisions on who will advocate for and work through these death-related tasks can be stressful, complicated by family resentments, and result in the exclusion of same-sex partners.

Non-death losses, including divorce, separation, and coming out, resulting in family abandonment, legal custody of children, housing crises, homelessness, unemployment, retirement, job termination, long-term diseases, incarceration, domestic violence, ongoing bullying, and harassment often result in interpersonal disenfranchisement. For many LGBTQIA+ persons, their capacity and willingness to reach out and seek support differ exponentially from their heterosexual counterparts (Hornjatkevyc & Alderson, 2011). Disenfranchised spaces (e.g., prisons, street life, shelters) deprive individuals from participating in grief care and rituals. These complicated and chaotic life events can often heighten emotional vulnerability and increase isolation.

Cumulative impacts of disenfranchised grief across the lifespan

Older LGBTQIA+ persons experience tremendous disparities in end-of-life and palliative care. Many in long-term care facilities endure inadequate, disrespectful, and abusive care due to their sexual orientation and gender identity (Stein & Berkman, 2019). These older adults may shy away from being openly identified as LGBTQIA+, fearful of not being given equal or safe treatment. They are often recipients of erroneous assumptions and derogatory statements from care providers (Kamen et al., 2015). In palliative, hospice, and long-term care, they fear identifying their family of choice and that their chosen surrogates will be ignored or disrespected (Neville & Henrickson, 2009). They dread being discriminated against, which may result in suboptimal care and poor preparation for legal advanced care planning (Haviland et al., 2020).

Palliative and end-of-life care require trust between the provider and LGBT-QIA+ patient. Sensitive to vulnerabilities, service delivery that highlights a series of relational transitions on the personal family, care advocate, and healthcare personnel networking levels, and the recognition of the patient's spiritual needs are essential to forge a humane, trusting connection (Cartwright et al., 2012). Ensuring a safe space creates the opportunity for self-disclosure, the assessment of family involvement, and it promotes continuity of care. The practice of inclusive communication, cultural humility, and active listening (Sprik & Gentile, 2019) must extend to the multi-dimensional transitions along a continuum of care from treatment, maximized quality of life, death, and bereavement, to the provision of after-care services to partners and family (Cloyes et al., 2018), as they process their grief to make sense of complex life-death events. Facilitating the death-life survival and recovery journey effectively could be achieved through ongoing LGBTQIA+-inclusive training, education, and practice for grief, mental health, and palliative care providers.

Allyship and advocacy

Allyship that highlights advocacy and accountability can contribute to creating meaningful, lasting, and sustainable partnerships to achieve LGBTQIA+ community integration and wellness goals. The legal protection and advocacy tide is constantly changing for K-12 LGBTQIA+ students as they face bullying, harassment, and more hostility that permeate the school landscape (Quantz, 2019). In a positive development at many academic institutions, LGBTQIA+ and straight student alliances have been forged to facilitate students' camaraderie, collegiality, and sense of belonging. International online and in-person sites have been established to create safe spaces for LGBTQIA+ youth to prevent suicide and promote peer support services, including the Trevor Project (www.thetrevor project.org), which provides 24/7 crisis intervention, research participation, and partnering with suicidologists to integrate LGBTQIA+ youth to a kinder world.

Globally, LGBTQIA+ community service centers invite LGBTQIA+ individuals of *all* ages to participate in social, recreational, work-training, health wellness, and mental health services both in person and online. These community-driven model organizations, led by LGBTQIA+ pioneers and supportive allies, have alleviated isolation, enhanced socialization and job skill sets, increased LGBTQIA+ human rights and resource banking, and provided a sense of belonging and community.

Aimed at addressing the many issues of LGBTQIA+ aging and building community and connection for LGBTQIA+ seniors, organizations like SAGE (www.sagenyc.org), offer innovative and interactive programs and services. The inclusion of trans individuals in the workplace and the emergence of active support and advocacy positively results in psychological safety, authenticity, and increased life satisfaction (Fletcher & Marvell, 2022).

Trans allyship in care settings starts with the collection of accurate and recent sexual orientation, sexual history, and gender identity data. Cognizant advocates must be mindful when analyzing this data to recognize chosen versus biological family dynamics, advocate for extended social networks' participation in decision-making, and proactively address inadequate, disrespectful, and/or abusive care or discriminatory treatment of their families and support networks (Stein et al., 2020).

Ethical considerations

LGBTQIA+ individuals are subjected to challenges that necessitate careful ethical review. When a same-sex couple divorces, extra steps must be taken to legally connect a child to their biological or non-biological parent (Meyer, 2022). Whether a child is conceived through artificial insemination, surrogacy, or adoption, same-sex partners must abide by different standards to establish a family. These traumatizing experiences create lifelong consequences for all parties involved.

Mental health advocates must be aware of several challenges that provoke grief for LGBTQIA+ partners, such as legal child custody cases, shared property divisions after a separation or divorce, inheritance legal disputes, housing crises after break-ups, HIV/AIDS sero-discordant couples' health care insurance eligibility, foster care and adoption eligibility, and foster or abortion versus pro-life decisions. Conversion therapy treatment continues to invade conflicting and traumatic ethical-legal and medical-mental health confrontations on its questionable merits, non-efficacy, and the tremendous lifelong harm it can inflict on young and adult LGBTQIA+ persons (Andrade & Campo Redondo, 2022). Attention to end-of-life care and after-life services must also focus on providers' ensuring that dying trans men and women are not be buried in their *dead names* (i.e., legal names) but in their chosen-trans names.

Strategies and interventions

Psychological trauma often serves as a connector to others who have experienced loss. There is a professional need to reject the viruses of homophobia, transphobia, violence, isolation, and prejudice; to embrace the fabrics of comfort, caring, and community; and to acknowledge that all humans, regardless of their sexual orientation and sexual constellation, struggle in their grieving and healing processes. Being able to access a varied array of culturally sensitive, language-competent, and compatible program plans for all grievers is vital in establishing an individual and communal base of support.

Confronting the conventional threshold of who is acceptable and embraced within the grieving communities and the commitment to facing clients' emotional landscapes are crucial in the initial encounter. An intransigent approach will not work because each individual story may have some similarities, but the range of differences in grief is unique and very personal. Rando (2003) suggested that a *life loss review* (LLR) for each traumatic life event must be explored, wherein the grieving person can begin to acknowledge the pain of their loss(es) and fully review their psychological defense processing to effectively release any mitigating behaviors associated with their loss(es); and process their *cognitive life raft* (Nord, 1996) as they review their relational adjustments, entitlements, or lack thereof.

Companioning grief, or reviewing previous sexual, emotional, and physical ties, identifying similarities and differences, then participating in the difficult task of letting go of the challenging past and embracing the present, engages the individual in the reconstruction of survival and resilience skills building (Meris, 2016; Southwick & Charney, 2018). *Mapping out and visually illustrating their traumatic narrative*, the griever or traumatized person is given permission to bridge the difficult emotional, financial, psychological, and social life adjustments necessary for them to forge ahead (Doka & Martin, 2010; Hostetler, 2012). Cultivating healthier and *individualized self-wellness agendas*, embracing positive events, identifying *grief triggers*, and *learning from setbacks* optimize body-mind re-engagements (Bonanno, 2021).

Cultural humility is knowing a clinician has more to learn and further explore with each client. Building on past encounters and highlighting the gains and trials that clients traversed, then focusing primarily on the present will allow continued bereavement-recovery (Carpenter, 2016; Lytle et al., 2015). Though obvious, it is worth noting that cultural similarities and differences are extremely complex. It is critical to be mindful that individuals grieve and respond to trauma and loss differently depending on their origins, ethnicity, and socioeconomic cultural base. A gay Puerto Rican man living on that island has varied sets of reactions, coping mechanisms, and traditions that differ significantly from those of a gay Puerto Rican-American man who was born and lives in New York City. There are myriad circumstances that influence how each person will process a death or non-death event. The key to being supportive is to ask questions that allow the person's story to unfold through their narration and personal timelines as they make meaning of their traumatic life events.

Most grievers and traumatized individuals find comfort participating in support groups. Support group engagement has the potential to help identify inner strengths, resources, and coping skills. LGBTQIA+ individuals' involvement in same-sex support groups has inspired the recognition of parallel processes that other survivors experienced, acknowledged the pain of loss, and discovered unique ways to commemorate and celebrate the deceased's legacies and transition from loss and trauma.

Summary

In this world of memes, where self-directed ventures discard the requisite compassion for others, the disenfranchised grief of the LGBTQIA+ communities is poorly understood and prioritized. At the crossroads of their multiple crises, the helping professional must acknowledge that these life challenges require processing, validation, and worthy life review as the underpinning of unique grief-trauma work. Reassessing both healthy and dysfunctional eco-systemic scans could afford LGBTQIA+ individuals the ability to discover the meanings of their personal and unique complicated grief (Worden, 2018). For most, the climate and societal conscience always require a wait-and-carefully-view disposition about what the road might have to provide in terms of genuine support and humane engagement.

What can be extrapolated from this life-death journey with LGBTQIA+ communities and the rejoining with life is the best-practice principle of redefining the word *compassion* to incorporate the sufferings of same-sex *and* opposite-sex grievers and those struggling with complicated losses and traumas into human traditions of unconditional support.

References

Alexander, R., Parker, K., & Schwetz, T. (2015). Sexual and gender minority health research at the National Institute of Health. *LGBT Health, 3*(1), 7–10. https://doi.org/10.1089%2Flgbt.2015.0107

Andrade, G., & Campo Redondo, M. (2022). Is conversion therapy ethical? A renewed discussion into the context of legal efforts to ban it. *Ethics, Medicine and Public Health, 20,* Article 100732. https://doi.org/10.1016/j.jemep.2021.100732

Blackwood, E. (2019). *The many faces of homosexuality.* Routledge.

Bonanno, G. (2021). *The end of trauma: How the new science of resilience is changing how we think about PTSD.* Basic Books.

Bristowem, K., Marshall, S., & Harding, E. (2016). The bereavement experiences of LGBT people who have lost a partner: A systematic review, thematic synthesis and modelling of the literature. *Palliative Medicine, 30,* 730–744. https://doi.org/10.1177/0269216316634601

Carpenter, M. (2016). The human rights of intersex people: Addressing harmful practices and rhetoric of change. *Reproductive Health Matters, 24*(47), 74–84. https://doi.org/10.1016/j.rhm.2016.06.003

Cartwright, C., Hughes, M., & Lienert, T. (2012). End-of-life care for gay, lesbian, bisexual and transgender people. *Culture, Health and Sexuality, 14*(5), 537–548. https://doi.org/10.1080/13691058.2012.673639

Cloyes, K. G., Hull, W., & Davis, A. (2018). Palliative and end-of-life care LGBT cancer patients and their caregivers. *Seminars in Oncology Nursing, 34*(1), 60–71. https://doi.org/10.1016/j.soncn.2017.12.003

Cook, S. H., Watkins, D. C., Calebs, B. J., & Wilson, P. A. (2016). Attachment orientation and sexual risk behavior among young Black gay and bisexual men. *Psychology and Sexuality, 7*(3), 177–196. https://doi.org/10.1080/19419899.2016.1168312

Coolhart, D., Ritenour, K., & Grodzinski, A. (2018). Experiences of ambiguous loss for parents of transgender youth: A phenomenological exploration. *Contemporary Family Therapy, 40*(1), 28–41. https://doi.org/10.1007/s10591-017-9426-x

Derbyshire, K. L., & Grant, J. E. (2015). Compulsive sexual behavior: A review of the literature. *Journal of Behavioral Addictions, 4*(2), 37–43. https://doi.org/10.1556/2006.4.2015.003

Descamps, M. J., Rothblum, E., Bradford, J., & Ryan, C. (2000). Mental health impact of child and sexual abuse, rape, intimate partner violence, and hate crime in the national lesbian health care survey. *Journal of Gay and Lesbian Social Services, 11*(1), 27–56. https://doi.org/10.1300/J041v11n01_02

Dodd, S. J., & Booker, L. C. (2017). Practice with lesbian individuals and couples. In G. P. Mallon (Ed.), *Social work practice with lesbian, gay, bisexual and transgender people* (3rd ed., pp. 66–89). Routledge.

Doka, K. J. (2008). Disenfranchised grief in historical and cultural perspective. In M. S. Stroebe, R. O. Hansson, H. Schut, & W. Stroebe (Eds.), *Handbook of bereavement research and practice: Advances in theory and intervention* (pp. 223–240). American Psychological Association. https://doi.org/10.1037/14498-011

Doka, K. J., & Martin, T. L. (2010). *Grieving beyond gender: Understanding the ways men and women mourn.* Routledge.

Douthat, D. (2022, April 13). How to make sense of the new LGBT cultural wars. *The New York Times.* www.nytimes.com/2022/04/13/opinion/transgender-culture-war.html

Fletcher, L., & Marvell, R. (2022). Furthering transgender inclusion in the workplace: Advancing a new model of allyship intentions and perceptions. *The International Journal of Human Resources Management,* 1–31. https://doi.org/10.1080/09585192.2021.2023895

Garner, A. (2022, June 28). Let's talk about sex. *The Advocate, 1122,* 19.

Gonzalez, J.-M., Sinclair, K. O., D-Augelli, A. R., & Grossman, A. H. (2017). Intersectionality and well-being among racial/ethnic minority and LGB youth: Extended family members as support against negative parental reactions to coming out. In R. Dimitrova (Ed.), *Well-being of youth and emerging adults across cultures* (pp. 123–144). Springer.

Haviland, K., Walters, C. B., & Newman, S. (2020). Barriers to palliative care in sexual and gender minority patients with cancer: A scoping review of the literature. *Health and Social Care in the Community, 29*(2), 305–318. https://doi.org/10.1111/hsc.13126

Hornjatkevyc, N., & Alderson, K. (2011). With and without: The bereavement experiences of gay men who have lost a partner to non-AIDS-related causes. *Death Studies, 35*(9), 801–823. https://doi.org/10.1080/07481187.2011.553502

Hostetler, A. J. (2012). Community involvement, perceived control, and attitudes towards aging among lesbians and gay men. *International Aging and Human Development, 77*(2), 141–167. https://doi.org/10.2190/AG.75.2.c

Human Dignity Trust. (2022). LGBT and the law. *Human Dignity Trust.* www.human dignitytrust.org/lgbt-the-law

Jenkins, T. M., & Short, S. E. (2017). Negotiating intersex: A case for revising the theory of social diagnosis. *Social Science and Medicine, 175,* 91–98. https://doi.org/10.1016/j.socscimed.2016.12.047

Kamen, C. S., Smith-Stoner, M., Heckler, C. E., Flannery, M., & Margolies, L. (2015). Social support, self-rated health, and LGBT-identity disclosure to cancer care providers. *Oncology Nursing Forum, 42*(1), 44–51. https://doi.org/10.1188/15.ONF.44-51

Lee, C., Oliffe, J. L., Kelly, M. T., & Ferlatte, O. (2017). Depression and suicidality in gay men: Implications for health care providers. *American Journal of Men's Health, 11*(4), 910–919. https://doi.org/10.1177/1557988316685492

Lytle, M., De Luca, S., Blosnich, J., & Brownson, C. (2015). Associations of racial/ethnic identities and religious affiliation with suicidal ideation among lesbian, gay, bisexual, and questioning individuals. *Journal of Affective Disorders, 178,* 39–45. https://doi.org/10.1016/j.jad.2014.07.039

Mangia, J. (2020, January 22). Gay men are dying from the crisis we're not talking about: No one's really grappling with the meth disaster. *New York Times.* www.nytimes.com/2020/01/22/opinion/gay-meth-addiction.html

McNutt, B., & Yakushko, O. (2013). Disenfranchised grief among lesbian and gay bereaved individuals. *Journal of LGBT Issues in Counseling, 7*(1), 87–116. https://doi.org/10.1080/15538605.2013.758345

Meris, D. (2016). Transformation through socially sensitive experiences. In D. L. Harris & T. C. Bordere (Eds.), *Handbook of social justice in loss and grief: Exploring diversity, equity and inclusion* (pp. 179–190). Routledge.

Meyer, I. H. (2003). Prejudice, social stress, and mental health in lesbian, gay, and bisexual populations: Conceptual issues and research evidence. *Psychological Bulletin, 129*(5), 674–697. https://doi.org/10.1037/0033-2909.129.5.674

Meyer, A. (2022, April 8). Oklahoma mother to be removed from baby's birth certificate because she's not the "gestational parent." *Nextstar Media Wire.* www.bigcountryhomepage.com/news/national-news/oklahoma-mother-to-be-removed-from-babys-birth-certificate-because-shes-not-the-gestational-parent/

Michael, C. (2007). Not found on the quilt: Gay widowers and their loss due to circumstances other than AIDS. *Dissertation Abstracts International: Section A. Humanities and Social Sciences, 68*(6-A), 2338.

Mortell, S. (2015). Assisting clients with disenfranchised grief: The role of mental health nurse. *Journal of Psychosocial Nursing and Mental Health Services, 53*(4), 52–57. https://doi.org/10.3928/02793695-20150319-05

Neville, S., & Henrickson, M. (2009). The constitution of "lavender families": A LGBT perspective. *Journal of Clinical Nursing, 18*(6), 849–856. https://doi.org/10.1111/j.1365-2702.2008.02457.x

Nord, D. (1996). Issues and implications of the counseling of survivors of multiple AIDS-related loss. *Death Studies, 20*(4), 389–413. https://doi.org/10.1080/07481189608252789

Norwood, K. (2013). Grieving gender: Trans-identities, transition, and ambiguous loss. *Communication Monographs, 80*(1), 24–45. https://doi.org/10.1080/03637751.2012.739705

Otterman, S. (2022, July 18). For monkeypox patients, pain is brutal and care is lacking. *New York Times*, A1, A13.

Patlamazoglou, L., Simmonds, J. G., & Snell, T. L. (2018). Same-sex partner bereavement: Non-HIV-related loss and new research directions. *OMEGA – Journal of Death and Dying, 78*(2), 178–196. https://doi.org/10.1177/0030222817690160

Patlamazoglou, L., Simmonds, J. G., & Snell, T. L. (2021). Grief in later life: Symbolic losses and unsolicited gains following the death of a same-gender partner. *Psychology and Sexuality*. Advance online publication. https://doi.org/10.1080/19419899.2021.2016915

Piatczanyn, S. A., Bennett, K. M., & Soulsby, L. K. (2016). "We were in a partnership that wasn't recognized by anyone else": Examining the effects of male gay partner bereavement, masculinity, and identity. *Men and Masculinities, 19*(2), 167–191. https://doi.org/10.1177/1097184X15583905

Quantz, M. (2019). Educator advocacy for queer students in schools. *Dialogues, 2*(1), 1–4. https://doi.org/10.33011/assembly.v2i1.479

Radosh, A., & Simkin, L. (2016). Acknowledging sexual bereavement: A path out of disenfranchised grief. *Reproductive Health Matters, 24*(48), 25–33. https://doi.org/10.1016/j.rhm.2016.11.005

Rando, T. (2003). *Treatment of complicated mourning*. Research Press.

Stack, L. (2022, July 29). In monkeypox, gay men confront a health crisis with echoes of the past. *New York Times*, A20.

Southwick, S. M., & Charney, D. S. (2018). *Resilience: The science of mastering life's greatest challenges* (2nd ed.). Cambridge University Press.

Sprik, P., & Gentile, D. (2019). Cultural humility: A way to reduce LGBTQ health disparities at the end-of-life. *American Journal of Hospice and Palliative Medicine*, *37*(6), 404–408. https://doi.org/10.1177/1049909119880548

Stein, G. L., & Berkman, C. (2019). Palliative and end-of-life care to the LGBT community. *Innovation in Aging*, *3*(Supplement 1), Article S623. https://doi.org/10.1093/geroni/igz038.2322

Stein, G. I., Berkman, C., O'Mahony S., Godfrey, D., Javier, N. M., & Maingi, S. (2020). Experiences of LGBT patients and families in hospice and palliative care: Perspectives of the palliative care team. *Journal of Palliative Medicine*, *23*(6), 817–824. https://doi.org/10.1089/jpm.2019.0542

Wheat, L. S., & Thacker, N. E. (2019). LGBTQ+ loss experiences and the use of meaning reconstruction with clients. *Journal of LGBT Issues in Counseling*, *13*(3), 232–251. https://doi.org/10.1080/15538605.2019.1627973

Worden, J. W. (2018). *Grief counseling and grief therapy: A handbook for the mental health practitioner* (5th ed.). Springer.

Questions for reflective practice

1. What are the loss and trauma challenges (socio-relational and ethical) unique to LGBTQIA+ communities?
2. What are some population-specific humane interventions that can be offered to LGBTQIA+ individuals who struggle with multiple death and non-death losses?
3. How can mental health practitioners address the diversity and multiplicity of cultural factors that impact the grief process and relational re-integration of LGBTQIA+ individuals?
4. As a grief, mental health, and wellness advocate, what effective strategies can you provide specifically to culturally diverse LGBTQI+ clients?

Supplemental electronic resources

- Association for Death Education in Counseling: www.adec.org
- LGBTQ+ Lifeline: 1-800-273-8255; suicidepreventionlifeline.org
- SAGE National LGBTQ+ Elder Hotline: 1–877–360-LGBT (5428); www.sagenyc.org; www.sageusa.org
- Trans Lifeline: www.translifeline.org
- The Trauma Foundation: www.thetraumafoundation.org
- The Trevor Project: 1-800-788-7386; www.thetrevorproject.org

8

The interplay of disenfranchised grief and systemic barriers from COVID-19 for African Americans

Theresa Libios and Edward F. Hudspeth

Though now in endemic status, the COVID-19 pandemic has residual effects on groups that have been marginalized. For many, discussions about COVID-19 bring up what might have previously been unimaginable: millions of deaths and long-term physical and mental impairments for those who contracted it but survived. If the world's population could be surveyed about their experiences with COVID-19, one might expect that the majority would report significant life changes. If asked about perceptions of how COVID-19 affects some differently than others, the typical person would not identify its effects on populations that have been marginalized. However, in medical, mental health, and sociological environments, the impacts of the pandemic initiated conversations about race, historical barriers, and community experiences related to inequities in the social determinants of health and mental health outcomes, such as poverty, food insecurity, insufficient housing, and healthcare access, which affect groups that have been disadvantaged and marginalized (Watson et al., 2020).

The emergence of the COVID-19 pandemic exacerbated disparities, unleashing an abundance of grief and mourning upon communities of color. Initially, African Americans, Latinx, and Indigenous peoples were at higher risk of contracting and dying from the coronavirus (Walsh, 2020). During the apex of the first two years of the pandemic, among these groups, African Americans died at higher rates than their counterparts. Furthermore, efforts to slow the spread of the coronavirus created consequences that were economically detrimental and weakened cultural rituals, familial practices, and community-based support systems that People of Color traditionally relied upon as buffers to stress. Support in times of grief is an essential ingredient in the mourning process; COVID-19 became an invasive, unexpected, and new source of grief that destroyed support systems and changed the mental health trajectory for

DOI: 10.4324/9781003292890-10

African American communities. As a result, the pandemic added an additional layer of adverse childhood experiences (ACEs) with lingering effects on African Americans' mental health (Sonu et al., 2021; Srivastav et al., 2021).

Given the exacerbation of grief and ACEs levied on African Americans during the pandemic, the application of existing grief models requires further clinician self-reflection and social-cultural adaptations to address this unique grieving process under these unprecedented circumstances. In this chapter, readers will note the intersection of grief, social-cultural issues, and multisystemic losses that African Americans experienced during the COVID-19 pandemic that may give rise to complex grief, consideration of layered ACEs, and interrupted mourning processes. The authors incorporate considerations for helping professionals practice effective, culturally responsive grief work with the African American community. The authors also aim to shed light on the complex and multisystemic losses that the COVID-19 pandemic has had and continues to have upon communities of color, specifically African Americans.

Perspectives on grief

Grief is generally viewed and accepted as the experience resulting from death- or non-death loss. Grief is culturally and socially normed and influenced by countless variables. *Disenfranchised grief* denotes grief that is not acknowledged, accepted, or does not align with socially accepted norms (Doka, 2008).

When considering disenfranchised grief experienced within African American culture, it is essential to explore the concept alongside the importance of cultural rituals (Piazza-Bonin, 2015). Culturally supported grief rituals are essential because they provide a corridor of emotional expression and community connection (Romanoff, 1998). Community and connection are important, threaded patterns that seem to forge bonds within the African American community.

Within the African American community, there is a lingering historical pain that is an accumulation of loss, historical trauma, inequities, racism, and discrimination. For the African American community, the first experience of loss can be traced back to families being torn apart for the purpose of slavery. As such, slavery is an example of grief and loss by way of family separation, physical and emotional pain, mistrust, deception, hate, lack of attachments, confinement, stress, and trauma. It is important to note that this chapter is not about slavery. However, mentioning slavery is pertinent because it offers context for understanding family (community) history. The characteristics of grief and loss surfaced from the normalized treatments of those enslaved. Though these experiences are far too numerous to mention, naming a few historical ones provides a foundation for understanding.

Family separations included children being taken away from their mothers and sold as property. Marriages had to be approved by slave owners, and even then, family members could be separated and sold, never to see their loved ones again. Infractions were met with whipping and lynching without age or gender limitations (Smithers, 2012). Consider the act of having your child taken from you to be sold. Consider being a husband or parent witnessing your wife or daughter's rape. Contemplate the act of being enslaved and the grief and loss it represents. Now, consider the magnitude of the experience and imagine not being able to openly display the emotions evoked by these experiences.

Slaves were prohibited from displaying emotions and were controlled by harmful physical and psychological measures. For those unfamiliar with the acts forced upon the enslaved, clinicians are encouraged to research the history to gain essential insight. Illustrations included rape, beatings, lynching, and other dehumanizing actions to subdue a culture's voice and right to exist (Granek & Peleg-Sagy, 2015). These actions required resilience that was illumined as strength, especially for Black women, hence the "Strong Black Woman" stereotype. African American grief is still seen as minimal or non-existent because scholars indicated that most European Americans believed African Americans did not feel pain or had a higher tolerance for pain (Henderson et al., 2021). Such treatments further ingrained a trauma that buried the grief of loss and maltreatment. Loss in any form was normalized yet unresolved.

Historically, for African Americans, loss and grief were felt in the form of loss of freedom, family displacement, loss of community, and loss of safety, each of which warranted a season of grieving. However, for this population, there has been no space for this type of grieving or an understanding of the need to grieve. This led to the conceptualization of how grief is associated with unresolved historical trauma presented as disenfranchised grief, physical ailments, shortened life span, mental health symptomatology, and psychological distress.

There is limited research analyzing the emotional and mental health effects of slavery and how those unique experiences have transformed generational/historical trauma into complex prolonged grief, because these historical events have been displayed, discussed, and documented devoid of the emotional experience. Henderson et al. (2021) indicated that historical traumas experienced by groups that have been marginalized have specific effects on current generations. Behaviors reflect the transgenerational transmission of cultural practices, such as the expression of grief or its lack of expression and the use of certain coping mechanisms. Over generations, the current effects of this transmission can be seen in ACEs responses (viz., anxiety, substance abuse, spirituality, coping norms, etc.) and physical trauma symptoms in response to threatening situations.

With this in mind, consider a community experiencing an accumulation of loss and trauma with no voice or corridor for expression. When someone experiences a traumatic event, cortisol is released, causing physical or emotional responses, sometimes referred to as "fight or flight" responses or reactions (Helsel, 2015). The body releases chemicals to facilitate a reaction or response. Three aspects of the nervous system may activate a response: The enteric nervous system (ENS) influences a freezing response; the sympathetic nervous system (SNS) influences the fight or flight response; and the parasympathetic nervous system (PNS) influences a resting state of being (Helsel, 2015). Now imagine the body needing to respond and react but the person cannot (Bowers & Yehuda, 2016). When slaves were sold, hanged, or violated, slave owners prohibited their outward expressions of grief and trauma; however, their inner reactions and responses were encapsulated in spiritual beliefs to one day be free.

Same pain, different era

The COVID-19 pandemic and the 2020 Black Lives Matters protests highlighted the broad spectrum of grief and how it is now viewed beyond the concept of losing a loved one. The narratives are fundamental to the embodiment of ACEs. The 2020 experience brought to light the distinct forms of grief that are ubiquitous among African Americans. The pandemic drew attention to the physical and mental health disparities facing African Americans. It also underscored the historical significance of mistrusting medical and mental health professionals, creating barriers to seeking treatment that people who have been marginalized often experience. The pandemic highlighted the importance of health care and the tragedy of mental health disparities to the forefront of international conversations. It underscored the historical significance of mistrust and stigma, which are associated with barriers to seeking treatment that people who have been marginalized often experience. How can a race of people that have been mistreated by another race turn for help to someone from the latter race that mistreated them? Given the low representation of African Americans in mental health fields, the question is one that partially explains the reticence People of Color have to seeking mental health services and further widens healthcare disparities.

COVID-19 dismantled superficial conversations about systematic racism and disparities and gave a small whisper of a voice to African Americans. It brought hidden, complicated grief that has been passed down from generation to generation to the surface. Communities united through media sources for a common cause, displaying kinship as a mechanism of essential, familial support. In African American communities, fractured social and support systems highlighted community disparities that were seen in having limited access to technology, health testing, mental health support, and general education about the virus and ways to protect oneself from it. As a result, these challenges brought the need for social change to the forefront of national and international conversations. COVID-19 added a layer to ACEs, imploring an exploration of complicated, disenfranchised grief. Disenfranchised grief can lead to prolonged grief disorder (PGD), which increases the chances of physical and mental health illnesses (Goldsmith et al., 2008).

Social aspects of disenfranchised grief

Some social aspects of disenfranchised grief are rooted in how African Americans are perceived to grieve and are grounded in behaviors resulting from intergenerational traumas. Historically, slaves were sold to different plantations at the owner's will. *Kinship* arose from a person or mentor taking care of the new slave that was brought to the plantation. Derived from the system of unmerited change (Crewe & Wilson, 2007), kinship was extended to those who were orphaned due to multiple facets of their activities. This type of kinship is a generational practice of support and connection. It is like having that family member everyone calls uncle or aunt, but no one remembers how or if they are blood relatives. It is the embodiment of community, support, and connection that is a prevalent custom among African Americans.

The historical perception that African Americans did not grieve or feel pain and had high endurance amplified other disenfranchisements and disparities during the height of the COVID-19 pandemic in 2020, such as lack of access to COVID testing and medical care and a lack of access to employment, education, and social connection. Social connection and kinship are significant components of support within the African American community that often arise from work, school, and community relationships. During the pandemic, the number of deaths increased and kinship connections decreased. With the high number of COVID-19 deaths came an increased need for mental health services within the African American community.

Community support was somewhat fractured during worldwide pandemic lockdowns, which increased mental health struggles and symptoms. Families were limited in how they could connect with each other. In the US, church services were canceled and only offered via social media in areas where many had limited access. Church and faith are major supportive factors within African American communities; therefore, two major lifelines were disconnected or limited, leaving a support void. So began a season of loss that transcended the physical loss of a human being. These types of losses are part of an ongoing process that characterizes complicated grief (Matthews et al., 2021).

Table 8.1 represents a fraction of the losses experienced and the impacts that made them disenfranchised, compounding the effects of ACEs in adults and adding another layer of ACEs for the current generation of children. Exploring this layer reveals how connected the nature of ACEs and COVID-19 are and underscores the social determinants of mental health and social systems (Watson et al., 2020).

With loss comes a grieving process; however, how does a population grieve when all they have known is loss? This loss is historical, prolonged, yet currently relevant. It is a loss that has been observed yet inadequately addressed. How can that same population of people grieve when it has never been a socially acceptable process? Accordingly, it is imperative to consider the general concept of disenfranchised grief to evaluate the social aspects, and acceptance can be analyzed by viewing African Americans' past and current experiences.

Cultural aspects of disenfranchised grief

There are several layers of cultural aspects to consider in how disenfranchised grief manifests for African Americans. Historical constraints on grief play a big part in how African Americans perceive and respond to grief. There is a cultural avoidance of talking about death and loss. When chronic illness is present, most of the time, African Americans abstain from having conversations about dying. Family, friends, and people in kinship roles take on the responsibility of care in the form of presence, caregiving, cooking (meals are culturally important), and sometimes sitting in silence. Once death has arrived, many African American Christians believe the person passes on to a higher entity, and planning the funeral begins.

Table 8.1 Types of Social Losses African Americans Experience Due to the COVID-19 Pandemic

Experience	Impact on African Americans
Illness: Some African Americans withheld their trust in healthcare systems due to historical mistreatment of people who have been minoritized. People were unable to visit hospitals due to protocols to minimize the spread of disease.	Some African Americans were reluctant to seek treatment when illness was manageable, had limited access to loved ones admitted to the hospital, and could not say goodbye to loved ones who died in the hospital.
Inability to gather: COVID-19 imposed confinement and then limited the number of people that could congregate in one place. Some churches had limited access to broadcast services, and some members had limited access to technology (no internet, poor connections, no supportive devices, etc.). Family gatherings ceased. Children converted to online education.	The loss of practicing faith in person limited the sense of belonging and connection people felt with their congregation. The limited access use of technology changed the quantity and quality of people's engagement with their spiritual community. Sunday dinners, birthday parties, etc., could not be held. Educational disparities broadened and economic inequities were highlighted for children with limited access to technology/internet. Children missed educational milestones and could not participate in collective activities (graduations, extracurricular activities, etc.)
Inability to provide basic needs: Lower-income workers were laid off during the pandemic.	Many lost their homes due to high eviction rates, which led to a loss of community. Food insecurity amplified social inequities and a greater need for social supports. Inability to interact with colleagues may represent a loss of social supports.
Increase in mental health symptoms: Added stressors due to illness, inability to gather, and inability to provide for basic needs augmented mental health needs. Lack of cultural awareness within mental health professions about the unique experiences of African Americans.	Mental health-market demands increased, which resulted in long waiting times to receive services. Lack of trust within the African American population to seek mental health services. Mental health disparities for African Americans increased.

Grief in a spiritual collective

Many African Americans grieve as a spiritual collective, and the Christian church and faith have been instrumental in offering coping skills and practices. For example, for many African American Christians, the church has been seen as the cornerstone of community offering healing, hope, support, unity, and a sacred place of worship. The *Black Church* has its history rooted in an era where White slave owners attempted to convert slaves to Christianity. Interestingly, *Exodus* was the book in the *Bible* that resonated most with African Americans, because it reverberated with slavery, emancipation, and reconstruction, similarly to The Great Migration and the Civil Rights Movement (Gates, 2021). Grief is processed within the *self* and within the *church*, allowing God to be a source of healing. *Faith* allows for the belief that loved ones have transitioned to a better place beyond an earthly presence. The transition comprises the Christian ritual of having a "wake" (viewing) and a "funeral" ceremony, uniting grievers and the community.

Following Christian traditions, the day of the funeral service is one in which close family meets to dress and accompany each other on the ride to the church in a procession. During the church service, special words are spoken, songs are sung, and sermons are given with words of encouragement to the family. Following the church service, the cemetery service involves additional words of homegoing, scriptures, and final words of goodbye. For African American Christians, these rituals may be conceptualized as a remembrance of the person's life, relief from the sickness that preceded their death, and homegoing celebrations that marked the return of their soul to their native Africa after enslavement (Moore et al., 2022). Once the services have concluded, a continued act of service to handle financial affairs is prominent. These Christian rituals, and rituals for African Americans of other faiths, were hindered during COVID-19, compounding disenfranchised grief and altering the connection process within African American communities.

As history dictates, once the deceased is buried, so is the grief, and then it is back to work. No conversations about the mental and emotional strain are had, nor are any conversations about unresolved feelings. During slavery, the enslaved were given one day to bury, and sometimes they were back to work within hours. Openly showing emotion was prohibited. This long-practiced ritual of not showing emotion has expanded through multiple forms of loss today, increasing complicated grief symptoms (Laurie & Neimeyer, 2008). Complicated grief emerges from discrimination, oppression, and marginalization when a lack of social justice continually retriggers these traumas for African Americans.

Acknowledgment of multiple forms of losses

Another disenfranchised layer of African American grief is the multiple forms of non-death losses: loss of safety and security, freedoms, police brutality, negative police contact, loss of innocence, incarceration, unemployment, racism, and a loss of voice. Lawson (2014) highlighted that African Canadians have fought and continue to fight for equality and against inequities, which is also true for African Americans. However, the space to grieve for what those struggles stand for and offer are absent.

When African American families are separated, there is little opportunity to process the losses. The community attempts to move forward with daily living because there is no time or space to grieve. Knight and Gitterman (2019) succinctly described ambiguous loss as disenfranchised: "Since the grief associated with ambiguous loss is not socially recognized, this leads to further pathologizing what is, in fact, an expected and understandable reaction to an already untenable loss" (p. 4). This experience suggests a question to ponder, "How does a population learn to grieve normalized losses?"

Relational aspects of disenfranchised grief

Understanding the relational factors involved in the nature and the transcendence of grief requires evaluating the transmission of individual behavioral patterns that are established at the junction of traumatic life experiences, intersecting identities, and communication patterns. Those behavioral patterns, through relationships and transgenerational transmission of family functioning, may amplify disenfranchised grief that develops as a result of larger cultural and societal influences. Family unit transmission is common and can be directly correlated to family functioning. Trauma is transmitted via family functioning and individual behaviors through styles of communication, family conflict, family dysfunction, and parental relationships or the lack thereof. It is important to note that trauma transmission can be direct or indirect. COVID-19 was experienced as a direct and an indirect transmission of trauma.

Although multiple forms of loss may have significant impacts, incarceration is a factor and an essential aspect of grief for African Americans that is infrequently conceptualized. According to Bocknek et al. (2009), incarceration is a type of ambiguous loss associated with absence. Boss (2016) defined *ambiguous loss* as "a situation of unclear loss that remains unverified and thus without resolution" (p. 270). Considering that African American males are incarcerated at higher rates than any other racial group in the US, this type of ambiguous loss may be prevalent.

Incarceration reveals a complex experience of loss that was further deepened during the COVID-19 pandemic. For example, when a husband, father, or brother is incarcerated, the community and family often lose a male figure, and new roles must be defined. A way of life is lost, survival is crucial, and there is no time to grieve. African American women step into roles that are supportive, resembling the position of matriarch (Hart-Johnson, 2014). When this happens, the women and children connected to the incarcerated are left with an untended void. It is crucial to highlight that incarceration amplifies attachment difficulties for children and an inability to grieve the loss of the relationships (Hart-Johnson, 2014); the person is still alive but inaccessible. Pandemic restrictions to curb coronavirus spread worsened this attachment difficulty through the prohibition of prison visits.

Cumulative impacts of disenfranchised grief across the lifespan

African Americans have a unique cultural experience that contributes to their disenfranchised grief (Boulware & Bui, 2016). To understand the African American population's experience of disenfranchised grief, one must understand the lifespan and history of their cumulative scars. The scars began with slavery, the separation of family, and disconnection from the generational rituals, resulting in the loss of a way of life and being.

Slavery is a generational and cultural experience whose impacts continue to influence the lifespan of the African American population. The experience of unresolved traumatic events over a lifespan often results in generational trauma. The trauma of slavery epitomizes transgenerational transmission by way of family narratives, childrearing based on social norms, and social experiences. These historical experiences, manifest as lower socioeconomic status (SES), systemic racism, and limited opportunities that influence community wellbeing. These challenges can be seen in the underpinnings of ACEs when applied to the African American Community.

Several authors refer to ACES coupled with adverse community environments as the *Pair of ACEs*, (Ellis & Dietz, 2017; Sonu et al., 2021), which take into account the effects of historical experiences. Superposing COVID-19 onto the Pair of ACEs highlights community restraints that affected the kinships, education, mental health, physical health, housing, and food security (Sonu et al., 2021) People of Color experienced at the height of the pandemic. Children who have been minoritized are reported to experience multiple ACEs exposures with greater frequency than those of dominant ethnicities, leading to lower SES, more mental health disorders, and increased physical health challenges (Hampton-Anderson et al., 2021).

Allyship and advocacy

Granek and Peleg-Sagy (2015) noted that African Americans' grief has gone largely unexplored as compared to their dominant cultural counterparts'. Thus, allyship and advocacy efforts begin with giving a voice to People of Color in the US and across the globe by increasing research with respect to past misfortunes that led to current mistrust. It is important to investigate grief and disenfranchised grief in this population because their suffering has been traumatic, complicated, and prolonged. Practitioners and researchers alike should challenge the oversight of research that does not take into account the fact that African Americans' grief and mourning do not resemble grief and mourning in Westernized culture. By doing so, clinical trust increases, which can decrease mental health outcome disparities.

Trust is earned in a manner that will acknowledge and address barriers to mental health. Some of those efforts can begin with understanding discrimination, racism, bias, stigma, lack of access to care, and lack of adequate mental health resources. Further, seeking to educate clinicians on the conditions that contribute to mental health barriers, seeking to understand how historical traumas contribute to current mental health diagnoses, and highlighting the need for increased awareness about how grief symptoms present within African American communities is paramount to building trust. Likewise, creating partnerships that aim to collaborate and to cultivate a system of healing begins with the community embracing individual healing as necessary. It is essential to acknowledge aspects of disenfranchisement before there is an effort to advocate for social change and to create a system of healing. Finally, facilitating relationships with religious organizations to create cohesive unity that increases access to mental health care and decreases mental health disparities is beneficial.

Ethical considerations

In a systematic literature review, Granek and Peleg-Sagy (2015) observed that most approaches to grief are based on commonality among Western traditions, validated outcomes for which were erroneously applied to African Americans.

The assumption that every population grieves in the same manner and for the same reasons overgeneralizes the emphasis on dominant cultural norms. The process of grief is specific to the individual and the individual's family, community, and culture. When helping African Americans through the grieving process, considerations for historically unique and culturally specific experiences, along with self-reflection and research to expand an understanding of historical influences (Sacks et al., 2021), should be undertaken. Conceptualizing the role of trust, which can support mental health-seeking behaviors and actions over time, must be explored. Gaining a deeper awareness of rooted responses and reactions that may seem normalized, by either the client or the clinician, will be helpful.

Ethical consideration should be given to multiple variables that may be contributing to disenfranchised grief, namely through biases, lived experiences, COVID-19, and the interconnectedness of how components of ACEs influence the client needing care and the clinician offering services. Evaluating the global interdependence of how mental health, physical health, and the intertwined connections highlights a need for support during the pandemic (Watson et al., 2020), because the experience of grief is not universal in its response or reaction (Granek & Peleg-Sagy, 2015).

Strategies and interventions

Taking into consideration the social determinants of mental health and ACEs is a beneficial start to the process of offering mental health services that focus on addressing disenfranchised grief, especially for People of Color. Current approaches to working with and understanding grief are heavily embedded within White frameworks but need to be refocused to incorporate the unique experiences of People of Color: ACEs; historical, systemic challenges; and the residual effects of COVID-19 (Hampton-Anderson et al., 2021).

Further, cultivating a clinical strategy that connects the individual and clinician to build a bridge of trust is warranted, because trust empowers the client to offer insight into their lived experience, which, in turn, offers vulnerability to their grief. Ortega-Williams et al. (2019) argued that to be effective, clinicians should connect historical experiences and generational traumas by using a colorism framework. The *colorism framework* takes into consideration and conceptualizes the interconnectedness of mass social trauma and how color has affected functioning (Ortega-Williams et al., 2019). By doing so, clinicians gain expanded insight into deeper individual and community experiences. Another approach is to consider ecological and multisystemic frameworks that focus attention on community adversities. Likewise, it is necessary to recognize how historical trauma affects current biosocial mental health and how those experiences are transmitted to descendants (Hampton-Anderson et al., 2021) to approach healing through a multidimensional lens (Henderson et al., 2021).

In summary of the literature, clinicians may identify treatment areas by reviewing the most common losses that contribute to disenfranchised grief with attention to individual experience:

- Loss of a loved one
- Loss of kinship
- Social injustices
- Microaggressions
- Loss of community connection
- Loss of financial security
- Divorce
- Incarcerations
- Health care disparities
- Minimal access to technology (infrastructure)
- Loss of educational opportunities
- Loss of innocence
- Loss of social safety

The list above is not exhaustive, and clinicians are encouraged to have deeper conversations with clients to explore individuals' specific experiences that contribute to disenfranchised grief (e.g., Albuquerque et al., 2021; Sneed et al., 2020; Sonu et al., 2021).

Clinicians should consider completing an in-depth intake that involves exploring general traumas and coping mechanisms. Obtaining this information will allow the clinician to have a multidimensional view of family history and highlight elements of the Pair of ACEs (Ellis & Dietz, 2017; Sonu et al., 2021) that may be contributing to symptomatology. Exploring coping behaviors may give insight into how disenfranchised grief is being masked as resilience, resulting in high stress levels and prolonged grief disorder (Boulware & Bui, 2016; Laurie & Neimeyer, 2008). It is important to also note that spiritual and social communion are often important activities within African American communities (Granek & Peleg-Sagy, 2017). Clinicians should seek to incorporate those elements into treatment plans when applicable.

Additionally, the complexities of African American disenfranchised grief experiences are not adequately addressed by any single model. Utilizing a flexible strategy and incorporating cultural humility, may prove to be the best approach, as there is still a tremendous amount of research needed to better understand African American disenfranchised grief.

Summary

Disenfranchised grief exists when grief is not acknowledged, accepted, or does not align with socially accepted norms (Doka, 2008). Similar to the Pair of Aces phenomenon, the long-term impact of disenfranchised grief is often unrecognized, as it may have been subtle, yet pervasive and detrimental across a lifespan. As conceptualized in this chapter, the COVID-19 pandemic added a new layer to the growing list of adverse experiences that may impact individuals, families, and communities. The pandemic compounded adversity and preexisting disparities in the African American population and added a fresh layer of disenfranchised grief to their mental health burden. To more fully conceptualize and effectively treat grief in this population, clinicians must consider historical and intergenerational trauma, preexisting disparities, the impacts of the ongoing pandemic, and their clients' intersecting identities. Moreover, clients' experiences, intertwined, potentially will create further disparities, marginalize, and compound existing grief and trauma, leading to reactions of avoidance, repression, and difficulty overcoming social barriers in an already overburdened community.

References

Albuquerque, S., Teixeira, A. M., & Rocha, J. C. (2021). COVID-19 and disenfranchised grief. *Frontiers in Psychiatry*, *12*, 638874. https://doi.org/10.3389/fpsyt.2021.638874

Bocknek, E. L., Sanderson, J., & Britner, P. A. (2009). Ambiguous loss and posttraumatic stress in school-age children of prisoners. *Journal of Child and Family Studies*, *18*(3), 323–333. https://doi.org/10.1007/s10826-008-9233-y

Boss, P. (2016). The context and process of theory development: The story of ambiguous loss. *Journal of Family Theory and Review*, 8(3), 269–286. https://doi.org/10.1111/jftr.12152

Boulware, D. L., & Bui, N. H. (2016). Bereaved African American adults: The role of social support, religious coping, and continuing bonds. *Journal of Loss and Trauma*, *21*(3), 192–202. https://doi.org/10.1080/15325024.2015.1057455

Bowers, M. E., & Yehuda, R. (2016). Intergenerational transmission of stress in humans. *Neuropsychopharmacology*, *41*(1), 232–244. https://doi.org/10.1038/npp.2015.247

Crewe, S. E., & Wilson, R. G. (2007). Kinship care: From family tradition to social policy in the African American community. *Journal of Health and Social Policy*, *22*(3–4), 1–7. https://doi.org/10.1300/j045v22n03_01

Doka, K. J. (2008). Disenfranchised grief in historical and cultural perspective. In M. S. Stroebe, R. O. Hansson, H. Schut, & W. Stroebe (Eds.), *Handbook of bereavement research and practice: Advances in theory and intervention* (pp. 223–240). American Psychological Association. https://doi.org/10.1037/14498-011

Ellis, W., & Dietz, W. (2017). A new framework for addressing adverse childhood and community experiences: The building community resilience (BCR) model. *Academic Pediatrics*, *17*, S86–S93. https://doi.org/10.1016/j.acap.2016.12.011

Gates, H. L., Jr. (2021). *The Black church: This is our story, this is our song.* Penguin Press.

Goldsmith, B., Morrison, R. S., Vanderwerker, L. C., & Prigerson, H. G. (2008). Elevated rates of prolonged grief disorder in African Americans. *Death Studies*, *32*(4), 352–365. https://doi.org/10.1080/07481180801929012

Granek, L., & Peleg-Sagy, T. (2015). Representations of African Americans in the grief and mourning literature from 1998 to 2014: A systematic review. *Death Studies*, *39*(10), 605–632. https://doi.org/10.1080/07481187.2015.1047059

Granek, L., & Peleg-Sagy, T. (2017). The use of pathological grief outcomes in bereavement studies on African Americans. *Transcultural Psychiatry*, *54*(3), 384–399. https://doi.org/10.1177/1363461517708121

Hampton-Anderson, J. N., Carter, S., Fani, N., Gillespie, C. F., Henry, T. L., Holmes, E., Lamis, D. A., LoParo, D., Maples-Keller, J. L., Powers, A., Sonu, S., & Kaslow, N. J. (2021). Adverse childhood experiences in African Americans: Framework, practice, and policy. *American Psychologist*, *76*(2), 314–325. https://doi.org/10.1037/amp0000767

Hart-Johnson, A. M. (2014). Symbolic imprisonment, grief, and coping theory: African American women with incarcerated mates. *Walden Dissertations and Doctoral Studies.* https://scholarworks.waldenu.edu/dissertations/146

Helsel, P. B. (2015). Witnessing the body's response to trauma: Resistance, ritual, and nervous system activation. *Pastoral Psychology*, *64*(5), 681–693. https://doi.org/10.1007/s11089-014-0628-y

Henderson, Z. R., Stephens, T. N., Ortega-Williams, A., & Walton, Q. L. (2021). Conceptualizing healing through the African American experience of historical trauma. *American Journal of Orthopsychiatry*, *91*(6), 763–775. https://doi.org/10.1037/ort0000578

Knight, C., & Gitterman, A. (2019). Ambiguous loss and its disenfranchisement: The need for social work intervention. *Families in Society*, *100*(2), 164–173. https://doi.org/10.1177/1044389418799937

Laurie, A., & Neimeyer, R. A. (2008). African Americans in bereavement: Grief as a function of ethnicity. *OMEGA – Journal of Death and Dying*, *57*(2), 173–193. https://doi.org/10.2190/OM.57.2.d

Lawson, E. (2014). Disenfranchised grief and social inequality: Bereaved African Canadians and oppositional narratives about the violent deaths of friends and family members. *Ethnic and Racial Studies*, *37*(11), 2092–2109. https://doi.org/10.1080/01419870.2013.800569

Matthews, J. J., Fonseca, F. D., & Varnado, J. C. D. (2021). Help-seeking behaviors of African Americans after a loss. *Journal of Multicultural Counseling and Development*, *49*(1), 60–71. https://doi.org/10.1002/jmcd.12206

Moore, S. E., Jones-Eversley, S. D., Tolliver, W. F., Wilson, B., & Harmon, D. K. (2022). Cultural responses to loss and grief among Black Americans: Theory and practice implications for clinicians. *Death Studies*, *46*(1), 189–199. https://doi.org/10.1080/07481187.2020.1725930

Ortega-Williams, A., Crutchfield, J., & Hall, J. C. (2019). The colorist-historical trauma framework: Implications for culturally responsive practice with African Americans. *Journal of Social Work*, *21*(3), 294–309. https://doi.org/10.1177/1468017319890083

Piazza-Bonin, E., Neimeyer, R. A., Burke, L. A., McDevitt-Murphy, M. E., & Young, A. (2015). Disenfranchised grief following African American homicide loss: An inductive case study. *OMEGA – Journal of Death and Dying*, *70*(4), 404–427. https://doi.org/10.1177/0030222815573727

Romanoff, B. D. (1998). Rituals and the grieving process. *Death Studies*, *22*(8), 697–711. https://doi.org/10.1080/074811898201227

Sacks, T. K., Savin, K., & Walton, Q. L. (2021). How ancestral trauma informs patients' health decision making. *AMA Journal of Ethics*, *23*(2), 183–188. https://doi.org/10.1001/amajethics.2021.183

Smithers, G. D. (2012). *Slave breeding: Sex, violence, and memory in African American history* [Kindle book]. University Press of Florida.

Sneed, R. S., Key, K., Bailey, S., & Johnson-Lawrence, V. (2020). Social and psychological consequences of the COVID-19 pandemic in African American communities: Lessons from Michigan. *Psychological Trauma: Theory, Research, Practice, and Policy*, *12*(5), 446–448. https://doi.org/10.1037/tra0000881

Sonu, S., Marvin, D., & Moore, C. (2021). The intersection and dynamics between COVID-19, health disparities, and adverse childhood experiences: Intersection/

dynamics between COVID-19, health disparities, and ACEs. *Journal of Child and Adolescent Trauma, 14*(4), 517–526. https://doi.org/10.1007/s40653-021-00363-z

Srivastav, A., Richard, C. L., McRell, A. S., & Strompolis, M. (2021). The unintended consequence of novel coronavirus (COVID-19) pandemic on racial inequities associated with adverse childhood experiences (ACEs): Findings from a population-based study. *Frontiers in Public Health, 9*, Article 701887. https://doi.org/10.3389/fpubh.2021.701887

Walsh, C. (2020, April 14). COVID-19 targets communities of color. *The Harvard Gazette.* https://news.harvard.edu/gazette/story/2020/04/health-care-disparities-in-the-age-of-coronavirus/

Watson, M., Bacigalupe, G., Daneshpour, M., Han, W.-J., & Parra-Cardona, R. (2020). COVID-19 interconnectedness: Health, inequity, the climate crisis, and collective trauma. *Family Process, 59*(3), 832–846. https://doi.org/10.1111/famp.12572

Questions for reflective practice

1. Throughout this chapter, the COVID-19 pandemic is described as an adverse childhood experience (ACE). What characteristics of the pandemic qualify COVID-19 as an ACE?
2. As part of treatment conceptualization and planning, what social and cultural factors must be considered at the intersection of ACEs, COVID-19, and disenfranchised grief for working with People of Color, in particular? Which phenomena are likely to amplify one's mental health burden at this intersection?
3. This chapter is framed around disenfranchised grief among African Americans. How might what you learned from this chapter inform your work and/or research with other People of Color?

Supplemental electronic resources

- Health Equity Initiative: www.healthequityinitiative.org/covid-19-and-health-equity-resources.html
- Racial Equity Tools: www.racialequitytools.org/
- IBrother, You're on My Mind: www.nimhd.nih.gov/programs/edu-training/byomm/toolkit.html
- Therapy for Black Girls: https://therapyforblackgirls.com/
- Therapy For Black Men: https://therapyforblackmen.org/

9
Disenfranchised grief for individuals with disabilities

Rochelle Ritzi and Marshall Lyles

Individuals with disabilities often experience a sense of grief and loss connected to their disability. When grief is not acknowledged or supported, it makes grieving challenging, if not impossible, for the individual with a disability to openly grieve in a healthy, productive, and meaningful way. This may include a persistent and perceived loss of what they wish life to be without a disability, or the persistent sense that they are perceived as different from those without a disability. Even the term *disability*, among those who have a disability, has been explored to determine respectfulness and sensitivity without ignoring the cultural, social, and relational life experiences of the person with a disability. For example, it is important to recognize the humanness of the person first, and then the disability. Yet, it is also important to recognize that many people with disabilities choose to integrate and claim their disability as part of their identity, such as the second author, using the words "disabled" and "chronically ill" as identifiers.

An alternative to person-first language is identity-first language (American Psychological Association [APA], 2020; Flink, 2021; Kenny, 2016). Identity-first language suggests that the word "disabled" is not a label to be avoided or shunned. Examples of an identity-first language are when people use the name of the disability as an identifier, such as "I am autistic," or "I am diabetic," or "Deaf person," or "blind person." When using person-first language, the person is emphasized rather than the person's disability; however, when using identity-first language, the disability becomes the focus, which *allows* the individual to claim the disability and choose their identity. According to APA's (2020) latest edition of the *Publication Manual*, it is acceptable to use person-first or identity-first language unless, or until, an author or researcher knows that a group prefers one option over the other, in which case, they should use the group's preferred approach (APA, 2020).

DOI: 10.4324/9781003292890-11

Allyship and advocacy for the disability community starts by asking individuals their preference and continues with education and awareness. This has been the first author's path, identifying as a Person of Colour and chronically ill when germane to the conversation. However, her allyship and advocacy integrated from lifelong connections to the Deaf community before she had embraced the term *chronic* regarding her life experience. Regardless of how we, the authors, arrived on our paths, our hope is that accommodation in the greater world will one day evolve to be naturally inclusive of all abilities and impairments, as well as how people desire to identify. Sadly, this is not currently the state of the existing world; therefore, the language around ability and disability must be navigated.

To maintain a balance of consistency and a respectful and sensitive tone throughout this chapter, at times we will utilize person-first language to emphasize that individuals with disabilities are people first. At times, we will utilize identity-first language such as "disability" and "disabled" to destigmatize the words. Ultimately, we hope readers will gain an integrated understanding that language identity in the disability community is important and will vary from individual to individual. Alternating between person-first and identify-first language also promotes an environment where language can move toward more inclusivity without denying members of the disabled community a collective identity when desired.

Social aspects of disenfranchised grief

When considering how the disabled community lives within the greater social construct of a non-disabled world, discussing "disability" becomes quickly complicated because no universal agreement exists on how to identify language and view this multifaceted concept (Waldschmidt, 2018). The ability/disability framework forces a binary (De Schauwer et al., 2021) that shifts those with societally perceived impairments into a marginalized "othered" position; yet, due to ableist systems, people with disabilities deserve acknowledgment and accommodation. Doka (1999) coined the term *disenfranchised grief* to name the phenomenon many have painfully experienced when not feeling free to openly grieve, acknowledging that people experience it for a multitude of societally constructed reasons. A denied and, therefore, unexpressed grief will not receive the social acknowledgment and care required and deserved for healing (Doka, 2008). Unfortunately, this denied and unexpressed grief increases the aloneness and pain carried by the isolated griever, even when they are part of a social environment.

It is not uncommon for individuals with disabilities to find themselves in an array of social situations where their grief is minimized or ignored. Those without disabilities are often unaware of using inclusive language or forward thinking regarding creating an environment that does not perpetuate disen-franchised grief (Haller & Preston, 2017). For example, a six-year-old child with type 1 diabetes is unable to "normally" participate in eating treats at a sleepover or a piece of cake at a birthday party without receiving increased attention from a caregiver. This increased attention often leaves children feeling *different* than their peers during a time when most children are trying to fit in. Creating an inclusive environment could include educating other parents and children of the child's dietary and medical needs; however, a child may also not want any additional attention and therefore respecting the child's preference may be more inclusive. In either event, the child has become different than her peers, leading to a sense of grief connected to her social environment.

Infertility or chronic illness that has social implications are other issues that fall under the umbrella of disability (Sternke & Abrahamson, 2015), and can lead to disenfranchised grief (McBain & Reeves, 2019). For example, a young person who is unable to become pregnant and attends a baby shower for their sibling or best friend may feel socially obligated to attend the baby shower even while they grieve their own loss regarding not having biological children. To perpetuate this grief, they may be told by other party attendees, "At least it's fun trying," or "Don't worry, you'll be next," or "Kids are so expensive – enjoy it." Comments such as these are painful and create an exclusive social environment where people who are unable to conceive or carry a baby to live birth do not feel they belong. If the attendee appeared sad during the baby shower, they might be viewed as selfish or jealous because the social obligation to be happy for others often does not allow for that same situation to accept or express the grief connected to it.

A further example could be a new father with multiple sclerosis who is reminded each time he holds his infant child that soon he will be unable to pick her up because she will weigh more than his capability to lift. This father celebrates the birth of his child while also mourning the inevitable progres-sion of his disability. Societal pressures of providing for his child and being a doting hands-on father may perpetuate his grief. Comments from others, such as, "At least you can hold her now," or "At least you were able to be a dad" may leave this new father feeling invalidated, deepening his grief feelings. It is also possible that some people overly sensationalize his being a father by applaud-ing him for performing common parenting tasks. In the disability community, this is called *inspiration porn* and it also perpetuates grief (Haller & Preston, 2017). In each of these scenarios, well-meaning people may not recognize that societal pressures of being "normal" can lead to disenfranchised grief.

Cultural aspects of disenfranchised grief

People in the disability community have forged a unique culture due to the shared common history of oppression and a bond of resilience (Waldschmidt, 2018). Those in the disability culture create literature, music, and other forms of art that express these shared lived experiences where people can be proud of who they are. Regardless of the disability, people in the disability community have encountered some level of oppression related to their disability, which connects them to a unique culture that provides validation and support.

It is important to acknowledge the multiple layers of culture in individuals with disabilities; these various layers play a role in how these individuals not only identify but also lead to additional levels of marginalization. The crossover between disability and disenfranchised grief intensifies when the person with the disability also carries other traditionally marginalized identities related to gender, race, and socioeconomic factors (Artiles, 2013; Crenshaw, 1989). There are many other people groups who have a history of societal exclusion, which increases in complexity when disability is introduced into their lived experience.

Another example is connected to infertility. Consider a transracial adoption where a child is adopted from an orphanage in a country that is different from their adoptive parents' home country. Well-meaning friends and family might comment on how lucky the child is for being adopted by such a loving family and brought to the US, while the child grieves the loss of the culture and familiar things left behind. The friends' words and the child's experience may exacerbate disenfranchised grief connected to the parents' infertility. Women and men facing infertility often feel an array of emotions, such as feeling rejected by their body or feeling disconnected from their social environments (Peterson et al., 2006), which often further complicates grief when their adopted child struggles to attach. The layers of grief may stem from shame from moments of feeling rejected by their child, or anger at the child's behavior, or thoughts of regret due to the intense parenting difficulties that are associated with raising a child with attachment problems.

Consider the Deaf community. For most in the Deaf community, not being able to hear is viewed as one type of human experience rather than a disability

(Duncan & O'Neill, 2020; Leigh et al., 2020). Deaf culture encompasses behaviors, values, and history among a community that uses sign language to communicate. It is common for those in the Deaf community to have pride in their identity as a Deaf individual and being Deaf is not viewed as something that needs to be fixed (Duncan & O'Neill, 2020). Individuals in the Deaf community, however, still desire and need access to accommodations to live within the greater hearing culture. Also, those in the Deaf community may still grieve the loss of not fitting into a larger community because the greater society considers Deaf individuals as different, treating them as less than capable of someone who is hearing.

Relational aspects of disenfranchised grief

Living with disability can usher in various losses of aspects of self (Charmaz, 1983), including disabled persons' relationships. For example, when adjusting to different relational roles, diminishing abilities, shifting autonomy, and other such dynamics, a person with disability may need to grieve the lived pain that directly results from their condition, but they also may need to mourn the "suffering . . . caused by an ableist environment" (Crosby, 2019, p. 624). Grief from identity loss and relational shifts tend to be poorly accepted and often misunderstood. Disabled people deserve to be empowered to name when and how they need to grieve and when they need to push back against an imposed agenda of what they should perceive as loss by those with whom they are in relationship or by society. People whose disabilities span a range of categories often already experience intense aloneness and isolation from simply carrying the "impairment" or "difference" that affects various relationship aspects. This includes humans facing mental illness (Andersson et al., 2015), learning disability (Musetti et al., 2019), intellectual disability (McVilly et al., 2006), autism spectrum disorder (Kasari & Sterling, 2013), and physical disability (Rokach at al., 2006).

Consider the example of the father with multiple sclerosis discussed earlier. Perhaps he married before any significant progression of the disease and is now grieving and experiencing the loss of his independence. His partner may also grieve his loss of independence due to the additional parenting roles required of the parent without disability. This could contribute to grief, frustration, and discord between the partners regarding parenting roles falling more on one parent than the other. Consider if the father also identifies as a Person of Colour and lives in an area of the US or another place in the world where systematic racism has created barriers to receiving quality medical care, thereby allowing faster disease progression and demonstrating an additional layer to stressors that affect and strain the relationship. This is a sampling of the complexities of disability and the layers of grief experienced by the disabled individual within their relationships; the examples are endless.

Relationships provide practical support, emotional support, support with decision-making, and opportunities to widen and strengthen existing support networks. Whether considering relationships within one's family of origin, in school or at work, or with friends and loved ones, those with disabilities may also face unique challenges. Children and adolescents with learning differences have healthier relationship success when they have experienced a psychosocial intervention that increased social support from teachers, parents, and peers (Musetti et al., 2019). Significant relationships can be rare or intermittent for many people with intellectual disability (McVilly et al., 2006). Women who experienced infertility grief expressed how their grief was disenfranchised by people in their lives (McBain & Reeves, 2019). Traumatic stress decreases in individuals with chronic illness when they have meaningful and healthy social support (Zeligman et al., 2018).

Cumulative impacts of disenfranchised grief across the lifespan

When considering the effects of disenfranchised grief on individuals with disabilities, or the people who care for them, it is important to consider how chronic feelings of silenced grief and invalidation can manifest as cumulative stress (Artiles, 2013; Castrillón, 2020). Not being able to conceive or carry a baby to live birth can also lead to cumulative stress (McBain & Reeves, 2019). Fear of the inevitable death of a chronically ill or disabled child also leads to cumulative stress (Todd, 2008). The impact of grief in parents who care for adult children with disabilities is also shown as cumulative stress (Fernández-Ávalos et al., 2020). Frequent hospital and other doctor visits are connected to disenfranchised grief and cumulative trauma and stress in cancer patients (Gabbay, 2021). Cumulative impact of disenfranchised grief and stress manifests in many ways, including resulting in traumatic stress.

Historically, researchers have published curiously little crossover between cumulative traumatic stress and disability exploration through the lifespan (Berger, 2004), likely a representation of the previously described disenfranchisement. However, with an overall increase in focus on posttraumatic stress disorder (PTSD) in mental health research, there has been more recent attention on the comorbidity of various disabilities and trauma symptoms (Antunes et al., 2018). This trend will likely intensify following the worldwide reckoning with COVID-19 (Lund et al., 2020).

Assessing for trauma symptoms in certain disabled/neurodiverse populations, such as those on the autism spectrum or with an intellectual disability, presents complications for under-trained clinicians (Kildahl et al., 2020). However, researchers indicate a strong need for medical and mental health providers to have adequate trauma assessment skills for this population, because both patients and their loved ones carry increased risk of posttraumatic stress (Wintermann et al., 2019). This is especially true among children processing losses associated with illness and disability, for whom posttraumatic stress only strengthens as the duration and intensity of the struggles persist (Pinquart, 2020).

The interaction between trauma and disability moves in more than one direction. In addition to those with disabilities having internal and societal struggles that set up traumatic internalization, those with PTSD resulting from a variety of non-health stressors may be at higher risk of developing other health conditions, causing potential accumulation of additional disabilities (Renna et al., 2018). Such compounded struggles further complicate the grief experience for these survivors.

Combatting disability-related trauma symptoms cannot rest only on the shoulders of those with disabilities. Disability is a societally created struggle and society needs to be part of the remedy. This occurs when others, including healing professionals, acknowledge and welcome the appropriate grief responses needed in the disabled community. Simultaneously, others cannot impose a grief agenda on people with disabilities who do not experience their differences as losses; this misattunement actually can further isolation and disenfranchisement. When proper social support remains available for those with illnesses and disabilities to make meaning around their own defined areas of experienced grief, significant posttraumatic growth can occur (Zeligman et al., 2018).

Allyship and advocacy

An ally is an individual who supports the cause of a marginalized group, such as disabled people, who is willing to use their privilege to learn from that group and strengthen the call for their cause. It is important to remember that people with disabilities may also belong to other marginalized groups, such as People of Color, people in the LGBTQIA+ community, people with low income, and other groups that have been marginalized. Whether readers identify as a disabled person, a person who cares for an individual with a disability, or someone who wants to advocate for people with disabilities or any other marginalized group, support is needed to create a society that is inclusive. In the case of those with a disability, an inclusive society includes a society that is educated about the disability community and provides easy access to accommodations.

An important step toward being an effective ally and advocate is to become educated about the basics of disability. This includes learning about types of disability and the laws and policies regarding disability. Structural-level changes must start with becoming aware of the existing laws to become aware of people and businesses who do not adhere to the laws, but also to know how existing laws are either inadequate or not easily accessible. Increasing disability awareness also means allies and advocates should learn about ableism, implicit biases, and microaggressions.

Language around disability continues to evolve and allies should keep themselves updated on language use and integrating disability etiquette. It is common to feel anxious about saying "the wrong thing," but anxiety should not keep people without disability from talking with and about disabled individuals. People should also avoid engaging in inspiration porn by over sensationalizing someone with a disability (Haller & Preston, 2017) or applauding individuals with disabilities for performing common tasks. As a general rule, ask individuals the language they prefer to use.

Inviting individuals with disabilities to be a part of the discussion is also an important trait of an ally and advocate. An important step in maintaining cultural humility regarding disability is to engage in conversations with people who have various types of disability to learn about their lived experiences. Using this knowledge base to become an active ally through sharing language etiquette, creating a space with accommodations, advocating in places of work or shopping, and sharing the experiences of disabled people within their communities is important in becoming an ally. For more insight and strategies on being an ally and advocate, consider the reflective questions and supplemental resources at the end of the chapter to learn more.

Ethical considerations

Despite the prevalence of disability in the US and globally, numerous ethical issues arise from interacting with individuals with disabilities (Johnson,

2016). The complexity of these ethical issues builds when one considers the overarching concept of disenfranchised grief in interaction. However, there are key elements to consider that can help people without disabilities maintain an ethical approach when interacting with the disability community. First and foremost, respecting the dignity, autonomy, equality, and diversity of every member of the disability community is vital. People with disabilities are people first. Treating disabled individuals with dignity, giving them autonomy and equality, and honoring their multiple and intersecting identities are prerequisites for holding space for an individual with a disability to grieve.

Gaining knowledge and increasing cultural humility of the disability community can also aid in increasing awareness on how to honor and hold space for those in the disability community to grieve. Without increasing a knowledge base of the types of grief unique to those with disabilities, people may unknowingly perpetuate disenfranchisement of grief, even when attempting to be an ally or advocate. Lastly, allies and advocates need to engage in self-reflection regarding personal biases and conflicts about individuals with disabilities. Without exploring and challenging core beliefs about those in the disability community, individuals who are not disabled will likely not be open to the change needed to create an inclusive environment, regardless of ability (Cornish & Monson, 2018).

Strategies and interventions

Strategies and interventions regarding increasing awareness about disenfranchised grief within the disability community can help decrease disenfranchised grief (Mortell, 2015). There are a host of etiquette tips; however, following a few general guidelines can be helpful in decreasing chances that a disabled person will be treated in a way that perpetuates disenfranchised grief. First, gain a sensitive and ethical understanding on how to interact with people with disabilities. Focus on the person first, and *if* it is germane to the conversation, ask how the individual wants to be identified. Always ask before giving assistance. For example, "Can I get the door for you?" or "Would you like help carrying that?" Avoid over sensationalizing an individual for common behaviors, such as praising the father with multiple sclerosis discussed earlier for typical parenting activities like playing with his child. Saying things similar to "He is so courageous" can lead to feelings of disenfranchised grief (Haller & Preston, 2017).

As a general rule, think before speaking. It is not uncommon for people without a disability to stumble over their words when trying to say the *right* thing. If someone says something that they regret, they should apologize. Avoid being patronizing. An adult in a wheelchair is a person. Speak to them as you would any other adult. Lastly, when interacting with someone with a disability who has an aid, an interpreter, or a companion, people should direct their conversation to the person they are speaking to. For example, if someone is speaking to a Deaf individual, they should look at the Deaf person and speak how they would speak to a hearing individual, not the interpreter. Actively gaining education and awareness on how to interact with the disabled community and subgroups in the community is an important step in decreasing the level of disenfranchised grief in this community. See the Supplemental Electronic Resources at the end of this chapter for more extensive lists of tips.

Only some of the grief explored thus far has been death-related grief, and it is important to explore additional detailed strategies directly related to death for supporting the disability community. To decrease disenfranchised grief is to recognize that people with disabilities need to process grief in similar ways as people without disabilities. Ensure that people in the disabled community are involved in planning and taking part in grieving rituals related to death, such as the visitation and funeral. Sometimes people withhold information from someone in the disabled community because there is a belief that the person has limited understanding of the process. However, it is more important to gain an understanding of *how* to deliver the information than debating *whether or not* the information should be delivered. Because someone with a disability may be at a higher risk for disenfranchised grief (Sapey, 2004), a death may complicate the grieving process. Professional counseling from a mental health provider familiar with and trained in working with individuals with disabilities should be considered for any intervention.

Summary

Those with disabilities experience interconnected levels of grief that are both hidden and seen, acknowledged and ignored, and this grief is typically overlapping and interdependent with systems that disadvantage and discriminate. When considering intersectionality (Crenshaw, 1989; see Chapter 2), individuals with diverse backgrounds, such as race, class, and gender, may experience more complex grief and loss that might initially be invisible to others. These various levels of disenfranchised grief that disabled individuals experience deserve recognition, exploration, validation, understanding, and empathy. Because the disabled community is embedded within the greater social construct of a non-disabled world, it is important to increase awareness and explore how people with disabilities navigate their lived experiences as "others" in the hope that being "othered" will no longer be a barrier socially, culturally, and relationally. Decreasing levels of cumulative effects of disen-franchised grief among people with disability depends on allies and advocates in the larger non-disabled community creating an inclusive environment for people with all levels of ability.

References

American Psychological Association. (2020). *Publication manual of the American Psychological Association* (7th ed.). Author. https://doi.org/10.1037/0000165-000

Andersson, G., Denhov, A., Bülow, P., & Topor, A. (2015). Aloneness and loneliness – persons with severe mental illness and experiences of being alone. *Scandinavian Journal of Disability Research, 17*(4), 353–365. https://doi.org/10.1080/15017419.2014.941927

Antunes, A., Frasquilho, D., Azeredo-Lopes, S., Neto, D., Silva, M., Cardoso, G., & Caldas-de-Almeida, J. M. (2018). Disability and common mental disorders: Results from the World Mental Health Survey Initiative Portugal. *European Psychiatry, 49*, 56–61. https://doi.org/10.1016/j.eurpsy.2017.12.004

Artiles, A. J. (2013). Untangling the racialization of disabilities: An intersectionality critique across disability models. *Du Bois Review: Social Science Research on Race, 10*(2), 329–347. https://doi.org/10.1017/S1742058X13000271

Berger, J. (2004). Trauma without disability, disability without trauma: A disciplinary divide. *JAC, 24*(3), 563–582.

Castrillón, N. (2020). The art and virtue of the care of a sick and disabled child. *Early Child Development and Care, 190*(14), 2171–2180. https://doi.org/10.1080/03004430.2018.1563893

Charmaz, K. (1983). Loss of self: A fundamental form of suffering in the chronically ill. *Sociology of Health and Illness, 5*(2), 168–195. https://doi.org/10.1111/1467-9566.ep10491512

Cornish, J. A. E., & Monson, S. P. (2018). Ethical issues in working with individuals with disability. In M. M. Leach & E. R. Welfel (Eds.), *The Cambridge handbook of applied psychological ethics* (pp. 285–301). Cambridge University Press.

Crenshaw, K. (1989). Demarginalizing the intersection of race and sex: A Black feminist critique of antidiscrimination doctrine. *University of Chicago Legal Forum, 1989*, 139–168. https://chicagounbound.uchicago.edu/cgi/viewcontent.cgi?article=1052&context=uclf

Crosby, C. (2019). Faithful to the contemplation of bones: Disability and irremediable grief. *South Atlantic Quarterly, 118*(3), 615–641. https://doi.org/10.1215/00382876-7616187

De Schauwer, E., Daelman, S., Vandenbussche, H., Sergeant, S., Van de Putte, I., & Davies, B. (2021). Desiring and critiquing humanity/ability/personhood: Disrupting the ability/disability binary. *Disability and Society, 36*(2), 286–305. https://doi. org/10.1080/09687599.2020.1735306

Doka, K. J. (1999). Disenfranchised grief. *Bereavement Care, 18*(3), 37–39. https:// doi.org/10.1080/02682629908657467

Doka, K. J. (2008). Disenfranchised grief in historical and cultural perspective. In M. S. Stroebe, R. O. Hansson, H. Schut, & W. Stroebe (Eds.), *Handbook of bereavement research and practice: Advances in theory and intervention* (pp. 223–240). American Psychological Association. https://doi.org/10.1037/14498-011

Duncan, J., & O'Neill, O. (2020). Person-first, identity-first and the language of deafness. *Deafness and Education International, 22*(1), 1–2. https://doi.org/10.1080/14 643154.2020.1720204

Fernández-Ávalos M. I., Pérez-Marfil, M. N., Ferrer-Cascales, R., Cruz-Quintana, F., & Fernández-Alcántara, M. (2020). Feeling of grief and loss in parental caregivers of adults diagnosed with intellectual disability. *Journal of Applied Research in Intellectual Disabilities, 34*(3), 712–723. https://doi.org/10.1111/jar.12842

Flink, P. (2021). Person-first & identity-first language: Supporting students with disabilities on campus. *Community College Journal of Research and Practice, 45*(2), 79–85. https://doi.org/10.1080/10668926.2019.1640147

Gabbay, G. (2021). A nonheroic cancer narrative: Body deterioration, grief, disenfranchised grief, and growth. *OMEGA – Journal of Death and Dying, 83*(2), 287–309. https://doi.org/10.1177/0030222819852836

Haller, B., & Preston, J. (2017). Confirming normalcy: "Inspiration porn" and the construction of the disabled subject? In K. Ellis & M. Kent (Eds.), *Disability and social media, global perspectives* (pp. 41–54). Routledge.

Johnson, E. (2016). Disability, medicine, and ethics. *AMA Journal of Ethics, 18*(4), 355–358. https://doi.org/jb5s

Kasari, C., & Sterling, L. (2013). Loneliness and social isolation in children with autism spectrum disorders. In R. J. Coplan & J. C. Bowker (Eds.), *The handbook of solitude: Psychological perspectives on social isolation, social withdrawal, and being alone* (pp. 409–426). Wiley.

Kenny, L., Hattersley C., Molins, B., Buckley, C., Povey, C., & Pellicano, E. (2016). Which terms should be used to describe autism? Perspectives from the UK autism community. *Autism. 20*(4), 442–462. https://doi.org/10.1177/1362361315588200

Kildahl, A. N., Helverschou, S. B., Bakken, T. L., & Oddli, H. W. (2020). "If we do not look for it, we do not see it": Clinicians' experiences and understanding of identifying post-traumatic stress disorder in adults with autism and intellectual disability. *Journal of Applied Research in Intellectual Disabilities, 33*(5), 1119–1132. https://doi.org/10.1111/jar.12734

Leigh, I. W., Andrews, J. F., Harris, R. L., & Gonzalas Avila, T. (2020). *Deaf culture: Exploring Deaf communities in the United States* (2nd ed.). Plural.

Lund, E. M., Forber-Pratt, A. J., Wilson, C., & Mona, L. R. (2020). The COVID-19 pandemic, stress, and trauma in the disability community: A call to action. *Rehabilitation Psychology, 65*(4), 313–322. https://doi.org/10.1037/rep0000368

McBain, T. D, & Reeves, P. (2019). Women's experience of infertility and disenfranchised grief. *The Family Journal: Counseling and Therapy for Couples and Families, 27*(2), 156–166. https://doi.org/10.1177%2F1066480719833418

McVilly, K. R., Stancliffe, R. J., Parmenter, T. R., & Burton-Smith, R. M. (2006). "I get by with a little help from my friends": Adults with intellectual disability discuss loneliness. *Journal of Applied Research in Intellectual Disabilities, 19*(2), 191–203. https://doi.org/10.1111/j.1468-3148.2005.00261.x

Mortell, S. (2015). Assisting clients with disenfranchised grief: The role of a mental health nurse. *Journal of Psychosocial Nursing and Mental Health Services, 53*, 52–57. https://doi.org/10.3928/02793695-20150319-05

Musetti, A., Eboli, G., Cavallini, F., & Corsano, P. (2019). Social relationships, self-esteem, and loneliness in adolescents with learning disabilities. *Clinical Neuropsychiatry, 16*(4), 133–140.

Peterson, B. D., Newton, C. R., Rosen, K. H., & Schulman, R. S. (2006). Coping processes of couples experiencing infertility. *Family Relations, Interdisciplinary Journal of Applied Family Studies, 55*, 227–239. https://doi.org/10.1111/j.1741-3729.2006.00372.x

Pinquart, M. (2020). Posttraumatic stress symptoms and disorders in children and adolescents with chronic physical illnesses: A meta-analysis. *Journal of Child and Adolescent Trauma, 13*(1), 1–10. https://doi.org/10.1007/s40653-018-0222-z

Renna, M. E., O'Toole, M. S., Spaeth, P. E., Lekander, M., & Mennin, D. S. (2018). The association between anxiety, traumatic stress, and obsessive – compulsive disorders and chronic inflammation: A systematic review and meta-analysis. *Depression and Anxiety, 35*(11), 1081–1094. https://doi.org/10.1002/da.22790

Rokach, A., Lechcier-Kimel, R., & Safarov, A. (2006). Loneliness of people with physical disabilities. *Social Behavior and Personality: An International Journal, 34*(6), 681–700. https://doi.org/10.2224/sbp.2006.34.6.681

Sapey, B. (2004). Impairment, disability, and loss: Reassessing the rejection of loss. *Illness, Crisis and Loss, 12*(1), 90–101. https://doi.org/10.1177%2F1054137303259738

Sternke, E. A., & Abrahamson, K. (2015). Perceptions of women with infertility on stigma and disability. *Sexuality and Disability, 33*(1), 3–17. https://doi.org/10.1007/s11195-014-9348-6

Todd, S. (2008). Silenced grief: Living with the death of a child with intellectual disabilities. *Journal of Intellectual Disability Research, 51*(8), 637–648. https://doi.org/10.1111/j.1365-2788.2007.00949.x

Waldschmidt, A. (2018). Disability – culture – society: Strengths and weaknesses of a cultural model of dis/ability. *ALTER – European Journal of Disability Research, 12*(2), 65–78. https://doi.org/10.1016/j.alter.2018.04.003

Wintermann, G. B., Petrowski, K., Weidner, K., Strauß, B., & Rosendahl, J. (2019). Impact of post-traumatic stress symptoms on the health-related quality of life in a cohort study with chronically critically ill patients and their partners: Age matters. *Critical Care, 23*(1), 1–10. https://doi.org/10.1186/s13054-019-2321-0

Zeligman, M., Varney, M., Grad, R. I., & Huffstead, M. (2018). Posttraumatic growth in individuals with chronic illness: The role of social support and meaning making. *Journal of Counseling and Development, 96*(1), 53–63. https://doi.org/10.1002/jcad.12177

Questions for reflective practice

1. What barriers still exist for people with disabilities?

    a. What physical, emotional, or mental barriers do I observe in my workplace or school?

    b. Have I challenged myself to read about ableism?

2. What was I taught about disabled people?

    a. How was disability discussed (or not discussed) in my family of origin?

    b. What messages have I been given from the world of media and entertainment?

    c. Where (and how) have I interacted with disabled people throughout my life?

3. What are my implicit biases regarding the disabled community? For example, what thoughts occur when I encounter someone who:

    a. Uses a wheelchair?

    b. Has a hearing or vision impairment?

    c. Has autism?

4. How can I become an ally and advocate in my local community?

    a. How, when, and where can I acknowledge and respect individual experiences and abilities?

    b. How can I leverage my privilege to advocate for the disabled community?

Supplemental electronic resources

- Communicating with and about People with Disabilities: www.cdc.gov/ncbddd/disabilityandhealth/materials/factsheets/fs-communicating-with-people.html
- Disability Impacts All of Us: www.cdc.gov/ncbddd/disabilityandhealth/infographic-disability-impacts-all.html#:~:text=61%20million%20adults%20in%20the,is%20highest%20in%20the%20South
- Examples of Disability Microaggressions in Everyday Life: www.vancouver.wsu.edu/equity-diversity/examples-disability-microaggressions-everyday-life#:~:text=Occurs%20when%20any%20aspect%20of,is%20normal%20or%20like%20mine
- How to be an Ally of the Disability Community: www.paraquad.org/blog/how-to-be-an-ally-of-the-disability-community/#:~:text=In%20summary%2C%20an%20ally%20is,group%20and%20amplify%20their%20cause
- National Network: Information, Guidance, and Training on the Americans with Disabilities Act: https://adata.org/learn-about-ada
- Stella Young. *I'm not your inspiration, thank you very much:* www.youtube.com/watch?v=8K9Gg164Bsw

10

The aftermath of sexual violence

Consequent grief and loss

Maria Haiyasoso

Renowned author, Isabel Allende (2001), aptly described in *Portrait in Sepia* that to honor truth, one must examine what exists versus creating a picture of what one hopes to see: "If what you want is the effect of painting, then paint, Aurora. If what you want is truth, learn to use your camera" (p. 12). The same holds true for those supporting survivors of sexual violence. Treatment providers for survivors of sexual violence focus on symptom reduction and other common effects (e.g., post-traumatic stress, anxiety, and depression), as they should. Yet, truth (to borrow from Allende) requires acknowledging the reality that grief often accompanies survivors' symptomatology associated with sexual violence.

The terminology used within this chapter warrants discussion. Sexual violence remains a term often used synonymously to describe sexual assault, sexual abuse, rape, and sexual misconduct. Definitions of sexual violence vary from jurisdiction to jurisdiction, which creates problems pertaining to eligibility for services and within the justice system. For example, if a state's sexual assault law excludes elements of intoxication and unconsciousness from their criminal statute, someone might not meet the criteria for charges of rape of a nonconscious person in that state, though they would be charged for the same crime in another state. For the purposes of this chapter, the author defines sexual violence as any form of coerced, forced attempts, or completed non-consensual sexual act. Common terms for individuals who experience sexual violence include *victim* and *survivor*. *Victim* routinely describes someone with recent experiences of sexual violence, or someone harmed by a crime or in the criminal justice system, and *survivor* references those further along in their recovery from the violence who navigate the short-term or long-term effects of sexual violence (Rape, Abuse and Incest National Network [RAINN], 2022). Recognizing that people may or may not identify with either of these terms or may identify with both terms, the author uses the term *survivor* in this chapter.

DOI: 10.4324/9781003292890-12

Social stigmas and myths around sexual violence include the notion that women largely lie about sexual violence, rape equals merely sex, and strangers predominately perpetrate sexual violence rather than partners, ex-partners, and acquaintances (Ullman, 2010). As a result of victim-blaming attitudes and persisting beliefs, survivors of sexual violence often do not report the violence. Survivors often contend with negative effects on their mental, emotional, and physical wellbeing, perhaps in isolation. Common effects include posttraumatic stress, depression, anxiety, disordered eating, and substance misuse (Dworkin et al., 2017).

Amidst the non-exhaustive list of presenting concerns above, a survivor exists and operates within several contexts. Thus, these concerns reach beyond the individual and bleed into the survivor's relationships and functioning within relational and interpersonal systems (e.g., family, work, school, and community). Many mental health professionals increasingly train and practice with clients' cultural contexts and cultural identities in mind (Ratts et al., 2016). Yet, more work needs to be done, considering marginalized communities remain most susceptible to sexual violence (Breidling et al., 2014; Smith et al., 2017) and to inequitable treatment in various settings. Survivors with identities that have been marginalized essentially experience revictimization, again and again, compounding their experiences of disenfranchised grief.

In this chapter, the author offers an examination of a commonly overlooked aspect of survivors' experiences – *disenfranchised grief*, or the lack of recognition for a loss due to a perceived lack of validity or social stigma (Doka, 1989). Survivors of sexual violence often contend with multiple losses, each carrying its own significant impact beyond the effects of being subjected to violent acts. Sexual violence leads to losses involving a diminished sense of safety, security, and stability at individual and systemic levels. Survivors often know their perpetrators, meaning such violence can lead to the loss of relationships as well. If helping professionals and society at large invalidate or do not acknowledge the survivors' grief of these losses, disenfranchised grief ensues. For survivors from groups that are commonly marginalized, this lack of recognition compounds the oppression they already experience.

In the next sections, the author overviews social, cultural, and relational elements of disenfranchised grief resulting from sexual violence. A step toward understanding how survivors' experiences of loss turn into disenfranchised grief requires an understanding of social, cultural, and relational contributions to these experiences. Though these domains are intricately linked, *social* refers to the influence of the broader societal context, *cultural* refers to the roles of culture and cultural identities, and *relational* refers to the influence of interpersonal interactions and relationships. The following sections contain a description of the lifelong impact of disenfranchised grief for survivors of sexual violence, a discussion of advocacy efforts to mitigate disenfranchised grief, considerations for the ethical practice among clinicians, and suggestions for interventions that address loss from a relational-cultural lens.

Social aspects of disenfranchised grief

Many in society automatically assume grief connects only to death, failing to recognize that grief transpires with non-death-related losses as well. Indeed, much non-death-related loss occurs when sexual violence occurs (Bordere, 2017). Survivors lose a sense of safety in the environment, in their physical bodies, and in their daily activities. The ease experienced in their daily functioning prior to sexual violence becomes lost and replaced with fear and uncertainty. If not acknowledged, the losses associated with sexual violence can lead to disenfranchised grief (Bordere, 2017).

To note the gravity of the harm caused by disenfranchised grief, one must understand the prevalence of sexual violence and the societal contribution to perpetuating this harm. Childhood sexual abuse (CSA) impacts one in 10 children before 18 years of age (Townsend & Rheingold, 2013), and in the US, one in five adult women and one in 14 adult men reportedly experience sexual violence in their lifetimes (Smith et al., 2018). The majority of cases involve women survivors, though sexual violence occurs across gender identification.

From their national survey data collected from all 50 states and the District of Columbia from 2010 to 2012, Smith and colleagues (2017) reported that a majority of women survivors (81%) of completed or attempted rape first experienced such victimization prior to 25 years of age, and 43% experienced sexual violence prior to age 18. For 31% of women survivors, their first victimization occurred between 11 and 17 years of age, and 13% experienced sexual violence for the first time at or before 10 years of age. Most men survivors (71%) of completed or attempted rape first experienced these violations prior to 25 years of age, and 51% of men survivors first experienced such victimization prior to age 18. For 25% of men survivors, their first victimization occurred between 11 and 17 years of age, and 26% of men survivors experienced sexual violence for the first time at or before 10 years of age (Smith et al., 2017). In another survey study, 12% of transgender participants reported histories of sexual violence in K-12 educational settings (Grant et al., 2011). Many respondents (15%) reported being sexually assaulted in prisons, 3% reported sexually assaults in higher education institutions, and 6% of respondents reported being sexually assaulted in their workplace, with undocumented noncitizens reporting rates of sexual assault in their places of employment at 19%, over three times the rate of the overall sample (Grant et al., 2011). Reported rates of sexual violence clearly reveal pervasive concerns across genders, ages, and settings.

Discourses in literature, media, and society commonly attribute blame to survivors of sexual violence. Prevailing social stigmas of women (e.g., a person possesses the capability to prevent an assault or they asked for it; Ullman, 2010) and men (e.g., men cannot experience sexual assault; only weak men experience sexual violence; Ullman, 2010), combined with the reported lack of disclosure from one in four transgender people who fear seeking help in incidents of violence (Human Rights Campaign & Trans People of Color Coalition, 2017) exacerbate silence about sexual violence as well as disenfranchised grief in survivors. The victim-blaming nature of sexual violence, stigma, and patterns of oppression nature inhibits disclosure and help-seeking, which leaves little room for any attention to survivors' grief.

For those who disclose, survivors often receive harmful messages. Many survivors receive negative social reactions from at least one member of their informal support system (Campbell et al., 2001). In turn, survivors often believe they deserved what happened, they should move on, they need to stop thinking about it, etc. They may receive feedback and advice from peers or those close to them to simply get over the assault. In reality, survivors commonly carry memories of the violence and grieve for the losses associated with the violence for a considerable amount of time.

Notably, another consequence of sexual violence includes unwanted/unplanned pregnancy. The ways in which people who become pregnant manage their unwanted/unplanned pregnancy can result in feelings of guilt, shame, and another layer of loss. The person confronting choices about a pregnancy that results from rape (e.g., to terminate their pregnancy, to carry their pregnancy to term and raise the child, or to make an adoption plan for the child) may experience loss of their envisioned life plan and the what-ifs associated with the choice they did *not* make. In some societies (e.g., Democratic Republic of the Congo; Onyango et al., 2016), people who become pregnant as a result of sexual violence may encounter abandonment by their partner and community in addition to the aforementioned social stigmas. Within some cultural groups, families and communities may reject or murder survivors, namely women and girls, if they disclose sexual assault because, with compromised virginity, their marriage prospects and family reputation become ruined

(Fontes & Plummer, 2010). It is reasonable to conclude that a survivor from those sociocultural groups who becomes pregnant as a result of rape could experience similar backlash. Thus, for those who suffer physical consequences of sexual violence, such as pregnancy or sexually transmitted diseases, myriad socioemotional and psychological consequences arise, including grief.

Society may perceive grief as a "soft" emotion to a sexually violent incident. People assume fear, terror, and anger represent appropriate emotions, and grief goes unacknowledged. Grief over the losses of personal agency, interpersonal agency, and sexual agency commonly occur and can underpin depression, anxiety, and suicidal ideation (Ebrahim et al., 2021). Treatment providers unknowingly contribute to disenfranchised grief already cultivated in social contexts if untrained to address and bear witness to that part of survivors' experiences.

Although societal influences exacerbate harm for survivors in several ways, recent activism efforts brought awareness of sexual violence to the fore. Movements such as the #MeToo movement, started by Tarana Burke, highlighted the longstanding patterns of sexual violence (Rister & McClure, 2019). After actress Alyssa Milano used the phrase "me too" on Twitter in response to the injustices of sexual violence, similar movements occurred on social media platforms in multiple languages including Arabic, Farsi, French, Hindi, and Spanish (Mahdavi, 2018). When societies and communities mobilize to resist the status quo and to raise awareness, survivors' experiences become acknowledged. So, too, should their grief.

Cultural aspects of disenfranchised grief

As previously noted, social stigma commonly influences views and discussions of acts of sexual violence. Critical aspects of culture also inform the way survivors experience their existence in society. Cultural identities, intersectional identities, and responses within cultural contexts also influence survivors' experience of the aftermath of sexual violence.

People with intersectional and marginalized identities experience a higher prevalence of estimates of sexual violence. In the US, 50% of multiracial women, 46% of Indigenous/Alaska Native women, 39% of non-Hispanic White women, 36% of non-Hispanic Black women, 29% of Hispanic women, and 23% of Asian/Pacific Islander women experienced some form of contact sexual violence involving physical contact during their lifetime (Smith et al., 2017). Over the span of their lifetime, 32% of multiracial men, 23% of Indigenous/Alaska Native men, 19% of non-Hispanic Black men, 19% of Hispanic men, 17% of non-Hispanic White men, and 9% of Asian/Pacific Islander men experienced one or more forms of sexual violence involving physical contact (Smith et al., 2017).

Before reviewing important data regarding women and men in the transgender community, note that the current author does not intend to separate the experiences of the respondents to the surveys, which examine the experiences of trans survivors of sexual violence, from those of cisgender people. Rather, the author aims to give voice to the multi-layered and severe disenfranchisement present for trans survivors, especially when over half of the respondents reportedly believed they were assaulted because of their transgender status, gender identity, or gender expression (Smith et al., 2017). According to Smith et al. (2017), of those who experienced forced sex, 20% reported one incident, 26% reported two incidents, 19% reported three to five incidents; another 19% reported six to 19 incidents, and 16% reported 20 or more incidents. In Grant et al.'s (2011) national transgender discrimination survey study, 64% experienced sexual violence. Black respondents in shelters for individuals without housing reported the highest rate of sexual assault at 33%, followed by Latinx at 31% (Grant et al., 2011).

Sexual violence occurs with a high prevalence on college campuses. Women aged 18–24 years are more vulnerable to sexual violence than at any other time in their lives (Sinozich & Langton, 2014). An estimated 30% of women college students and 11% of men college students experience sexual violence and other violence on campus (Conley et al., 2017). Many survivors elect not to disclose to law enforcement or the institution (Sabina & Ho, 2014) for reasons including fear of not being believed, fear of retaliation, impeded progress toward earning their degree, social stigma, and unwanted attention. Prevailing myths and beliefs also contribute to silencing survivors, because students potentially lack knowledge about sexual violence, leading them to endorse rape myths, such as the stranger rape myth, and to assign blame to victims (Baldwin-White, 2021). In addition to mental health consequences, many college students report higher levels of substance use, risky behaviors, lower academic performance, and sexual dysfunction after a sexual assault (Jordan et al., 2014). Potter and colleagues (2018) discussed the loss of human capital, or the individual knowledge, skills, and value they would bring to their economy, when sexual violence against college students occurs. They discussed the effect on all aspects of survivors' lives (i.e., physical and mental health, individual and societal human capital losses, financial costs, and emotional weight for survivors' families), and a need for compassionate care that honors the survivors' losses. Grief over these losses profoundly informs survivors' post-assault realities and should be conceptualized as such.

Relational aspects of disenfranchised grief

By definition, disenfranchised grief transpires through a relational process, in which one party's grief remains unacknowledged or minimized by another. Relational-cultural theorists categorize invalidation of this nature as characteristic of chronic disconnection where one party frequently receives nonempathic responses and repeatedly feels inhibited by another party and unable to share or display their genuine experience (Jordan, 2018). In unpacking the relational influence on disenfranchised grief, one can quickly see that sexual trauma and resultant losses impact the *self* via the inevitable functioning of the *self-in-relationship*. Others' actions (e.g., the violence) and responses (e.g., social responses or stigma) affect survivors and their subsequent relational interactions.

The majority of survivors across genders know their perpetrators. The most common perpetrators were intimate partners or acquaintances prior to the sexual violence (Smith et al., 2017). Acknowledging sexual violence as an intentional violation from one person to another person leads to graver consequences related to psychological distress for survivors, especially knowing the violence derived from a person (or people) whom the survivor trusted. Survivors often struggle with losses associated with self-trust and trusting others after betrayal and violation (Ebrahim et al., 2021).

Keshet et al. (2019) found that women survivors of sexual assault presented with more severely impaired self-perception than women who reported histories in which their main trauma related to motor vehicle accidents or to bereavement resulting from an unexpected death. More specifically, survivors in their sample ($N = 108$) reported lower levels of self-esteem and lower self-evaluations of resilience and intimacy than their counterparts. When assessing trauma symptom severity in survivors of sexual assault, Deitz et al. (2015) found that survivors' internalization of social stigmas about sexual violence significantly predicted symptom severity. In other words, trauma involving interpersonal violations is associated with a reduced sense of self. Toxic messaging and social stigma negatively impact survivors; however, if survivors believe those messages, their self-perception suffers further and trauma symptom severity increases. In addition to an increase in trauma severity, survivors experience a shift in identity and a loss of their former selves (Ebrahim et al., 2021).

Taken together, relational violations inherent in sexual violence cause survivors to often lose relational abilities to connect with others from a place of trust (self and others) and with a coherent sense of self. If nonoffending family members and loved ones validate and believe survivors, avoid making shaming and misinformed comments, and acknowledge the multiple losses, their acknowledgment fosters a supportive grief process (Bordere, 2017). Relational support provides the means to move from chronic disconnection and disenfranchised grief to connection after sexual violence.

Cumulative impacts of disenfranchised grief across the lifespan

Grief over the losses associated with sexual violence occurs with or without the recognition of others and devoid of broader sociocultural and relational support. When not recognized, the grief evolves into disenfranchised grief, adding to the consequences of the violence. Over the lifespan, survivors must manage their grief and an accumulation of symptoms and attempt to cope.

In cases of CSA, for example, the sexual violations deleteriously impact survivors' personal and relational health in childhood and into their adulthood. Aside from losing their childhood, physical bodily integrity, and psychological safety, they often lose safety in relationships through adulthood (Haiyasoso & Trepal, 2019; Herman, 2015). Many develop an unhealthy association with sexual activity, preventing healthy functioning in adult sexual relationships (Leonard et al., 2008), and experience marital dissatisfaction (Liang et al., 2006). Nelson and Wampler (2000) analyzed psychological distress symptoms, relationship quality, and couple/family cohesion in couples ($N = 161$) with one or both partners reporting histories of child sexual or child physical abuse and in couples with no reported abuse history. They revealed statistically significant positive correlations for mental health issues in couples with an abuse history and suggested that couples tend to "mirror symptomatology" (p. 177). Further, couples with at least one partner reporting a history of child abuse evidenced less relationship satisfaction and higher levels of psychological distress symptoms than couples without an abuse history (Nelson & Wampler, 2000).

In parenting their children, CSA survivors often struggle with physical connection, trusting others, and fear of threats to their children's safety (Haiyasoso & Trepal, 2019). The loss of safety and intrapersonal and interpersonal trust impede survivors' relational functioning into adulthood. Survivors of sexual assaults in adulthood grieve losses related to shifts in worldview, view of self-agency, and abilities to safely participate in relationships with others. If not addressed, their mourning remains an isolated process throughout their lives.

Allyship and advocacy

People dealing with non-death loss, such as sexual violence, need support in their lives at every level. Advocates and professionals in community agencies and in educational, medical, and mental health settings possess the ability to dispel myths about sexual violence and to work toward dismantling social stigma. Educating professionals (e.g., law enforcement, prosecutors, academicians) about survivors' losses and the psychological and physical costs to survivors can begin with partnering on awareness campaigns on campuses and communities. Bordere (2017) highlighted the need for higher education institutions to examine students' bereavement leave policies and to provide explicit survivor support assistance within their institutions' existing resources and accommodations. Additionally, considering that college students primarily turn to friends as their main source of support after experiencing violence, college campuses must develop or enhance current programming to educate all students and to equip bystanders with skills and knowledge to safely support survivors (Choi et al., 2021).

Mental health professionals address the sequelae of survivors' trauma by assessing the symptoms of common stress-related disorders and mood disorders. To thoroughly address the aftermath of sexual violence, however, clinicians should examine survivors' experiences of grief. In her foundational work, Herman (2015) suggested that clinicians first establish safety, then facilitate survivors' remembering and mourning, and help survivors reconnect to life. Thus, an appraisal of mourning and how one makes sense of the memories of the violence remains an integral part of the recovery model.

Ethical considerations

Mental health professionals working with youth and adult survivors of sexual violence focus on establishing a sense of safety and stability at the outset (Kress et al., 2018). Building a strong therapeutic relationship and safe environment requires intentionality, time, and accounting for trauma severity, the intensity of losses, presentation of symptoms, presence or absence of relational support, and the capacity to activate internal coping strategies. Clinicians should stay mindful of ethical codes safeguarding clients from harm (e.g., American Counseling Association [ACA], 2014; National Association of Social Workers [NASW], 2021) and assess if safety, connection, and client capacity are such that they can address clients' loss in a safe manner. Addressing loss in a way that pulls a survivor outside of their coping capacity can further harm those who grapple with loss in isolation.

Cultural norms and responses from one's cultural group inform survivors' experiences of trauma and associated losses. Thus, clinicians should inquire about survivors' cultural identities and cultural contexts. Amaya and Gray (2021) described the utility of assessing cultural values in assessments and adapting evidence-based treatments to better suit multicultural populations, because their presenting concerns and responses to treatment are not necessarily reflected in research conducted largely on White, middle-class populations.

Furthermore, mental health professionals must examine their implicit biases and practice with cultural humility, or "the ability to maintain an other-oriented interpersonal stance, even under the strain of cultural differences between the client and counselor" (Davis et al., 2016, p. 483) to avoid imposing their own values in the therapy setting. Sharing information about various cultural values potentially offers additional insights for clients to consider; yet, coercing a client to shift their values to address loss and sexual trauma defies ethical mandates of clients' rights to self-determination (ACA, 2014; NASW, 2021). Notably, Amaya and Gray (2021) provided examples of common values in some Latinx communities (i.e., gender-based roles, familism, religion/spirituality, interpersonal engagement/respect). As clinicians learn about these cultural values, they should explore what constitutes healthy responses to trauma within each set of beliefs or norms versus challenging the values by propping them up against those of the dominant culture and discussing them as flawed. In sum, mental health professionals are ethically obligated to remain culturally humble and attentive in their practice.

Strategies and interventions

Clinicians who do not acknowledge grief and loss as a result of sexual violence inadvertently contribute to survivors' disenfranchised grief. Clinicians should address survivors' grief and loss with a focus on individual and broader socio-cultural and relational contexts. The following suggestions for strategies and interventions aim to target survivors' experiences of loss and can be used in conjunction with trauma-informed treatment models.

The extent to which a traumatic event becomes central to survivors' identity and daily life relates to survivors' self-perceptions following sexual violence (Keshet et al., 2019). Thus, mental health professionals should examine survivors' trauma centrality to (a) learn how they conceptualize their life and activities, and (b) examine how they conceptualize their identity in the aftermath of the loss (e.g., victim vs. survivor, capable vs. incapable, trustworthy vs. dishonest). Questions clinicians might ask include:

- "What changes have you noticed in the way you see yourself/the world/ others since the violence occurred?"
- "What differences have you noticed about this loss/grief experience in comparison to your previous experiences of loss/grief?"

Mental health professionals operating ethically attend to cultural identities and cultural values. When working with survivors from backgrounds that have been minoritized, clinicians should consider cultural values that frame a survivor's experience. In the previous example of familism in many Latinx communities, a clinician might explore with open inquiries such as:

- "Tell me about your relationship with your family members."
- "What does decision making look like in your family?"

If learning that the family plays a central role for the client and the client's family lives with messages or negative beliefs around disclosing intrafamilial sexual violence, the clinician should further assess for the grief that possibly accompanies losing familial relationships. The clinician considers working with the survivor to recognize that becoming healthy individually also allows them to serve as a healthy member of the family who can contribute to the family's well-being (Amaya & Gray, 2021). In any case, clinicians must avoid generalizations and learn about cultural values directly from the client as they further examine compounded marginalization.

Survivors from the dominant culture may be unaccustomed to compounded marginalization while encountering injustices common in sexual violence. Shame, a frequent response to sexual violence, can lead them to experience the some of the silencing, isolating, and disempowering oppression that people who have been marginalized often face. From an RCT perspective, shame contributes to lowered sense of worth, reduced ability to authentically exist in relationships with others, and chronic disconnection (Jordan, 2018). Clinicians should remain aware of possible implications to survivors' experiential reality related to the world and their place in it. For those from the dominant culture, their assumptions about the world may shatter (Attig, 2010), triggering an existential crisis of meaning (see Chapter 3 for more information). Mental health professionals need to attend to the shift in meaning above and beyond sexual violence and recognize the grief related to losses of privilege (Bordere & Danforth, 2020). Clinicians may ask:

- "Can you share your experiences with 'using your voice' before/after the violence?"
- "How do the responses you received from_____ (fill in with reporting agency, educational institution, family members, peers) fit/not fit with your general experiences outside of the sexual violence?"

Considering that people can dually experience privilege (e.g., access to legal assistance and resources, knowledge of relevant systems, identification within one or more areas of the dominant culture, access to relational support, perceived as credible/believable/capable/worth protecting) *and* discrimination or oppression (e.g., lack of access to legal assistance and resources, lack of knowledge of relevant systems, no identification within areas of the dominant culture, no access to relational support, not perceived as credible/believable/capable/worth protecting), clinicians exercising cultural humility should learn about survivors' experiences of navigating the violence and related losses with combinations of privilege/oppression and power/disempowerment in mind. From an RCT perspective, U.S. and Western societies traditionally ascribe to *power-over* dynamics in which some parties/systems (i.e., those with privilege) possess control and dominance that may oppress others (Jordan, 2018). Relational-cultural theorists encourage a *power-with* approach instead, which involves shared power, collaboration, and empowering others (Jordan, 2018). Clinicians strive to better understand when survivors encounter *power-over* versus *power-with* dynamics in their pre- and post-assault experiences by inviting the following inquiries:

- "Tell about times when you felt empowered and steady, even if afraid, when sharing your story about the violence and your needs thereafter."
- "Tell about times when you felt shut down, disempowered, disbelieved, and unheard when sharing your story the violence and your needs thereafter."

Relatedly, assessing *relational images*, or the internal representations of how one expects to function within relationships, allows clinicians to guide clients through an exploration of inner frameworks and an examination of those that enhance self-worth and those that contribute to chronic disconnection

(Jordan, 2018). Relational images become particularly important for treatment because survivors normally disclose to their close friends before ever reporting the crimes (Choi et al., 2021), and responses from others heavily influence how survivors feel about the violence. Mental health professionals may assist survivors through questions such as:

- "What relationships prompt a sense of safety in you?"
- "What relationships feel unsafe?"
- "Where do you feel free to be authentic?"
- "Where do you feel afraid to be yourself?"
- "What relationships allow you to be vulnerable?"

With the survivor's permission, clinicians can support the relationships that engender safety by providing those in the survivors' inner circle with psychoeducation or resources (e.g., Bordere, 2017). Offering educational tools to help survivors' support network can mitigate unintentional but insensitive, ill-informed statements that push survivors further into their grief.

Summary

Survivors of sexual violence experience compounding subjugation. They become disenfranchised through society's views and manner of addressing (or not addressing) sexual violence. Then, survivors subjected to violence become further disenfranchised through a lack of acknowledgment of their grief due to the unrecognized or stigmatized losses associated with sexual violence. Women, notably those with multiple intersectional identities that have been marginalized, experience sexual violence at the highest rates; for them, their disenfranchised grief compounds their oppression. Allies, advocates, policymakers, and mental health professionals can and should work to dispel myths and change social stigmas that pervade societal, cultural, and relational responses to survivors and ignore their grief.

References

Allende, I. (2001). *Portrait in sepia: A novel* (M. S. Peden, Trans.). Harper Collins.

Amaya, S., & Gray, M. J. (2021). Cultural considerations in the treatment of Latina survivors of sexual assault. *Journal of Loss and Trauma, 26*(8), 714–732. https://doi.org/10.1080/15325024.2021.1926175

American Counseling Association. (2014). ACA *code of ethics and standards of practice*. www.counseling.org/resources/aca-code-of-ethics.pdf

Attig, T. (2010). *How we grieve: Relearning the world* (2nd ed). Oxford University Press.

Baldwin-White, A. (2021). College students and their knowledge and perceptions about sexual assault. *Sexuality and Culture, 25*(1), 58–74. https://doi.org/10.1007/s12119-020-09757-x

Bordere, T. (2017). Disenfranchisement and ambiguity in the face of loss: The suffocated grief of sexual assault survivors. *Family Relations, 66*(1), 29–45. https://doi.org/10.1111/fare.12231

Bordere, T., & Danforth, L. (2020). Sexual assault, loss, and the journey to justice. In D. Harris (Ed.), *Non-death loss and grief* (pp. 256–269). Routledge.

Breidling, M. J., Chen, J., & Black, M. C. (2014). The National Intimate Partner and Sexual Violence Survey (NISVS): 2011 prevalence and characteristics of sexual violence, stalking, and intimate partner violence victimization, *MMWP, 63*(SS08), 1–18. www.cdc.gov/mmwr/preview/mmwrhtml/ss6308a1.htm

Campbell, R., Ahrens, C. E., Sefl, T., Wasco, S. M., & Barnes, H. E. (2001). Social reactions to rape victims: Healing and hurtful effects on psychological and physical health outcomes. *Violence and Victims, 16*(3), 287–302. https://doi.org/10.1891/0886-6708.16.3.287

Choi, Y. J., Rai, Abha, R., Hyunkag, C., Son, E., Soonok, A., & Yun, S. (2021). Help-seeking behaviors for intimate partner violence among college students: Implications for intimate partner violence prevention and intervention. *Violence and Victims, 36*(4), 548–564. https://doi.org/10.1891/VV-D-20-00124

Conley, A. H., Overstreet, C. M., Hawn, S. E., Kendler, K. S., Dick, D. M., & Amstadter, A. B. (2017). Prevalence and predictors of sexual assault among a college sample. *Journal of American College Health, 65*(1), 41–49. https://doi.org/10.1080/07448481.2016.1235578

Davis, D., DeBlaere, C., Brubaker, K., Owen, J., Jordan II, T. A., Hook, J. N., & Van Tongeren, D. R. (2016). Microaggression and perceptions of cultural humility in counseling. *Journal of Counseling and Development, 94*(4), 483–493. https://doi.org/10.1002/jcad.12107

Deitz, M. F., Williams, S. L., Rife, S. C., & Cantrell, P. (2015). Examining cultural, social, and self-related aspects of stigma in relation to sexual assault and trauma symptoms. *Violence Against Women, 21*(5), 598–615. https://doi.org/10.1177/1077801215573330

Doka, K. J. (1989). *Disenfranchised grief: Recognizing hidden sorrow.* Lexington Press.

Dworkin, E. R., Menon, S. V., Bystrynski, J., & Allen, N. E. (2017). Sexual assault victimization and psychopathology: A review and meta-analysis. *Clinical Psychology Review, 56*, 65–81. https://doi.org/10.1177/1524838018813198

Ebrahim, B. K., Fouche, A., & Walker-Williams, H. (2021). Losses associated with childhood sexual abuse in women survivors: A scoping review. *Trauma, Violence, and Abuse, 23*(5), 1695–1707. https://doi.org/10.1177/15248380211013137

Fontes, L. A., & Plummer, C. (2010). Cultural issues in disclosures of child sexual abuse. *Journal of Child Sexual Abuse, 19,* 491–518. https://doi.org/10.1080/10538 712.2010.512520

Grant, J. M., Mottet, L. A., Tanis, J., Harrison, J., Herman, J. L., & Keisling, M. (2011). *Injustice at every turn: A report of the national transgender discrimination survey.* National Center for Transgender Equality and National Gay and Lesbian Task Force. https://transequality.org/sites/default/files/docs/resources/NTDS_ Report.pdf

Haiyasoso, M. D., & Trepal, H. (2019). Survivors' stories: Navigating parenthood after surviving child sexual abuse. *Journal of Counseling and Development, 97*(3), 281–292. https://doi.org/10.1002/jcad.12268

Herman, J. L. (2015). *Trauma and recovery: The aftermath of violence from domestic abuse to political terror.* Basic Books. (Original work published 1992)

Human Rights Campaign & Trans People of Color Coalition. (2017). *A time to act: Fatal violence against transgender people in America 2017.* http://assets2.hrc.org/ files/assets/resources/A_Time_To_Act_2017_REV3.pdf

Jordan, C. E., Combs, J. L., & Smith, G. T. (2014). An exploration of sexual victimization and academic performance among college women. *Trauma, Violence, and Abuse, 15*(3), 191–200. https://doi.org/10.1177/1524838014520637

Jordan, J. V. (2018). *Relational-cultural therapy* (2nd ed.). American Psychological Association. https://doi.org/10.1037/0000063-000

Keshet, H., Foa, E. B., & Gilboa-Schechtman, E. (2019). Women's self-perceptions in the aftermath of trauma: The role of trauma-centrality and trauma-type. *Psychological Trauma: Theory, Research, Practice, and Policy, 11*(5), 542–550. https://doi. org/10.1037/tra0000393

Kress, V. E., Haiyasoso, M. D., Zoldan, C. A., Headley, J. A., & Trepal, H. (2018). The use of relational-cultural theory in counseling clients who have traumatic stress disorders. *Journal of Counseling and Development, 96*(1), 106–114. https:// doi.org/10.1002/jcad.12182

Leonard, L. M., Iverson, K., & Follette, V. M. (2008). Sexual functioning and sexual satisfaction among women who report a history of childhood and/or adolescent sexual abuse. *Journal of Sex and Marital Therapy, 34*(5), 375–384. https://doi. org/10.1080/00926230802156202

Liang, B., Williams, L. M., & Siegel, J. A. (2006). Relational outcomes of childhood sexual trauma in female survivors: A longitudinal study. *Journal of Interpersonal Violence, 21*(1), 42–57. https://doi.org/10.1177/0886260505281603

Mahdavi, P. (2018, March 6). "How #MeToo became a global movement." *Foreign Affairs*. www.foreignaffairs.com/articles/2018-03-06/how-metoo-became-global-movement

National Association of Social Workers. (2021). Code of ethics of the National Association of Social Workers. *NASW*. www.socialworkers.org/About/Ethics/Code-of-Ethics/Code-of-Ethics-English

Nelson, B. S., & Wampler, K. S. (2000). Systemic effects of trauma in clinic couples: An exploratory study of secondary trauma resulting from childhood abuse. *Journal of Marital and Family Therapy*, 26(2), 171–184. https://doi.org/10.1111/j.1752-0606.2000.tb00287.x

Onyango, M. A., Burkhardt, G., Scott, J., Rouhani, S., Haider, S., Greiner, A., Albutt, K., Mullen, C., VanRooyen, M., & Bartels, S. (2016). A qualitative analysis of disclosure patterns among women with sexual violence-related pregnancies in Eastern Democratic Republic of Congo. *PLoS ONE*, 11(10), 1–13. https://doi.org/10.1371/journal.pone.0164631

Potter, S., Howard, R., Murphy, S., & Moynihan, M. M. (2018). Long-term impacts of college sexual assaults on women survivors' educational and career attainments. *Journal of American College Health*, 66(6), 496–507. https://doi.org/10.1080/07448481.2018.1440574

Rape, Abuse and Incest National Network. (2022). Key terms and phrases. *RAINN*. www.rainn.org/articles/key-terms-and-phrases

Ratts, M. J., Singh, A. A., Nassar-McMillan, S., Butler, S. K., & McCullough, J. R. (2016). Multicultural and social justice counseling competencies: Guidelines for the counseling profession. *Journal of Multicultural Counseling and Development*, 44(1), 28–48. https://doi.org/10.1002/jmcd.12035

Rister, A., & McClure, C. I. (2019). The Me Too movement: A qualitative content analysis of news featuring #MeToo. *The Northwest Journal of Communication*, 47(1), 153–185.

Sabina, C., & Ho, L. Y. (2014). Campus and college victim responses to sexual assault and dating violence: Disclosure, service utilization, and service provision. *Trauma, Violence, and Abuse*, 15(3), 201–226. https://doi.org/10.1177/1524838014521322

Sinozich, S., & Langton, L. (2014). Rape and sexual assault victimization among college-age females, 1995–2013. *U.S. Department of Justice*. https://bjs.ojp.gov/content/pub/pdf/rsavcaf9513.pdf

Smith, S. G., Chen, J., Basile, K. C., Gilbert, L. K., Merrick, M. T., Patel, N., Walling, M., & Jain, A. (2017). The national intimate partner and sexual violence survey (NISVS): 2010–2012 state report. *National Center for Injury Prevention and Control, Centers for Disease Control and Prevention*. www.cdc.gov/violenceprevention/pdf/nisvs-statereportbook.pdf

Smith, S. G., Zhang, X., Basile, K. C., Merrick, M. T., Wang, J., Kresnow, M., & Chen, J. (2018). The national intimate partner and sexual violence survey (NISVS): 2015 data brief – updated release. *National Center for Injury Prevention and Control, Centers for Disease Control and Prevention.* www.cdc.gov/violenceprevention/pdf/2015data-brief508.pdf

Townsend, C., & Rheingold, A. A. (2013). Estimating a child sexual abuse prevalence rate for practitioners: A review of child sexual abuse prevalence studies. *Darkness to Light.* www.d2l.org/wp-content/uploads/2017/02/PREVALENCE-RATE-WHITE-PAPER-D2L.pdf

Ullman, S. (2010). *Talking about sexual assault: Society's response to survivors.* American Psychological Association.

Questions for reflective practice

1. Professional and personal development involves self-reflection. What might prevent you from listening for themes of grief and loss when a survivor of sexual violence discloses their experiences?
2. Compounded injustice occurs when disenfranchised populations (minoritized, marginalized people) also experience disenfranchised grief as survivors of sexual violence. Describe ways you can intentionally highlight this fact with survivor clients.
3. Connection exists as a biological imperative, and relationships influence the quality of life and physical health. Yet, U.S. and other Western societies normalize rugged individualism and personal responsibility (i.e., we are responsible for seeking independence and taking care of ourselves by ourselves). How might this impact a survivor's experience of loss after sexual violence? What if the survivor possesses intersecting, marginalized identities? How might this awareness impact your work with survivors?

Supplemental electronic resources

- National Center for PTSD: www.ptsd.va.gov/understand/types/sexual_trauma_male.asp
- Rape, Abuse & Incest National Network (RAINN): www.rainn.org/national-resources-sexual-assault-survivors-and-their-loved-ones
- Unapologetically Surviving (podcast): https://unapologeticallysurviving.com/rec/podcasts/

11

Addressing violence and loss in schools

Amanda Winburn and Mary Bess W. Pannel

Before children reach adulthood, almost all will experience the death of someone or loss of something very important to them. Millions of students encounter loss each year, and they experience a range of significant losses. Loss and grief, when not addressed, can become complicated and extended (Ferow, 2019). It is important for school systems to understand how students make sense of these losses, as well as what school-based counselors can do to help support students. The authors explore varying forms of loss and grief most common in elementary and secondary students.

Students' grief

Children and adolescents experience social-emotional developmental milestones (e.g., learning to resolve conflict, developing academic and or career identities, engaging in first romantic relationships) within the school system environment. Many of these developmental milestones may include some form of loss, which could lead to grief (Hannon et al., 2019). Age and development level are critical factors in experiencing grief (Çakar, 2020). The literature dedicated to the needs of grieving students is minimal; however, there is a consensus supporting the standard that grieving children and adolescents should be offered support from their family systems and school-based counselors. Although grieving parents are often considered particularly vulnerable, their grieving children might also experience personal or interpersonal difficulties in verbally expressing their feelings about their grief (Flahault et al., 2018).

Disenfranchised grief

Doka (1989) defined *disenfranchised grief* as "the grief that persons experience when they incur a loss that is not or cannot be openly acknowledged, publicly

DOI: 10.4324/9781003292890-13

mourned, or socially supported" (p. 4) According to Corr et al. (1999), a constant for youth is informal death education, and formal death education programs provide support and context within schools, which can be used to benefit youth and their support systems. Oftentimes, school-based counselors are called upon to assist grieving students with death- and non-death losses, including disenfranchised grief, through informal and formal education programs. Counselors can suggest structured routines, awareness, and education within the classroom to support the entire school environment and assist grieving youth.

Elementary students

For elementary students, grieving is a developmental process. Elementary students are at developmental stages of beginning to learn how to form relationships and characteristically may have limited to no experience with change. Thus, change in the form of learning to emotionally cope with loss, can be extremely challenging when a friend, teacher, or family member is no longer in their life. Elementary students often encounter disenfranchised grief when relationships with parents, other family members, friends, teachers, support professionals, and pets change or end, because their grief experiences are not acknowledged or supported. Although these developments are often a normal part of life, caregivers and school-based counselors should be aware that if elementary students experience grief that these changes may lead to academic or behavioral challenges in school (Protivnak et al., 2020).

Grieving the loss of a significant relationship can also lead to short- and long-term psychological and physiological challenges in school-aged children. According to Flahault et al. (2018), the most common short-term behaviors are "anxiety, depression, behavioral problems, poorer school attainment, social withdrawal, and feelings of insecurity and vulnerability" (p. 483). Some risk factors can also increase a child's vulnerability, such as a surviving parent's depression and/or the risk of low quality of care they provide their child. This low level of care could result in long-term consequences for the child that could possibly lead to psychiatric disorders during adulthood, such as suicidality. For grieving children, strong and healthy relationships exhibited in family cohesion among nuclear and extended family and kinship caregivers may determine positive levels of self-regulation skills and can also contribute to resilience. These positive relationships can allow bereaved children to have healthy levels of self-esteem, appropriate expression of feelings, insight and awareness among family members, and the ability to maintain a positive understanding during the experience of loss (Flahault et al., 2018).

Secondary students

Students within secondary school levels can express grief in similar ways to elementary-aged students, however, these student populations differ from younger children and from adults in their expressions of grief. The process of coping with loss and the response to grieving in older children and adolescents are more multifaceted than that of younger children, given their developmental stage. In older adolescents, "identity development, gaining autonomy, separation from parents, defining career choices and the formation of close relationships" (Çakar, 2020, p. 28), could potentially have a more significant impact on the grieving process during these developmental stages. In essence, adolescents experience grief differently because they experience themselves in relationship and as part of relationships differently. At varying levels, adolescents begin to process grief existentially, with an understanding of their own mortality. Parallel to this increased awareness comes an increased empathy for others, which can be overwhelming for some adolescents, triggering symptoms of anxiety and depression. Moreover, the associated biopsychosocial changes in the transition from childhood to adulthood increase the risks of problems related to physical and mental health and social functioning (Feigelman et al., 2017).

Similar to elementary-age children, behavioral problems and emotional reactions that could arise following stressful life events are associated with decreases in their overall mental wellbeing. Grief in adolescents can also amplify developmentally normal boundary testing and moodiness, resulting in a decrease in school attendance, decrease in academic achievement, and increases in negative behaviors (e.g., aggression, defiance, irritability). In supporting youth, it is essential to view these behaviors and responses through a grief lens to avoid further disenfranchising the grief experience. School-based counselors, parents/caregivers, peers, and other adults in supportive roles can create support systems in protecting and strengthening students' mental health, which is considered vital in developing healthy coping skills for loss and grief.

Recognized and unrecognized types of loss affecting schools

The most common form of recognized loss is the death of a loved one. Common experiences of loss are more likely to be addressed by parents, caregivers, or school-based counselors. In many instances, systems are in place to support students who experience this type of grief. Despite this support, some students may not have the coping skills to effectively understand their feelings and regulate their emotions following a loss (Protivnak et al., 2020).

As Doka (1989) indicated, elementary-aged students are often unintention-ally marginalized. This is partly due to adults' lack of awareness that children often do not understand the nuanced experience of grief and critically need care and support to be able to process grief and loss (Protivnak et al., 2020). When adult support systems do not provide opportunities for students to grieve recognized or unrecognized losses, these students are then potentially excluded or deprived from experiencing and understanding the grieving pro-cess. Therefore, even when acknowledged, youths' grief can become disen-franchised when the grief is not adequately processed by the youth.

Another point of consideration is that school environments are the natural arena in which students of all ages learn to develop relationships with peers and adults outside of their family (e.g., teachers, school-based counselors, sports coaches). Protivnak et al. (2020) indicated that "early friendships are extremely important because of social support, learning, social comparison, affiliation, and the need to engage in activities" (p. 6). The concept of a rela-tionship can be new to many students, and friendships are one of their "first independent self-directed experiences" (Protivnak et al., 2020, p. 6), thus relational losses at this stage are novel and deeply painful. Disenfranchised grief connected to relationship losses that may be unidentified or indistin-guishable by school-based counselors include: a friend moving away; death of a pet or giving a pet away; parental miscarriage or stillbirth; incarcera-tion of a family member; family disruption; deployment of a family member; parental job transfer; parental incapacitation (e.g., serious physical or mental illness); teacher or school staff leaving; and death of a non-family member (e.g., neighbor). Students who experience disenfranchised grief may exhibit academic and behavioral problems, but because this type of grief and loss regularly goes unrecognized, school-based counselors and support systems may miss the connection. To avoid diminishing and further disenfranchising youths' grief experiences, especially non-death losses, school personnel must view the youth holistically.

Dimensions of loss

Grief is often portrayed as the characteristic response to a loss, in that it is closely associated with the symptoms, feelings, and expressions of mourn-ing and bereavement. Appropriate responses to loss continue to be debated. Some researchers suggested that loss and grief are perceived and experienced in completely unique and personal ways according to culture, developmental stages, support systems, and the success or failure of past experiences and present attitudes (Baker et al., 2009). Conversely, there have been various efforts to categorize reactions to loss into specific stages. Such concepts for grieving may be unsupportive because these only provide basic knowledge and specific approaches in how people ought to experience loss. Grief is difficult to categorize and "one size" does not fit all. Loss and grief have multiple dimensions, and, in many instances, one type of loss can lead to or trigger another type of loss, resulting in a complexity of losses (Baker et al., 2009).

The American Institute of Health Care Professionals (2012) outlined common dimensions of loss:

1. *Shock or apparent lack of feeling* – feelings are ignored, or the griever often shows no emotion or feelings.
2. *Physiological changes* – feelings or symptoms are connected to the body's reaction to stress, such as stomach aches and headaches.
3. *Regression* – feelings or symptoms include increased dependency on adults.
4. *Disorganization* – feelings or symptoms include confusion about what will happen in the future and questioning who will be the caretaker or responsible adult support system.
5. *Explosive emotions* – feelings or symptoms appear in a wide range, varying from anger to hyperactivity.
6. *Acting out* – feelings or symptoms include going to great lengths to be noticed by others.
7. *Hyper-maturity* – feelings or symptoms include taking on the role of an adult.
8. *Fear* – feelings or symptoms include being scared or anxious.
9. *Guilt* – feelings or symptoms include magical thinking in wishing past experiences had caused the loss of the loved one.
10. *Relief* – feelings or symptoms include egocentrism in which life can return to "normal."
11. *Sadness* – feelings or symptoms include extreme sadness.
12. *Reconciliation* – feelings or symptoms include finding and understanding a new "normal."

For example, a grieving elementary-aged child could display symptoms of regression when being dropped off at school. When carpool drop-off is a typical, daily routine for grieving children, the act of separation from a living caregiver could bring about fears and worries about not seeing the living caregiver again. In turn, this could lead to outward expressions based on the traumatic loss of the deceased parent, such as refusal to leave the car or physical or verbal aggression towards others when encouraged to separate.

Psychological trauma

Dutil (2019) identified symptoms, such as additional emotional and behavioral challenges, cognitive impairment, as well as increased hyperarousal sensitivity, or flight-or-fight tendencies, in students experiencing trauma and traumatic grief. Students experiencing trauma display impairments in academic and social functioning, and in some cases, some students may face school discipline due to these impairments. Therefore, it is critical that students have support systems in place (e.g., school-based counselors, teachers, school counselors, school administrators) that are aware, are sensitive, and understand trauma and traumatic grief. Increasing school personnel self-efficacy through consultation, collaboration, and professional development is imperative to responding positively and proactively to students experiencing trauma (Dutil, 2019).

Promoting resilience and wellness as students grow, develop, and experience developmental changes is fundamental in addressing and supporting students that experience traumatic grief and loss events. It is imperative that school-based counselors collaborate in implementing psychoeducational curricula and crisis interventions, such as large and small group counseling, to address student's safety, social and emotional wellness, and academic success. Additionally, student support systems should consistently and collaboratively address barriers in providing access to resources needed for students experiencing traumatic grief (Dutil, 2019).

Secondary trauma

Promoting resilience and wellness also extends beyond students' needs, because those that support students in their grief experiences are also subject to experiencing secondary trauma. Ferow (2019) highlighted that parents and caregivers, school-based counselors, and other school personnel who support students are often impacted and affected by grief as well. Self-care practices are essential in reducing symptoms of secondary trauma, especially when working with students that are experiencing grief and loss. It is vital that anyone assisting students through their traumatic experiences and grief practices self-care. All school-based counselors and helping professionals should be mindful of secondary trauma and implement daily self-care routines to effectively care for themselves and the students they serve (Ferow, 2019).

School violence

School officials and lawmakers have a moral and legal obligation to protect children in their schools. School stakeholders are continually going to great lengths to protect children from the potential dangers that exist because children's safety and security is vital to creating a positive academic environment. A school culture that does not provide both security and safety for their students and employees can shortchange students a fair and equitable opportunity to learn and experience academic growth. In the aftermath of critical incidents, such as the 1999 Columbine High School shooting and other acts of school violence, school officials and lawmakers have refocused on methods to protect children through various policy and legislative initiatives (Birkland & Lawrence, 2009). As such, one important step has been to pass state statutes designed to reduce the amount of bullying in schools, as well as punish those who perpetrate such acts.

According to Paolini (2015), there are two primary causes of school violence: bullying (87%), as well as both non-compliance and/or side effects from psychiatric drugs (13%). Most school shooters indicated that they were victims of bullying that left severe and lasting effects (Paolini, 2015). These individuals likely experienced humiliation and embarrassment, which provoked feelings of anger, frustration, and revenge. According to the Safe School Initiative, prior to the violent act committed, 73% of perpetrators felt resentment or ill will towards at least one of their victims; 59% of school shootings occurred during the school day; and in 73% of attacks one or more students and faculty were killed (Vossekuil et al., 2002).

Some researchers have attributed the increase of school violence to information being readily available on the Internet, exposure to violence, media, and video games. Anderson et al. (2010) found that exposure to media violence can increase aggression amongst users, and those users are more likely in turn to be interested in acquiring and using guns after exposure to gun violence in films. Mental illness has also been linked to school violence. According to Vossekuil et al. (2002), 25% of perpetrators of mass shootings had been treated for mental illness, and more than 75% had symptoms of mental illness before the attack. Unfortunately, adolescents have been identified as the least likely group to receive mental health services (Evans et al., 2006), despite the significant need demonstrated in schools and communities. Teplin et al. (2002) estimated that approximately 65–70% of the more than 2 million children and young adults who formally enter the juvenile justice system have at least one diagnosable mental health disorder. This creates a significant expense to society and future generations. The mental wellness of students should be viewed and funded as a public health issue. This type of response would include universal interventions targeting all students to prevent aggressive behaviors.

Range and complexities

The term *school violence* can include a wide array of behaviors that contribute to an unsafe educational environment. Typically, it's used as an umbrella term that includes behaviors such as bullying, peer victimization, and verbal or physical aggression. The most feared form of school violence includes serious injury or loss of life, which have been evidenced in shootings at Columbine High School and Sandy Hook Elementary School (National Threat Assessment Center, 2019). In 2022, the US experienced another great tragedy at Robb Elementary School in Uvalde, Texas. Time will tell how these great tragedies inform policies and procedures regarding school safety and gun violence.

Although loss of life in schools is rare, incidents of targeted school violence have been the catalyst for increased legislation, funding, preventative programs, and intervention strategies (Kupchik et al., 2015). The consequences of violent school behaviors can be damaging to witnesses, victims, and perpetrators (Ttofi et al., 2012). Walters (2021) recently found that there are clear associations between experiencing acts of school violence and anxiety, depression, and poor educational outcomes. Fowler et al. (2009) found a positive relationship between exposure to school violence and a number of negative mental health and behavioral outcomes, including posttraumatic stress disorder (PTSD), depression, anxiety, aggression, poor academic achievement, and risky sexual behavior. These difficulties have the potential to impact behaviors such as suicidal ideation, anger, and aggression. A climate pervaded by violence may affect students' attendance and academic and social engagement capacities at school; poor attendance, low academic performance, and school connectedness also potentially impact poor student outcomes (Thapa et al., 2013).

School safety and active shooter drills

Following the Sandy Hook Elementary School shooting in 2012, national school trends yielded a general response of adding additional school resource officers (SROs), surveillance, and visual security measures to most school districts around the US (Kupchick et al., 2015). The federal government primarily funded this increase in security under the "Now is the Time Policy" (King & Bracy, 2019). Between 2017 and 2018, federal data showed over 70% of school districts have school-based law enforcement officers. However, researchers have found that security is only part of an effective strategy to combat school violence (Na & Gottfredson, 2013). An increased security presence also may have negative consequences for students, such as increases in student arrest, school disciplinary actions, and in perceived negative school climate (Mowen & Freng, 2019). Preparing for the worst-case scenarios also may contribute to a negative school climate.

Currently, 95% of all U.S. schools have some type of a lockdown procedure (Musu et al., 2019). These emergency drills typically focus on worst-case scenarios to prepare students and school staff for fires, tornados, earthquakes, and violence. An ongoing challenge in today's school system is to safely prepare and protect the school student body from potential outside threats while providing a quality educational environment that feels safe enough to promote learning. In addition to teaching children language arts, math, and science, educators are now tasked with the responsibility of providing students with preparedness for real-life threats to the academic environment. During active shooter drills, students typically practice three main responses: fleeing, barricading themselves in a room, and distracting and actively resisting the shooter (Jonson et al., 2018). Children as early as preschool age are required to participate in lock down drills, wherein they are required to remain quiet, huddle with other students, and remove themselves from doors and windows. Of course, there can be consequences for going through these drills; Huskey and Connell (2021) posited it is possible for such drills to impact a student's psychological wellbeing. If a student experiences these drills and enters a state of fear versus a sentiment of safety, then the drill could have the opposite effect of what is intended.

Trauma-informed allyship and advocacy

The Every Student Succeeds Act (2015) provided school districts with guidelines to offer trauma-informed programming to support safe, supportive educational environments. Since that time, trauma-informed programming has reduced discipline referrals and has had a positive impact when school districts make changes to their climate and culture (Dorado et al., 2016). This type of delivery system has great potential, because the majority of students receive most of their supportive services within the K-12 system. School stakeholders, such as teachers, counselors, and administrators, are already involved as allies in their students' lives through their existing relationships with them and providing a substantial source of support to their them and their community. Offering trauma-informed interventions inside the schools is viewed by many (practitioners and academics) as a practical approach with the potential to reduce school discipline and classroom disruptions, serve the whole child, and offer a more understanding and accepting learning environment, which ultimately offers benefits to the entire school community.

The importance of employing trauma-informed schools is crucial to the growth and development of children and adolescents. Perfect et al. (2016) found that approximately two-thirds of school-age children are likely to have experienced at least one traumatic event by 17 years of age. *Trauma-informed schools* are educational environments that are responsive to the needs of trauma-exposed youth through the application of evidenced-based interventions and system changing strategies (Chafouleas et al., 2015). Personnel and their ability to have a basic understanding of trauma and how trauma affects learning and behavior in the academic setting is a vital component (Substance Abuse and Mental Health Services Administration [SAMHSA], 2014; Cole et al., 2013). As school personnel increase their understanding of trauma and implement universal screening to identify the needs of students, they may work towards prevention and intervention programs to advocate for student's needs. Price et al. (2016) stated that schools also should focus on hiring additional mental health professionals (e.g., school counselors) and on implementing restorative practices that reduce the threat of violence. Such professionals lead the implementation of strategies and interventions to increase belonging and problem-solving strategies that could improve school climates and reduce the risk of violent thoughts and behaviors being enacted in schools.

Ethical considerations

Teachers, counselors, administrators, and other helping professionals in the K-12 system must be aware of evidenced-based interventions and should also understand ethical and legal concerns when working with grieving students and their parents. This includes, but is certainly not limited to, knowing the specific codes of ethics that apply to one's profession and the laws that govern them. For example, professional school counselors are governed by the ASCA (2022) *Ethical Standards for School Counselors* and relevant state laws.

Informed consent, confidentiality, along with other considerations, should all be weighed when working with grieving students and their parents. A parent or legal guardian must give written consent before a school-based therapist can provide services for treatment. Informed consent provides students and families with information concerning the provider's professional credentials, types of services, goals, and limitations within the therapeutic approach and/or interventions.

When working with grieving families, confidentiality is very important. Helping professionals, such as school counselors or school-based therapists, must ensure students and their guardians understand the boundaries and limits of confidentiality. School counselors are required to maintain students' confidentiality unless legally obligated to disclose information or if there is a reasonable belief that the student is at risk of "serious and foreseeable harm" (American School Counselor Association, 2019). School counselors are required by law to report all instances of abuse or neglect of students. Additional ethical codes may apply to school-based therapists, depending on their specific profession and professional association memberships.

Strategies and interventions

Addressing grief, loss, and disenfranchised grief with children and adolescents is necessary to promote wellness as students move through developmental stages into early adulthood. Losing a loved one, friend, or classmate following a traumatic event can be extremely difficult and cause students to experience extreme stress, anxiety, depression, and grief. These events can often be complex and be entangled with varying factors that compound the experience and loss. Each loss or trauma typically increases the odds for behavioral issues or mental health impairment (Layne et al., 2014). Researchers have examined varying grief interventions for children and adolescents and typically have found small to moderate effect sizes (Rosner et al., 2010). Generally, tertiary interventions that target students who struggle with grief symptoms demonstrate the most significant differences (Hagan et al., 2016).

Play-based therapy is an effective modality to address traumatic grief and loss in children (Turner, 2020) and may also facilitate understanding of active shooter drills. Play allows children to conceptualize and make sense out of violence, death, loss, and fear. In the context of active shooter drills, *playing at violence* allows children to practice scenarios of "bad guy-play" to gain mastery instead of being the victim (Delaney, 2017). Some adults may not feel comfortable with this type of play. However, Berson and Baggerly (2009) showed that engagement in this type of play allows children to examine and understand traumatic events and Holland (2003) posited that it gives school stakeholders a way to productively process the realities of active shooter drills with children in a developmentally appropriate way.

Older children and adolescents may benefit from cognitive-behavioral interventions. An example of a current school-based intervention is the cognitive-behavioral intervention for trauma in schools (CBITS) program. CBITS is an adaptation of trauma focused-cognitive behavioral therapy (TF-CBT) that uses student group work for trauma and grief symptoms and has been implemented in K-12 schools throughout the US (Jaycox et al., 2012). This intervention utilizes individual sessions, parent meetings, and training sessions for educators; it has been studied in diverse populations such as Indigenous peoples, rural low-income, and urban African American students, yielding positive treatment outcomes (Ngo et al., 2008).

School personnel that illustrate a successful adaptation of evidenced-based interventions to meet the needs of students suffering from grief and loss yield such program results. Researchers have shown CBITS to be effective and beneficial for schools in a variety of student populations and can treat various types of psychological trauma, while creating a safe and therapeutic academic environment (Dutil, 2019). Employing other strategies, such as play-based interventions, have also returned highly effective results with elementary aged children coping with traumatic loss (Turner, 2020). With student populations experiencing grief and loss at increased rates, lack of access to mental health services in rural and urban communities increases the need for schools to provide these types of services.

Professional school counselors should adhere to the American School Counselor Association (ASCA) National Model (2019), which promotes academic, career, and social/emotional development of all students. According to the ASCA National Model, the counseling process in a school setting is designed to help identify issues, causes, alternatives, and possible outcomes so students and families can make decisions and take appropriate actions (Marino et al., 2015). Direct services, including guidance lessons within the classroom, individual student planning, and responsive services, are delivered throughout the schools' overall curriculum (ASCA, 2019). Additional services can range from individual counseling, small and large group counseling, and family counseling. These types of services help students in K-12 schools overcome grief and loss issues that impede their academic achievement, personal development, and overall school success. Although further research is warranted to develop additional interventions and curriculum for grief and loss in school settings, the potential for negative academic and behavioral outcomes necessitates additional resources be allocated so schools have the resources needed to intervene when students experience loss.

Summary

Grief has a tremendous impact on students. Schools recognize the need for additional support; however, they often find themselves ill prepared and under-resourced to meet students' needs when they are experiencing grief and loss, disenfranchised grief, and/or trauma-related symptoms. Individual, classroom, and universal/school wide interventions can be utilized to address both academic and behavioral difficulties within a K-12 student population. Moving forward, schools should prioritize professional development, utilize trauma-informed practices, and provide students with greater access to mental health services to respond to students' needs.

References

American Institute of Health Care Professionals. (2012). *Child grief counseling and bereavement education: Dimensions of child grief.* https://aihcp.net/2012/07/27/child-grief-counseling-and-bereavement-education-dimensions-of-child-grief/

American School Counselor Association. (2019). *The ASCA National Model: A framework for school counseling programs* (4th ed.). Author.

American School Counselor Association. (2022). *ASCA ethical standards for school counselors.* www.schoolcounselor.org/About-School-Counseling/Ethical-Legal-Responsibilities/ASCA-Ethical-Standards-for-School-Counselors-(1)

Anderson, C. A., Shibuya, A., Ihori, N., Swing, E. L., Bushman, B. J., Sakamoto, A., Rothstein, H. R., & Saleem, M. (2010). Violent video game effects on aggression, empathy, and prosocial behavior in eastern and western countries: A meta-analytic review. *Psychological Bulletin, 136*(2), 151. https://doi.org/10.1037/a0018251

Baker, A. E. Z., Procter, N., & Gibbons, T. (2009). Dimensions of loss from mental illness. *The Journal of Sociology and Social Welfare, 36*(4), 25–52.

Berson, I. R., & Baggerly, J. (2009). Building resilience to trauma: Creating a safe and supportive early childhood classroom. *Childhood Education, 85*(6), 375–379. https://doi.org/10.1080/00094056.2009.10521404

Birkland, T. A., & Lawrence, R. G. (2009). Media framing and policy change after Columbine. *American Behavioral Scientist, 52*(10), 1405–1425. https://doi.org/10.1177/0002764209332555

Çakar, F. S. (2020). The role of social support in the relationship between adolescents' level of loss and grief and well-being. *International Education Studies, 13*(12), 27–40. https://doi.org/10.5539/ies.v13n12p27

Chafouleas, S. M., Johnson, A. H., Overstreet, S., & Santos, N. M. (2015). Toward a blueprint for trauma-informed service delivery in schools. *School Mental Health*, 8(1), 144–162. https://doi.org/10.1007/s12310-015-9166-8

Cole, S. F., Eisner, A., Gregory, M., & Ristuccia, J. (2013). Creating and advocating for trauma-sensitive schools. *Massachusetts Advocates for Children*. https://traumasensitiveschools.org/tlpi-publications/download-a-free-copy-of-a-guide-to-creating-trauma-sensitive-schools/

Corr, C., Adams, D. W., Davies, B., Deveau, E., de Veber, L. L., Martinson, I. M., Noone, M., Papadatou, D., Pask, E., Stevens, M. M., & Stevenson, R. G. (1999). Children, adolescents, and death: Myths, realities, and challenges. *Death Studies*, 23(5), 443–463. https://doi.org/10.1080/074811899200957

Delaney, K. K. (2017). Playing at violence: Lock-down drills, "bad guys" and the construction of "acceptable" play in early childhood. *Early Child Development and Care*, 187(5–6), 878–895. https://doi.org/10.1080/03004430.2016.1219853

Doka, K. J. (1989). Disenfranchised grief. In Doka, K. J. (Ed.), *Disenfranchised grief: Recognizing hidden sorrow* (pp. 3–11). Lexington Books.

Dorado, J. S., Martinez, M., McArthur, L. E., & Leibovitz, T. (2016). Healthy Environments and Response to Trauma in Schools (HEARTS): A whole-school, multi-level, prevention and intervention program for creating trauma-informed, safe and supportive schools. *School Mental Health*, 8(1), 163–176.

Dutil, S. (2019). Adolescent traumatic and disenfranchised grief: Adapting an evidence-based intervention for Black and Latinx youths in schools. *Children and Schools*, 41(3), 179–187. https://doi.org/10.1093/cs/cdz009

Evans Cuellar, A., McReynolds, L. S., & Wasserman, G. A. (2006). A cure for crime: Can mental health treatment diversion reduce crime among youth? *Journal of Policy Analysis and Management: The Journal of the Association for Public Policy Analysis and Management*, 25(1), 197–214. https://doi.org/10.1002/pam.20162

Every Student Succeeds Act, 20 U.S.C. § 6301 (2015). www.congress.gov/114/plaws/publ95/PLAW-114publ95.pdf

Feigelman, W., Rosen, Z., Joiner, T., Silva, C., & Mueller, A. S. (2017). Examining longer-term effects of parental death in adolescents and young adults: Evidence from the National Longitudinal Survey of Adolescent to Adult Health. *Death Studies*, 41(3), 133–143. https://doi.org/10.1080/07481187.2016.1226990

Ferow, A. (2019). Childhood grief and loss. *European Journal of Educational Sciences*, 1–13. https://doi.org/10.19044/ejes.s.v6a1

Flahault, C., Dolbeault, S., Sankey, C., & Fasse, L. (2018). Understanding grief in children who have lost a parent with cancer: How do they give meaning to this experience? Results of an interpretative phenomenological analysis. *Death Studies*, 42(8), 483–490. https://doi.org/10.1080/07481187.2017.1383951

Fowler, P. J., Tompsett, C. J., Braciszewski, J. M., Jacques-Tiura, A. J., & Baltes, B. B. (2009). Community violence: A meta-analysis on the effect of exposure and mental health outcomes of children and adolescents. *Development and Psychopathology*, *21*(1), 227–259. https://doi.org/10.1017/S0954579409000145

Hagan, M. J., Ingram, A. M., & Wolchik, S. A. (2016). Evidence-based interventions for childhood grief in children and adolescents. In *The handbook of evidence-based interventions for children and adolescents* (pp. 67–83). Springer.

Hannon, M. D., Mohabir, R. K., Cleveland, R. E., & Hunt, B. (2019). School counselors, multiple student deaths, and grief: A narrative inquiry. *Journal of Counseling and Development*, *97*(1), 43–52. https://doi.org/10.1002/jcad.12234

Holland, P. (2003). *We don't play with guns here: War, weapon and superhero play in the early years*. Open University Press.

Huskey, M. G., & Connell, N. M. (2021). Preparation or provocation? Student perceptions of active shooter drills. *Criminal Justice Policy Review*, *32*(1), 3–26. https://doi.org/10.1177/0887403419900316

Jaycox, L. H., Kataoka, S. H., Stein, B. D., Langley, A. K., & Wong, M. (2012). Cognitive behavioral intervention for trauma in schools. *Journal of Applied School Psychology*, *28*(3), 239–255. https://doi.org/10.1080/15377903.2012.695766

Jonson, C. L., Moon, M. M., & Hendry, J. A. (2018). One size does not fit all: Traditional lockdown versus multi-option responses to school shootings. *Journal of School Violence*, *19*, 154–166. https://doi.org/10.1080/15388220.2018.1553719

King, S., & Bracy, N. (2019). School security in the post-Columbine era: Trends, consequences, and future directions. *Journal of Contemporary Criminal Justice*, *35*(3), 274–295. https://doi.org/10.1177/1043986219840188

Kupchick, A., Brent, J. J., & Mowen, T. J. (2015). The aftermath of Newtown: More of the same. *British Journal of Criminology*, *55*, 1115–1130. https://doi.org/10.1093/bjc/azv049

Layne, C. M., Briggs, E. C., & Courtois, C. A. (2014). Introduction to the special section: Using the Trauma History Profile to unpack risk factor caravans and their consequences. *Psychological Trauma: Theory, Research, Practice, and Policy*, *6*(S1), S1–S8. https://doi.org/10.1037/a0037768

Marino, R. C., Thornton, M. D., & Lange, T. (2015). Professional school counselors address grief and loss: A creative group counseling intervention. *VISTAS Online*, Article 66. www.counseling.org/docs/default-source/vistas/article_66965a22f16116603abcacff0000bee5e7.pdf?sfvrsn=4

Mowen, T. J., & Freng, A. (2019). Is more necessarily better? School security and perceptions of safety among students and parents in the United States. *American Journal of Criminal Justice*, *44*(3), 376–394. https://doi.org/10.1007/s12103-018-9461-7

Musu, L., Zhang, A., Wang, K., Zhang, J., & Oudekerk, B. A. (2019). *Indicators of school crime and safety: 2018* (Publication no. NCES 2019–04/NCJ 252571). National Center for Education Statistics, U.S. Department of Education, and Bureau of Justice Statistics, Office of Justice Programs, U.S. Department of Justice. https://nces.ed.gov/pubs2019/2019047.pdf

Na, C., & Gottfredson, D. C. (2013). Police officers in schools: Effects on school crime and the processing of offending behaviors. *Justice Quarterly, 30*(4), 619–650. https://doi.org/10.1080/07418825.2011.615754

National Threat Assessment Center. (2019). *Protecting America's schools: A U.S. Secret Service analysis of targeted school violence.* U.S. Secret Service, Department of Homeland Security. www.secretservice.gov/sites/default/files/2020-04/Protecting_Americas_Schools.pdf

Ngo, V., Langley, A., Kataoka, S., Nadeem, E., Escudero, P., & Stein, B. D. (2008). Providing evidence-based practice to ethnically diverse youths: Examples from the Cognitive Behavioral Intervention for Trauma in Schools (CBITS) program. *Journal of the American Academy of Child and Adolescent Psychiatry, 47*, 858–862. https://doi.org/10.1097/CHI.0b013e3181799f19

Paolini, A. (2015). School shootings and student mental health: Role of the school counselor in mitigating violence. *Vistas Online*, Article 90. www.counseling.org/docs/default-source/vistas/school-shootings-and-student-mental-health.p

Perfect, M., Turley, M., Carlson, J. S., Yohannan, J., & Gilles, M. S. (2016). School-related outcomes of traumatic event exposure and traumatic stress symptoms in students: A systematic review of research from 1990 to 2015. *School Mental Health, 8*(1), 7–43. https://doi.org/10.1007/s12310-016-9175-2

Price, J. H., Khubchandani, J., Payton, E., & Thompson, A. (2016). Reducing the risks of firearm violence in high schools: Principals' perceptions and practices. *Journal of Community Health, 41*(2), 234–243. https://doi.org/10.1007/s10900-015-0087-0

Protivnak, J. J., Scott, H., Herman, E. R., & Matos, D. (2020). Addressing the unrecognized grief of elementary students experiencing relationship loss. *Journal of School Counseling, 18*(28). https://eric.ed.gov/?id=EJ1281110

Rosner, R., Kruse, J., & Hagl, M. (2010). A meta-analysis of interventions for bereaved children and adolescents. *Death Studies, 34*(2), 99–136. https://doi.org/10.1080/07481180903492422

Substance Abuse and Mental Health Services Administration. (2014). *SAMHSA's concept of trauma and guidance for a trauma-informed approach* (HHS publication no. [SMA] 14–484). https://store.samhsa.gov/sites/default/files/d7/priv/sma14-4884.pdf

Teplin, L. A., Abram, K. M., McClelland, G. M., Dulcan, M. K., & Mericle, A. A. (2002). Psychiatric disorders in youth in juvenile detention. *Archives of General Psychiatry, 59*(12), 1133–1143. https://doi.org/10.1001/archpsyc.59.12.1133

Thapa, A., Cohen, J., Guffey, S., & Higgins-D'Alessandro, A. (2013). A review of school climate research. *Review of Educational Research, 83*(3), 357–385. https://doi.org/10.3102/0034654313483907

Ttofi, M. M., Farrington, D. P., & Lösel, F. (2012). School bullying as a predictor of violence later in life: A systematic review and meta-analysis of prospective longitudinal studies. *Aggression and Violent Behavior, 17*(5), 405–418. https://doi.org/10.1016/j.avb.2012.05.002

Turner, R. (2020). Playing through the unimaginable: Play therapy for traumatic loss. *International Journal of Play Therapy, 29*(2), 96. https://doi.org/10.1037/pla0000116

Vossekuil, B., Fein, R. A., Reddy, M., Borum, R., & Modzeleski, W. (2002). *The final report and findings of the Safe School Initiative: Implications for the prevention of school attacks in the United States.* United States Secret Service and United States Department of Education. https://www2.ed.gov/admins/lead/safety/preventingattacksreport.pdf

Walters, G. D. (2021). School-age bullying victimization and perpetration: A meta-analysis of prospective studies and research. *Trauma, Violence, and Abuse, 22*(5), 1129–1139. https://doi.org/10.1177/1524838020906513

Questions for reflective practice

1. Recall your experiences within the school setting as a youth. What losses do you recognize as an adult that you did not recognize as a child? Of these losses, which were directly attributed to the school setting and/or perpetuated by the school system?
2. As a youth, what external losses did you experience that were not acknowledged or adequately addressed by the school system? What would have been different for you if these losses had been acknowledged?
3. With consideration for the influence of culture and diversity, what losses impact the current generation of youth that were not part of the landscape of your youth? In your perception, what is different for today's youth? How will you educate yourself to provide culturally curious treatment?

Supplemental electronic resources

- The Alcove Center for Grieving Children and Families: https://thealcove.org/
- American Academy of Child and Adolescent Psychiatry: www.aacap.org/
- Association for Death Education and Counseling: www.adec.org

- The Dougy Center for Grieving Children and Families: www.dougy.org/
- Linda Goldman: Helping children with grief and trauma: www.grieving children.net/
- National Alliance for Children's Grief: https://childrengrieve.org/
- OUR HOUSE Grief Support Center, School Personnel Toolkit: Supporting Grieving Students in the age of COVID-19 and beyond: www.nea.org/sites/default/files/2020-10/Our-House-ESP-COVID-Toolkit.pdf

Part III

Disenfranchised grief impacting families

12

Loss within the margins of childrearing

Disenfranchised grief in parenting

Mandi Meléndez

The act of becoming a parent initiates a shift in identity and creates a new relational "we" that is entirely outside both parent and child. For a time, the parent may only tentatively sense the child's individuality, perhaps filling in the unknown aspects of personality with hopes or expectations. But the child's inner self grows as the body does, which invites a continuous and dynamic recalibration of the intrapersonal and interpersonal experiences within the parent-child relationship. Diana Gabaldon (1992) eloquently described this phenomenon in her novel *Dragonfly in Amber*:

> Babies are soft. Anyone looking at them can see the tender, fragile skin and know it for the rose-leaf softness that invites a finger's touch. But when you live with them and love them, you feel the softness going inward, the round-cheeked flesh wobbly as custard, the boneless splay of the tiny hands. Their joints are melted rubber, and even when you kiss them hard, in the passion of loving their existence, your lips sink down and seem never to find bone. Holding them against you, they melt and mold, as though they might at any moment flow back into your body.
>
> But from the very start, there is that small streak of steel within each child. That thing that says, "I am," and forms the core of personality.
>
> In the second year, the bone hardens and the child stands upright, skull wide and solid, a helmet protecting the softness within. And "I am" grows, too. Looking at them, you can almost see it, sturdy as heartwood, glowing through the translucent flesh.
>
> The bones of the face emerge at six, and the soul within is fixed at seven. The process of encapsulation goes on, to reach its peak in the glossy shell of adolescence, when all softness then is hidden under the nacreous layers of the multiple new personalities that teenagers try on to guard themselves.

DOI: 10.4324/9781003292890-15

> In the next years, the hardening spreads from the center, as one finds and fixes the facets of the soul, until "I am" is set, delicate and detailed as an insect in amber.

(p. 55)

As a people, we are socialized to believe that raising children is both our birthright and our obligation to the world in return for our own creation. Carrying forward the human population, creating and shaping the future generation, and reveling in the privilege of doing so is the assumed highest calling for many people. Children may be gifted baby dolls, complete with the accoutrements of the work of parenting, like bottles, diapers, and strollers. In grade school, children may already be planning how many of their own to have someday and what to name them, "playing house" at recess, and appointing familial roles for peers. Literature written for young adolescents instills the idea that as parents they will need to accept their self-sacrificial lot, as when a father in a popular young adult series told his son, "When you become a parent, you may understand this. One of my hardest jobs as a father, one of my greatest duties, was to realize that my own dreams, my own goals and wishes, are secondary to my children's" (Riodan, 2010, p. 472).

Some newlyweds complain they are already being asked when they will start their own family by family and strangers alike. This implies, of course, that a family is not composed of two adults, but must include offspring. In several countries, including Ireland, tradition holds that the top layer of the wedding cake be saved and served at the christening of the firstborn child, cementing the relationship between marriage and procreation. Couples who are childless after some time together are often assumed to have wanted children but have been unable to fulfill their dreams. Those who struggle with infertility can feel not only incomplete as a family but may also feel incomplete or faulty as human beings under the weight of social expectation when unable to conceive or carry a child. Those who terminate a pregnancy may live with shame for not "meeting" the challenge of this assumed privilege of childrearing or feel grief or guilt over their belief that abortion was the correct choice. The world views the creation and upbringing of children as a duty and a privilege of being human. Indeed, many parents will readily acknowledge that having children has been the greatest and most central joy of their lives.

But what of parents for whom parenting has been tinged with unspeakable loss, disappointment, and grief? Or those whose experience of their actual child does not meet their expectations of the child they were committing to raise? More challenging still is the sense that in becoming a parent, one loses the right or ability to even think thoughts that solely care for the self. In her song, "The Mother," Brandi Carlile (2018) poignantly described how a mother's thoughts become preoccupied by worry for her child to the detriment of her own mental space. The inability to speak freely of grief related to identity shifts as a result of parenting, and thus seeking support and connection around this grief, becomes an anchor that pulls the grieving parent down as they struggle more fiercely to cling to the parent identity while sinking under the weight of the burden.

The disenfranchised grief of childrearing

Disenfranchised grief can be defined as grief that is encountered by those who have experienced a loss that is not or cannot be publicly acknowledged, openly mourned, or socially supported (Doka, 1999). Disenfranchised grief poses an emotional dilemma: to suffer in silence with often overwhelming outcomes or to suffer the potential ignominy of perceived social failure. People experiencing grief around unmet expectations and the identity shift of parenting may find their emotions so at odds with widely held beliefs about parenting that they cannot even allow themselves to think their private thoughts if those thoughts are deemed unloving towards their children. In turn, the griever will seek more formal sources of support, and mental health providers should be equipped to care for the disenfranchised parts of the parent-griever (Doka, 2020).

If the nature of disenfranchisement is denial of the mourner's right to grieve, then supporters must privilege the parent's grief to welcome the self of the parent into wholeness (Attig, 2004). Parents may fear the resultant impact of defining the edges of their grief on the child and family; however, continuing to juxtapose their child's growth with the depreciation of unnamed parts of themselves carries with it the potential for exponential damage to all, including the child. As Swiss psychologist Carl Jung (1954/2014) opined, "There can be no doubt that it is of the utmost value for parents to view their children's symptoms in the light of their own problems and conflicts" (p. 42).

The parent who finds marked loss within the margins of childrearing may find themselves isolated with their sadness, anger, and disappointment, as so few are able to articulate the grief of parenting a living child, and fewer still are willing to share for fear of sanction. "Mothers have martyred themselves in their children's names since the beginning of time. We have lived as if she who disappears the most, loves the most. We have been conditioned to prove our love by slowly ceasing to exist" (Doyle, 2020, p. 128). Relationships, and even larger webs of social functioning, crave homeostasis. Attempts to step away from the accepted narrative of parenting as perhaps an exasperating but altogether worthwhile enterprise have the potential to disrupt one's existence so entirely that well-meaning confidants will deny, dismiss, or correct a parent who attempts to share their grief. Even Mother's Day and Father's Day, celebrated in numerous countries throughout the world, focus the idealized lens on the role of parenting as one of joyful self-sacrifice. Mother's and Father's Day cards and gifts that imply a parent is simply average are considered jokes. Meanwhile even capitalism has not yet found a share of the market for cards noting the sorrows and losses that many parents experience on these holidays. Parents of a deceased child would certainly suffer on these holidays in a way that some sensitive friends and family may take note of and support. But for those who have experienced infertility, pregnancy loss, abortion, or losing a child to adoption or foster care, there will likely be little to no acknowledgment of them or their pain. Perhaps even more ambiguous than these losses is the complex array of emotions arising on holidays to celebrate parents when those parents experience parenting as a signifier of their own failings.

The double bind in the disenfranchised grief of parenting

Parents the world over are taught that having and raising children is central to the human experience. In Moorhead's (2005) article, anthropologist Barry Hewlett described the beliefs of a group of African Indigenous people, "To the Aka, your children are the very value of your life. The idea of a child as a burden would be incomprehensible there . . . children are the energy, the life force of the community" (p. 1). Although many parents would agree, those who disagree would feel the double bind of shame by dissent and their inability to express or seek support for it. In Jamaica, tradition holds that friends and family donate a tree to the parents of a new baby, under which the placenta will be buried to nourish the tree, to symbolize the family's attachment to the land now that they have created a child. To be an adult without a child might be considered a disconnection from the culture and the homeland itself, magnifying the loss sustained. This polarity, that parenting a child must either be central to the person's identity and value or be a hidden shame in the lack of this identity and value, further disenfranchises the grief. It may be more helpful, and more resonant, if our society were to appreciate the shift in identity and value as well as the grief particular to parenting.

Becoming a parent includes marked shifts in intrapersonal and interpersonal identity grounded in cultural, social, and relational expectations. This shift in identity has been well documented in popular media and research, but little has been explored about the grief that may accompany the parenthood experience. Aside from expected sacrifices in sleep, money, and free time, parents may experience myriad losses that defy quantification. Intrapersonally, parents may experience loss of physical and psychological freedom to make self-interested decisions. These decisions might include complex changes like those in changing jobs, homes, or relationships, or even simpler choices, such as whether to seek or avoid certain foods, exercise, media, or medication. They may experience a loss of felt safety for themselves in relation to their child, resulting in a diminishment of previously appreciated aspects of identity, such as engaging in travel and other potentially riskier activities.

Interpersonally, parents may feel unprepared to experience new needs or desires to maintain, intensify, or distance from their family of origin, community, or culture. Parents at all stages of the child's development may experience a diminished sense of efficacy, loss of dreams and expectations about who they might be as a parent, who their child would be, how their relationships, communities, and cultures would interact with and support their child and their parent self. Parents may feel shame if they consider these losses, much less speak about them, thus amplifying the covert nature of the grief and deepening the sense of isolation. More damaging than the experiences of loss surrounding parents is the inability to express the grief and find resonance in the community. The parent experiencing disenfranchised grief is often unable to articulate the loss or identify the source of grief.

Maccallum and Bryant (2008) asserted that the primary task of bereavement is to revise "self-identity to incorporate the reality of the loss and enable the development of new goals, life roles, and attachments that are independent of the loss" (p. 719). This assumes the person is able to identify the loss, which may not be the case with parents who are suppressing grief. Parents may also experience a variety of mental health concerns, including anxiety, depression, or substance abuse rooted in the experience of shame around the felt losses of being a parent. Thus, a mental health provider's primary task is to support the existence and identification of the loss, so the parent is better able to integrate it and effectively engage with their new role and attachments.

Additionally, by right of the child development process, parents must continually change roles and shift personal identity. Throughout the child's maturation process, the parent will need to hone their identity in relationship to the child and the child's developing independence and, at times, may feel more or less connected to their child. The child's natural weaving in and out of developmental phases may create a sense of turmoil for the parent as they work continually to meet the demands of each new developmental season.

The social disconnection inherent in disenfranchised grief

Parents who can identify and articulate their grief may in return be met with both implicit and overt resistance as relational partners and society at large diminish or deny the grief experience. Parents who attempt to define the loss experience in all but the blandest terms, even with significant appreciation of concurrent gains in becoming a parent, may be met with dismissiveness or outright denial by their relational partners. This is in keeping with the concept of homeostasis, explored in family systems theory and others, whereby relational partners may send messages that maintain the relationship rather than change it (Bowen, 1966; Schwartz, 1998). Engagement of parental grief with the larger society may be limited by an unwillingness to acknowledge these losses in a more public capacity if they are met with negative feedback within the family system. Cultural institutions may be called upon to strengthen parent identity while simultaneously prescribing a predictable set of rules and expectations that minimize or deny parents' grief.

Those who have experienced pregnancy but do not have a child, such as those impacted by baby loss or pregnancy termination, may experience simultaneous and enigmatic pressures as the pregnancy has physically ended but the parental sense of attachment may endure (Lang et al., 2011). Due to stigma, politicization, lack of a standardized societal response to perinatal loss, and public perceptions that a fetus may not be a "real child," those grieving a perinatal loss may feel unsafe or unable to share their grief and thus are reluctant to seek support among family, friends, or even in medical or therapeutic settings (Goldblatt Hyatt, 2021; Lang et al., 2011; Sawicka, 2016).

Although social integration is greater for parents than it is for nonparents (Nomaguchi & Milkie, 2003), the inability to articulate and share grief deepens the feeling of disconnect. This has the potential to compound the disenfranchised grief as the feeling of disconnect moves from within a person to between people and entities. Grieving parents may feel they are at the center of a vortex, where self-disconnect fosters relational disconnect from partners; in turn, the disconnect widens and strengthens the cyclone and spins out to include social and community disengagement toward a fractured relationship with the culture in which the parent exists. This has the potential to turn back inwards and reach through the parent to the child. Bruce (2000) described a cycle of disenfranchisement, wherein a parent who is unable to integrate their continuing grief may be perpetually overwhelmed by it, finding themselves less able to support their children, their families, and themselves, and thus aggravating and reinforcing the grief.

Cultural aspects of disenfranchised grief

Parents may suffer in silence over the ways their child is not who they expected. People are enculturated to predict and control the variables we believe will determine who a child might become, with rituals in nearly every world culture around expectations for the child. For example, the Igbo Indigenous people of Nigeria encourage parents to select an articulate relative to chew alligator pepper and then share saliva with the newborn, so the child will be as well-spoken as the relative offering the blessing. In the eastern cape of Africa, Sifudu custom dictates a new baby be passed through the smoke of Sifudu tree leaves so they will never be timid, shy, or anxious. In many cultures, rituals circumscribe a child's prospects. In Armenia, a baby who has cut their first tooth is tempted with sweets to crawl towards objects predicting their future career and contribution to the world. A tractor might indicate a future farmer, a cake could point to the next baker in the family. What goes unsaid is that many futures are excluded from the ritual simply due to the parentally approved parameters. In this manner, parents whose child is not what they expected (or wanted) may find their grief impossible to articulate.

Although there are innumerable ways in which a parent may feel grief around a child or parenting not being as hoped, it is no less difficult for parents to speak of this loss for fear of outing themselves as a parent who does not meet the expectations of parental adoration and martyrdom. One client described:

> I love my kid. But I don't like him very much, which feels like an awful thing to say. I would be horrified if he ever knew I said that. And it's not even his fault or something he did. He is just . . . not that intelligent. And I don't want that to be the only thing that counts! But I am smart, and so is [his other parent], and we just assumed he would be as well. I resent having to explain things that seem obvious, and I feel embarrassed when people meet him and see him for what he is. But I can't say that, so I try different ways to avoid these feelings, to change him or change others' view of him. But what I really wish is that I could stop wishing to change him. He's just not like me, in the way I thought was most important.

Another client described a burgeoning awareness that becoming a parent had been a mistake that was impossible to correct. She had thought she wanted a child, and after nearly a decade still deeply missed the person she had been before becoming a mother: a woman who could make choices about her own happiness, who was untethered, and whose energy was spent in creative self-directed pursuit. She described her parenting performance as "more than adequate" and yet felt deep shame for not finding the fulfillment so many others seemed to in this role.

Despite these challenges, there is reason to believe that with support for all a parent's grieving parts, they may come to integrate the wanted and expected with the unwanted and unexpected in their child. Solomon (2012) stated:

> To look deep into your child's eyes and see in him both yourself and something utterly strange, and then to develop a zealous attachment to every aspect of him, is to achieve parenthood's self-regarding, yet unselfish, abandon. It is astonishing how often such mutuality had been realized – how frequently parents who had supposed that they couldn't care for an exceptional child discover that they can. The parental predisposition to love prevails in the most harrowing of circumstances. There is more imagination in the world than one might think.
>
> (p. 6)

Relational aspects to disenfranchised grief

Individual parents are not the only ones to experience the negative impact of their disenfranchised grief. Couples with children report lower relationship satisfaction than those without. New parents are likely to experience challenges in their romantic relationship as they adjust to their new family structure. Among them, new parents report pervasive postpartum sexual concerns that are moderately distressing and related to lower relationship satisfaction (Schlagintweit et al., 2016).

Countless researchers also have demonstrated the deep connection between parent and child wellness. Maternal emotional distress is a strong predictor of internalizing problems in children (Bayer et al., 2011). Studies of grieving refugee parents have found that caregivers' grief is directly associated with their children's emotional challenges (Bryant et al., 2021). For example, in families where one parent has died, it is the surviving parent's functioning that most influences the children's wellbeing and adjustment to loss (Haine et al., 2008). Unresolved grief in the remaining partner may even impact the parent-child attachment in subsequent pregnancies (O'Leary, 2004).

The attachment relationship between parent and child has profound implications for both participants. These include social, emotional, cognitive, and behavioral components, with each person creating an internal representation or *working model* of the relationship and its participants. This working model influences the participants' behaviors such that they reflect and maintain the relationship (Goldberg, 2000). Thus, if a parent is grieving or otherwise distressed, both the child and the parent will be impacted personally and interpersonally as they make sense of themselves and the other through the lens of grief. If the child eventually becomes a parent, then attachment trauma has the potential to prolong and amplify insecure attachment as each new generation carries forward the undigested grief of the progenitors.

Cumulative impacts of disenfranchised grief across the lifespan

Disenfranchised grief in parenting will have a cumulative effect across the lifespan and intergenerationally, radiating out towards the previous and the next generations. New parents may find themselves macerating in multifaceted grief, which may feel unspeakable as they are embraced by a community congratulating them on their "bundle of joy." Or a parent may find that they are ill-equipped to offer nurturance to their own child because they are so unfamiliar. As van der Kolk (2015) explained:

> If your parents' faces never lit up when they looked at you, it's hard to know what it feels like to be loved and cherished. If you come from an incomprehensible world filled with secrecy and fear, it's almost impossible to find the words to express what you have endured. If you grew up unwanted and ignored, it is a major challenge to develop a visceral sense of agency and self-worth.
>
> (p. 296)

Conversely, parents may become simultaneously more and less forgiving of their own experiences of being parented as they navigate the waters of parenthood themselves. That which seemed impossibly challenging for their own parents, perhaps unconditional love, protection, or sensitive emotional response, may feel intuitive and automatic to the adult child as a parent, thus deepening the divide between adult child and now grandparent. Alternatively, previously misunderstood aspects of parenting may now resonate with deep empathy and compassion for the parent of the adult child. The exhaustion, confusion, anxiety, and stress inherent in the early stages of parenting may allow the new parent to see their own parents' dysfunctional behavior in a new light, as they themselves grapple with and at times fail to meet the overwhelming demands in this new position and identity.

Consequently, the parent and adult child's working model may shift as the adult child's unmet childhood needs may be joined with a new empathy for their own parents' demands at a similar stage. This season of growth and development is ripe with opportunity to break the bondage of intergenerational trauma, but these adult children will need to navigate several experiences of disenfranchised grief, including their own childhood losses, as well as the loss of their fantasized or idealized parent (Zupanick, 1994).

Allyship and advocacy

Childrearing is integral to our society and indeed the continuation of human existence, which creates a burdening dynamic for parents experiencing grief around parenting. Parents face a variety of challenges to truthfully expressing, or even considering, losses incurred in the face of what society proclaims should be the greatest joy of their lives. To effectively ally with parents in grief, mental health providers will first need to normalize feelings of grief in parents and the wide array of grief experiences surrounding parenthood. Communicating this to the world at large will require sensitivity and determination, as societal norms will suggest rejection of anything that may challenge the existing narrative around parenting.

Providers might consider writing, offering therapy groups, presenting to the public and specifically to groups of parents, and educating fellow therapists on the complexity and widespread experience of grief in parenting. Encouraging a stance of both/and, such that parents may simultaneously hold seemingly contradictory feelings of love and loss around parenting, enhances the individual's capacity to integrate all parts of their parenting experience. In essence, anything that invites the grief of parenthood to exist within the parent and between the self and the other will support the grieving parent.

Ethical considerations

As the most vulnerable party, the child of the grieving parent must be protected first and foremost. Clinicians providing support to the grieving parent must include the child's physical and emotional safety as a primary consideration in all engagements. A parent grappling with disenfranchised grief may find themselves unmoored by their awareness and may move towards unintended neglect or endangerment. Even in the absence of abuse, the child's attachment and attunement with the primary caregiver are of vital importance to healthy development. Parenting experts and neuroscientists have shared that the common thread to raising happy, healthy children is for them to feel safe and protected from danger, to be seen and loved, soothed when hurting, and secure that the relationship and the world are reasonably predictable (Siegel & Bryson, 2011). These goals may be challenging for the grieving parent to meet. Therapists should offer support to clarify and enhance the parental focus on these needs, and to resource the parent and child when they are not able to adequately meet these needs.

Mental health providers must remain alert for signs of children's unmet needs and advocate for social, cultural, and relational support for the child and the parent. Often, parents believe that by serving their child, they are also serving themselves, when the opposite is true. When a parent's emotional needs are met, they are empowered to see and serve their child's needs. Unfortunately, children grow relentlessly toward adulthood and may not be paused in this process, no matter how desperately the parent may need a break while seeking self-knowledge and acceptance.

When a parent's own growth process leaves little bandwidth for meeting the needs of the child, additional supports for the child may be found in the community. Individual and developmentally appropriate therapy for the child is appropriate, in addition to seeking and strengthening the child's relationships with caretakers and supporters like other parents, extended family, close friends, teachers, coaches, and faith leaders. Indeed, the bigger and thicker the therapeutic web of support for the child, the freer the parent will be and feel to pursue self-knowledge. In turn, this provides a more solid foundation upon which the child may grow. Thus, everything that supports parental growth is in service to the child. Parents who work towards integration of disenfranchised grief in parenting provide a solid foundation upon which their own children may thrive. With the weight of silence lifted, the parent can chart their own course while also providing secure presence for their child to do the same.

Strategies and interventions

Most of the literature on disenfranchised grief suggests that we must enlarge the circle of what constitutes legitimate grievers to enfranchise those who are disenfranchised. For the previously explored reasons, as well as the myriad obligations and exhaustion that are typical to raising children, parents may find themselves sparsely supported and unable to think about the grief of parenting. Mindfulness, meditation, prayer, and movement can be supportive to parents working to permit their own thoughts of loss to rise to the previously impenetrable surface. Likewise, journaling or poetry have the potential to connect the emotions to consciousness.

Enlarging the therapeutic web of support for parents requires direct and vocal support by those who are deemed experts and who are less vulnerable to censorship by peers. Mental health providers give voice to those less empowered. Thus, a primary strategy of support is the simple-but-no-less challenging task of drawing attention to parents' disenfranchised grief. Speaking with personal and professional peers may initiate previously unheard conversations that become the proverbial stone on a still pond, sending ripples of energy toward shores desperate for support. Offering sanctuary and confidential engagement, either through individual therapy or moderated groups of like-minded peers, may give shape to the abstract emotions of grief in parenting and strengthen the known while crystallizing the unknown for parents.

Rituals provide an opportunity to construct and/or restore a sense of meaning in the wake of loss (Hall, 2001). Parents exploring their grief around parenting may need new rituals that engage the polarity of what is and what is not, what has been and what will now no longer be. Confucius (1533/2001) taught, "When it comes to ritual, it is better to be spare than extravagant" (Bay yi, 3:4). This is taken to mean that ritual should be focused on simplicity and not be draining but restorative (Cline, 2020). Daily rituals, such as meditation, expressions of gratitude, or time spent in nature may be the balm needed for the wounds that appear as disenfranchised grief is shaped into knowing and integration.

Summary

Parenting creates a window of opportunity for unsurpassed love, joy, and healing, as well as the potential for indescribable anxiety, loss, and anguish. Parents' disenfranchised grief, once found and integrated, has the capacity to break generational cycles, heal old wounds, and enable them to exist in wholeness. The therapist's job is simultaneously the most complex and the most simplistic: Allow the grief to come. Be prepared for the many ways grief might show up in parents, so that when it shyly emerges, we are ready to invite it into the room. Allow the grief to take shape and develop just as a child does: a thought and a feeling breathed into existence, soft and malleable at first, slowly forming into forged steel, the strength that carries the soul forward.

References

Attig, T. (2004). Disenfranchised grief revisited: Discounting hope and love. OMEGA – Journal of Death and Dying, 49(3), 197–215. https://doi.org/10.2190/P4TT-J3BF-KFDR-5JB1

Bayer, J. K., Ukoumunne, O. C., Lucas, N., Wake, M., Scalzo, K., & Nicholson, J. M. (2011). Risk factors for childhood mental health symptoms: National longitudinal study of Australian children. Pediatrics, 128(4), e865–e879. https://doi.org/10.1542/peds.2011-0491

Bowen, M. (1966). The use of family theory in clinical practice. *Comprehensive Psychiatry*, 7(5), 345–374. https://doi.org/dqm2tx

Bruce, E. J. (2000). Grief, trauma and parenting children with disability. *Grief Matters: The Australian Journal of Grief and Bereavement*, 3(2), 27–31.

Bryant, R. A., Edwards, B., Creamer, M., O'Donnell, M., Forbes, D., Felmingham, K. L., Silove, D., Steel, Z., McFarlane, A. C., Van Hooff, M., Nickerson, A., & Hadzi-Pavlovic, D. (2021). Prolonged grief in refugees, parenting behaviour and children's mental health. *Australian and New Zealand Journal of Psychiatry*, 55(9), 863–873. https://doi.org/10.1177/0004867420967420

Carlile, B. (2018). The mother [Song]. On *By the way, I forgive you*. Low Country Sound; Elektra.

Cline, E. (2020). *Little sprouts and the Dao of parenting: Ancient Chinese philosophy and the art of raising mindful, resilient and compassionate kids.* Norton.

Confucius. (2001). *The original analects: Sayings of Confucius and his followers* (Brooks, E. B., &, Brooks, T., Trans.; Bay yi, 3:4). Columbia University Press. (Original work published 1533)

Doka, K. J. (1999). Disenfranchised grief. *Bereavement Care*, 18(3), 37–39. https://doi.org/10.1080/02682629908657467

Doka, K. J. (2020). Disenfranchised grief: An exposition and update. In J. D. Morgan (Ed.), *Readings in thanatology* (pp. 275–283). Routledge.

Doyle, G. (2020). *Untamed*. The Dial Press.

Gabaldon, D. (1992). *Dragonfly in amber*. Delacorte Press.

Goldberg, S. (2000). *Attachment and development*. Routledge.

Goldblatt Hyatt, E. D. (2021). Counseling women who have terminated a pregnancy due to fetal anomaly (TOPFA): The ACCEPT model. *Clinical Social Work Journal*, 49(1), 52–63.

Haine, R. A., Ayers, T. S., & Sandler, I. N. (2008). Evidenced-based practices for parentally bereaved children and their families. *Professional Psychological Research*, 39(2), 113–121. https://doi.org/10.1037/0735-7028.39.2.113

Hall, C. (2001). Reconstructing meaning in the wake of loss: Creating "meaning full" ritual activities. *Grief Matters: The Australian Journal of Grief and Bereavement*, 3(4), 51–53.

Homeyer, L. E., & Sweeney, D. S. (2021). *Sandtray therapy: A practical manual* (4th ed.). Routledge.

Jung, C. G. (2014). *The development of personality: Papers on child psychology, education, and related subject: Vol. 17 Collected works of C. G. Jung* (G. Adler, Ed., & F. C. Hull, Ed., & Trans.). Princeton University Press. (Original work published in 1954) https://doi.org/10.1515/9781400850839

Lang, A., Fleiszer, A. R., Duhamel, F., Sword, W., Gilbert, K. R., & Corsini-Munt, S. (2011). Perinatal loss and parental grief: The challenge of ambiguity and disenfranchised grief. *OMEGA – Journal of Death and Dying, 63*(2), 183–196.

Maccallum, F., & Bryant, R. A. (2008). Self-defining memories in complicated grief. *Behavior Research and Therapy, 46*(12), 1311–1315. https://doi.org/10.1016/j.brat.2008.09.003

McGoldrick, M., Gerson, R., & Petry, S. S. (2020). *Genograms: Assessment and intervention* (3rd ed.). Norton.

Moorhead, J. (2005, June 15). Are the men of the Aka tribe the best fathers in the world? *The Guardian.* www.theguardian.com/society/2005/jun/15/childrensservices.familyandrelationships

Nomaguchi, K. M., & Milkie, M. A. (2003). Costs and rewards of children: The effects of becoming a parent on adults' lives. *Journal of Marriage and Family, 65*(2), 356–374. https://doi.org/10.1111/j.1741-3737.2003.00356.x

O'Leary, J. (2004). Grief and its impact on prenatal attachment in the subsequent pregnancy. *Archives of Women's Mental Health, 7*(1), 7–18. https://doi.org/10.1007/s00737-003-0037-1

Riodan, R. (2010). *The red pyramid.* Disney Hyperion Books.

Sawicka, M. (2016). Searching for a narrative of loss: Interactional ordering of ambiguous grief. *Symbolic Interaction, 40*(2), 229–246.

Schlagintweit, H. E., Bailey, K., & Rosen, N. O. (2016). A new baby in the bedroom: Frequency and severity of postpartum sexual concerns and their associations with relationship satisfaction in new parent couples. *The Journal of Sexual Medicine, 13*(10), 1455–1465. https://doi.org/10.1016/j.jsxm.2016.08.006

Schwartz, R. C. (1998). Internal family systems family therapy. In F. M. Dattilio, F. M., & M. R. Goldfried (Eds.), *Case studies in couple and family therapy: Systemic and cognitive perspective* (pp. 331–352). Guilford Press.

Siegel, D. J., & Payne Bryson, T. (2011). *The whole-brain child: 12 revolutionary strategies to nurture your child's developing mind.* Bantam Books.

Solomon, A. (2012). *Far from the tree: Parents, children and the search for identity.* Scribner.

van der Kolk, B. A. (2015). *The body keeps the score: Brain, mind, and body in the healing of trauma.* Penguin Books.

Zupanick, C. E. (1994). Adult children of dysfunctional families: Treatment from a disenfranchised grief perspective. *Death Studies, 18*(2), 183–195. https://doi.org/10.1080/07481189408252650

Questions for reflective practice

1. Sit in quiet introspection and meditate on the question: "Who could I have been/who would I be if I were not a parent?" Notice the responses, including the rejection of responses, that arise within the solitude of your thoughts. What makes it difficult to hear your own thoughts? What is ambiguous in these projections, and what is concrete? How do these connect with what is socially, relationally, and culturally acceptable in your family of origin and in the family you founded?
2. The person of the therapist must be constantly explored and understood to facilitate optimal client support. Create a sand tray (e.g., Homeyer & Sweeney, 2021) or a collage that shows your world of what *is*, what *has been*, what *could be*, and what *could have been*. Where do these worlds touch and foster connection and integration, and where do they diverge from one another?
3. The creation of a human life is irreversible. Even after death, the life does not cease to have existed. For a parent who may be grieving because of or around the existence of their child, what strengths will need to be developed or nurtured for them to carry forward with acceptance and awareness? Write a "prescription" that meets the needs of the whole parent, including physical care and intrapersonal and interpersonal support.
4. Create a genogram (e.g., McGoldrick et al., 2020) depicting the perceived strength of parent and child relationships in your own family, as well as the expected losses of parenting within and between generations. What are the intergenerational trends? What would you like to carry forward, and what would you like to grow through and out of? Project into the future, including any children you may have and how you could imagine them as parents. What would you like to see stay the same? What would you like to see change?

Supplemental electronic resources

- American Academy of Pediatrics Parenting Website: www.healthy children.org
- The Compassionate Friends: www.compassionatefriends.org
- Glow in the Woods for babylost mothers and fathers: www.glowinthe woods.com
- Parenting After Trauma with Robyn Gobel podcast: https://podcasts. apple.com/us/podcast/parenting-after-trauma-with-robyn-gobbel/ id1543535062
- Parenting for Brain (supported by AAP and APA): www.parentingfor brain.com

13
African American sibling loss

A sister's perspective

Tangela C. Sawyerr

Society has dictated how and for whom one grieves, and this hierarchy has fostered a culture of bereavement inequity. Though adult sibling loss can be the most traumatic experience of a person's life, it is often unrecognized within academia and the larger society. Sibling grief is influenced by identity, culture, family dynamics, and societal expectations. Individuals of diverse backgrounds are more vulnerable to multiple forms of oppression due to their overlapping social identities. Therefore, the current author will explore the role of intersectionality and how social systems and structures contribute to the oppression and marginalization of siblings during their bereavement. It will also illuminate the importance of intersectionality, allyship, and culturally affirming grief support for those experiencing sibling loss.

Intersectionality and sibling loss

The intersectionality framework originated through the Black Feminist movement to explore, challenge, and critique how antiracist and feminist movements overlooked the unique challenges faced by Black women within politics and feminism (Crenshaw, 1989). In addition to addressing marginalization by oppressive structures, intersectionality draws attention to vulnerabilities faced by groups that have been minoritized. It highlights how social inequities impact vulnerability during existential circumstances (Kuran et al., 2020), which can be a determinant in sibling bereavement. For example, social inequity involving health care, education, and socioeconomics can impact levels of vulnerability due to lack of access to services based on cultural barriers, linguistics, financial burdens, and institutional mistrust (Kuran et al., 2020). Moreover, if individuals lack access due to systemic inequities, the increased vulnerability will impact coping and management skills during times of crisis (Kuran et al., 2020). An intersectional lens encapsulates the lived reality of bereaved siblings

DOI: 10.4324/9781003292890-16

by examining cultural backgrounds, mourning traditions, social norms, and existing power structures to discern methods to alleviate vulnerabilities and promote grief equity and social justice. In utilizing this framework, clinicians can better understand sibling needs, be authentically present, and engage in culturally affirming education and practices when serving this population.

From this perspective, grief and intersectionality are inexplicably intertwined. They are influenced by race, gender, socioeconomics, and sexual identity; and they extend to kinship, manner of death, and societal responses to loss. Grief is not a siloed event, and adult siblings must engage with systems and structures that fail to recognize their loss and endorse their marginalization, which stifles productive grieving. Due to the correlation between identity, oppression, and social systems, there must be an acute understanding of how power and positionality influence marginalization (Allen, 2016). Recognizing the importance of intersecting identities within these systems and structures ensures equity, social justice, and diversified treatment responses (Allen, 2016). The following is a composite vignette designed to illustrate the role of intersectionality during adult sibling bereavement.

Belinda's story

Belinda is a 52-year-old African American female mourning the loss of her sister, Sandra. Sandra died suddenly from a heart attack at age 54, leaving behind an ex-husband and two teenage daughters. Sandra had a history of hypertension and was always stressed in her marriage and by her lack of financial resources. Belinda recalled her sister as her best friend and was a source of support during Sandra's marital and financial struggles. Losing her sister devastated Belinda, and she felt isolated and excluded unless she completed tasks or comforted her mother. Adding to her grief, Sandra had no life insurance, and the family expected Belinda to cover funeral expenses resulting in an unexpected financial setback. Furthermore, Belinda, a state agency accountant, was only given three days of bereavement leave. Upon her return to work, coworkers casually offered condolences but did not engage her even when she was seen crying at her desk. Two weeks later, a supervisor informed Belinda that her exhibited mourning was making her coworkers uncomfortable and advised her to take some vacation time to "get herself together." Belinda, a devout Baptist, also sought comfort from her church. Like her work experience, Belinda shared that the church's expectation was for her to move forward with life. When Belinda expressed her frustration and anger with a church member, she was told she should not question God's divine will.

Belinda reported suffering from insomnia and depression, and due to her varied experiences of disenfranchisement, she became socially withdrawn. As such, she sought professional intervention. Belinda's efforts to get "outside" help were met with criticism from her mother and her fellow church members, who stated that she should have been able to manage her grief without consulting "strangers." Ignoring the backlash, Belinda attended an initial session with a White female counselor. During this session, Belinda shared her story and symptoms, including persistent crying, repeated headaches, and feelings of isolation and anger. Belinda was asked, "It has been a month since your sister died. Why are you still crying?" Belinda questioned the therapist's response and was told, "In society, Blacks have greater exposure to death, so I assumed you were used to handling loss." Belinda abruptly left the session and never returned. Only after she spoke with an acquaintance was Belinda linked with a culturally affirming therapist who was integral in helping Belinda manage her grief and make meaning of her loss.

Complexities of adult sibling bereavement

Adult sibling loss is underappreciated and linked to the unwarranted assumption that it has nominal significance on surviving siblings (Marshall, 2013). This supposition exists because adult siblings often live independently, have their own families, and have individualized interests. Due to life transitions, sibling contact can decrease, yet the relationship is significant (Jenson et al., 2018). In some cases, the sibling bond grows more robust due to mutual interests and shared perspectives about life and family, which has a profound impact when death occurs. However, not all sibling relationships are good. In these instances, siblings have sparse or no contact, and death can result in guilt due to the inability to resolve previous conflicts or in relief if the relationship was a source of stress and anxiety (Wright, 2016).

The death of an adult sibling represents the loss of an attachment formulated at birth or early in life that impacts survivors' general wellbeing (Walsh, 2019). Furthermore, researchers studying sibling loss in adulthood suggest elevated mortality rates (Rostila et al., 2012) and increased risk of strokes and myocardial infarctions (Rostila et al., 2013a, 2013b). The physical and psychological ramifications of adult sibling loss imply that the sibling bond is a distinct phenomenon that cannot be neglected. Therefore, understanding the role of intersectionality is essential in helping to alleviate grief symptomatology for this disenfranchised group (Moore et al., 2022).

Given that the US and many other countries around the world embody individuals from diverse cultural, religious, and ethnic backgrounds, readers would be remiss to ignore how structural inequities impact the lived reality of their occupants. Because bereaved adult siblings have multiple roles in life, they can endure simultaneous forms of oppression. Power and privilege determine who receives access and becomes disenfranchised (Doka, 1989). Power and privilege extend to the grief paradigm with social messages declaring who is worthy of grief based on perceived societal positioning and circumstance of loss (Doka, 1989). This messaging unintentionally leaves siblings questioning whether their grief is justified and decreases wellbeing without tangible support. Through an intersectionality lens, it is crucial to understand the role of societal positionality and how privilege and oppression manifest during bereavement (Moore et al., 2022), as evidenced by a lack of sibling bereavement resources, support groups, and societal minimalization of loss. These disparities emit false indications about the value placed on adult sibling loss and contribute to further inequity by social systems.

Experiences of societal disenfranchisement

More than 80% of Americans were raised in the same household with a sibling (Jenson et al., 2018). However, researchers have demonstrated that sibling relationships may go unacknowledged when a sibling's death occurs (Marshall, 2013). The social nullification of this critical loss can be emotionally catastrophic, leading to decreased self-worth or depressive symptoms. For example, hearing phrases such as "The worst loss a person can experience is the loss of a child," or having one's grief minimized because it was "only sibling loss" causes disenfranchisement for bereaved siblings and condones oppressive attitudes and practices. Additionally, bereavement groups primarily focus on child, parental, or spousal losses. For example, suppose a sibling attends a support group where they are the only sibling griever or Person of Color. In this case, a lack of recognition or invalidation within the bereavement group can cause further alienation and vulnerability based on intersecting identities, thus compounding their disenfranchised grief.

Wilson et al. (2021) suggested that disenfranchisement in adulthood extends to employers' lack of support, allocated bereavement leave, and inability to address grief in the workplace. Belinda suffered a lack of empathy and diminished grief experience on the job. Moreover, the negative framing of her exhibited grief and extended leave suggestion demonstrated employers' issues in addressing grief with their employees. Belinda was not given an option to consult with a licensed professional, nor was she referred to the Human Resources department for bereavement support services. Unfortunately, Belinda lacked emotional support and expressed that, "No one seemed to understand why I could not 'move on' after the loss of my sister." Grief cannot be resolved in less than a week. Hence, siblings often return to work before they can genuinely process their loss (Wilson et al., 2021), and they contend with structural inequities that promote disenfranchisement.

When sibling loss results from unnatural causes (e.g., suicide, homicide, accident), social stigmas can worsen grieving processes and foster increased isolation and vulnerability (Tasker & Wright, 2020). Furthermore, law enforcement and media outlets utilize invasive protocols to achieve their agencies' desired goals to the detriment of traumatized persons. Thus, an intersectional lens is also needed to examine the impact of media and law enforcement on sibling experiences with traumatic bereavement. For example, if the deceased is a member of a group that has been minoritized, in many cases, media outlets may use provocative language and unflattering depictions that shape public perception and empathy based on the death circumstance. This illustrates how oppressive social systems bolster biases during bereavement and why power and privilege should be analyzed when researching or working with Communities of Color (Grinage, 2019).

For these reasons, it is crucial to recognize the impact of racism and discrimination when working with communities that have been minoritized (Rosenblatt & Wallace, 2021). Moreover, repercussions of racism and discrimination will generate varied outcomes because lived experiences, culture, and traditions vary by and within ethnic subcultures (Artiga & Ubri, 2017; Findling et al., 2019a, 2019b; Yip et al., 2021). Persons from African American, Latinx, Asian American, Indigenous, and immigrant communities that have been minoritized face similar health care, housing, and employment disparities, culminating in depreciated physical and emotional wellbeing (Artiga & Ubri, 2017; Findling et al., 2019a, 2019b; Yip et al., 2021). Death and non-death losses that result from racism, colonization, migration, and forced assimilation compound trauma and bereavement responses for populations that have been minoritized because it influences how and in what ways siblings grieve (Parkes et al., 2015).

In some cultures, sibling bereavement may result in an outward display or in subdued grief expressions, which can be misinterpreted by those working in institutional settings causing the biased allocation of support. Grief is also aggregate due to separation and inaccessibility to supportive services in countries of origin (Parkes et al., 2015). Additionally, cultural bereavement rituals may not be recognized in Western culture, leaving adult siblings unable to practice honored grieving rites, disenfranchising and invalidating one's identity (Parkes et al., 2015). Due to the intersectionality of racialized trauma, ethnicity, and the multi-layered manifestation of bereavement, it is necessary to explore these components to ensure the honoring of cultural traditions while understanding and validating the totality of the bereaved adult sibling experience.

Therapeutic environments should be safe spaces for bereaved clients of color. However, bias and prejudice can make therapeutic environments another venue for discrimination and disenfranchisement. In Belinda's case, the first clinician had cultural biases that manifested during the initial session, which derailed the therapeutic alliance. This negative interaction offended Belinda, left her unwilling to seek further interventions, and lent credence to cultural beliefs against seeking professional help. African Americans' grief experiences embody loss and amassed contributions of historical racism, systemic inequity, and dehumanization (Grinage, 2019). This disparity continues within bereavement because Black grief is not viewed as a priority (Rosenblatt & Wallace, 2021). The intersection of society, racial identity, and disenfranchised grief create complex experiences for bereaved adults as they navigate varied interpersonal dynamics following the loss of a sibling. If those practicing bereavement work cannot understand the interconnectedness of lived experience, grief, and privilege, adult siblings may endure secondary traumatization, leaving them at increased risk of emotional harm.

The intersectionality and influence of culture on grief responses

In many African American Christian communities, common death traditions include funerals or homegoing services to pay homage to the deceased (Rosenblatt & Wallace, 2021). The family carefully plans the final arrangements and obituary, and services are typically held within one week after death (Moore et al., 2022). The ceremony is led by a designated clergyperson and may include scripture readings, gospel selections, and praise dancing (Rosenblatt & Wallace, 2021). Family presence and a vast gathering symbolize status and respect for the deceased. Immediately after the funeral and interment, family and friends return to the church or designated location for the repast, a Christian tradition in which mourners gather to eat, share stories, and pay respects to the family (Moore et al., 2022). Funerals can be somber and joyous as African Americans are more apt to display grief through outward emotion, including crying, wailing, and fainting, than their European American counterparts (Rosenblatt & Wallace, 2021).

Religious beliefs and traditions in the African American community are often practiced because they are paramount to one's identity and culture (Rosenblatt & Wallace, 2021). However, if a bereaved sibling fails to exhibit expected cultural grief responses, they can experience disenfranchisement from others in the religious community. The lack of visible grief assumes that the sibling may have held some unknown animosity or dislike towards the bereaved. Conversely, grieving siblings who express frustration or anger over a loss may face criticism from their religious circle, who may, in turn, misinterpret the response as a sign of wavering faith and disrespect towards God. From an intersectional lens, religion can be oppressive when expected grieving boundaries do not align, negatively impacting bereaved siblings and their responses to loss. It is important to stress that human emotion cannot be structured to fit an unspoken template for grief expression (Worden, 2018). Anger and frustration are normal grief responses and may prompt an individual to question their faith when a loss occurs, especially if the manner of death is sudden or tragic (Worden, 2018). Questioning a higher power or authentically sharing unpleasant thoughts are not a cause for reprimand, but an opportunity for empathetic dialogue.

Relational aspects of disenfranchised grief

During bereavement, kin and informal supports provide solace in the African American community (Rosenblatt & Wallace, 2021). In this context, the term *kin* or *kinship* encompasses more than the nuclear family. It includes extended relatives, friends, and church members who have close relationships with the bereaved and assist the family in the immediate days following a loss (Rosenblatt & Wallace, 2021). In adulthood, siblings naturally take on tangible roles as caretakers for family members and have decision-making capacities regarding housing and medical care. However, sibling loss inevitably affects family dynamics (Marshall, 2017). Subsequently, role changes can increase surviving siblings' stress levels as they prepare funeral arrangements and assume care for elderly parents or young children left behind (Marshall, 2017).

In Belinda's case, she assumed a familial leadership role and discovered that her position resulted in less recognition of her loss as she was expected to handle estate matters and care for her mother. Belinda was not ready for this responsibility, which meant she would have to devote more time to her mother and incur additional expenses related to her sister's estate. She was frustrated because she had to manage family responsibilities while grieving in silence. Belinda also felt that all the focus was on her mother while her well-being was ignored. It is crucial to recognize the vulnerability of adult siblings during bereavement due to family positionality and unequal bereavement status. When siblings encounter dismissive attitudes or emotional unavailability towards their grief, they may experience disenfranchisement from informal support systems and internalize their emotions (Marshall, 2013).

Physical death is not a singular event and culminates in secondary losses that may go unacknowledged (Worden, 2018). For example, in the case of siblings, corresponding deficits may include the loss of a friend and confidant. In addition, there may be a rupture in the relationship with other family members. In Belinda's case, her sister was the link to her nieces, and the death may cause distance due to new living arrangements and subsequent parental choices. Furthermore, the unexpected funeral costs were a financial burden leaving Belinda to incur a financial setback and increased responsibilities for the care of her mother. By extension, Belinda endured her mother's emotional unavailability, which often occurs after a child's death. The impact of parental unavailability is exacerbated after sibling death because adult siblings often function as a source of strength for their parents and one another; the loss of this normal functioning is deepened by the permanence of the loss (Marshall, 2013). Moreover, the intimacy of existing relationships may be irreparably changed, leaving adult siblings isolated and apprehensive about seeking solace from grieving family and friends. Lastly, the death of her sister resulted in Belinda questioning her faith. Spiritual dilemmas are not uncommon after death, and survivors grapple with reasons why the death occurred, preventability, and the role religion plays in their bereavement (Worden, 2018).

Through an intersectional lens, power dynamics within familial relationships can be explored to ascertain how traditional and cultural expectations foster or hinder bereaved siblings' mourning processes (Walsh, 2016, 2019). This exploration includes gender roles and birth order to define anticipated behaviors from surviving siblings in adherence to family structures (Walsh, 2016, 2019). In addition, it is necessary for sibling grievers to discuss their loss and how familial and informal support impacts their grief. A nuanced understanding of these intersecting points would benefit professionals in formulating bereavement strategies to assist siblings in maintaining relational ties and navigating their bereavement while working through emotional and spiritual challenges.

Cumulative impacts of disenfranchised grief throughout the lifespan

From an intersectionality standpoint, social inequities are not the result of solitary circumstances, but rather a combination of overlapping experiences related to power, privilege, and racial trauma (Moore et al., 2022).

For bereaved adult siblings, the consequences of limited support, validation afforded after death, and subsequent secondary losses result in repeated disenfranchisement. Sibling loss in the context of disenfranchisement over time can lead to a myriad of manifestations that inevitably stunt the ability to productively process losses causing adverse health outcomes without proactive interventions (Rostila et al., 2012). Due to documented consequences resulting from unacknowledged loss and accompanying aggregate oppressions, clinicians must examine the cumulative effects of disenfranchised grief over time to holistically serve adult siblings during bereavement.

Advocacy and allyship

Allyship is a serious commitment when engaging with populations that have been minoritized, such as African American, Latinx, Asian American, Indigenous, and immigrant peoples. It is more than performative action (e.g., showing up at protests and chanting slogans). Allyship through the lens of intersectionality calls for active learning, engagement, and dialogue about uncomfortable topics related to race, power, and privilege. It calls for meeting siblings who have been minoritized where they are on the grief continuum and consciously implementing culturally affirming interventions to alleviate therapeutic disparities (Rosenblatt & Wallace, 2021). An ally focusing on intersectionality recognizes they are not an expert in the oppression experienced by others and remains cognizant of the lived experiences of discrimination against Communities of Color from established social institutions. Understanding these realities makes allyship a transformative practice in which attitudes and beliefs become inclusive and empathetic, fertilizing ground for allies to encourage the client to consider ways to combat injustices (Sue et al., 2016) when doing so is consistent with the clients' goals.

Along with intersectionality, allyship addresses social challenges that can deter siblings from seeking help for their bereavement, including linguistic barriers and citizenship status. Immigration can result in the loss of social systems (family ties) and traditions that are crucial during mourning, including attending sibling burials in their countries of origin (Lipscomb & Salinas, 2020; Parkes et al., 2015). These post-migration losses may be exacerbated by the transnational sibling's inability to be physically present due to financial or immigration status; the disconnection from cultural and traditional mourning practices can disenfranchise immigrants from varied ethnic groups (Lipscomb & Salinas, 2020; Parkes et al., 2015).

By extension, allyship examines the impact of colonization, forced assimilation, and the inability to practice traditional grieving rituals for Indigenous Americans (Dennis & Washington, 2018). Discriminatory social conditions are woven into the narratives of populations that have been minoritized within the US. An intersectional lens addresses mistrust of institutions, the lingering impact of colonization, and search for solutions to these social dilemmas to increase bereavement equity and promote validating self-identity and cultural attachment (Sue et al., 2016). It also advocates for the incorporation of ethnic bereavement traditions, fostering resilience and promoting healthy grief processes.

Bereaved siblings can suffer from disenfranchisement due to resource inaccessibility. It is essential to have available, accessible, and culturally affirming supports to help adult siblings process their grief, maintain continuing bonds, and find ways to incorporate deceased siblings into present-day life (Klass et al., 1996). Clinicians should be able to advocate for bereavement resources, establish connections with ethnic and religious organizations in Communities of Color, and diversify the therapeutic community (Moore et al., 2022). Grief therapists who incorporate intersectionality recognize that diversity matters, and visible cultural representation may alleviate some clinician mistrust due to levels of cultural familiarity and shared experiences. However, regardless of provider ethnicity, boundaries should be clearly articulated to minimize problematic situations within the therapeutic setting.

Ethical considerations

Clinicians may serve as a primary source of support for adult siblings who have endured loss and disenfranchised bereavement. Bereavement work aims for independent functionality, fruitful relationships, and productive life readaptation (Worden, 2018) following sibling loss. Unfortunately, a clinician's unconscious inclination to assist grieving persons by resolving their problems can be detrimental to bereaved clients (Harris & Winokuer, 2016). If clinicians have blurred boundaries, the therapeutic environment may foster client dependency and failure to progress in treatment (Harris & Winokuer, 2016). Likewise, clinicians must carefully consider their own emotional investment to ensure they do not vicariously use the client to work out their own unresolved issues (Harris & Winokuer, 2016). Therefore, clinicians must recognize instances of countertransference and seek supervision or refer to other clinicians when necessary.

Sibling loss in adulthood is profoundly impactful, and these multi-layered relationships may encompass positive or negative grief responses (Marshall,

2013). Clinicians encounter clients from varied ethnicities and cultures. As such, they should be prepared to discuss death and bereavement within a social justice context. Because grief is expressly unique, theory-driven frameworks are a useful reference point but should not supersede the lived experiences, culture, and traditions of groups that have been minoritized (Rosenblatt & Wallace, 2021). Additionally, clinicians should avoid antiquated stage-based models. Instead, they should incorporate dynamic iterative understandings into the therapeutic process, going back and forth through different tasks of mourning or allowing bereaved siblings to recapitulate details as needed to come to new levels of grief acceptance. Clinicians should ensure that their professional practice is culturally affirming and continuously adjust their practice to incorporate the client's intersecting identities (Moore et al., 2022).

In Belinda's case, the clinician must address the Black woman, sister, daughter, church member, and employee to fully understand her disenfranchisement through the prism of each identity and navigate how to validate her experiences, normalize her grief, and allow her to process her sibling and secondary losses constructively. The operationalization of intersectionality in grief work aids practitioners in understanding how inequities influence behaviors associated with grief (Allen, 2016). For Belinda, those inequities presented themselves at work, church, and in the mental health system. As such, clinicians are duty-bound to educate themselves about the interconnection between social positionality, the importance of disenfranchised grief, and how they can impact bereaved siblings' lives (Allen, 2016).

Strategies and interventions

Grief is a multi-faceted phenomenon in which societal standards and obsolete bereavement timelines cause harm to those suffering from sibling loss. Validation and normalizing the grief experience can be beneficial in alleviating negative emotions and initiating restorative work. In fact, for some, sibling loss spurs a quest to find meaning and purpose by constructing positive narratives that stimulate healthy transformation (Neimeyer, 2016). This development not only frames the loss in a manageable way for the client but also propels them to nurture relationships and to find new joy in life.

It is important to note that sibling relationships do not end with physical death (Klass et al., 1996). As such, clinicians and bereaved siblings can explore continuing bonds and implement strategies to integrate deceased siblings into their present life (Klass et al., 1996). Continuing bonds demonstrate that deceased siblings are still influential in the lives of the bereaved, and their intentional inclusion in the current lives of surviving siblings can facilitate more significant healing and increased emotional wellbeing (Klass et al., 1996).

Because bereavement is a delicate encapsulation of emotions and lived experiences, it is essential to understand the interconnectedness of race and culture in grieving practices within diverse populations (Parkes et al., 2015). Immigration and acculturation affect bereavement due to the loss of honored traditions in one's country of origin and the host country's dominant grieving practices (Lipscomb & Salinas, 2020). In addition, the disconnect between familial and community support and language can aggregate grief in communities that have been minoritized (Lipscomb & Salinas, 2020). As such, grief expressions may present in unfamiliar ways that others may judge or dismiss. Subsequently, clinicians must avoid assumptions before assessing their clients' family dynamics and cultural backgrounds (Sue et al., 2016). Instead, there should be a respectful and open dialogue about cultural perspectives of loss and grief traditions and how secondary losses contribute to the bereavement experience (Parkes et al., 2015).

Clients should lead this conversation because they are experts in their lived experiences. This reciprocal exchange allows clients to share what death means to them, its societal impact, and how cultural expressions are stigmatized when they differ from the expected norms of the prevailing culture. For example, suppose traditional grieving practices involve wearing specific apparel and outward verbal and non-verbal displays of emotion. In that case, professionals unfamiliar with their clients' cultural expressions can misinterpret grief, causing further social alienation. Clinicians should also examine the significance of family structures and role expectations following a loss (Walsh, 2019). In some cultures, grief is a collective experience, and adaption must be employed to include family members (Parkes et al., 2015). Therefore, understanding cultural traditions through a structured family lens can help clinicians assess whether individual or family intervention would best serve bereaved clients.

Exploring the incorporation of writing, art, and music brings added dimension bereavement work (Worden, 2018). Creative expressions can aid clients in identifying feelings related to grief and secondary losses, build self-efficacy, and validate their experiences in ways that embrace cultural traditions. It may also provide contextual insight into a client's worldview and perspectives concerning racialized trauma and social inequities that may be difficult to verbalize. Clinicians must be cognizant of historical and ongoing discrimination because populations that have been minoritized suffer varied grief experiences across their lifespans (Rosenblatt & Wallace, 2021). When clinicians self-reflect and recognize clients' social conditions, they are more apt to effectively address identified concerns, strengthening the therapeutic alliance (Sue et al., 2016). Finally, a clinician's ability to engage with bereaved groups requires adaptability and willingness to understand that although grief is a universal experience, intersectionality and multicultural interventions are essential for addressing bereavement needs.

Summary

The death of an adult sibling is a frequently ignored form of familial loss. This grief inequity endorses dismissive narratives and disenfranchisement for adult sibling grievers. Adult sibling loss must be acknowledged with the same reverence as parental, child, or spousal deaths. In addition, conceptualizing the grief continuum through a lens of intersectionality expands the traditional viewpoint of bereavement. Clinicians viewing grievers through the lens of intersectionality may assist them in navigating structural oppression and societal dismissal of their sibling relationship. Moreover, it ensures that the therapeutic process epitomizes the lived experiences of adult siblings. Only when validation of the total lived experience exists can positive strides be made in accepting loss, making meaning, and continuing bonds for these unique grievers.

References

Allen, J. (2016). Critical social work in action. In *Handbook of social justice in loss and grief: Exploring diversity, equity, and inclusion* (pp. 21–39). Routledge.

Artiga, S., & Ubri, P. (2017). *Living in an immigrant family in America: How fear and toxic stress are affecting daily life, wellbeing, and health.* The Henry K. Kaiser Family Foundation. www.kff.org/racial-equity-and-health-policy/issue-brief/living-in-an-immigrant-family-in-america-how-fear-and-toxic-stress-are-affecting-daily-life-well-being-health/

Crenshaw, K. (1989). Demarginalizing the intersection of race and sex: A Black feminist critique of antidiscrimination doctrine, feminist theory and antiracist politics. *The University of Chicago Legal Forum, 1989*(1), Article 8, 139–167. https://chicagounbound.uchicago.edu/uclf/vol1989/iss1/8

Dennis, M., & Washington, K. T. (2018). Ways of grieving among Ojibwe elders. *OMEGA – Journal of Death and Dying, 78*(2), 107–119. https://doi.org/10.1177/0030222816679661

Doka, K. (1989). *Disenfranchised grief: Recognizing hidden sorrow.* Lexington Books.

Findling, M., Bleich, S., Casey, L., Blendon, R., Benson, J., Sayde, J., & Miller, C. (2019a). Discrimination in the United States: Experiences of Latinos. *Health Services Research, 54*, 1409–1418. https://doi.org/10.1111/1475-6773.13216

Findling, M., Casey, L. S., Fryberg, S. A., Hafner, S., Blendon, R. J., Benson, J. M., Sayde, J. M., & Miller, C. (2019b). Discrimination in the United States: Experiences of Native Americans. *Health Services Research, 54*(S2), 1431–1441. https://doi.org/10.1111/1475-6773.13224

Grinage, J. (2019). Endless mourning: Racial melancholia, black grief, and transformative possibilities for racial justice in education. *Harvard Education Review, 89*(2), 227–250. https://doi.org/10.17763/1943-5045-89.2.227

Harris, D., & Winokuer, H. R. (2016). *Principles and practice of grief counseling* (2nd ed., pp. 197–212). Springer.

Jenson, A., Fingerman, K., & Whiteman, S. (2018). "Can't live with or without them:" Transitions and young adults' perceptions of sibling relationships. *Journal of Family Psychology, 32*(3), 385–395. https://doi.org/10.1037/fam0000361

Klass, D., Silverman, P. R., & Nickman, S. L. (1996). *Continuing bonds: New understandings of grief.* Taylor & Francis.

Kuran, C. H. A., Morsut, C., Kruke, B. I., Krüger, M., Segnestam, L., Orru, K., Naevestad, T., Airola, M., Keranan, J., Gabel, F., Hansson, S., & Torpan, S. (2020). Vulnerability and vulnerable groups from an intersectionality perspective. *International Journal of Disaster Risk Reduction, 50*, 101826. https://doi.org/10.1016/j.ijdrr.2020.101826

Lipscomb, A., & Salinas, P. (2020). The mis-bereavement of transnational deaths: Exploring grief and bereavement experiences among Latinx immigrants in the United States. *London Journal of Research in Humanities and Social Sciences, 20*(5), 7–15.

Marshall, B. (2013). *Adult sibling loss: Stories, reflections and ripples.* Baywood Publishing.

Marshall, B. (2017). Sibling loss in adulthood: Narrative reflections. *Sibling loss across the lifespan: Research, practice, and personal stories* (pp. 101–109). Taylor & Francis.

Moore, S., Jones-Eversley S., Tolliver W., Wilson, B., & Harmon, D. (2022). Cultural responses to loss and grief among Black Americans: Theory and practice implications for clinicians. *Death Studies, 46*(1), 189–199. https://doi.org/10.1080/07481187.2020.1725930

Neimeyer, R. A. (2016). Meaning reconstruction in the wake of loss: Evolution of a research program. *Behaviour Change, 33*(2), 65–79. https://doi.org/10.1017/bec.2016.4

Parkes, C., Laungani, P., & Young, B. (2015). *Death and bereavement across cultures.* Routledge.

Rosenblatt, P. C., & Wallace, B. R. (2021). *African American Grief.* Taylor and Francis.

Rostila, M., Saarela, J., & Kawachi, I. (2012). The forgotten griever: A nationwide follow-up study of mortality subsequent to the death of a sibling. *American Journal of Epidemiology*, *176*(4), 338. https://doi.org/10.1093/aje/kws163

Rostila, M., Saarela, J., & Kawachi, I. (2013a). Fatal stroke after the death of a sibling: A nationwide follow-up study from Sweden. *PLoS One*, *8*(2), e56994–e56994. https://doi.org/10.1371/journal.pone.0056994

Rostila, M., Saarela, J., & Kawachi, I. (2013b). Mortality from myocardial infarction after the death of a sibling: A nationwide follow-up study from Sweden. *Journal of the American Heart Association*, *2*(2), Article e000046. https://doi.org/10.1161/JAHA.112.000046

Sue, D. W., Rasheed, M. N., Rasheed, J. M. (2016). *Multicultural social work practice: A competency-based approach to diversity and social justice* (2nd ed., pp. 403–491). Wiley.

Tasker, S., & Wright, K. (2020). Exploring aspects of health and wellbeing in siblings of young homicide survivors. *Illness, Crisis, and Loss*, *28*(1), 71–94. https://doi.org/10.1177/1054137317742560

Walsh, F. (2016). *Strengthening family resilience* (3rd ed.). Guilford Press.

Walsh, F. (2019). Loss and bereavement in families: A systemic framework for recovery and resilience. In B. H. Fiese (Ed.), *APA handbook of contemporary family psychology: Foundations, methods, and contemporary issues across the lifespan* (Vol. 1, pp. 649–663). American Psychological Association.

Wilson, D., Punjani, P., Song, Q., & Low, G. (2021). A study to understand the impact of bereavement grief on the workplace. *OMEGA – Journal of Death and Dying*, *83*(2), 187–197. https://doi.org/10.1177/0030222819846419

Worden, J. W. (2018). *Grief counseling and grief therapy: A handbook for the mental health practitioner*. Springer.

Wright, P. M. (2016). Adult sibling bereavement: Influences, consequences, and interventions. *Illness, Crisis and Loss*, *24*(1), 34–45. https://doi.org/10.1177/1054137315587631

Yip, T., Cheah, C., Kiang, L., & Hall, G. (2021). Rendered invisible: Are Asian Americans a model or a marginalized minority? *American Psychologist*, *76*(4), 575–581. https://doi.org/10.1037/amp0000857

Questions for reflective practice

1. How knowledgeable are you about adult sibling loss and its impact on the family unit?
2. What culturally affirming methods would you utilize to address the multidimensional aspects of loss and disenfranchisement experienced by bereaved adult siblings?

3. How can you adopt an intersectionality framework in your practice with populations that have been minoritized to ensure that clients receive holistic care during bereavement?
4. How does working with clients of different faith traditions and cultures influence your service provision?
5. How have your personal beliefs and expectations about grief and loss caused disenfranchisement for someone experiencing loss? What steps do you need to take to avoid this practice?

Supplemental electronic resources

- Adult sibling loss: A grief resource for clinicians, social workers, and experts in the field: https://tangela07.wixsite.com/my-site
- The Compassionate Friends: www.compassionatefriends.org
- Twinless Twins Support Group International: https://wwwtwinlesstwins.org

14
The grief of parenting "borrowed children"

A foster parent perspective

Theresa Fraser

If one theme is ever present in the child welfare system, it is the experience of grief. Removed children often grieve for their families of origin; biological parents grieve for the loss of their removed children and family life. Workers in the child welfare system often voice that they experience heartache, if not vicarious trauma, because they do not feel they can spend the time they would like to help families. This contributes to high staff turnover, which leads to children and foster families experiencing the loss of workers with whom they have a relationship (Canadian Association of Social Workers [CASW], 2018; Casey Family Homes, 2017). Individuals who provide daily care for children can also experience secondary grief and disenfranchised grief, particularly when they care for or even love children who are not legally theirs.

Children are apprehended from their family of origin by a representative of the state (sometimes referred to as Children's Aid or the Department of Community Services) when there is concern that they have experienced neglect, abuse, or exposure to domestic violence. They can then be placed with individuals who are connected to the child through the child's family of origin or are in the role of extended family or friends. In some locations in North America, this might be known as *kin care* or *kinship foster care*. If no such support exists, children are then placed with a "professional" family that has been vetted and is approved to provide care for financial reimbursement (United Nations General Assembly, 2009). These placements are known as *foster homes* or *foster care*.

When children are placed in foster care, their caregivers are referred to as *foster parents* or *foster carers*. Though these individuals take on a parenting role, they lack legal and biological connections to the children they are raising. Many foster parents view their role as often marginalized for many reasons summarized herein, the most important being when a decision is made for the

DOI: 10.4324/9781003292890-17

child to leave the foster home without taking into consideration the foster parents' views, lenses, or feelings. Foster families may fear that the children are returning to an unsafe situation, and they may truly care for the children for whom they are financially remunerated to provide care. Many foster parents are told that they are not supposed to love their foster children, but shouldn't all children experience a loving home, even if the caregivers are foster parents?

According to Doka (2002), disenfranchised grief is a form of grief that is not acknowledged or socially accepted. Though this concept is generally related to bereavement, the current author counters that disenfranchised grief for the foster parent is often connected to the lack of voice or impact on the treatment plan for the youth with whom they live and the subsequent loss of a child they have come to love. Foster children may have left the foster family system with little notice, preparation, or foster-parent input on the placement change. This grief can impact subsequent service delivery, as foster parents are told by child welfare representatives to be clear about their role and not love children, yet children who have experienced trauma require loving environments (Children's Bureau, 2014). As a result, the grief that foster parents experience can be disenfranchised because foster parents "are not accorded a 'right to grieve'" (Doka, 2002, p. 5).

Resource workers

Brown et al. (2015) met with 68 highly experienced family support workers who worked in child welfare (M_{years} = 18) and more specifically in foster care (M_{years} = 9) to discuss their roles when working with foster families (Brown et al., 2015). After answering questions, 14 resource worker volunteers utilized Trochim's (1989) concept system to group data. Although ten areas of job responsibilities were categorized, surprisingly, none specifically identified helping foster family members address grief or loss within the fostering experience (Brown et al., 2015). In comparison, this writer's experience (as a foster parent of 30 years, a foster care resource worker for five, and a therapist for over 15) supports Mullings's (2010) observation that foster parents are eager to have their grief noticed and supported.

The impact of grief on the foster family system

Foster families state that they desire both education and support to manage the ongoing experience of loss for themselves and family members. For example, foster parents identified that even though they experience continuous loss (Edelstein et al., 2001), there is little formal support (e.g., counseling) available for their biological children, whom Fraser (2015) described as the "silent partners" in the fostering family. Williams (2017) interviewed birth children of foster parents in Ireland to discuss feelings they had about foster children leaving the home. Birth children reported mixed feelings; they mourn the loss of foster siblings, perhaps feel a sense of relief they are gone, or fear for the future of the foster child, especially if the foster child shared details of their previous life experiences with the biological children (Williams, 2017). Sadly, the birth children also reported feelings of guilt and shame akin to survivor's guilt because they did not experience trauma as the foster children had (Williams, 2017). Birth children also were able to identify their fears about how these losses impacted their parents (Williams, 2017).

The current author often referred to their foster children as "borrowed children." This was because the children were neither biologically nor legally theirs. This term helped younger biological children understand that they could not keep the foster children in their lives, even though they cared for them while they resided with their family. When children left, the author carefully explained the reasons for the departure to their biological children while also respecting the privacy of the child who had left. The referring agency did not always support this practice, even though research supports this intervention to help remaining children come to terms with the reasons for the move, so they did not personalize the reasons (Williams, 2017).

Biological children's reactions to placement changes need to be acknowledged, given that each loss builds on the last and, without intervention or support, there can be long-term negative consequences, such as health issues, relationship issues, and closure of foster homes (Newquist et al., 2020). An additional study completed in the United Kingdom by Lynes and Sitoe (2019) noted that stories from foster parents (carers) were similar, though some indicated that they were shocked about the impact of grief and how this grief could be triggered by reminder events. Also, there were some respondents who stated that they did not feel as impacted by subsequent losses as the losses associated with their first fostering experience (Lynes & Sitoe, 2019).

Social aspects of disenfranchised grief

Many generalizations and stereotypes are connected to the fostering experience and may contribute to the diminished view of treatment partnership and/or voice by day-to-day caregivers. Waldon Family Services (2018), a foster care agency in the US, dispelled several misconceptions about foster parents, notably that foster care is financially challenging or lucrative; that foster parents have to be a certain age, heterosexual and/or married, own their own home, or have previous parenting experience to provide care; and that they are incapable of indicating what child would be a match for their family. Waldon Family Services (2018) also dispelled myths about foster children, notably that all foster children are involved in the legal system, that they have experienced sexual abuse, and that they lack medical insurance.

Misconceptions about who foster parents are can be perpetuated by the media in movies and television shows (Grimm & Darwell, 2015). The media can ultimately present foster parents as uncaring individuals who take in children for the money they receive as a per diem. Portrayals such as these can contribute to foster parents feeling isolated in their communities, particularly when they are in roles where they need to advocate strongly for services (e.g., school resources) but lack time to be involved in committees (e.g., parent–teacher associations).

Several harsh realities exist for foster families. They may have the house that police cars visit, strangers seem to frequent, and children of various social locations (e.g., gender, race, social class, age, ability, religion, sexual orientation, etc.) seem to hang around. They may lose contact with extended family and friends who may lack an understanding of the family life of a foster parent, thus making them and their family more vulnerable, particularly in times where they may need support.

Foster parenting: characteristics and support

Foster parents can be young or old when they engage in the home study licensing process. Their personal characteristics, skills, and social location (Fraser & Ventrella, 2019) contribute more to matching the specific needs of a child placed in their home. In some cases, matching is not taken into consideration, even when it was indicated as important at the foster parent licensing stage because there is nowhere else for a specific child to go at a specific time. Foster parents do not have to own their own home but need to provide a home that can be a house or an apartment that they may also share with extended family members in urban or rural communities. The condition of the home is more important to the placement of a foster child than home ownership. Factors such as the location of the home to community resources and a private place for a foster child to be in (such as their own bed or bedroom) dictate which home is a good match for a particular foster child.

Foster parents can be single or married. In the *Obergefell v. Hodges* decision (576 U.S. 14–556; 2015), the U.S. Supreme Court ruled that gay marriages in all 50 states could not be banned or dissolved under the Fourteenth Amendment due process and equal protection clauses in the U.S. Constitution. This ruling did not bring the same parity to fostering or adoption for same-sex couples. As of today, there is still no national law in the US that addresses LGBTQIA+ discrimination in regard to non-birthing same-sex parent adoption or foster care approval. These laws are managed state by state. For example, on June 17, 2021, a Catholic Church-affiliated agency in Philadelphia, Pennsylvania, won a Supreme Court case after refusing to place children in same sex foster homes. The ruling indicated that religious rights were paramount over LGBTQIA+ rights (Hurley & Chung, 2021). Loss of the ability to parent due to sexual orientation is another example of disenfranchised grief. It is important to note that Canadian same-sex couples can both foster and adopt.

Many foster parent agencies provide training to foster parents, even those who have never parented in the past. Training usually includes topics such as non-violent crisis intervention, first aid, trauma history, and government regulations. Foster parents who have specific post-secondary education related to the care of children and youth are also likely to be contracted, whether they have their own children or not. However, their training rarely includes discussion on the intense impact of loss that foster parents and/or family members feel when the child moves and leaves the care of the foster family, further disenfranchising their grief.

Foster children

Each foster child is an individual with individual strengths, challenges, and needs, embedded in a system with its own challenges and needs. Some foster children require specialized interventions with adults that have specialized training, while others require a family setting until they can return to their family of origin. Some children require an adult who is available 24 hours a day due to their complex physical or mental health needs. These could require the adults to attend multiple appointments with specialists in a week, meetings with other child welfare staff, or the provision of extra attention during the day for children who experience ongoing school suspensions or expulsions due to the lack of resources in their school communities to address their complex needs.

Some foster children have had an early connection with the juvenile justice system, while others have only engaged with a police service due to being victimized (cf. Courtney et al., 2007). Though abuse and neglect are consistent reasons for children being apprehended from their biological families, there are foster children who have parents who are ill, incarcerated, or have, sadly, died. Each foster child has their own story, and, as all trauma specialists know, even siblings can have different reactions to similar environmental experiences. Trauma is a subjective experience based on the individual's age, development, previous exposure to trauma, and familial or individualized challenges, resources, culture, and ethnicity (American Psychological Association [APA], 2022). Foster parents must also be cognizant of the grief and loss that has been experienced for each child in their care and provide support and treatment to address these individualized experiences so that children can develop and thrive emotionally, physically, and intellectually (Van Holen et al., 2019).

It is also important to note that racial/ethnic children who have been minoritized are disproportionately represented in out-of-home placements (Kirk & Griffith, 2008; Kirton, 2016; Mikell Montgomery, 2022). This is particularly troubling, given Mikell Montgomery's (2022) statement that "the value and humanity assigned to Black families by the child welfare system are shown by its expectation of dismemberment" (p. 149). These racial/ethnic disparities are also present in reunification decisions (viz. LaBrenz et al., 2021).

LGBTQIA+ and gender nonbinary youth are also overrepresented when compared with their heterosexual and cisgender peers (Schaub et al., 2022). Many LGBTQIA+ and nonbinary youth may not feel safe or willing enough to disclose those parts of their identity to actors in social care systems at all levels (e.g., foster parents, foster siblings, other youth in foster care, social workers, etc.), for fear of confidentiality risks and safety concerns around potential discrimination and violence (Schaub et al., 2022). Foster and residential social care systems are "often ill-equipped to meet the needs of transgender and nonbinary youth" (Schaub et al., 2022, p. 1). Prince et al. (2021) observed that "sexual and gender minority youth experience greater foster-related stressors than their peers," augmenting their "risk for anxiety/depressive, posttraumatic stress disorder, self-harm, and suicidality" (p. 1643). Baams et al. (2019) found LGBTQIA+ youth had poorer school functioning (e.g., grades, fights in school, victimization), higher substance use, and poorer mental health outcomes than their heterosexual counterparts in foster care. The challenges facing LGBTQIA+ youth are significant under any circumstances, and they would be amplified if the family system is unable or unwilling to support them.

The culture of foster family life

The fostering family could consist of romantic partners, adults and their adult parents, or even adult siblings. They may include one or more foster children as well as biological or adopted children. One or more parents may work. There is often at least one child welfare representative that is assigned to the family as a resource person. Each foster child may also have a social worker appointed or responsible for them. Therefore, it is possible that each foster family may have as many as five additional professionals with whom they are in contact at least monthly. In addition to being patient, persevering, psychologically stable, humorous, tolerant, caring, empathetic, warm, and open-minded, foster parents need to be flexible to engage with each of the professionals assigned to them (Van Holen et al., 2019).

Foster parents may feel like the culture of their family of origin is directly impacted by the other adults with whom they share parenting decisions. For example, they may not be able to attend church services if these do not align with the faith of foster children, or they may not be able to go on vacation if the timing does not align with court proceedings or visits with their biological family. They may need to adapt their meal planning to address the cultural or religious traditions of all children placed in their home.

Depending on the philosophy of child welfare staff, the foster parent may be regarded as an equal partner in the treatment planning for the foster child or as little more than a driver and babysitter. Child welfare staff may show up with little warning and expect the foster family to drop all plans to support an impromptu meeting. This lack of communication and discussion can demonstrate to foster parents how little their input into plans, interventions, scheduling, and involvement in team consultations is respected.

Some child welfare staff may expect the foster parent to increase their responsibilities, such as providing backup support for school staff when they are unable to support the child in the school milieu. There can often be the misperception that they are home doing nothing. The culture of foster-family life can therefore be ever changing due to the impact team members have on day-to-day functioning. This can mean that practices such as the ability to engage in self-care, church attendance, or adult peer activities are impacted by the needs of the children that are placed in the home or the child welfare staff that are intended to support the foster family system. Foster parents can consequently feel that their voice is sometimes lost because they are parenting by committee. This dynamic can also precipitate feelings of disenfranchised grief.

Cultural aspects of disenfranchised grief

Foster parents may feel isolated from child welfare staff; they may also experience isolation from friends and family because of the lifestyle that foster parents have to create and maintain with the aforementioned challenges. For example, if they create a milieu where new children enter and leave the family system regularly, they may need to create a quiet household, much like that of a new infant's home. Extreme behaviors may flare up, including verbal or physical aggression, and these are not easily understood by families whose children have not experienced a traumatic past. Therefore, when foster families provide care to children who have specific needs resulting from intersecting identities, attachment disruptions, and/or traumatic experiences, they may need to create a household structure where specialized needs are anticipated to create a safe environment for each child in their care (Fraser, 2011).

When placements abruptly end or children move, foster families may feel pressured not to publicly articulate their feelings of grief. Public grief over placement changes may be viewed as a weakness within the foster family, given that the children are neither legally nor biologically theirs; hence the term *borrowed children*. It is also difficult to suppress feelings of love that may develop while caring for foster children, deepening the silence and the disenfranchisement of the experienced grief. As Mullings (2010) eloquently elaborated:

> When a foster child is removed from one foster home and sent to another, it complicates the grief and loss process. Moving the child is seen as a placement breakdown, and it is also a public event, given the number of individuals who are aware of the breakdown, including agency personnel, the children and their friends, schoolteachers, and so forth. There is no recourse for the public shame that foster mothers feel – but I can tell you, shame is a lot easier to manage than losing a child.
>
> (p. 170)

Sometimes, agencies may be in such dire need that they will ask to place another child in the home more quickly than is appropriate for the foster family. The family may view their role as more of a calling than a job; hence, they will not refuse the next child in need of a bed when they haven't yet processed the loss of the previous child. Instead, their grief must be processed privately, underscoring the disenfranchised nature of their loss. Loss can precipitate somatic symptoms, such as headaches and sleep disruption, and even emotional feelings of depression, including a lack of purpose. Additionally, symptoms could include rumination of negative thoughts about self, the world, and the future (Eisma et al., 2022).

The very culture of the foster family community encourages isolation, given that foster parents are not permitted to publicly share their loss according to rules of confidentiality. Family and friends may not understand loss reactions, given the children were never "theirs" to begin with or were more difficult to parent due to their physical/mental health needs, trauma histories, and/or attachment disruption histories. Therefore, this culture of silence and isolation perpetuated in and around foster families complicates the loss experience; this culture also leads to a lack of social support that other families have access to. Lastly, the cost of verbalizing loss or communicating disagreement with social work or case management decisions can be that the foster family is viewed as being difficult, uncooperative, or not up for the job.

Being under a microscope

Many foster parents will articulate that they feel like they are constantly under a microscope and, as professional parents, are held to a higher standard than other community families. This is affirmed when involved with the child's other microsystems, including school, medical services, etc. If foster parents are consistently feeling judged by other team members, service providers, biological families, and the community, then it is understandable that they will be less open to sharing their vulnerabilities, including feelings of loss. "Foster mothers have little decision-making power, their mothering skills criticized and challenged constantly, yet they are expected to meet the needs of children, their biological family, and the agency consistently whether changes happen suddenly or gradually" (Mullings, 2010, p. 166).

Relational aspects of disenfranchised grief

Foster parents address grief in their work in many ways and from multiple sources (Edelstein et al., 2001), including the foster child's grief. Foster children's grief may be triggered by holidays or experiences embedded in the day-to-day milieu. At times, foster children may grieve the experiences that other children around them may have, such as a family visit that they may not be able to personally experience due to their own family constellation. They may also grieve a disconnection from their culture(s) of origin or from having access to adult models representative of aspects of their intersecting identities (e.g., race, gender, sexual orientation, etc.).

Children may communicate their grief in behavioral ways that have relational consequences by arguing, stealing, or expressing anger at foster parents, whom they may see as the reason they were first removed from their biological homes. These behaviors can be extreme yet minimized by other members of the treatment team, who may only view the behaviors from an intellectual lens as compared to a relational or somatic lens. Foster parents also may minimize the child's grief experience by not acknowledging that even when abused, children grieve the loss of their relational ties to their family of origin.

When foster parents share feelings of loss and grief, these can be met with reminders from team members, family, friends, or the community that they knew the expectations going into fostering and had to anticipate that transitions would be difficult, namely, that the children are not theirs. Also, though it is understandable that they should have feelings, they should always guard their hearts. This can also be true in cases where a placement breaks down or foster parents have requested a placement change. No one accepts a child with the intention that the placement will be unsuccessful. Also, the breakdown impacts all members of the family and can sometimes precipitate feelings of failure, shame, and embarrassment in the foster family, their own community, and the larger community. If foster parents' role is only seen as a job, then it may be confusing for outsiders to recognize that they may have a dialectical reaction to the placement change. "Relationships are disenfranchised when they are not granted social approval and losses are not recognized when their significance is not recognized by society" (Corr & Corr, 2013, p. 143). Foster parents may also personally feel like they have failed in their role or even feel incompetent as foster parents.

Allyship and advocacy

Many foster families will verbalize feeling fearful of advocating for the foster child or for themselves because the foster child is not theirs and will feel threatened by the information that another placement can be procured. Of course, these feelings are expected given foster parents' lived experience with disenfranchisement and marginalization. It can also be difficult for foster families to seek allies, given that they often work in isolation and are required to keep confidentiality, thus clinicians serve as powerful allies and advocates.

One significant area of advocacy is related to sexual and reproductive health. Sexual and reproductive health are persistent areas of concern for foster care youth and emancipated youth. Moreover, due to the instability many foster children experience, sexual health and quality sex education are often overlooked (Brandon-Friedman, 2019). Foster children also do not receive adequate socialization about sex and relationships (Diamant-Wilson & Blakey, 2019). As a result, foster care youth are more likely to develop HIV (Ahrens et al., 2010), engage in risky sexual practices, have sex for money or drugs, and engage in casual sex (Ahrens et al., 2010; Courtney et al., 2007). The stakes are high because children born to mothers in foster care are likely to be placed themselves by the time they are two years old (Welshonce & Shafer Aglietti, 2022). To advocate for foster families and foster youth, clinicians are encouraged to broach the subject of sexual and reproductive health with all foster children at developmentally appropriate levels. Ongoing conversations about sex and relationships normalize a topic that is often viewed as taboo.

Conversations related to sexual identity are equally important. The more social workers identified themselves as allies through their own personal experiences with LGBTQIA+ people, the more Schaub et al. (2022) noted improved "attitudes, beliefs, and behaviors towards LGBTQ[IA]+ youth in care," especially when supervisors provided direct services, and had "direct knowledge of the LGBTQIA+ community and affirm and validate LGBTQIA+ young people's experiences" (p. 12). van Bergen et al. (2020) also underscored the need for social services and mental health providers working with families to demonstrate an openness to LGBTQIA+ youth talking openly about their sexuality, further recognizing that "a child's disclosure [coming out] continues to strongly impact the quality of the parent-child relationship and emphasizes the role of professionals to harmonize conflict and communication issues in families" (p. 16).

Similarly, when racial/ethnic children who have been minoritized are placed with dominant culture families, clinicians should explicitly explore antiracist attitudes and ask for their commitment to maintaining connections to the child's ethnic community and culture (Mikell Montgomery, 2022). LaBrenz et al. (2021) suggested providing training to child welfare workers to reduce implicit bias in placement and service provision activities.

Ethical considerations

The National Foster Parent Association (NFPA) Code of Ethics, ratified in August 2021, identifies competencies foster parents need to possess across 18 principles. This document states that the foster family (in their provision of family foster care) provides opportunities for healing growth and development for infants through teens so that safe and nurturing relationships are created that will last a lifetime (NFPA, 2021). There is no domain that directly identifies the importance of self-care or self-advocacy for the foster parent. Only the 10th principle addresses the importance of professional development for the foster parent, but only in relation to the care that can be provided for the foster child.

Recognizing that there are consequences to disenfranchised grief, all members of the foster child's network need to ensure that strategies are adhered to and that interventions are provided for all involved in direct care, especially given that it is likely that remaining children (i.e., biological, legal, adopted, or foster children) can be impacted by their care providers' disenfranchised grief experiences. Without transparency and intervention, remaining children may experience personal guilt and responsibility while viewing the caregivers' grief experience (Williams, 2017).

Social work practice could also benefit from employing cultural humility concerning foster children's intersecting identities, including racial/ethnic identity, sexual orientation, and gender-diverse aspects.

Strategies and interventions

Pre-service foster training needs to include the impact of separation on attachment styles and relationships for all members of the fostering family. Ongoing training needs to increase understanding of the impact of loss. Remaining family members are sometimes impacted and the family's availability to provide future care (Edelstein et al., 2001). Such interventions can include pre-service psychoeducation on grief and loss, peer support from more seasoned foster parents, counseling for all members of the fostering family, and involvement in post discharge visitation, where possible (Lynes & Sitoe, 2019). The children of foster parents who experience repetitive loss require confidential support outside of the home so they can process their disenfranchised grief (Williams, 2017).

Grief psychoeducation needs to be provided at every stage of the fostering cycle of service provision. This can include pre-foster parent licensing and training, ongoing training, and consultation with resource workers. Therapy may be required for foster parents' children (i.e., legal, adopted, or biological) and for foster parents themselves. Resource workers need education about how long it may take to overcome feelings of grief and loss when there is a placement change. Specific attention needs to be paid to the children of foster families. Although everyone grieves differently, grief needs to be acknowledged to overcome disenfranchisement, given that the placement change involves real people and not files or case studies. Positive parenting practices and family functioning predicted fewer foster child behavior problems in a systematic review of 40 studies concerning foster and kinship care (Washington et al., 2018). Therefore, supporting foster families through further psychoeducation and training on parenting styles could be beneficial to building greater harmony in foster families.

It is important for all involved in child welfare to be aware that foster parents need to have a voice in what is happening to their foster child, themselves, and their entire family. There can be many opportunities to share and hear voices, including at the beginning (foster parent licensing stage), case conferences, annual foster parent reviews, meetings with other professionals, and specifically during progress or long-term planning meetings. Without these, foster parents perceive and experience having little control over life decisions, such as medical appointments, placement needs, or even foster children moving. Therapists who work with foster children can help by asking to have direct contact with foster parents and negotiating appointment times with them, given that they are often the individuals who transport children to and from medical and treatment appointments.

Additionally, Prince et al. (2021) recommended implementing family-based interventions to reduce child removal and out-of-home placement based on learning of a child's LGBTQIA+ identity. They explained that such interventions should be tailored "to stabilize and shift parenting behaviors to acceptance . . . to prevent child welfare involvement" (p. 1651).

When interventions are not provided to address disenfranchised grief, the subsequent impact can decrease foster home availability (Newquist et al., 2020) and the development of secondary mental health presentations, such as depression and vicarious trauma. Consequences can also include feelings of anger or guilt that can precipitate feelings of wanting to emotionally distance from potentially meaningful relationships.

Summary

Newquist et al. (2020) emphasized that foster parents play a crucial role in keeping the child welfare system functioning. Therefore, child welfare staff need to gain a stronger understanding of how to help foster parents manage placement changes or the removal of children from their homes, as well as ensure that their voice and expertise is part of treatment planning while vulnerable children need foster care services.

Child welfare workers (seen as employees) have access to employee assistance programs, but foster families are not often provided similar resources, even though they do the bulk of direct care work and are most at risk for disenfranchised grief. Without such acknowledgment of the impact of repetitive and intense loss, disenfranchised grief continues, which can impact the care of future children placed in foster homes.

Lastly, acknowledgment that foster families often care deeply for and may love their borrowed children needs to be underscored for all other service professionals. It needs to be underscored that the fostering relationship is not one that is easily developed nor easily dismantled, and foster families are engaging with the grief that the child experiences as well as their own. With this acknowledgment, it is hoped that formalized interventions can be provided to ensure that grief is acknowledged, prepared for, and addressed for all involved in the care of children requiring out-of-home or alternative care.

References

Ahrens, K. R., Richardson, L. P., Courtney, M. E., McCarty, C., Simoni, J., & Katon, W. (2010). Laboratory-diagnosed sexually transmitted infections in former foster youth compared with peers. *Pediatrics, 126*(1). https://doi.org/10.1542/peds.2009-2424

American Psychological Association. (2022). *Children and trauma: Update for mental health professionals 2008.* American Psychological Association. www.apa.org/pi/families/resources/children-trauma-update

Baams, L., Wilson, B. D. M., & Russell, S. T. (2019). LGBTQ youth in unstable housing and foster care. *Pediatrics, 143*(3), Article e20174211. https://doi.org/10.1542/peds.2017-4211

Brandon-Friedman, R. A. (2019, March 6–9). 88. The impact of sexual identity development on the sexual health of former foster youth. In L. D'Angelo & J. Nagata (Chairs), *Gender/sexual minority youth health* [Research Poster Symposium]. Society for Adolescent Mental Health and Medicine Annual Meeting, Washington, DC.

Brown, J. D., Rodgers, J., & Anderson, L. (2015). Roles of foster parent resource workers. *Journal of Child and Family Studies, 24*(6), 1551–1558. https://doi.org/10.1007/s10826-014-9959-7

Canadian Association of Social Workers. (2018). *Understanding social work and child welfare: Interviews with child welfare experts.* www.casw-acts.ca/files/attachements/CASW_Child_Welfare_Report_-_2018.pdf

Casey Family Homes. (2017). How does turnover affect outcomes and what can be done to address retention. *Casey Family Homes.* www.casey.org/turnover-costs-and-retention-strategies/

Children's Bureau. (2014). Parenting a child who has experienced trauma. *Child Welfare Information Gateway*. www.childwelfare.gov/pubpdfs/child-trauma.pdf

Corr, C. A., & Corr, D. M. (2013). Historical and contemporary perspectives on loss, grief, and mourning. In D. K. Meagher & D. E. Balk (Eds.), *Handbook of thanatology: The essential body of knowledge for the study of death, dying, and bereavement* (2nd ed., pp. 163–176). Routledge.

Courtney, M. E., Dworsky, A., Havlicek, J., Perez, A., & Keller, T. (2007). *Midwest evaluation of adult functioning of former foster youth: Outcomes at age 21*. Chapin Hall Center for Children at the University of Chicago. www.chapinhall.org/wp-content/uploads/Midwest-Eval-Outcomes-at-Age-21.pdf

Diamant-Wilson, R., & Blakey, J. M. (2019). "Strap up:" Sexual socialization and safer sex practices among African American youth in foster care. *Child Abuse and Neglect, 88*, 466–477. https://doi.org/10.1016/j.chiabu.2018.08.007

Doka, K. J. (2002). Disenfranchised grief. In C. D. Bryant & D. L. Peck (Eds.), *Encyclopedia of death and the human experience*. SAGE. https://doi.org/10.4135/9781412972031.n122

Edelstein, S. B., Burge, D., & Waterman, J. (2001). Helping foster parents cope with separation, loss, and grief. *Child Welfare, 80*(1), 5–25.

Eisma, M. C., Buyukcan-Tetik, A., & Boelen, P. A. (2022). Reciprocal relations of worry and rumination and psychopathology symptoms after a loss: A prospective cohort study. *Behavior Therapy, 53*(5), 793–806. https://doi.org/10.1016/j.beth.2022.01.001

Fraser, T. A. (2011). *Adopting a child with a trauma and attachment disruption history: A practical guide*. Loving Healing Press.

Fraser, T. A. (2015, September 16). *Supporting biological children: The invisible partners in fostering* [Conference Session]. Ontario Association of Foster Families Conference. Niagara Falls, ON, Canada.

Fraser, T. A., & Ventrella, M. (2019). *A tapestry of relational child and youth care competencies*. Canadian Scholars' Press.

Grimm, B., & Darwell, J. (2015, May 7). Foster parents: Reality v. perception. *National Center for Youth Law*. https://youthlaw.org/news/foster-parents-reality-v-perception

Hurley, L., & Chung, A. (2021, June 17). U.S. Supreme Court upholds Catholic agency's right to reject LGBT couples as foster parents. *National Post*. https://nationalpost.com/news/world/u-s-supreme-court-rules-for-catholic-group-in-lgbt-rights-dispute-3

Kirk, R. S., & Griffith, D. P. (2008). Impact of intensive family preservation services on disproportionality of out-of-home placement of children of color in one state's child welfare system. *Child Welfare, 87*(5), 87–105.

Kirton, D. (2016). (In)sufficient?: Ethnicity and foster care in English local authorities. *Child and Family Social Work, 21*(4), 492–501. https://doi.org/10.1111/cfs.12166

LaBrenz, C. A., Findley, E., Graaf, G., Baiden, P., Kim, J., Choi, M. J., & Chakravarty, S. (2021). Racial/ethnic disproportionality in reunification across U.S. child welfare systems. *Child Abuse and Neglect, 114*, Article 104894. https://doi.org/10.1016/j.chiabu.2020.104894

Lynes, D., & Sitoe, A. (2019). Disenfranchised grief, the emotional impact experienced by foster carers on the cessation of placement. *Adoption and Fostering, 43*(1), 22–34. https://doi.org/10.1177/0308575918823433

Mikell Montgomery, D. (2022). "They don't understand us and are afraid of us": Black social workers' perspectives on the role of anti-Blackness within foster care service provision to Black children. *Child Welfare, 100*(1), 141–164.

Mullings, D. V. (2010). Temporary mothering: Grieving the loss of foster children when they leave. *Journal of the Motherhood Initiative, 1*(2), 165–176.

National Foster Parent Society. (2021). *Foster parent code of ethics.* https://nfpaonline.org/ethics#:~:text=The%20National%20Foster%20Parent%20Association%20encourages%20child%20welfare%20professionals%20to,%2C%20service%2C%20and%20social%20justice

Newquist, J., Ladd, L. D., & Cooley, M. E. (2020). Processing the removal and managing the moves or removals of foster children: A qualitative exploration of foster parents' experiences. *Child and Adolescent Social Work Journal, 37*(5), 537–545. https://doi.org/10.1007/s10560-020-00652-w

Obergefell v. Hodges, 576 U.S._ (2015). www.supremecourt.gov/opinions/14pdf/14-556_3204.pdf

Prince, D. M., Ray-Novak, M., Gillani, B., & Peterson, E. (2021). Sexual and gender minority youth in foster care: An evidence-based theoretical conceptual model of disproportionality and psychological comorbidities. *Trauma, Violence, and Abuse, 23*(5), 1643–1657. https://doi.org/10.1177/152483802110131

Schaub, J., Stander, W. J., & Montgomery, P. (2022). LGBTQ+ young people's health and well-being experiences in out-of-home social care: A scoping review. *Children and Youth Services Review, 143*, Article 106682. https://doi.org/10.1016/j.childyouth.2022.106682

Trochim, W. M. (1989). Concept mapping: Soft science or hard art? *Evaluation and Program Planning, 12*(1), 87–110. https://doi.org/10.1016/0149-7189(89)90027-x

United Nations General Assembly. (2009). Guidelines for the alternative care of children, UN document A/RES/64/142. *United Nations.* www.unicef.org/protection/alternativecare Guidelines-English.pdf van Bergen, D. D., Wilson, B. D. M., Russel, S. T., Gordon, A. G., & Rothblum, E. D. (2020). Parental responses to coming out by lesbian, gay, bisexual, queer, pansexual, or two-spirited people across three age cohorts. *Journal of Marriage and Family, 83*(4), 1116–1133. https://doi.org/10.1111/jomf.12731

Van Holen, F., Geys, L., West, D., Gypen, L., & Vanderfaeillie, J. (2019). Characteristics of successful foster families according to Flemish foster care workers. *Children and Youth Services Review, 107*, Article 104519. https://doi.org/10.1016/j.childyouth.2019.104519

Waldon Family Services. (2018, May 31). Common foster care myths and misconceptions. *Walden Family Services.* https://waldenfamily.org/common-foster-care-myths-and-misconceptions/

Washington, T., Wrenn, A., Kaye, H., Priester, M. A., Colombo, G., Carter, K., Shadreck, I., Hargett, B. A., Williams, J. A., & Coakley, T. (2018). Psychosocial factors and behavioral health outcomes among children in foster and kinship care: A systematic review. *Children and Youth Services Review, 90*, 118–133. https://doi.org/10.1016/j.childyouth.2018.04.030

Welshonce, T., & Shafer Aglietti, R. (2022). KidsVoice's two-generation advocacy: Helping former foster youth succeed as young parents. *Children's Rights Litigation, 24*(3), 1–5.

Williams, D. (2017). Grief, loss, and separation: Experiences of birth children of foster carers. *Child and Family Social Work, 22*(4), 1448–1455. https://doi.org/10.1111/cfs.12366

Questions for reflective practice

1. If service providers believe in stakeholder voice, how can the child welfare system and those who work in it ensure that space is made for voices: the foster child's, the foster parents', and the biological or other foster children?
2. What services should be made available for the biological or legal children of foster parents to decrease their disenfranchised grief experience? How and by whom could these services be provided? How can these members of the family's foster team be engaged in the process?
3. Where can foster parents voice concerns or complaints without the threat of losing current or future foster children?
4. How can peer support groups be created to create more community for foster families?

Supplemental electronic resource

- AdoptUSKids for LGBTQIA+ families: 1-888-200-4005 or emailing info@adoptuskids.org
- The Annie E. Casey Foundation: www.aecf.org/topics/adoption
- Children's Welfare Information Gateway: www.childwelfare.gov/topics/outofhome/resources-foster-families/
- National Foster Parent Association: https://nfpaonline.org/

15
The sacrifice of service

Grief and loss within the military community

Christina Watts-Figueroa and Alton R. McCallum, Jr.

According to the Department of Defense (DOD; 2020), there are 2.5 million military personnel in the U.S. military. The U.S. military comprises an active-duty component (51.4%) and a reserve component (47.1%). Within the active-military component, there are: Air Force (24.7%), Army (36.1%), Navy (25.6%), Marines (13.6%), and the newly created Space Force (Military One Source, 2021). The reserve component consists of the Ready Reserves and the Retired Reserves containing: Air Force Reserve, Air National Guard, Marine Corps Reserve, Army National Guard, Army Reserve, Coast Guard Reserve, and Navy Reserve. Military personnel falls into two broad categories, officers and enlisted. The military is approximately 70.2% White, and 29.8% identify as a racial minority (e.g., Hispanic/Latino, Black/African American, Asian), with 81.1% male and 18.9% female. Approximately 37.5% of the military have families (i.e., children, spouses, or adult dependents), with 41.5% of military-related children between birth and five years old. According to Schaeffer (2021), of the 19.1 million veterans, 89.3% are male, and 10.7% are female. The current veteran population consists of every era of conflict since World War II (i.e., WWII, Korean Conflict, peacetime only, Gulf War, Vietnam Era, and Post 11 September 2001 [9/11]). The post-9/11 veterans are the youngest veteran-era served by the Department of Veterans Affairs (DVA), with about 5.1 million predicted to be served by 2021 (DVA, 2019).

Military members, veterans, and their families are a unique population within the US. While there are many reasons family members decide to serve (e.g., financial, travel, family legacy), servicemembers do so with at least some understanding that their decision involves sacrifice. The U.S. military and veteran community has made many sacrifices, most notably in the two decades since 9/11, wherein personnel from all branches of the U.S. military have faced multiple deployments, increased risk of death or physical injury, moral injury, family separation, and physical and mental impairments. The authors outline the sacrifice of service and subsequent bereavement and grief that persist within military families.

DOI: 10.4324/9781003292890-18

Military and veteran communities' experiences with grief

Military personnel and veterans experience a range of grief anomalies. Normative bereavement and grief last between 6 and 12 months and typically resolve without clinical intervention. However, servicemembers and veterans could be prone to higher incidents of clinical grief due to their comorbidity with other mental health disorders, such as posttraumatic stress disorder (PTSD), due to their potentially high exposure to violent and/or accidental deaths (APA, 2022).

Complicated grief diagnoses have evolved from persistent complex bereavement disorder (PCBD) to prolonged grief disorder (PGD; American Psychiatric Association [APA], 2022). APA (2022) defined PGD as a prolonged grief reaction that is maladaptive after the death of someone with whom a person was close. Additional criteria for PGD include the presence of a minimum of three of the following symptoms: identity disruption, a marked sense of disbelief about the death, intense emotional pain, difficulty reintegrating into activities or relationships, emotional numbness, the feeling that life is meaningless after the death, and intense loneliness. Other significant criteria for this disorder are the duration and severity of one's reactions exceeding social, cultural, and religious norms (APA, 2022). Culturally, adaptive grief can vary widely, ultimately impacting norms identified by the diagnosis (APA, 2022). Pervasive and intertwining comorbidities complicate these grief trajectories among servicemembers, such as PTSD and other pre-existing conditions.

Ambiguous loss

Servicemembers, veterans, and their families endure frequent experiences of ambiguous loss and disenfranchised grief. *Ambiguous loss* is a loss that is uncertain or ultimately incomplete, resulting from the uncertainty of a person's return or receiving no death verification (Boss, 1999). For example, if a service member becomes a prisoner of war (POW), the family members suffer ambiguous emotional and cognitive losses with ongoing uncertainty about the service member's physical wellbeing (Shalev & Ben-Asher, 2011). There is a finality to death loss, with events that lead one through parts of the bereavement process, like death notification, funerals, death certificates, and role changes. However, with ambiguous loss, doubt about the permanence of the loss prevents and delays acceptance, thus impacting how the griever processes the loss. Another example is when a service member or veteran suffers a traumatic brain injury (TBI) or personality-altering mental state, such as untreated depression or PTSD. A loved one's personality can change after injury or prolonged traumatic exposures, resulting in psychological absence or differences in relationships (Shalev & Ben-Asher, 2011). These changes can alter how the family functions and create role changes, ultimately impacting the servicemembers and their family's quality of life.

Another overlooked period of ambiguous loss comes during the adjustment period after a military member retires, leaves, or is discharged from the military as they identify their next *mission* or career. For military family members, transitioning out of the military means no longer belonging to the military while simultaneously not belonging to civilian culture. The adjustment is further complicated if the veteran has difficulty connecting to others in the civilian community, deepening their isolation and sense of loss. The transiency of military culture moves personnel and their families to different states within the US or to various countries worldwide and prevents military families from putting down roots or defining themselves by one culture. Many military families have transcultural experiences from moving around or learning to integrate these experiences into their own lives; as a result, many families develop a *third culture*.

Third culture

The *third culture* is developed by a person who has transcultural experiences in their lifetime, resulting in adopting and integrating customs, beliefs, attitudes, and norms (de Waal & Born, 2021). The third culture is common among military children born abroad or with a parent from another culture. Sociologists Drs. Ruth and John Useem established this term in the 1960s after observing the experiences of young American children living abroad in India. Useem and Useem (1967) noted that blending the dominant family culture with the second culture creates the third culture. Leaving behind a culture can create ambiguous loss and several forms of disenfranchised grief among servicemembers and their families.

Disenfranchised grief occurs when one's grief is minimized due to the lack of recognition by others, including how the grievers grieve culturally (Doka, 2002). The military and veteran community often experiences a great deal of non-death losses due to the nature of the job. A prime example of disenfranchised grief occurs during permanent changes of station (PCS), where military members and their families are forced to move every two to four years on average. The military culture often emphasizes being *mission ready*, which requires the individual to put the mission (i.e., field training, deployment, inventory, or even physical training) over anything else, including self and family. Unfortunately, military families are also expected to focus on the mission and do not receive the time or outlet to grieve as necessary. Primary stressors common to military families include combat-related death, deployment, family and friend network instability, frequent change of duty stations, divorce, financial stress, physical injury, and suicide; thus, disenfranchised grief in the military community profoundly impacts all domains of the military family's life. Add to that the blend of cultures that military families develop (i.e., culture[s] of origin, third culture, military culture) and the way a family grieves may not be well perceived or received by either military personnel or civilians in their current location, further disenfranchising their grief.

Social aspects of disenfranchised grief

Social connection is critical to those in the military community. The loss of social relationships can increase feelings of isolation and lead to a loss of identity for military members and their families. Isolation is one aspect many families face during PCS or deployments as part of the ongoing transitions within the military culture. Military personnel and their immediate families move away from their families of origin, friends, co-workers, teachers, doctors, and pets, thus creating additional isolation. Due to these ruptures, military families may develop internalized beliefs about saying goodbye and building relationships.

Disenfranchised grief may appear as a feeling of loneliness, isolation, and loss of belonging. Military members and their families may mourn the process of meeting new people, trusting new friends with their children, and (potentially) disconnecting from their past-proximity friends. Although this process is complex for adults, it can profoundly impact children due to the constant disruptions in their relationships. According to the DOD (2020), military children move anywhere from six to nine times between kindergarten and high school. As a result, children are faced with multiple losses related to those moves and do not often get the opportunity to grieve these losses. This further complicates critical developmental years and creates impacts across the lifespan.

Members of the military community may experience a strong sense of loss and have difficulty grieving the relationships they left behind after separating from the military. The way the servicemember is discharged from the military has a direct impact on their family and can continue to complicate the family's losses. *Discharge status* is a description of a servicemember's formal release from their military service obligation. Several servicemember discharge statuses exist: honorable, other than honorable, general, bad conduct, medical, or dishonorable. Military retirements and honorable discharges are regarded as the most respectable forms of military discharge. Other discharge types are subject to judgment from others and feelings of shame. Moving to a new community may make it difficult to move forward depending on discharge status, job availability, marital status, and desire to create new connections.

Children of military families can face multiple losses socially each time they have to move because of a permanent change of station (PCS), a deployment, or their parents' separation or divorce. Doka (2008) suggested that mourning is a socially acceptable expression of grief. Many are unaware of how children need to grieve and assume their experience is similar to adults' experiences when this is usually not the case.

Cultural aspects of disenfranchised grief

The military culture's foundation encompasses resiliency, loyalty, and patriotism. Ganz et al. (2021) noted that military communities pride themselves on core values set forth by individual branches. In addition, military community values deepen within individual units, such as combat arms or support units. The military culture influences the social norms that shape how those within the community will grieve. The military community is one founded on grit and pride to push through, which is a sentiment that extends to military personnel and family members that communicates avoiding help, primarily when related to mental health needs (Ganz et al., 2021). Although many military families have adopted the U.S. military as a third culture, their racial and ethnic identities are still a vital part of their identity and often play a role in their grieving process.

Mental health services

Seeking out mental health services has historically been publicly stigmatized within the military community; however, over the last two decades, there has been an organizational shift to increase mental health support. Organizational shifts to increase support for mental health is vital but largely depend on supportive leadership (McGuffin et al., 2021). If leadership is destructive and does not provide command support, servicemembers will be unable to address life stressors by seeking help, further complicating grief (McGuffin et al., 2021).

Intergenerational cultural beliefs about grief and mental health can impact a family's ability to grieve or to seek services. According to Doka (2002), the way families grieve is dependent on the cultural rules passed down to the family. These rules can either align with the U.S. military culture or misalign with their other cultural grieving practices. Active-duty funerals are not always representative of the diversity within the US and, as a result, can create a sense of disenfranchisement for those grieving who come from complex cultures (Doka, 2002). Ultimately, moral injury can further complicate the grief experience because individuals are influenced by their own cultural beliefs about death.

Suicide loss

The Department of Veteran Affairs (2019) reported that suicide is the leading cause of death in veterans aged 18 to 55. A statistically significant increase in suicides was completed from 2015 to 2020 (DOD, 2020) and 519 servicemembers and 202 family members died by suicide in 2021 DOD (2022). Seamon-Lahiff et al. (2021) named shame related to financial issues, combat-related trauma, relational stress, and moral injury as risk factors correlated to this increase. One's experience with combat can violate their belief system so much that it ultimately increases the association with suicidality (Kelley et al., 2019). Many of those who served may experience core symptoms of moral injury, such as guilt, shame, or existential crisis, which ultimately can impact secondary outcomes like suicidal thoughts, anxiety, and depression (Battles et al., 2021). Families who lose a loved one to suicide often struggle to find a sense of community due to the shame they may feel or the loss of access to the resources they once had.

Experiences among surviving family members of non-deployed servicemembers may carry a greater sense of shame or stigma. Servicemembers who do not deploy historically have not had the same screening level for suicide as those actively deployed (Kang et al., 2015). Ultimately, due to the overt focus on mental toughness common in military culture, many may not pursue help from professionals, resulting in suicide deaths (Kang et al., 2015). Due to the value of patriotism, heroism is associated with military personnel dying in combat (Cacace et al., 2022). Families can experience disenfranchised grief due to shame related to missing signs of suicidal ideation and because they may not understand what led to the death, as it cannot be further explained by deployment stress. Family members may not want to share their military affiliation to avoid assumptions about why their loved one is not with the family. In breaking this silence, their loved one may not receive the same honorable rituals allowed to those who died a military-related death.

Servicemembers who have been marginalized

Stigma related to mental health in the military and veteran community has decreased since 9/11; however, many members of the Black, Indigenous, and Persons of Color (BIPOC) military community that have been marginalized may continue to experience stigma, complicating their disenfranchised grief partly due to the underutilization of mental health services (De Luca et al., 2016). Some subcommunities (i.e., LGBTQIA+ and BIPOC) may share other life and disenfranchised grief experiences within the larger community. For example, a person from a minority racial/ethnic background may not believe in mental health treatment, which may cause internal conflict within the person or family seeking help. Children from these subcommunities may struggle to navigate their families' culture and tremendous military influence.

Recent cultural and social shifts have shed light on the collective disenfranchised grief experiences of many BIPOC in the US, including military and veteran families. Women's issues in the military also came to the forefront after the murder of U.S. Army Specialist Vanessa Guillén. Many military women disclosed their personal experiences with sexual assault and began to demand change, resulting in the introduction of H.R.8270, the I am Vanessa Guillén Act of 2020 (2019–2020) to make military sexual harassment a criminal act (Paybarah, 2020). As a result, the military chose to reevaluate its current capacity to address diversity, equity, and inclusion issues and to address bias within leadership (Military One Source, 2020). Although these changes are occurring, it relies on leadership to identify the impact of trauma and grief on their troops and provide space to grieve disenfranchisement related to oppression, sexism, homophobia, and other diversity issues.

Diagnostic issues

Within the diagnosis of PGD, there is an allowance for cultural norms that cause persistent grief and loss. APA (2022) stated in Criterion E, "the bereavement reaction clearly exceeds expected social, cultural, or religious norms for the individual's culture and context" (p. 321). Servicemembers and their families may not make "exceeding" displays of grief because military culture and the veteran community hide and mask the grieving process through a sense of responsibility and duty to servicemembers. When military/family members actively participate in the balancing act for grief displays in this culture, they may not qualify for a PGD diagnosis. Therefore, when grieving stems from combat and heavy training times, it is necessary to specify traumatic bereavement.

Relational aspects of disenfranchised grief

One of servicemembers' most significant and invisible sacrifices is the negative impact their service has on their families and other relationships. Military personnel and veterans express their grief about missing out on their children's many milestones and developmental phases due to military separation, duty, and mission readiness. Although servicemembers receive training on reintegration, mental health professionals' training does not adequately address grief related to the ongoing separation from family members and subsequent relational ruptures. During wartime, families continue to experience ongoing stressors related to adjustment and continued ruptures in attachment bonds due to the mobility of the culture and continuous military separations. Common ruptures include divorce, deployment, geographical separation, separation due to medical necessity (i.e., wounded warrior, physically and mentally), incarceration, parental emotional detachment, and death. Unfortunately, minimizing others' experiences with attachment wounds associated with deployment, family separation, and loss associated with changing duty stations is common within the military community.

Impact of attachment

Families who have experienced multiple military separations may begin to minimize their experiences and feelings, resulting in their children not expressing their feelings, thoughts, or beliefs about their grief experiences. In general, children also may not understand their experience as grief but may exhibit emotional and behavioral signs of grief. Children begin to externalize their feelings through behavioral issues and emotional dysregulation that impact attachment and attunement in parent-child relationships. Furthermore, children of military communities share many similarities in their grief compared to their civilian counterparts, including loss of appetite, depressed mood, difficulty sleeping, fear of being alone or away from a caregiver, regression in behaviors, and anxiety (Webb, 2010).

The stress of multiple deployments and military separations can take an enormous toll on families, and divorce is one of the most considerable losses. Divorce is a common experience for many families in the US (40–50%) and is not necessarily unique to the military (Abdel-Sater, 2022). Although many in society accept divorce as a shared experience, many often do not acknowledge the grief experienced by the loss. For military children, a divorce can mean further community instability. For example, some military children are born overseas or have a parent from another country. If their parents' divorce, the service member must have a family care plan, or that child may go with the other parent. Family care plans ensure that military members' children are cared for during military separation. Children who move away from their military community may initially struggle to adapt, find it challenging to share their experiences, and find it difficult to build new relationships.

How a child grieves also depends on overall family functioning. When the family support system is robust and stable during reintegration, discussions about loss, grief, and sacrifice of service can help the family unit overcome its suffering. Conversely, when there is family dysfunction, there is not enough safety to properly grieve within a socially expected or acceptable timeframe. Doka (2002) noted that many who experience disenfranchisement in their bereavement and mourning rituals are unable to process their grief fully. Rituals and practices of grief expression are essential for one to heal.

Cumulative impacts of disenfranchised grief across the lifespan

Military and veteran communities face many hardships because war exposure and constant transition create compounding losses. Cumulative impacts on the lifespan include increased anxiety, depression, substance use, moral injury, attachment ruptures, and lifecycle disruptions. For example, when a service member dies tragically at a young age (e.g., combat, suicide), it increases the survivors' risk of complications with the grieving process due to missed opportunities in life events with the deceased (Harrington, 2017).

Identity loss is a common experience for veterans and their families. According to Webb (2010), the degree to which a military member connects with military culture impacts the intensity of the loss felt at the time of separation from the military. Veterans may also resist adopting civilian identities (Albertson, 2019) due to feelings of loss and grief associated with leaving behind military life and culture.

Special considerations for military children and adolescents

Children and adolescents of military families will experience grief related to their military family's experience differently due to their developmental stage and cognitive abilities. The developmental stage most commonly forms children's experiences of grief; however, culture also strongly influences the grieving process. Children who do not have the needed support to process their grief fully will struggle to build lasting relationships and may continue to develop a deep sense of unfinished business throughout their lifespan. Some families experience and struggle to express grief related to their servicemembers' or veterans' mood and personality changes related to war exposure and moral injury.

The direct impact of deployment on children has resulted in higher rates of mental health services provided in the first decade of the global war on terror. During the initial years of the post-9/11 era, outpatient mental health visits for children doubled from around 1 million to 2 million (National Center for Children in Poverty, 2010). Preschool-aged children of deployed soldiers were twice as likely not to meet developmental stage milestones, resulting in ongoing challenges with social relationships, speech, language, and physical issues (St. John & Fenning, 2020). Adolescents who lived with a family member serving in the military experienced a disproportionate number of adverse childhood experiences (ACEs) compared to their civilian counterparts, which has led to a significant number of suicide attempts within the population (Clements-Nolle et al., 2021). The need for increased mental health services with providers who have competency in grief, military culture, and family therapy is vital to addressing the disenfranchisement many in the community feel.

A military or veteran child's grief will manifest only as much as their family system has allowed it to. Children's cultural beliefs and influences could impact how they process their grief. Although grief is healthy for any individual, understanding a person's adverse life experiences and the availability of opportunities to mourn their losses privately and publicly will determine if the grief becomes disenfranchised.

Allyship and advocacy

Military and veteran post-9/11-era communities have received more support from the American people than in previous wartimes. Although there has been increased research and resources related to PTSD, moral injury, substance use, deployments, and reintegration, minimal research is available about disenfranchised grief. Very little knowledge and few resources exist for those who did not experience a combat loss. Disenfranchised grief may directly and negatively impact military families' social, cultural, and relationship factors and, therefore, their quality of life.

Over recent years, many advocates for the military community have highlighted the need for further mental health support for all military families, including those who have less than honorable discharges from the military and increased loss due to suicide. Previously, families who lost a loved one to suicide or dishonorable discharge from service would not be afforded the same benefits as those who experienced combat losses. Organizations like the Tragedy Assistance Program for Survivors (TAPS) have shifted resources to support those families impacted by suicide. Due to the stigma associated with deaths by suicide, many families have not been able to grieve within their community or the military community.

Ethical considerations

A primary ethical consideration is acquiring cultural knowledge of the military and veteran families and their communities. Clinicians working with military families must become familiar with the U.S. military culture and each branch's unique subculture. In the last two decades, the military has established clear competencies with military personnel: military ethos, military organizations and roles, stressors and resources, and treatment resources and tools (Atuel & Castro, 2018). Learning about customs, rituals, norms, language, and beliefs related to the military is essential. Practicing cultural humility with this population is vital to support any military or veteran family navigating their disenfranchisement. *Cultural humility* is a commitment to lifelong cultural learning and the ability to become reflective practitioners, which involves ongoing self-evaluation while examining power imbalances within a community or system (Tervalon & Murray-García, 1998).

An important ethical consideration is acknowledging the mental health professional's biases and assumptions about military culture and military experiences. The military's role in foreign affairs is politicized, impacting their ability to seek assistance, especially when living outside predominantly military communities. If a mental health professional has negative personal experiences with the military or conflicting political views, this might impair their ability to support the military community or lead them to avoid working with it. Assumptions about how a military member should act or present in therapy can also create ethical issues. A military member's or veteran's presentation of symptoms in mental health has also influenced the intersectionality of their race, gender, religion, ethnicity, sexual orientation, rank, and branch. Exploration of assumptions and biases specifically related to beliefs about war, military culture, personal experiences with the military community, and foreign policy is vital to ensure ethical practice when working with this community.

Another ethical consideration is providing access to equitable mental health services. According to the DVA (2019), post-9/11 veterans had far higher uninsured rates than their non-veteran counterparts, regardless of gender. Depending on their location, veterans and their families may not find clinicians versed in their military culture or resources. The veteran's discharge status or socioeconomic status can also impact their ability to receive mental health services due to not receiving benefits, such as mental health access or ongoing insurance. As a result of the lack of mental health resources and increased risk for suicide loss, the DVA has increased access to telehealth services to reduce the barriers associated with lack of transportation, childcare, or finances (Jacobs et al., 2019).

Providing a medical diagnosis, including mental health disorders, is another ethical consideration for children and adolescents of active-duty service-members, because some diagnoses may impede their ability to serve later in the U.S. military. Using strengths-based language in clinical documentation and assigning appropriate diagnoses is vital when working with these families and military members to support them better throughout their lifespan.

The military community comprises many complex subcultural systems and families with diverse backgrounds. Increased diversity calls on mental health professionals to explore the intersectionality and third culture's impact on grieving rituals and beliefs. Providers who learn about the complexities and spectrum of family systems within the military community are better prepared to navigate these families' challenges. Burgin and Prosek (2021) noted that using culturally responsive treatments will prove more significant and have better outcomes for military families.

Strategies and interventions

Historically, the military community has had access to cognitive-behavioral health services that are evidence-based and time-limited. The challenge with treating military and veteran families for grief-related issues is that grief is not time-limited. Mental health therapies and interventions that help families move toward healing will also build continued resiliency within the family system.

Many theories and approaches to grief and bereavement work well within military and veteran communities. The TAPS model was established and created for military survivors by Major Bonnie Carroll, a survivor herself. This model is a peer-based program that provides care through three phases: stabilization, hopeful reappraisal, and positive integration (Dooley et al., 2019). Stabilization establishes trust and provides a safe environment through immediate care and assistance. According to Dooley et al. (2019), hopeful reappraisal builds hope by confronting loss with support and empathy while establishing new life roles and activities by envisioning a positive future. Positive integration is helping survivors achieve a renewed sense of meaning in life through positive integration of the loss into life growth, learning, and patterns (Dooley et al., 2019).

According to Einat and Talya (2022), various factors affect military members during their bereavement process, including unit-specific mourning rituals, the inability to grieve on the battlefield, and their ability to grieve authentically. These factors can invite increased shame during grief, as many in the military community do not want to appear weak. Many individuals experiencing disenfranchised grief often feel shame because they do not understand what they are truly experiencing. According to Boss (2010), mental health providers must employ several strategies: normalizing and validating grief experiences, revising attachments or bonds with the deceased person, finding meaning, and re-establishing hope. Strategies that could better support each military member or veteran include individual therapy, peer support groups, and changes at the organizational level in recognizing disenfranchised grief.

Family therapy is a recognized treatment modality to address attachment-related issues within the family system because families can help serve as a protective factor (Diamond et al., 2021). To better address family issues, engaging the family in family therapy or play therapy can be beneficial in facilitating connection, attunement, communication, and addressing challenging issues (Villarreal-Davis et al., 2021). The benefits of increasing family engagement reduce overall stress related to the military culture. Mental health treatments that address children's grief experiences in a developmentally appropriate way, such as play therapy, play-based interventions, or family therapy, can support military families and their children. These developmentally appropriate approaches are inclusive of all children. Schaefer and Drewes (2014) suggested that using play in family therapy to increase resiliency can support families by reducing isolation, nurturing relationships, developing meaning-making, and enhancing attachment.

Expressive arts therapy interventions, such as painting, poetry, writing, and mask making, have proven to be practical approaches to supporting a client experiencing grief because of their ability to capture a client's narratives. Kwong (2021) emphasized the value of expressive therapies in addressing grief and loss as a holistic approach; they offer a decentering approach allowing individuals to make new meaning about their experiences. Many who survived a suicide loss or attempt stayed silent for years because others expressed discomfort with talking about it. Strouse et al. (2021) highlighted art therapy as a non-pathological and non-verbal approach to addressing one's grief. Nonlinguistic narrative approaches, such as somatosensory narratives expressed through movement, sound, and rhythm (Malchiodi, 2020), can allow military personnel and veterans to embody their grief, allowing for a deeper level of expression. Strouse et al. (2021) noted that items like light memory books provide those grieving with a tangible object that can be taken home and continue to honor the lost life.

Summary

Grief is a universal experience that crosses all cultures, races, religions, and genders. How one grieves, however, is influenced by many factors. Military families and communities are no strangers to grief experiences; however, grief can be further complicated by a series of adverse life events, masked by adherence to military culture, or simply dismissed. Establishing appropriate resources and care is vital to better address disenfranchised grief experiences and proactively address mental health needs within the military community. Acknowledgment of families' losses and grief will create opportunities for permission to grieve. Understanding all the losses and the ambiguity connected to military culture will increase mental health practitioners' ability to support military families. Creating opportunities for families and military personnel to grieve the more marginalized losses is also crucial as the socially accepted ones. Families must make meaning of their losses to avoid further disenfranchisement. Proving access to peer support, appropriate treatment modalities, and stigma reduction related to losses can improve relationships, foster resilience, and provide spaces for healing.

References

Abdel-Sater, R. (2022). Marriage dissolution in the United States: A survival analysis approach. *Journal of Divorce and Remarriage, 63*(4), 235–261. https://doi.org/10.1 080/10502556.2022.2042788

Albertson, K. (2019). Relational legacies impacting on veteran transition from military to civilian life: Trajectories of acquisition, loss, and reformulation of a sense of belonging. *Illness, Crisis, and Loss, 27*(4), 255–273. https://doi. org/10.1177/1054137319834773

American Psychiatric Association, DSM-5 Task Force. (2013). *Diagnostic and statistical manual of mental disorders: DSM-5*™ (5th ed.). American Psychiatric Publishing, Inc. https://doi.org/10.1176/appi.books.9780890425596

Atuel, H. R., & Castro, C. A. (2018). Military cultural competence. *Clinical Social Work Journal, 46*(2), 74–82. https://doi.org/10.1007/s10615-018-0651-z

Battles, A. R., Jinkerson, J., Kelley, M. L., & Mason, R. A. (2021). Structural examination of moral injury and PTSD and their associations with suicidal behavior among combat veterans. *Journal of Community Engagement and Scholarship, 13*(4), 1–14. https://doi.org/10.54656/vlkw1083

Boss, P. (1999). *Ambiguous loss: Learning to live with unresolved grief.* Harvard University Press.

Boss, P. (2010). The trauma and complicated grief of ambiguous loss. *Pastoral Psychology, 59*(2), 137–145. https://doi.org/10.1007/s11089-009-0264-0

Burgin, E. E., & Prosek, E. A. (2021). Culturally responsive play therapy with military-connected children and families: Opportunities for rigorous research. *International Journal of Play Therapy, 30*(4), 221–230. https://doi.org/10.1037/pla0000151

Cacace, S., Smith, E. J., Cramer, R. J., Meca, A., & Desmarais, S. L. (2022). Military self-stigma as a mediator of the link between military identity and suicide risk. *Military Psychology, 34*(2), 237–251. https://doi.org/10.1080/08995605.2021.1994329

Clements-Nolle, K., Lensch, T., Yang, Y., Martin, H., Peek, J., & Yang, W. (2021). Attempted suicide among adolescents in military families: The mediating role of adverse childhood experiences. *Journal of Interpersonal Violence, 36*(23–24), 11743–11754. https://doi.org/10.1177/0886260519900976

De Luca, S. M., Blosnich, J. R., Hentschel, E. A. W., King, E., & Amen, S. (2016). Mental health care utilization: How race, ethnicity and veteran status are associated with seeking help. *Community Mental Health Journal, 52*(2), 174–179. https:// doi.org/10.1007/s10597-015-9964-3

Department of Defense. (2020). *2020 demographics profile of the military community.* https://download.militaryonesource.mil/12038/MOS/Reports/2020-demograph ics-report.pdf

Department of Defense. (2022). *Department of defense annual report on suicide in the military: Calendar year 2021*. www.dspo.mil/Portals/113/Documents/2021%20 ASR/FY21%20ASR.pdf?ver=1F9QARTc2gfXMGIoqum0Mw%3d%3d

Department of Veterans Affairs. (2019). *Post 9/11 veteran's profile 2017*. www.va.gov/ vetdata/docs/SpecialReports/Profile_of_Veterans_2017.pdf

de Waal, M. F., & Born, M. P. (2021). Where I'm from? Third Culture Kids about their cultural identity shifts and belonging. *International Journal of Intercultural Relations, 83*, 67–83. https://doi.org/10.1016/j.ijintrel.2021.04.004

Diamond, G., Diamond, G. M., & Levy, S. (2021). Attachment-based family therapy: Theory, clinical model, outcomes, and process research. *Journal of Affective Disorders, 294*(1), 286–295. https://doi.org/10.1016/j.jad.2021.07.005

Doka, K. J. (Ed.). (2002). *Disenfranchised grief: New directions, challenges, and strategies for practice*. Research Press.

Doka, K. J. (2008). Disenfranchised grief in historical and cultural perspective. In M. S. Stroebe, W. Stroebe, & R. Q. Hanssen (Eds.), *Handbook of bereavement research and practice: Advances in theory and intervention* (pp. 223–240). American Psychological Association. https://doi.org/10.1037/14498-011

Dooley, C. M., Carroll, B., Fry, L. E., Seamon-Lahiff, G., & Bartone, P. T. (2019). A model for supporting grief recovery following traumatic loss: The Tragedy Assistance Program for Survivors (TAPS). *Military Medicine, 184*(7–8), 166–170. https://doi.org/10.1093/milmed/usz084

Einat, Y., & Talya, E. (2022). "Crying in my uniform, for sure": A qualitative thematic analysis of loss and grief among soldiers after losing a comrade in combat. *OMEGA – Journal of Death and Dying*. Advance online publication. https://doi.org/10.1177/00302228221090749

Ganz, A., Yamaguchi, C., Koritzky, B. P. G., & Berger, S. E. (2021). Military culture and its impact on mental health and stigma. *Journal of Community Engagement and Scholarship, 13*(4), Article 10. https://doi.org/10.54656/ZZHP1245

Harrington, C. (2017). Meaning making in wartime bereavement: Lessons learned from bereaved parents and siblings. *OMEGA – Journal of Death and Dying, 76*(2), 103–121. https://doi.org/10.1177/0030222816643084

I am Vanessa Guillén Act of 2020, H.R. 8270, 116th Congress (2019–2020). www. congress.gov/bill/116th-congress/house-bill/8270/all-actions?s=1&r=1

Jacobs, J. C., Blonigen, D. M., Kimerling, R., Slightam, C., Gregory, A. J., Gurmessa, T., & Zulman, D. M. (2019). Increasing mental health care access, continuity, and efficiency for veterans through telehealth with video tablets. *Psychiatric Services, 70*(11), 976–982. https://doi.org/10.1176/appi.ps.201900104

Kang, H. K., Bullman, T. A., Smolenski, D. J., Skopp, N. A., Gahm, G. A., & Reger, M. A. (2015). Suicide risk among 1.3 million veterans who were on active duty during the Iraq and Afghanistan wars. *Annals of Epidemiology, 25*(2), 96–100. https://doi.org/10.1016/j.annepidem.2014.11.020

Kelley, M. L., Bravo, A. J., Davies, R. L., Hamrick, H. C., Vinci, C., & Redman, J. C. (2019). Moral injury and suicidality among combat-wounded veterans: The moderating effects of social connectedness and self-compassion. *Psychological Trauma: Theory, Research, Practice and Policy, 11*(6), 621–629. https://doi.org/10.1037/tra0000447

Kwong, M.-K. (2021). Making meaning out of intersectionality through expressive arts therapy: A case study. *Creative Arts in Education and Therapy, 6*(2), 127–140. https://doi.org/10.15212/CAET/2020/6/24

Malchiodi, C. A. (2020). *Trauma and expressive arts therapy: Brain, body and imagination in the healing process.* Guilford Press.

McGuffin, J. J., Riggs, S. A., Raiche, E. M., & Romero, D. H. (2021). Military and veteran help-seeking behaviors: Role of mental health stigma and leadership. *Military Psychology, 33*(5), 332–340. https://doi.org/10.1080/08995605.2021.1962181

Military One Source. (2020). *2020 demographics report.* www.militaryonesource. mil/data-research-and-statistics/military-community-demographics/2020-demo graphics-profile/

Military One Source. (2021). *How the military supports diversity and inclusion.* www.militaryonesource.mil/military-life-cycle/friends-extended-family/ military-diversity-and-inclusion/

National Center for Children in Poverty. (2010). *Trauma faced by children of military families: What every policymaker should know.* www.nccp.org/publication/ trauma-faced-by-children-of-military-families/

Paybarah, A. (2020, October 21). Vanessa Guillen died "in the line of duty," Army officials say. *The New York Times.* www.nytimes.com/2020/10/21/us/vanessa-guillen-death.html

Schaefer, C. E., & Drewes, A. A. (2014). *The therapeutic powers of play: 20 core agents of change* (2nd ed.). Wiley.

Schaeffer, K. (2021). The changing face of America's veteran population. *Pews Research Center.* www.pewresearch.org/fact-tank/2021/04/05/the-changing-face-of-americas-veteran-population/

Seamon-Lahiff, G. E., Dooley, C. M., Bartone, P. T., & Carroll, B. (2021). Risk factors for complicated grief in the military community. OMEGA – *Journal of Death and Dying.* Advance online publication. https://doi.org/10.1177/00302228211016218

Shalev, R., & Ben-Asher, S. (2011). Ambiguous loss: The long-term effects on the children of POWs. *Journal of Loss and Trauma, 16*(6), 511–528. https://doi.org/10 .1080/15325024.2011.576983

St. John, L. V., & Fenning, P. (2020). Supporting the behavioral and mental health needs of military children. *Preventing School Failure, 64*(2), 99–105. https://doi.org/10.1080/1045988X.2019.1680945

Strouse, S., Hass-Cohen, N., & Bokoch, R. (2021). Benefits of an open art studio to military suicide survivors. *The Arts in Psychotherapy, 72*, Article 101722. https://doi.org/10.1016/j.aip.2020.101722

Tervalon, M., & Murray-García, J. (1998). Cultural humility versus cultural competence: A critical distinction in defining physician. *Journal of Health Care for the Poor and Underserved, 9*(2), 117. https://doi.org/10.1353/hpu.2010.0233

Useem, J., & Useem, R. (1967). The interfaces of a binational third culture: A study of the American community in India. *Journal of Social Issues, 23*(1), 130–143. https://doi.org/10.1111/j.1540-4560.1967.tb00567.x

Villarreal-Davis, C., Watts-Figueroa, C., & Turner, R. (2021). Serving together: Play therapy to foster attachment in grieving military families. *International Journal for Play Therapy, 30*(4), 231–243. https://doi.org/10.1037/pla0000168

Webb, N. B. (Ed.). (2010). *Helping bereaved children: A handbook for practitioners* (3rd ed.). Guilford Press.

Questions for reflective practice

1. What cultural considerations should mental health practitioners explore before working with military members and their families?
2. What are some expected losses the military community experiences that can complicate grief or be ambiguous?
3. How does the intersectionality of gender, race, and rank impact feelings of disfranchisement?
4. How does disenfranchised grief impact military children and adults along the vital developmental stages of their lifespan?

Supplemental electronic resources

- National Alliance for Children's Grief: https://childrengrieve.org/
- Military One Source: www.militaryonesource.mil/
- Sesame Street for Military Families: https://sesamestreetformilitaryfamilies.org/
- TAPS: Tragedy Assistance Program for Survivors: www.taps.org/

16

Ovdje nisam, a tamo me nema

The silenced complicated, complex grief of Bosnian refugees

Selma Zakomac-Baćevac and Meyleen M. Velasquez

Wars erupt and bring unimaginable violence and significant trauma, inflicting pain and grief on those who survive. About 82 million refugees reside worldwide (United Nations High Commissioner for Refugees [UNHCR], 2021). Every war-torn community has a history of shared loss and unspoken pain that goes unnoticed throughout generations. Mental health professionals are critical partners in supporting refugee populations and developing programs that accurately address the complexities of grief. The authors explore the genocide and the survival of the Bosnian community to recommend effective treatment for refugees.

Positionality or *social location* refers to intersecting identities, such as race, gender, and religion, and their positions of power and privilege in society (Jacobson & Mustafa, 2019). An individual's social identity shapes their interests and how they interpret their world. For example, the first author, Selma Zakomac-Baćevac, is a Bosnian resettled refugee who survived the Siege of Sarajevo and escaped the horrors of the Bosnian war with her family in 1994. In 1997, Selma and her family became resettled refugees in the US. The second author, Meyleen M. Velasquez, is a Venezuelan immigrant. Her maternal family is Cuban, and her paternal family is Colombian. Meyleen grew up with the maternal side of her family, who sought political asylum in Venezuela following the start of the Cuban revolution. In 1995, Meyleen and her family fled Venezuela and migrated to the US.

Refugees' silent disenfranchised grief

Refugees experience a higher level of posttraumatic stress disorder (PTSD) and other mental health complications than populations that have not experienced resettlement (Miller & Rasmussen, 2017). Refugee survivors also

DOI: 10.4324/9781003292890-19

experience more severe symptomatology than war-affected civilians who were not displaced. Survivors hold the pain of losing culture, language, traditions, family support system, and lives. When war was brought to their country's doorstep, a whole community of people experienced human rights violations and lost the freedom to live without fear for their lives.

Bosnian refugees also experienced unique losses while displaced during the war (Human Rights Watch, n.d.). Survivors lost homes, opportunities to attend school or work, access to healthcare, and social networks, and they were forced into exile. Many Bosnians suffered torture and witnessed loved ones' rapes and murders. Mental health professionals must obtain training on the intersections of environmental stressors and trauma effects in grief treatment (Hagl et al., 2015).

Disenfranchised grief

Disenfranchised grief refers to overlooked, invalidated, and unsupported loss (Doka, 2008). Societal culture and values dictate which grief is worthy of recognition and which is not. Zoll (2019) stated that "grief is disenfranchised when others avoid talking to someone about a painful loss or use a cliché that minimizes that loss" (para. 1). When war erupts, people often do not have time to plan when they will leave or what to take with them. Escaping is the priority, and physical survival overshadows everything else. Survival implies that people focus on the reality of being alive and ignore other layers of loss. For communities resettling in a new country, the acknowledgment and expression of grief intersect with trauma, shock, and adjustment to the host country. Many parts of the survival experience take time, often generations, to recognize and grieve, adding to the reality of disenfranchisement.

The complicated grief experienced as a refugee remains taboo. Shame, guilt, and sadness develop after surviving atrocities when one knows that others did not survive. Bosnian people lost lives, safety, and their homeland, among multiple other complexities explored herein. The layers of loss when escaping genocide, such as leaving behind all possessions, are disenfranchised experiences. War and genocide severed connections to meaningful customs in Bosnian people's culture and practices around grief (Keyes & Kane, 2004).

Clinicians must collaborate with survivors to explore all the different pieces of the individual's lived experience beyond the bereavement of having lost loved ones to death. Additionally, war survivors who stayed in Bosnia have a different experience than individuals who had to flee. Refugees often do not have an opportunity to grieve due to the adjustment demands of resettling in a new country, like learning a new language and finding work to support family.

A brief history of Bosnian refugees

Bosnia and Herzegovina (BIH) is a small, heart-shaped, Southeast European country in the Balkans. BIH has a complex and painful past; understanding this will help readers deliver more compassionate and attuned care for Bosnian and other refugee communities. The Bosnian Kingdom fell in 1463 (Malcolm, 1996). Since then, the Bosnian people have endured several hundred years of colonization, occupation, wars, genocide, and forced mass migration, during which their identity, land, and history were lost. Losing this identity has been the center of much sadness and pain for many generations.

Upon declaring independence from the former Yugoslavia in 1992, war erupted in BIH (Malcolm, 1996). This war, led by Serbian and Bosnian Serb forces, lasted three years and was the worst bloodshed in Europe since World War II. It produced horrific genocides with over 200,000 civilian deaths, rape camps, and over 2 million refugees (Malcolm, 1996; United Nations, n.d.-a). Millions of people forcibly started their lives away from their families, homes, and country. This conflict changed the region and became a symbolic part of the ethnic wars that followed the fall of communism in Eastern Europe (Malcolm, 1996).

Additionally, the Bosnian War highlighted the dangerous rhetoric of fascism against Bosnian Muslims. Many Bosnian refugees were harmed by their next-door neighbors because they identified as Muslim or carried a Muslim-resembling name. The remnant of historical trauma at the intersections of identity and multiple losses passes from generation to generation, changing one's genetic expression and regulation and affecting one's long-term stress response and physical health outcomes (Ramo-Fernández et al., 2015; Sangalang & Vang, 2017).

Resettlement of Bosnian refugees

Worldwide, one out of every 95 people is forcibly displaced from their homes (UNHCR, 2020). Syria, Ukraine, Venezuela, Afghanistan, South Sudan, Myanmar, and the Democratic Republic of the Congo are currently countries with the highest number of displaced individuals (UNHCR, 2020, 2022). Although some communities receive higher media coverage, others go unnoticed or are forgotten. Anti-Black sentiment and Islamophobia impact attention and outcomes for refugee communities (McNeil, 2020).

By comparison, Bosnians' experiences with resettlement are twofold: Most were first displaced from their homes within Bosnia (i.e., from one region to another), then they had to rebuild again after being displaced from their home country to the US or elsewhere in the world. Resettlement agencies in the US provided Bosnian refugees with little to no support in adjusting to a new system and way of life (Owens-Manley & Coughlan, 2000). Most refugees arrived as family units, consisting of parents and children. Refugee children were enrolled in schools that provided English as Second Language (ESL) classes. Some adults had access to sponsored English classes and began working at low-paying, entry-level jobs. State agencies encouraged and expected refugees to quickly integrate and assimilate.

This expectation is dangerous, because a connection to one's culture of origin is a protective factor, and assimilation correlates with a higher risk for mood and anxiety disorders (Behrens et al., 2015; Teruya & Bazargan-Hejazi, 2013). Mental health outcomes are favorable when communities receive support in adjusting while maintaining a connection with their culture of origin. Clinicians must consider the complexity of different aspects of complicated grief that persist in survivors' daily lives and throughout their refugee community's experience.

Trauma

Families resettle in new countries with traumatic experiences still fresh in their minds. For generations, their suffering has been overlooked, locked away, and suppressed. Host-country supports can fail to address the emotional impact of losses, traumas, and disenfranchised grief. Diagnostic criteria and treatment for PTSD may not address vital features of a refugee's experience, such as yearning and continuing to search for their lost loved ones (American Psychiatric Association, 2022; Momartin et al., 2004). The reality that life will never be the same speaks to the trauma and grief inherent in the refugee experience.

Anxiety and depression

Depression and anxiety are common in refugees and often lead to serious mental health problems (Hameed et al., 2018). Many Bosnian refugees have few resources for managing emotional complications, and most keep them secret. Survivors struggle with an intense sense of personal threat, reflected in symptoms like anxiety, hypervigilance, and nightmares (Silove et al., 2010). The grief of anxiety and depression is complicated for people because there is much shame involved in needing support. The internalized expectation is to suppress and ignore distress, further contributing to survivors' experience of disenfranchised grief. Clinicians need to know that these expectations are integral to survival. Many families do not have an opportunity to explore what they feel amid the chaos. These conversations were and might still be taboo for some, leading to intense feelings of shame.

Shame

Bosnian refugees frequently do not address shame when describing their war experiences. Many experienced degrading and humiliating environments and situations when seeking safety, refuge, and protection (International Criminal Tribunal for the former Yugoslavia [ICTY], 2011), including dehumanizing and dangerous living conditions, lack of basic human needs, sexual violence, physical violence, and survival conditions beyond comprehension. During resettlement, Bosnian refugees continued to experience humiliation, degradation, and powerlessness (Human Rights Watch, n.d.). Many will describe how scared they were of their surroundings when they first moved to the US. Navigating this new world was a terrifying experience.

Bosnian families experienced shame in asking for help or assistance. Even in the direst of circumstances, they felt that they were supposed to be able to handle whatever life threw at them. Shame became a form of disenfranchised grief that went unacknowledged. Resettlement agencies in the US were often unprepared to handle trauma-related cases because the reality of ethnic cleansing goes beyond physical abuse and torture. Many survivors also faced a lack of acceptance from members of the dominant community based on their country of origin and religion.

Xenophobia and Islamophobia

Many Americans do not receive foreigners well. *Xenophobia*, an aversion, or discrimination against people from other countries, is prevalent in American society (McNeil, 2020). The Trump administration introduced the Muslim travel ban and declared to build a wall to prevent South American asylum seekers from entering the country. These conversations and policy changes create a dangerous climate for those who do not hold dominant identities and values. Although most Bosnian refugees pass for White bodies, they are not entirely accepted in society as White bodies.

It is essential to understand the impacts of discrimination against refugees, the impact of Islamophobia on religious identity, and the associated grief and disenfranchised grief it brings. Bosnian refugees carry names that would be hard to pronounce or write in English, with some characters that do not exist in the English language. Many Bosnians are proud of their name and associate it with their ancestors. Their names carry significant meaning and identity for the entire Bosnian experience. Many will say that the only reason they were persecuted and became refugees was because of their name (Malcolm, 1996). Persecution continues in the US, so many Bosnians felt the need to shorten or change their names, relinquishing another aspect of their identity to the ideals of assimilation and integration.

Dominant U.S. culture upholds beliefs that value Christian religion, democracy, capitalism, and whiteness. In principle, this culture is available to all, so long as they are White or "pass" for White. This reality is why the American Dream has been such a powerful myth, with promises that anyone who works hard enough will be able to provide for their family, achieve success, and pursue life, liberty, and happiness. Being or passing for White provides access to the American Dream and carries an unspoken obligation: Those who pass for White must adhere to the dominant culture. Those who are unable or unwilling to adhere to dominant culture will be stripped of their whiteness and be considered non-White bodies.

In this sense, whiteness is conditional; it must be earned and re-earned daily through hard work and moral behavior based on dominant cultural expectations. The authors recognize the very real privileges light-skinned and White bodies have that Brown and Black bodies do not hold. We invite the reader to explore the idea that the full benefits of whiteness are not automatically given to everyone with fair skin once they transgress dominant cultural expectations. To embody whiteness, one must look White and follow the rules of White supremacy, "because we are born into an already written script that tells us what to expect from strangers due to their skin color, accents, and social status, the whole of humanity is coded as white" (Eddo-Lodge, 2018, p. 85). Acceptance into the dominant community is often lost when it is discovered that the individual does not follow a Judeo-Christian religion or when one speaks with an accent.

Moreover, some Bosnian-Muslim women refugees wear a hijab head covering. Many women removed their hijab to find employment. Others kept their hijab to declare their faith and identity openly. Mental health providers must be aware of the systemic oppressions that Bosnian and other refugee communities experience at the intersection of xenophobia and Islamophobia.

Ambiguous loss

In July 1995, Serbian and paramilitary forces executed approximately 8,000 Bosnian men and boys in Srebrenica, BIH (United Nations, n.d.-b). Three years earlier, in Prijedor, BIH, the same troops murdered over 4,600 Bosnian men (ICTY, 2014). The perpetrators of these crimes attempted to cover up the evidence by reburying the bodies in mass gravesites throughout Bosnia. The International Commission on Missing Persons (ICMP, 2010) has found most of these sites and identified the victims through DNA analysis of their remains. Through its missing persons and repatriation programs, ICMP has facilitated the return of many victims' remains to their families for burial according to Islamic funeral rites. However, the memories of kidnapped children, soldiers missing in action, family separation during the war, deportation, and natural disasters can result in *ambiguous loss*. This type of disenfranchised loss results from a loved one's physical absence but emotional presence because there is no proof of death (Boss, 2004). Bosnian refugees who had family members captured by Serbian soldiers, killed, or who simply disappeared experience ambiguous grief. Ambiguous loss becomes disenfranchised grief because society expects survivors to move on.

The loss of a loved one is a tragedy, and the loss of someone who disappears without a trace is an unbearable mystery that creates ambiguous loss and disenfranchised grief. There is no closure, no physical body, and no grave. The loss remains alive in their minds because there are no remains or witnesses to bring peace. This type of trauma causes constant suffering and can lead to hopelessness, desperation, and depression. The reality of genocide left many refugees with tremendous, unrecognized grief, erasing multiple aspects of culture and identity vital to healing.

Cultural and identity loss

Most Bosnians made assimilation and integration efforts for survival and protection. The safety of their families was a priority, but many survivors lost a part of themselves in the process. They left their home, language, and traditions for a new life. Many were unable to return to their homes due to lack of resources or fear. Their grief was disenfranchised because others could not see it. They often felt isolated because others did not understand the pain. Unfortunately, this is a reality that many survivors face when obtaining clinical services.

Survivors lose a sense of belonging, safety, and familiarity. Upon arrival in the US, many were placed in areas with no access to other Bosnians. Bosnian refugees come from collective cultures where neighbors' daily visits and coffee time were lost. Grieving for one's culture can be as crucial as suffering from other losses, but it is rarely recognized by helping professionals. This disenfranchisement leads to feelings of shame and isolation that might be hard to understand for individuals who are not members of the family or community.

Family loss

Families were torn apart by genocide and war, leaving children fatherless and spouses without support. As men were killed, many women were widowed with no financial means to support themselves or their families (Somun-Krupalija, 2011). In some cases, women lost husbands, brothers, fathers, sons, uncles, and cousins in the same violent incident. They had to leave everything behind in Bosnia as they escaped war-torn areas on foot through minefields or in buses to refugee camps. Those who escaped experienced a disenfranchised loss because they had to focus on moving forward and surviving. Nickerson et al. (2011) found that loss and grief significantly impacted individual and family mental health outcomes for Bosnian refugees. They posited that family support is vital to preventing and recovering from psychiatric conditions conducive to survival. Clinicians working with survivors must explore the impact of family loss on mental wellbeing.

Parenting

Bosnian refugee parents grieve their own losses and losses resulting from their children's experiences. Parents' focus was on re-establishing daily life and providing for the family. Many parents came to the US without any education or financial resources and had to work several jobs to make ends meet. They had little time to spend with their children, who were left alone for most of the day. Although many had university degrees, they were overqualified for minimum-wage jobs. Some who had worked as doctors and engineers never found work in their fields after resettlement. Guilt from being absent from their children so often complicates parents' grief for not being able to raise their children as they had envisioned. Everything happened and continues to happen in survival mode, so children become parentified in raising themselves.

Parentification is a risk factor for mental health problems that many refugee children might experience. In *parentification*, a child takes on extra responsibilities when the parents are unable to do so or are absent due to death or displacement (Rizkalla et al., 2020). Parentification can lead to problems with general mental health and interpersonal relationships, anxiety, and people-pleasing tendencies. For example, a child without a father must take over tasks like cleaning and cooking for the family. The child might feel responsible for not letting their mother cry, for trying to cheer her up, and for protecting their siblings from experiencing what they did as refugees. Many lacked access to care because some adults distrust mental health professionals (Renner, 2021). The second generation of Bosnian refugees is growing up in the US. Many still suffer from disenfranchised stress-related problems caused by witnessing violence, being separated from loved ones, or experiencing parentification.

Language loss

Although parents want their children to be successful after resettlement, they feel a sense of loss when they notice their child no longer understands what they say or has forgotten how to speak their native language. As children begin to learn the host-country's language and adopt its use, their parents and grandparents lose the ability to communicate with them, which represents another disenfranchisement, having a family member that is alive but not having "access" to them in meaningful ways. For example, children lose interest in learning the language, because they become more comfortable speaking English and assimilating to American culture (Weine et al., 2004). Parents often feel a sense of shame when they cannot communicate outside of the Bosnian community and realize that they will never be able to integrate fully into the host country if they cannot speak the language fluently.

Material loss

Bosnian refugees' material losses were significant. Some had lost virtually all their possessions as their homes were burned and destroyed, while others were able to salvage a few treasured objects before fleeing. In what is now Republika Srpska, most refugees' homes were occupied, and the land that belonged to their families for generations was stolen (Human Rights Watch, n.d.). They lost land, livestock, businesses, the ability to live off the land, and other material resources fundamental to their economic survival. Many Bosnian refugees lost all physical reminders of their lives before the war, including pictures and family heirlooms. The continued occupation of their homes is a daily reminder of this disenfranchised loss. Many survivors carry guilt when faced with this reminder, as some survived while others did not.

Survivor guilt

For instance, Bosnian refugees often work long hours to avoid feelings of guilt at having survived when so many perished in war or in concentration camps (Sabic et al., 2014). This guilt often forces people to send money to support those who remain behind. Hard work provides an escape from painful memories that would haunt them if they did not keep busy and an outlet for honoring their dead relatives. For many survivors of terror, productivity might be a way to dissociate from traumatic experiences, further leading to disenfranchisement (Paperny, 2017).

Nostalgia, hope, and dreams

The disenfranchised grief of lost hopes and dreams is not something many refugees allow themselves to be sad about and grieve for. Parents who have lost their homes and possessions may repeatedly tell these stories to their children to remind themselves of what was left behind and to retain hopes and dreams of being able to return home one day. In the meantime, they try to carry on with their lives as best they can. Unfortunately, returning home is not always possible due to complexities in mental health, shame, grief, loss, and personal history.

One way that professionals can support survivors is to be mindful of questions and statements such as, "Oh! You've never been back home?!" This is dismissive, hurtful to the listener, and makes many assumptions about survivors' experiences. A clinician might erroneously assume that the client has access to the financial and emotional means to travel back to their home country. Professionals need to explore the relationship between their own assumptions, privileges, and biases.

Bosnian refugee women

Many women experienced sexual harassment and rape as weapons of mass destruction during the war (Reid-Cunningham, 2008). Groups of soldiers regularly invaded neighboring cities and kidnapped and gang raped women in front of their families (Hansen, 2000; Stiglmayer, 1994), augmenting women's hypervigilance of their surroundings. Many of the survivors carry shame and profound sadness. After being assaulted, some survivors lost their husbands because they were seen as damaged (Skjelsbæk, 2006). However, most suffer silently, unable to communicate their trauma to anyone, even their closest family members.

Many survivors had little to no family support after losing their parents and siblings. Women carried out responsibilities overlooked by society: caring for family members and elderly parents, preparing food and water, finding shelter and clothing, and ensuring safety. Women held an immense responsibility as they lived through the worst atrocities that a human being can experience as victims of war and victims of a patriarchal culture that devalued their worth as human beings.

Allyship and advocacy

Over the past few years, there has been an alarming increase in the number of refugees and asylum seekers traveling from Syria, Iraq, Afghanistan, Ukraine, and elsewhere to seek safety in the West (UNHCR, n.d.a). Unfortunately, there is not much done to center the voices of refugees when developing support systems. Advocates can call upon the media to uphold their responsibility to share stories accurately in ways that highlight the needs of communities that historically have been marginalized. Many conversations about refugees tend to be racist, sexist, xenophobic, and Islamophobic (Grandi, 2021). The narrative surrounding refugees often excludes refugees' voices. Unfortunately, when it does include their voices, it avoids supporting the communities that have been the most marginalized among refugees, such as gender and sexual minorities and the Roma itinerant community. This lack of representation is problematic because it perpetuates oppression, stereotypes, and misconceptions. This inequity leads to discriminatory policies and practices that negatively impact the refugees' lives.

Grandi (2021) identified people being turned away after fleeing war zones to seek safety in other countries as one of the most pressing issues societies face today. Refugees' voices are muted, although politicians', activists', journalists', and academics' are amplified. Providers and program administrators must listen and collaborate in all aspects of project development and assessment with people that have lived refugee experiences so refugees may tell their stories.

Speaking and listening to each other's stories is a way of recognizing shared humanity. Stories can also serve as a basis for action: They can provide clues about what is essential in other people's lives, how they feel about it, and what they do about it. Stories can help identify problems, issues, or opportunities that otherwise may have gone unnoticed.

We implore clinicians working with refugee clients to obtain training and consultation from professionals with lived refugee experience. Without this knowledge, one could inadvertently cause harm by attempting to apply standard therapeutic techniques without an understanding of their appropriateness for different communities that have been marginalized. Mental health professionals are responsible for ensuring that the person they are learning from practices an anti-oppressive framework to avoid working with someone who upholds harmful ideas like denialism and racism.

Advocating for Bosnian refugees includes eliminating *denialism*, which attempts to silence victims and erase the reality of wars and genocides (Parent, 2016). Denialists contest that genocide took place, and they attack those who affirm that it took place. Denialism remains one of the most significant obstacles in seeking justice for Bosnian victims, and is one of many examples of this injustice in history. The Armenian genocide, the Holocaust, and the Cambodian genocide are all horrific events that have also led to denial or silencing (Parent, 2016). Denialism is one of the main reasons many perpetrators were never held accountable for their actions.

The term *genocide* has become controversial due to denialist phenomena. Though many books on denialism are available, there has been very little research into the denialism specific to the Bosnian war and genocide. Providers must be aware of their positions on genocide and ethnic cleansing as they seek to support refugee populations. They must also ensure that they know where different referral sources stand on denialism to prevent referring clients to a provider or a resource that will cause harm.

Ethical considerations

The word assimilation evokes fears of losing one's culture and language in the face of a dominant culture. There are many reasons for this fear: past experiences with assimilation and the horrors of genocide. For many Bosnian refugees, assimilation means giving up or being forced to give up their Bosnian identity. It is imperative for clinicians working with refugees to see and process their own implicit biases toward refugee populations. *Implicit biases* are unconscious beliefs about others that often contradict conscious views (FitzGerald & Hurst, 2017) and favor a person's in-group. Implicit biases are inherently connected to one's positionality as they filter through worldviews and societal discourses.

Discourses refer to the formation of meaning in social matters, such as compliance, mental health, and interventions. Discourses affect how we define helping fields, allocate resources, and determine who receives services. A deep awareness of one's values, beliefs, and experiences can help clinicians advance social justice, especially considering that the client-therapist relationship is naturally unbalanced. Clinicians retain power as the service provider, and most providers in the US are members of dominant communities. Engagement in regular critical self-reflection and critique can support equitable and ethical practice.

All mental health professions have a code of ethics that outlines a clinician's cultural considerations when working with diverse populations. The onus of providing inclusive care that advances liberation falls on the clinician. Providers must familiarize themselves with their professional codes of ethics and learn from the community they serve because the mental health field has historically excluded communities that have been marginalized from being critical partners in their healing. This might mean engaging in didactic learning about the Bosnian community from community members. To provide ethical care, clinicians acknowledge that people are the experts in their stories. Clinicians and organizations must take steps to provide services in the client's preferred language. Access to care surpasses having the financial means to pay for services and includes providing services that are culturally matched and appropriate. Only then can clinicians collaborate with clients toward interventions.

Strategies and interventions

Processing trauma is significant in working with refugees. Many refugees live with survival mechanisms decades after the war (Weine et al., 2004). Processing trauma and survival mechanisms is impossible without allowing individuals to express their grief without fear of judgment and stereotypes.

Processing traumatic grief

One step that providers can take is to engage in didactic learning about all forms of war trauma from individuals with lived experience and an anti-oppressive lens. This learning must be coupled with appropriate training and supervision. Figure 16.1 shows the different forms of war trauma as three concentric circles of loss. The innermost circle represents personal losses, including deaths, injuries, and illnesses of family members and friends; physical assaults; loss of sexual integrity; forced displacement; forced relocation; loss or damage to homes and other property; loss of employment and livelihood; and loss of community and social networks. The second circle represents the visible signs of a disrupted society: damaged buildings (e.g., hospitals, factories, schools, churches, synagogues, and mosques) and destroyed infrastructure (e.g., roads, bridges, water systems, electricity grids, and communications

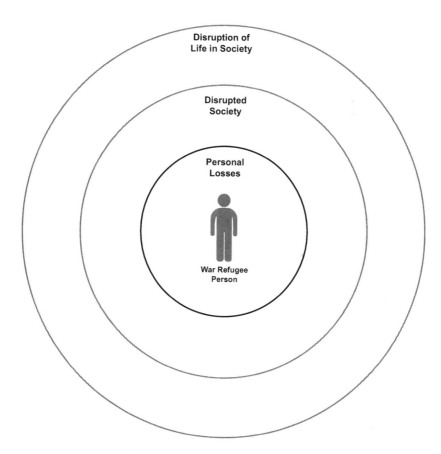

Figure 16.1 Concentric circles of loss experienced in war trauma. Reprinted with permission from Selma Zakomac-Baćevac. Copyright 2022.

Note. The darker the lines, the more the loss is acknowledged by the refugee person and their environment. The lighter the lines, the less likely the loss is to be acknowledged by the environment, despite it being deeply felt by the refugee person.

systems). The third circle encompasses the broader disruption to life in society: shortages of fuel and food, limited access to clean water and adequate sanitation facilities, unreliable/failed transportation systems that impede access to medical care and other critical services, failed law enforcement that makes people feel unsafe in their own homes and neighborhoods, interrupted education for children whose schools have been destroyed or are used for other purposes during conflicts, and a lack of essential services (e.g., trash collection) that add to a sense of social chaos.

Seeing survival mechanisms as positive attributes

The different ways humans survive struggle represent their internal drive, willpower, and love. Supporting refugee clients to accept their survival mechanisms as necessary resources is essential to their ability to see their strength and bravery in all aspects of who they are. Helping the client verbalize and develop a relationship with their survival mechanisms takes time and deep trust. Asking clients how their survival mechanisms have helped them and how they would like to thank this part of themselves can open their ability to positively see this part of themselves and break the shame they may be masking to honor the ways individuals survived.

Trust is essential to effective treatment. Helping refugee clients build trust within the therapeutic relationship will take time. The provider's desire to learn about the client's culture through the client's eyes is essential to the clinical relationship. It is not enough to learn about the Bosnian war through movies or a book. Engaging in curious conversations with clients is a way to name what might be present in that individual's life. However, asking clients about their culture cannot serve as the primary education for the provider, as this is harmful. Seeking supervision or consultation from helping professionals with lived experience, training specific to the refugee's culture, and immersing oneself in research will demonstrate that the clinician has done their due diligence without placing further responsibility on the client to educate them. Clinicians need to make actionable and culturally attuned efforts to move the connection and trust to a deeper level where clients can share more deeply.

Summary

The cultural and identity loss experienced by Bosnian refugees evokes grief, disenfranchised grief, ambiguous loss, and trauma. The loss of home, culture, and community is experienced as a death of the self. Bosnian refugees' experiences of displacement are characterized by physical relocation and also by the death and destruction of their culture. In addition to experiencing material losses, Bosnian refugees often experience cultural losses following resettlement. Bosnian refugees are often left feeling invisible and voiceless in the context of psychological research and service provision. Providers working with refugee communities must consider the complexities of the grief experience and their own implicit biases and take steps to build trust beyond a superficial clinical relationship.

References

American Psychiatric Association, DSM-5 Task Force. (2013). *Diagnostic and statistical manual of mental disorders: DSM-5™* (5th ed.). American Psychiatric Publishing, Inc. https://doi.org/10.1176/appi.books.9780890425596

Behrens, K., del Pozo, M. A., Großhennig, A., Sieberer, M., & Graef-Calliess, I. T. (2015). How much orientation towards the host culture is healthy? Acculturation style as risk enhancement for depressive symptoms in immigrants. *International Journal of Social Psychiatry, 61*(5), 498–505. https://doi.org/10.1177/0020764014560356

Boss, P. (2004). Ambiguous loss. In F. Walsh & M. McGoldrick (Eds.), *Living beyond loss: Death in the family* (pp. 237–246). W.W. Norton.

Doka, K. J. (2008). Disenfranchised grief in historical and cultural perspective. In M. S. Stroebe, R. O. Hansson, H. Schut, & W. Stroebe (Eds.), *Handbook of bereavement research and practice: Advances in theory and intervention* (pp. 223–240). American Psychological Association. https://doi.org/10.1037/14498-011

Eddo-Lodge, R. (2018). *Why I'm no longer talking to White people about race.* Bloomsbury.

FitzGerald, C., & Hurst, S. (2017). Implicit bias in healthcare professionals: A systematic review. *BMC Medical Ethics, 18,* Article 19. https://doi.org/10.1186/s12910-017-0179-8

Grandi, F. (2021, March 21). High commissioner's message on the international day for the elimination of racial discrimination. *United Nations High Commissioner for Refugees.* www.unhcr.org/news/press/2022/3/62370dc44/high-commissioners-message-international-day-elimination-racial-discrimination.html

Hagl, M., Powell, S., Rosner, R., & Butollo, W. (2015). Dialogical exposure with traumatically bereaved Bosnian women: Findings from a controlled trial. *Clinical Psychology and Psychotherapy, 22*(6), 604–618. https://doi.org/10.1002/cpp.1921

Hameed, S., Sadiq, A., & Din, A. U. (2018). The increased vulnerability of refugee population to mental health disorders. *Kansas Journal of Medicine, 11*(1), 1–12.

Hansen, L. (2000). Gender, nation, rape: Bosnia and the construction of security. *International Feminist Journal of Politics*, 3(1), 55–75. https://doi.org/10.1080/14616740010019848

Human Rights Watch. (n.d.). *Abuses against minorities after the war*. www.hrw.org/reports/2000/bosnia/Bosn005-06.htm

International Commission on Missing Persons. (2010, July 9). *DNA results of the International Commission on Missing Persons reveal the identity of 6,481 Srebrenica victims*. www.icmp.int/press-releases/dna-results-reveal-6481-srebrenica-victims/

International Criminal Tribunal for the former Yugoslavia. (2011). Inside the tribunal [Video]. ICTY. www.youtube.com/watch?v=nCwORJDn0sQ

International Criminal Tribunal for the former Yugoslavia. (2014). Crimes before the ICTY: Prijedor [Video]. ICTY. www.icty.org/en/outreach/documentaries/crimes-icty-prijedor

Jacobson, D., & Mustafa, N. (2019). Social identity map: A reflexivity tool for practicing explicit positionality in critical qualitative research. *International Journal of Qualitative Methods*, 18, 1–12. https://doi.org/10.1177/1609406919870075

Keyes, E. F., & Kane, C. F. (2004). Belonging and adapting: Mental health of Bosnian refugees living in the United States. *Issues in Mental Health Nursing*, 25(8), 809–831. https://doi.org/10.1080/01612840490506392

Malcolm, N. (1996). *Bosnia: A short history*. New York University Press.

McNeil, T. (2020, September 24). The long history of xenophobia in America. *Tufts Now*. https://now.tufts.edu/articles/long-history-xenophobia-america

Miller, K. E., & Rasmussen, A. (2017). The mental health of civilians displaced by armed conflict: An ecological model of refugee distress. *Epidemiology and Psychiatric Sciences*, 26(2), 129–138. https://doi.org/10.1017/S2045796016000172

Momartin, S., Silove, D., Manicavasagar, V., & Steel, Z. (2004). Complicated grief in Bosnian refugees: Associations with posttraumatic stress disorder and depression. *Comprehensive Psychiatry*, 45(6), 475–482. https://doi.org/10.1016/j.comppsych.2004.07.013

Nickerson, A., Bryant, R. A., Brooks, R., Steel, Z., Silove, D., & Chen, J. (2011). The familial influence of loss and trauma on refugee mental health: A multilevel path analysis. *Journal of Traumatic Stress*, 24(1), 25–33. https://doi.org/10.1002/jts.20608

Owens-Manley, J., & Coughlan, R. (2000). Adaptation of refugees during cross-cultural transitions: Bosnian refugees in upstate New York. In *Levitt report* (pp. 87–93). www.hamilton.edu/levitt/pdfs/owens-manley_refugee.pdf

Paperny, T. (2017, February 16). Do some trauma survivors cope by overworking? *The Atlantic*. www.theatlantic.com/health/archive/2017/02/do-some-trauma-survivors-cope-by-overworking/516540/

Parent, G. (2016). Genocide denial: Perpetuating victimization and the cycle of violence in Bosnia and Herzegovina (BiH). *Genocide Studies and Prevention: An International Journal, 10*(2), 38–58. https://doi.org/10.5038/1911-9933.10.2.1369

Ramo-Fernández, L., Schneider, A., Wilker, S., & Kolassa, I.-T. (2015). Epigenetic alterations associated with war trauma and childhood maltreatment. *Behavioral Sciences and the Law, 33*(5), 701–721. https://doi.org/10.1002/bsl.2200

Reid-Cunningham, A. R. (2008). Rape as a weapon of genocide. *Genocide Studies and Prevention, 3*(3), 279–296. https://doi.org/10.3138/gsp.3.3.279

Renner, C. (2021, May 6). Trauma and PTSD still affect Bosnian community. *The Webster Journal.* https://websterjournal.com/2021/05/06/trauma-and-ptsd-still-affect-bosnian-community/

Rizkalla, N., Mallat, N. K., Arafa, R., Adi, S., Soudi, L., & Segal, S. P. (2020). "Children are not children anymore; they are a lost generation": Adverse physical and mental health consequences on Syrian refugee children. *International Journal of Environmental Research and Public Health, 17*(22), Article 8378. https://doi.org/10.3390/ijerph17228378

Sabic, D., Blattner, C., & Polk, J. D. (2014). Bosnian refugees: Screening and treatment in an immigrant population. *Journal of Osteopathic Medicine, 114*(8), 617–618. https://doi.org/10.7556/jaoa.2014.126

Sangalang, C. C., & Vang, C. (2017). Intergenerational Trauma in refugee families: A systematic review. *Journal of Immigrant and Minority Health, 19*(3), 745–754. https://doi.org/10.1007/s10903-016-0499-7

Silove, D., Momartin, S., Marnane, C., Steel, Z., & Manicavasagar, V. (2010). Adult separation anxiety disorder among war-affected Bosnian refugees: Comorbidity with PTSD and associations with dimensions of trauma. *Journal of Traumatic Stress, 23*(1), 169–172. https://doi.org/10.1002/jts.20490

Skjelsbæk, I. (2006). Victim and survivor: Narrated social identities of women who experienced rape during the war in Bosnia-Herzegovina. *Feminism and Psychology, 16*(4), 373–403. https://www.doi.org/10.1177/0959353506068746

Somun-Krupalija, L. (2011). Gender and employment in Bosnia and Herzegovina: A country study. *International Labor Office.* www.ilo.org/wcmsp5/groups/public/ – dgreports/ – gender/documents/publication/wcms_170832.pdf

Stiglmayer, A. (1994). *Mass rape: The war against women in Bosnia-Herzegovina.* University of Nebraska Press.

Teruya, S. A., & Bazargan-Hejazi, S. (2013). The immigrant and Hispanic paradoxes: A systematic review of their predictions and effects. *Hispanic Journal of Behavioral Sciences, 35*(4), 486–509. https://doi.org/10.1177/0739986313499004

United Nations High Commissioner for Refugees. (2020). Global trends: Forced displacement in 2020. *UNHCR.* www.unhcr.org/flagship-reports/globaltrends/

United Nations High Commissioner for Refugees. (2021, June 18). Figures at glance. *UNHCR*. www.unhcr.org/il/en/global-figures-at-a-glance#:~:text=How%20 many%20refugees%20are%20there,under%20the%20age%20of%2018

United Nations High Commissioner for Refugees. (2022). Operational data portal: Ukraine refugee situation. *UNHCR*. https://data.unhcr.org/en/situations/ukraine

United Nations High Commissioner for Refugees. (n.d.-a). Operations data portal: Refugee Situations. *UNHCR*. https://data.unhcr.org/en/situations

United Nations High Commissioner for Refugees. (n.d.-b). What is resettlement? *UNHCR*. www.unhcr.org/en-us/resettlement.html

United Nations International Criminal Tribunal for the Former Yugoslavia. (n.d.). The conflicts. *ICTY*. www.icty.org/en/about/what-former-yugoslavia/conflicts

Weine, S., Muzurovic, N., Kulauzovic, Y., Besic, S., Lezic, A., Mujagic, A., Muzurovic, J., Spahovic, D., Feetham, S., Ware, N., Knafl, K., & Pavkovic, I. (2004). Family consequences of refugee trauma. *Family Process, 43*(2), 147–160. www.doi. org/10.1111/j.1545-5300.2004.04302002.x

Zoll, L. S. (2019). Disenfranchised grief: When grief and grievers are unrecognized. *The New Social Worker*. www.socialworker.com/feature-articles/practice/ disenfranchised-grief-when-grief-and-grievers-are-unrecogniz/

Questions for reflective practice

1. What are some limiting personal views and beliefs about refugees a clinician might hold?
2. How can a clinician become aware of internalized racism or dominant privilege? How might these affect their client-therapist relationships?
3. What steps can a clinician take to become familiar with a refugee's experience outside of reading or watching movies about the refugee experience?
4. What advocacy steps can a clinician take to help refugees feel more welcome, secure, and supported in their resettlement?

Supplemental electronic resources

*   Children's book: *Adem and the Magic Fenejr* by Selma Baćevac
*   International Criminal Tribunal for the former Yugoslavia 1993–2017: www.icty.org/
*   Lived experience book: *Zlata's Diary* by Zlata Filipovic
*   War Childhood Museum: https://warchildhood.org/

Conclusion

The authors of this volume have offered their knowledge, experience, and heartfelt beliefs about what it means to experience disenfranchised grief and grief-related discrimination, marginalization, and oppression. Though the chapters contained in this book do not represent all forms of disenfranchised grief and are not representative of all grief experiences or trajectories, they serve as an excellent starting point to begin the conversations necessary for individual, systemic, and social healing.

We leave you, Dear Reader, with a profound *Untitled* poem from one of our authors, Marshall Lyles (n.d.), reprinted here in its entirety with his gracious permission. It beautifully articulates the pain and isolation described in each of the chapters in this volume.

To the
Unwanted
Chronically haunted
Tired and daunted
Who are
Omitted and
Oppressed
Occasionally depressed
Waiting for a
Moment's rest

To the
Unbelieved
Misperceived
Too often grieved
Who just need
Justice and
A witness

To those on the
Outside
Forced to down size
Downcast
Outcast
Just so over
Getting
Passed over

Others' poor vision
And power hungry indecision
Others' attempts at
Division
Don't make you
Invisible
Your voice is
Undeniable
Their sins
Unjustifiable

Stand
One more day
Speak
One more line
Stay you
Be you
All of you

Used with permission from Marshall Lyles (n.d.).
www.marshalllyles.com/poetry.html

We hope these words spark advocacy within your heart and a spirit of understanding for clients who walk through your doors. We believe in the ripple
effect of change, and this encapsulates our wish for you and your clients:
However each of you may have been made to feel disenfranchised in your
identity or in your grief that you may carry on through your ordeals and society's struggles with (in)justice, with your communities' support, and with an
active hope that your story and your voice will make a difference as all of you
are heard and recognized in dismissing the disenfranchisement.

Index

Page numbers in *italics* refer to figures. Page numbers in **bold** refer to tables.

abandonment 7, 26, 70, 72, 128–129
ableism 11, 162
abortion 5, 59, 63, 131, 208, 210
Abrams, J. A. 86
abuse 7; environment 64; symptoms 72
academic performance 81
acceptance 8–9
accountability 36
active-duty funerals 261
adaptive grief 257
addictions and self-destructive behaviors 123
adult sibling loss 224
adverse childhood experiences (ACEs) 15, 139, 141, 147, 265
advocacy *see* allyship and advocacy
African American/Black women 64
African American Community 78, 143, 147
African Americans, healthcare barriers for: allyship and advocacy 148; cultural aspects 143–146; cumulative impacts 147–148; ethical considerations 148–149; mental health 139; perspectives 139–142; relational aspects 146–147; social aspects 142–143; strategies and interventions 149–151
African American sibling loss: allyship and advocacy 230–231; culture, intersectionality and influence of 227–228; cumulative impacts of 229–230; ethical considerations 231–232; intersectionality and influence of culture 227–228; intersectionality and sibling loss 222–225; racism and discrimination 226; relational aspects 228–229; sibling bereavement 226–227; societal disenfranchisement, experiences 225–227; strategies and interventions 232–234; unnatural causes 226
African Diaspora 5–6, 9
aggression 194
Ali, S. R. 10
Allende, I. 170
allyship and advocacy: African Americans, healthcare barriers for 148; African American sibling loss 230–231; biracial individuals, social and systemic barriers for 109–110; Bosnian refugees 284–285; childrearing 216; disabilities, individuals with 161–162; healing spaces 50–51; identity loss 35–36; LGBTQIA+ community 130; liberation psychology 51; mental health workers 51–52; parenting "borrowed children" 247–248; racial trauma, untangling 85; sexual violence 178; spiritual trauma 70–71; trauma-informed, school violence 195–196
Almeida, R. V. 34–35
Amaya, S. 179
ambiguous loss 26–27, 146–147, 257–258, 280; definition 26; and disenfranchised grief 25–27
American Academy of Child and Adolescent Psychiatry (AACAP) 102

American Association for Marriage and Family Therapy (AAMFT) 85
American Civil War 9
American community 139
American Counseling Association (ACA) 35–37, 85–86, 109–110, 179
American Institute of Health Care Professionals 191
American Psychological Association (APA) 81, 155, 243, 257
American School Counselor Association (ASCA) National Model 197–198
Anderson, C. A. 193
anesthetization 43
anger and depression 52
anti-Black racism/sentiment 82, 276
anti-miscegenation legislation 100
anxiety 8, 26, 194; Bosnian refugees 277–278; and depression 43, 80
Armenian genocide 285
Artiga, S. 10
art therapy 269
Association for Multicultural Counseling and Development (AMCD) 85–86
Association for Spiritual, Ethical, and Religious Values in Counseling (ASERVIC) 71, 88
attachment styles and patterns 3–4, 6, 214–215, 263–264
Attig, T. 61, 62, 181
authenticity 34
autism spectrum disorder 159
autonoetic consciousness 7
avoidance 87
awareness 50

Baams, L. 243
Baggerly, J. 197
Baker, D. 82
Becker, C. B. 11
Bent-Goodley, T. B. 64
bereaved adult siblings 230
bereavism 27
Berson, I. R. 197
Bindley, K. 27–28
biological and adopted children 7–8
biopsychosocial effects of grief 29–30

biracial individuals 99–100; allyship and advocacy 109–110; bicultural grief 108; discrimination and microaggressions 107–108; ethical considerations 111; identity development 99, 106–107; interracial couple 101–106; interracial marriages 100–101; and multiracial individuals 101; social and systemic barriers for 99–112; strategies and interventions 112; systemic and social barriers 109; uniqueness 106–109
bisexual identity 127
Black, Indigenous, and Persons of Color (BIPOC) military community 262
Black Americans 35
Black Feminist movement 222
Black-Hispanic interracial couples 102
Black Lives Matter movement 103–104, 141
Black women: grief of 27–28; maternal grief 83; matriarchs 83; teenage girls 89
Bland, S. 82
Bocknek, E. L. 146
body-based memory 50
Bordere, T. C. 36, 178
borrowed children 240
Bosnia and Herzegovina (BIH) 276, 280
Bosnian refugees: allyship and advocacy 284–285; ambiguous loss 280; anxiety and depression 277–278; cultural and identity loss 280–284; disenfranchised grief 275–276; ethical considerations 285–286; family loss 281; history 276; language loss 282; loss experienced in war trauma 287; material loss 282–283; nostalgia, hope, and dreams 283; parenting 281–282; refugees' silent disenfranchised grief 274–275; resettlement 276–279; shame 278; strategies and interventions 286–288; survivor guilt 283; trauma 277; women 283–284; xenophobia and islamophobia 278–279
Boss, P. 26, 30–33, 35–36, 146–147, 268
Bowlby, J. 6, 44
Breen, L. J. 14–15
broaching grief 14–15
Brown, A. 104–105, 239
Brown, M. 79, 82, 102
Bruce, E. J. 212

Bryant, R. A. 211
bullying 89
Burgin, E. E. 267
Burke, T. 174

Cambodian genocide 285
Canadian Association of Social Workers (CASW) 238
Carbado, D.W. 24
Casellato, G. 44
Casey Family Homes 238
Chan, C. D. 29
Chao, R. C. 111
Cheryan, S. 107
childhood/children: abuser 4; behavior problems 250; cultural beliefs and influences 265; welfare representative 244
childhood sexual abuse (CSA) 172
childrearing: allyship and advocacy 216; cultural aspects 213–214; cumulative impacts 215; disenfranchised grief 209–210; ethical considerations 216–217; mental health providers 217; parenting 210–211; relational aspects 214–215; self-knowledge and acceptance 217; social disconnection inherent 212; strategies and interventions 217–218
church and faith, African American communities 143
Civil Rights Movement 79
classism 11, 27
client's culture 72–73
clinical depression 8
clinical training programs 13–14
cognitive-behavioral health services 267–268
cognitive-behavioral intervention for trauma in schools (CBITS) 198
cognitive dissonance 64
cognitive impairment 192
cognitive life raft 131
collective coping 88
colonialism 9
colorism framework 149–150
community building 52
companioning grief 132

Complex ACES and Complex Aid (CAsCAid) Group 16
complicated spiritual grief (CSG) 59–60, 72
compulsive sexual addictions 122
confidentiality 196–197, 247
Confucius 218
Connell, N. M. 195
conscious breathing 88
consciousness-raising and public awareness 110
constant reassurance 50
contemplative prayer 73
continued bereavement-recovery 132
coping 30; skills for loss and grief 189; strategies 87
co-regulation 6
corporate policies 5
cortisol 141
counselor identity development 29
counselor self-awareness 71
countertransference 71; see also spiritual trauma
covert discrimination 33
COVID-19 pandemic 138, 141–144
Crenshaw, K. 24–25, 158, 164
criminalization 120
critical race theory (CRT) 109
cultural aspects, disenfranchised grief: African Americans, healthcare barriers for 143–146; childrearing 213–214; chronic illness 143; disabilities, individuals with 158–159; LGBTQIA+ community 127–128; non-death losses, multiple forms 146; parenting "borrowed children" 245–246; service sacrifice 260–263; sexual violence 174–176; social losses African Americans experience **144**; spiritual collective 145
cultural humility 5, 13, 29, 52, 72, 81, 103, 105, 111–112, 129, 132, 163, 266
culture/cultural: barriers 222; comfort 111; competence 110; construct 86; -context model 31, 34–35; identity 29–30; and identity loss 280–284; importance 5; influences 12; as mezzo-level influences 10; opportunities 111; practices, transgenerational transmission of 141; sensitivity 121; trauma 82

cumulative impacts: African Americans,
   healthcare barriers for 147–148;
   African American sibling loss 229–230;
   childrearing 215; disabilities, individuals
   with 160–161; LGBTQIA+ community
   129; service sacrifice 264–265; sexual
   violence 177–178
Curtin, N. 31

Daniels, J. 86
Davis, D. E. 111
Deaf community 155–156, 158–159
death: after police contact 5; loss 8, 72–73;
   -related grief 164; -related tasks 128; row
   inmates 5
decision making and coping processes 26
Deitz, M. F. 176
demographics and diversity 35
denialism 285
Department of Veterans Affairs (DVA) 256,
   261
depression 8, 26, 80, 122, 194, 224, 250
devaluation 11
developmental disorders 26–27
diagnosable mental illness 85
disabilities, individuals with: allyship and
   advocacy 161–162; cultural aspects
   158–159; cumulative impacts 160–161;
   ethical considerations 163–164; people
   born with or who develop 8; -related
   trauma symptoms 161; relational aspects
   159–160; social aspects 156–158;
   strategies and interventions 163–164
discharge status 259–260
discourses 286
discrimination 6, 9, 69, 100, 108, 120;
   and inequality experiences 24; and
   microaggressions 107–108; oppression and
   marginalization 8–9
disenfranchised grief 33, 275–276;
   acknowledgment 4; cultural impacts of
   46–48; definition 25–26, 42, 121, 156;
   exclusion 5; griever 5–6; impacts across
   lifespan 29–30; processing levels 31;
   relational aspects of 48–49; relationship
   3–4; response to 29; social aspects
   of 142–143; social impacts 45–46;
   stigmatization 5; viewpoint 6

disenfranchisement 8, 10, 264
disengagement, social and community 212
disillusionment 63
disorganization 191
disruption of spiritual practice 72
divorce 4, 7, 59, 264
Doka, K. J. 3–5, 25–26, 42, 44, 72–73, 82,
   121, 156, 190, 239, 260–261, 264
domestic violence 64
dominant cultural counterparts 148
Dominguez, K. M. 52
"Don't Say Gay" bill 128
Dooley, C. M. 268
dream deferred 12
Drewes, A. A. 269
Durkin, T. 34–35
Dutil, S. 192

Einat, Y. 268
Eisenberger, N. I. 50
elementary-aged child 191
elementary students, school violence 188
emotion/emotional 50; coping strategies 88;
   distress 80; experiences 53; explosive 191;
   fortitude 84; and insecurities 105–106;
   memories interface 50; reactions 87;
   regulation 50; strength 80, 84; support 7;
   suppression 87; unavailability 229; verbal
   and non-verbal displays 233; vulnerability
   129
empathic failure 7, 105
employment loss 27
empty chair technique 73
end-of-life care 131
end-of-life/death ritual 26
English as Second Language (ESL) 277
environmental stressors and trauma effects
   275
episodic memories 50
ethnic-racial identity development 102
ethnocentrism 27
European colonialism 9
Every Student Succeeds Act (2015)
   195–196
evidenced-based interventions 196
exclusion 5
existential shattering 62
expressive arts therapy interventions 269

faith-based communities 60
familism 180–181
family: dysfunction 264; loss 281;
    positionality and unequal bereavement
    228–229; separations 140; therapy
    268–269; unit transmission 146
fear 191
feelings: of empowerment 34; expression 44;
    stunned/shocked/dazed 8
female slave 79
feminine wisdom 68
Ferow, A. 192
"fight or flight" responses 141
Flahault, C. 188
flight-or-fight tendencies 192
Floyd, G. 15–16, 79, 82
foster children 7–8, 242–243
foster family: community 246; life, culture
    244
foster homes/foster care 238
foster parents 7–8, 241–242; foster carers
    238–239; licensing stage 250
Fowler, D. N. 64, 194
Fox, J. 61
Fraser, T. A. 240
freezing response 141
funeral and burial rites 11, 84

Gabaldon, G. 207
Ganz, A. 260
Garrison, M. 31
gay people/gay: community 122; couple
    intimacy connections 122; men's
    experiences 122; same-sex marriages 106;
    widowers from HIV/AIDS 120–133
gender discrimination 36–37
genocide 285
Gitterman, A. 146
Goff, P. A. 37
Gordon, J. A. 89
Grandi, F. 284
Granek, L. 108, 148–149
Grant, J. M. 175
Gray, M. J. 179
Greif, G. 102
grief: anomalies 257; effects types 43; equity
    and social justice 64, 223; griever 5–6;
    inequity 10; and intersectionality 223;

practitioners 16; psychoeducation 249;
    reaction 4; triggers 132
Grilley, P. 49
Guillén, V. 262
guilt 63, 191
gun violence 89; in schools 193–195

Haines, S. K. 11, 13
Harris, D. L. 36, 106–107
healing: circles 35; spaces 50–51
health disparities 9–10
healthy biracial identity development 107
hearing phrases 225
Helbert, K. 53
help-seeking behaviors 30
Henderson, Z. R. 141
Herman, J. L. 178
heroism 261–262
heterosexism 27
Hewlett, B. 210
Hill, L. 10
historical unresolved grief 8
Hoffman, L. 62
Holinger, D. P. 43–44
Holland, P. 197
homicide 79
hope and healing during mourning 86
Hughes, L. 12–13
humanity 79
human rights protections 120
humiliation and embarrassment 193
humility 110
Hunter, A. G. 110
Huskey, M. G. 195
hyperarousal sensitivity 192
hyper-maturity 191

identity denial 107
identity development 106
identity disruption 257
identity loss 264; allyship and advocacy
    35–36; definitions and background 25–27;
    disenfranchised grief impacts across
    lifespan 29–30; ethical considerations
    36–37; identity strategies 30–35;
    intersectionality in processing 27–28
immigrants 5
immigration 230

implicit biases 285–286
incongruence 43
Indigenous Americans 9
Indigenous peoples' right 9
individualized self-wellness agendas 132
infertility 4, 157–158
informed consent 196–197
insecurity: with God 72; and vulnerability
    feelings 188
insomnia 224
inspiration porn 158
institutional inequities 27
institutional racism 89, 104
intellectual disability 160
interconnectedness 149–150
intergenerational cultural beliefs 261
intergenerational trauma 6, 15–16
internalized oppression 11
International Commission on Missing
    Persons (ICMP) 280
International Criminal Tribunal for the
    former Yugoslavia (ICTY) 278
interpersonal conflicts 26
interpersonal-intimate partner violence 124
interpersonal violence 15
interracial couples 99–106; challenges 102;
    interracial couple grief 103–104; meaning
    making for 105–106; parenting biracial
    children 102–103; parenting practices
    102; privilege and systemic racism 104;
    systemic and social barriers 104–105
interracial marriages 99–101
intersectionality 24–25, 224; identity
    markers 27; and influence of culture;
    disabilities 158, 164, 227–228; and sibling
    loss 222–225; treatment approach 35
intersex and bisexual persons 123–124
intra-LGBTQIA+ sub-group 120
Inventory of Complicated Spiritual Grief
    (ICSG) 72
Islamophobia 276, 278–279
isolation 120, 124, 259

Jiggetts, V. D. 27, 36
Johnston, M. P. 107
Jordan, J. 105
Judeo-Christian religion 279
Jung, C. 209

K-12 system 195–196; educational setting
    172–173; LGBTQIA+ students 130;
    schools 198
Kahn, K. B. 37
Kauffman, J. 84
Keshet, H. 176
Killian, K. D. 105
Kim, J. Y. 10
kin care 238
King, K. M. 14
kinship foster care 238
Klassen, D. K. 15
Knight, C. 146
Konrad, C. 14
Kwong, M. -K. 269

LaBrenz, C. A. 248
language loss 282
Lantz, M. M. 111
Latinx communities 179–180
Levine, P. 45, 50
Lawson, E. 82, 146
lesbians 124; see also gay people/gay
Leslie, L. A. 105
LGBT-medical/mental health clinic 126
LGBTQIA+ community 4, 24; allyship and
    advocacy 130; culture sensitivity 121;
    cumulative impacts 129; discrimination
    242; ethical considerations 130–131; gay
    men experiences 122; gay widowers from
    HIV/AIDS 120–133; grief and challenges
    in 120–133; intersex and bisexual persons
    123–124; intolerance 89; lesbian women
    124; relational aspects of 128–129; sex
    work and incarceration, trans women
    with histories 123; social/cultural aspects
    127–128; strategies and interventions
    131–132; trans men experiences 123;
    trans women with histories 123; youth 243
liberation psychology 51
liberatory consciousness framework 25, 36
life loss review (LLR) 131
Livingston, G. 104–105
loneliness 259
longing/yearning 8
loss: African American sibling 229–230;
    ambiguous 25–27, 146–147, 257–258,
    280; of belonging 259; death 8, 72–73;

employment 27; experienced in war
  trauma 287; family 281; identity 25–26,
  35–36; language 282; material 282–283;
  maturational 30; non-death 7–8, 63–64,
  172; physical 4; post-migration 230;
  psychosocial 8; racial grief and 108;
  recognized and unrecognized 189–192;
  suicide 261–262, 267; symbolic 8;
  unresolved trauma and 7
Love, B. J. 27, 36
Lynes, D. 240

Maccallum, F. 211
macro/societal-level of processing 36
"mammy" 79
marginalization 4, 6, 9–10, 64, 222–223
marital dissatisfaction 177
Martin, T. 82
Martín-Baró, I. 51
mass social trauma 149–150
material loss 282–283
maturational losses 30
McCoyd, J. L. M. 29–30
meaning making 32–33, 71
meatpackers 11
media violence 193
meditation 73
mental health: precarity 16; professionals 30,
  32–33; symptomatology 140
mental health and social services (MHSS)
  professionals 121
mental mapping 7
#MeToo movement 174
microaggressions 100, 102, 107–108
Milano, A. 174
military 256–257; see also service sacrifice
Miller, J. B. 34
minimization 87
mirror symptomatology 177
misconceptions, foster parents 241
misdiagnose grief 8
monkeypox epidemic 122
monoracial couples 102
monoracism 107
Monroe, B. 34
Montgomery, M. 243
mood disorders 178
Moore, S. E. 35

Moorhead, J. 210
moral injury 62–63, 68, 72
Morin, B. 107
mothers/maternal: emotional distress 214;
  mourning 83
motivation 107
mourning 11, 87–88, 230
Mullings, D. V. 239, 245
multicultural counseling competencies
  (MCCs) 111
multiculturalism 29, 99; counseling literature
  14; knowledge and awareness 111
multiethnic 99
multiple sclerosis 159–160
multiracial/multiraciality 99, 109, 101
Murray-García, J. 103
mutual empathy 34

Nadal, K. L. 107
National Association of Social Workers
  (NASW) 179
national counseling organizations 85
National Foster Parent Association (NFPA)
  Code of Ethics 248–249
national transgender discrimination survey
  175
Nayak, S. 108
Neimeyer, R. A. 54, 72, 105
Nelson, B. S. 177
neurobiology 6–7
neuroception 7
Nickerson, A. 281
niqab (face veil) in Islam 9
non-death grief 8, 31; losses 7–8, 63–64,
  172; rituals 26
nonlinguistic narrative approaches 269
non-native speakers 4
non-traditional approach 35
non-violent crisis intervention 242
nostalgia, hope, and dreams 283
"Now is the Time Policy" 195
nuclear family 128

Obergefell v. Hodges 242
Olivier, H. 34
"one-drop rule" 102, 106, 109
oppression 6, 13, 64
Ortega-Williams, A. 149–150

overlapping social identities 24
Owen, J. 111

Panchuk, M. 60–61
Paolini, A. 192
Papa, A. 8
parasympathetic nervous system (PNS) influences 141
parental rights 128
parent-child attachment 214
parent-child relationships 263
parentification 282
parenting: allyship and advocacy 247–248; "borrowed children" 238–251; Bosnian refugees 281–282; childrearing 210–211; cultural aspects 245–246; ethical considerations 248–249; foster family system, impact 239–240; relational aspects 246–247; resource workers 239; social aspects 240–244; strategies and interventions 249–250
partner infidelity 28
patriarchal hierarchy 63–64, 67–68
patriotism 261–262
Peleg-Sagy, T. 108, 148–149
People of Color 109, 141, 147–149
Perfect, M. 196
perfectionism 87 permanent changes of station (PCS) 258–260
persistent complex bereavement disorder (PCBD) 257
personality-altering mental state 257–258
personal protective equipment 11
Peskin, H. 11
Pew Research Center 100–101
physical: communications of grief 43; death 229; disability 159; losses 4; trauma symptoms 141
physiological changes 191
Piazza-Bonin, E. 84
Pietrantoni, L. 59
play-based therapy 197
pleasure and intimacy 122
Pliske, M. 15
portrayals 241
positionality 274
positive attributes 288
positive integration 268

post-9/11 era 265
post-migration losses 230
postmortem profiling 82
Poston, W. S. C. 106
posttraumatic growth 59–60
posttraumatic stress disorder (PTSD) 8, 29–30, 160–161, 194, 257, 274–275, 277
Potter, S. 175
poverty 11, 15, 89
power-over systems 11
Porges, S. 6–7
Powers, S. 53
Pranayama 53
Prati, G. 59
pre-service psychoeducation 249
pregnancy: abortion 5, 59; miscarriage 4, 212; rape 173
Price, J. H. 196
Prince, D. M. 243, 250
principle of colorism 106
prisoner of war (POW) 257
privilege and systemic racism 30, 104
prolonged grief disorder (PGD) 142, 257
Prosek, E. A. 267
Protivnak, J. J. 190
psychiatry 9
psychic tears 43
psychological distress 140
psychological ramifications 224
psychological trauma 63, 124, 192; see also moral injury
psychosocial losses 8
public humiliation 67
public worship 59

racial/racism 9, 11, 82, 89; discrimination 78, 102, 226; disenfranchised grief 100; ethnic children 243; ethnic disparities 243; grief and loss 108; identity 110; inequalities 9–10; justice 109; privilege 105; socialization 110; subtexts 82
racial trauma 16, 79, 229–230; for African Americans 78–79, 81–84; allyship and advocacy 85; Black youth and young adults in treatment 88–89; ethical considerations 85–86; historical oppression and racial trauma 80–81; informal supports 88; psychoeducation

and breathing room 87–88; race and racism 87; spiritual coping resources 88; strategies and interventions 86–89; Strong Black Woman (SBW) schema 80; super woman schema 86–87
racist 37; discourses 82; societal attitudes 83
Rando, T. 8, 131
Rape, Abuse and Incest National Network (RAINN) 170
recognized and unrecognized loss 189–192
reconciliation 191
refugees 5; see also Bosnian refugees
regression 191
relational aspects: African Americans, healthcare barriers for 146–147; African American sibling loss 228–229; childrearing 214–215; disabilities, individuals with 159–160; disconnection 34; of disenfranchised grief 48–49; identity 30; images 181–182; LGBTQIA+ community 128–129; parenting 246–247; service sacrifice 263–264; sexual violence 176–177
relational cultural theory (RCT) 31, 33–35, 176, 180–182
relational influences 12–13
relational resilience 34
relational support systems 30
relational violations 177
relationship break-ups 122
relearning 62
relief 191
religion/religious: and African Americans 88, 145, 228; community 60; cultures 33; faith 59–60; intolerance 9; racism 9; religiosity and spirituality 60; and spiritual abuse victims 64; trauma 60
resilience 15, 33
Rollins, A. 110
Rosen, J. E. 102
Rosenblatt, P. C. 87

sacredness 50–51; immanence 60; moral injury 63
sadness 191
Safe School Initiative 193
same-sex marriage rights 121

same-sex sexual behavior 122
sanctuary and confidential engagement 218
Satchidananda, S. 53
Schaefer, C. E. 269
Schaeffer, K. 256
Schaub, J. 248
school-based therapist 196–197
school resource officers (SROs) 194–195
school violence: causes 193; coping skills for loss and grief 189; dimensions of loss 190–191; disenfranchised grief 187–188; elementary students 188; ethical considerations 196–197; humiliation and embarrassment 193; insecurity and vulnerability feelings 188; media violence 193; psychological trauma 192; range and complexities 194; recognized and unrecognized loss 189–192; school-based counselors 188–189; school safety and active shooter drills 194–195; secondary students 189; secondary trauma 192; strategies and interventions 197–198; students' grief 187–189; trauma-informed allyship and advocacy 195–196
Seamon-Lahiff, G. E. 261
secondary students 189
secondary trauma 192
self-advocacy 249
self and community 36
self-awareness 14, 87
self-blame 16
self-care 192, 249
self-compassion 87
self-confidence 81
self-critique 103
self-deficiency 16
self-directed experiences 190
self-disenfranchisement 11, 17, 84
self-efficacy 233
self-empathy 34
self-esteem 16, 107
self-identify 109
self-identity 60–61, 122, 211
self-in-relationship 176
self-isolation 124
self-knowledge and acceptance, childrearing 217
self-loathing 124

self-reflection 103, 139
self-reported engagement 107
self-sacrifice 80, 210
self-silencing 80, 87
self-transcendence 60
self-worth 122
sense of self 25–26
separateness 50–51
service sacrifice: allyship and advocacy 265–266; attachment, impact of 263–264; cultural aspects 260–263; cumulative impacts across lifespan 264–265; diagnostic issues 262–263; ethical considerations 266–267; grief anomalies 257; mental health services 260–261; military and veteran communities' experiences 257–259; military children and adolescents 265; military retirements and honorable discharges 260; relational aspects 263–264; servicemembers 262; social aspects 259–260; strategies and interventions 267–269; suicide loss 261–262
severe acute respiratory syndrome (SARS) 126
sexism 27, 64
sex/sexual: -based discrimination 25; behavior 194; bereavement 122; health and quality sex education 248; identity 248; intimacy 122; offenders, family members of 5; orientation 69, 127; and race discrimination 28; and reproductive health 247–248; -role perceptions 64; vulnerability 122; work and incarceration, trans women with histories 123
sexual violence: allyship and advocacy 178; cultural aspects 174–176; cumulative impacts 177–178; definitions 170; ethical considerations 178–179; as intentional violation 176; myths and beliefs 175; relational aspects 176–177; social aspects 172–174; social stigmas and myths 171; strategies and interventions 179–182; unwanted/unplanned pregnancy 173; validity or social stigma 171; victim and survivor 170
shame 63, 278; and self-esteem 16–17
shattered assumptions 62

Shay, J. 62–63
shock or apparent lack of feeling 191
siblings: bereaved adult 230; bereavement 222, 226–227; grief 222; see also African American sibling loss
Siegel, D. J. 7, 15
silencing pain 84
single-axis framework 24
Sitoe, A. 240
slave masters 79
slavery 78–79, 139–140, 147–148
Smigelsky, M. A. 72
Smith, S. G. 172
social alienation 233
social attitude 28
social categories 30
social connection and kinship 142–143
social-cultural adaptations 139
social culture and values 275
social determinants, mental health and social systems 143
social disconnection 212
social disenfranchisement 11, 225–227
social dominance theory 111
social engagement 7
social functioning 209–210
social identity 30, 32
social inequities impact 222
social influences 11
social injustices 34
social integration 212
social justice 46, 145
social location 274
social marginalization 35
social minimalization of loss 225
social nullification 225
social pain and physical pain 50
social prejudice and institutional oppression 121
social psychologists 37
social rejection and empathic failures 83
social stigmatization 5
social and structural barriers 27
socioeconomic status (SES) 28, 147
Solomon, A. 214
somatosensory narratives 269
Southern Poverty Law Center 81

spirituality/spiritual 72–73; abuse 72; community 31, 64; concept 60; coping 88; and leadership 70; practices 88

spiritual trauma 61–62; allyship and advocacy 70–71; culture and faith 69–70; ethical considerations 71–72; existential shattering 62; experiences and faith 66–67; and milestones 65–66; moral injury 62–63, 68–69; patriarchal hierarchy 63–64; patriarchal influence and gender 67–68; religious institutions 61; and spiritual leadership 68–69; strategies and interventions 72–73; trauma and 61–64

stigmatization 5, 31

strengths-based language 267

stress 178, 264

Stroebe, M. 44

Strong Black Woman (SBW) 83; schema 80; stereotype 140

Strouse, S. 269

structural and social inequalities 27

substance abuse 5

Substance Abuse and Mental Health Services Administration (SAMHSA) 196

Sue, D. W. 111

suicide/suicidality 5, 59, 63, 72, 122, 243; loss 261–262, 267; rate 88–89; see also moral injury

surveillance 194–195

survivor guilt 283

symbolic losses 8

sympathetic nervous system (SNS) 141

synchronicity 6

systematic racism and disparities 142

systemic inequities 10

systemic oppressive forces 32–33

systemic racism 108, 147

Taku, K. 15

talk therapy 112

Talya, E. 268

Taylor, B. 79, 82

Teplin, L. A. 193–194

Tervalon, M. 103

theory-driven frameworks 232

therapeutic group-type treatments 35

therapist-client relationship 35

third culture 258–259

Todd, A. R. 104

Toporek, R. L. 86

toxic spirituality 69–70

Tragedy Assistance Program for Survivors (TAPS) 266, 268

trans allyship 130

transgender people 123, 127

trauma 26, 89; Bosnian refugees 277; imprints 50; -informed allyship and advocacy 195–196; -informed care 15–16; -informed strategies 13; injury 4; memories 50; -related emotions 50; stress 160; trigger 34

trauma focused-cognitive behavioral therapy (TF-CBT) 198

traumatic brain injury (TBI) 26–27, 257–258

Trevor Project 130

Trochim's concept system 239

turbans in Sikhism 9

unaddressed disenfranchised grief 49–50

unconscious beliefs 286

underscoring racism 100

unexpected funeral costs 229

unresolved grief 214

unresolved trauma and losses 7

unspoken grief 42–54

Useem, J. 258

Utsey, S. O. 88

van der Kolk, B. A. 49–50, 53, 215

verbal aggression 191

verbal and nonverbal expression 43

verbal and physical abuse 126

vicarious trauma 250

victim-blaming 28, 171, 173

Vietnam War 125

violence 15; -repression-bullying 121; school behaviors 194; see also school violence

visual security 194–195

vulnerabilities 70, 223

Waldon Family Services 240–241

Wallace, B. R. 87

Walter, C. A. 29–30

Walters, G. D. 194

Wampler, K. S. 177

Webb, N. B. 264
Wheat, L. S. 13–14
white bodies 278
whiteness 279
widowers 121–122
Wilkins, E. J. 84
Williams, R. K. 79, 83, 240
Wilson, D. 225–226

women and race-based discrimination 25
Worden, J. W. 31–32, 35

xenophobia 278–279

yarmulkes, in Judaism 9
yoga 53
Young, J. L. 105

9781032268903